Lauren St John is the author of *Walkin' After Midnight: A Journey to the Heart of Nashville)* of which Steve Earle said 'This book is about my Nashville, the town I've called home for 26 years and have come to love in spite of itself' and four other books. Born in Zimbabwe, she has written extensively for the *Sunday Times* and the *Independent*.

For more information on Lauren St John visit
www.4thestate.com/laurenstjohn

Hardcore Troubadour

Hardcore Troubadour
The Life and Near Death of
Steve Earle

Lauren St John

FOURTH ESTATE · *London* and *New York*

This paperback edition first published in 2003
First published in Great Britain in 2002 by
Fourth Estate
A Division of HarperCollins*Publishers*
77–85 Fulham Palace Road
London, w6 8jb
www.4thestate.co.uk

1 2 3 4 5 6 7 8 9

A catalogue record for this book is available
from the British Library

ISBN 1-84115-6116

Typeset in Sabon by
Palimpsest Book Production Limited
Polmont, Stirlingshire
Printed and bound in Great Britain by
Clays Ltd, St Ives plc

for Kellie

'I have a low tolerance for mediocrity in music and life. I'm into pain and joy and the in-between doesn't interest me.'

Steve Earle, *Washington Post*, 1986

'Music is supposed to be entertaining and if it touches you emotionally, so much the better. Or sometimes you do it to save your own life, not anybody else's. That's mostly why I write. I'm not trying to change anybody else's life or the world, I'm trying to keep from blowing my own brains out. That's the real point.'

Guy Clark, Nashville, 2001

Prologue

'Don't worry, David, I'm on my way.'

Heroin-roughened, Steve Earle's voice at the other end of the telephone line still sounded confident and reassuring. It had a familiar sardonic edge to it, as if he hadn't lived through six marriages, a police choking, numerous lawsuits, tequila runs, drug busts and emotional tidal waves; as if he hadn't smashed through the conventions of folk, country and biker rock; as if, at any moment, he could run off a string of caustic one-liners, like 'I'm planning to have at least one wife for every letter of the alphabet' or 'Capital punishment means never having to say you're sorry.'

For two interminable days in 1992, his attorney, Englishman David Simone, had been sitting under the chandeliers of the Essex Hotel in mid-town New York with a multi-million-dollar record contract in his briefcase. It was a long time since Steve had written a song and longer still since his performing career had imploded in a haze of crack smoke. His immediate family excepted, most people had given up on him. But Simone had persisted. Somehow he'd managed to talk Mercury and Virgin Records into putting up rival bids for Steve for amounts which, Simone would have been the first to admit, far exceeded what his wayward client was worth. Virgin had supplied Simone with several first-class air tickets to England and accommodation at New York's glamorous Essex Hotel during the final phase of meetings. Each label had a day to convince Steve to sign with them.

The night before the first meeting, Steve failed to arrive at the hotel. Simone went to bed and awoke to find that his client had gone missing. He'd last been seen at the airport in Nashville but, for reasons unknown, he'd never made it to the plane. Four stressful hours later, Steve was on the phone with some garbled story about illness striking and the ticket being lost. He was charmingly apologetic and disingenuously disorganized. Simone moved all the meetings back twenty-four hours and dispatched a new air ticket. Steve called him from the gate at the airport. He was, he reassured Simone, on his way.

It was the last time Simone heard from him for three years. In the harrowing days that followed, he came to discover that Steve had sold his ticket at the gate for $100 and gone to a crack house. 'He never turned up and, obviously, we never did the deal. And it was devastating – not because of the deal, but emotionally for me. Because this guy who was so special was just killing himself.'

1

Life and Death in Texas

It was death that Jack Earle brushed in dreamy flights across America, though he never thought of it like that. Life lived too large in him. A strapping sixteen-year-old with big kind hands and the skin the colour of the iron-rich Texas earth, he looked down on the sweeping landscapes and felt invincible. There was a freedom about it. He loved to go up and bore holes in the virgin sky, to strike out into the unknown with a shaky compass. 'The old aircraft always smelled of gasoline and dope, the paint that they used on the fabric. That *smell* – I just lived for that smell. Terrify most people nowadays.'

For the most part Jack had no idea where he was going, or how many rolls of masking tape it would take to get the plane he was collecting airborne when he arrived. *Trade-A-Plane* guided his destiny like some fifties astrological chart. The owner of the Jacksonville, Texas airfield where he spent his days (an old barnstormer on a motorbike) consulted the magazine on a monthly basis. Jack, who'd been obsessed by flying ever since he could remember and had cadged or worked for lessons until he'd earned his first solo flight at sixteen and his passenger licence at seventeen, waited around the airfield in the hope that the old man would make a deal. If that happened, he'd send Jack and another boy to fetch the aircraft. They flew as far as Ann Arbor, Michigan, Ohio and California, encountering planes they'd never seen or heard of, before figuring out how to fly them back. Jack's favourites were J-3 Piper Cubs and Aeronca Chiefs and Champs. Often the very fabric of the planes was worn out and starting to rot. The boys would patch them together with masking tape, kick the aged engines into life and go.

'We got real good at changing oil and unsticking valves. Those little aeroplanes, you'd have ones that had been sitting out in the field for two or three years without even starting. You'd throw in the oil, change it by hand about a jillion times, crank it up and clear all the birds' nests and cobwebs out of it and depart. And it was great. We thought nothing of it. Now I kinda shudder when I think.'

Most of the aircraft were old and slow – sixty-five horse-power or less. Jack reasoned that if one of them quit, he'd most likely have time to find a safe place to land. Only once did he ever see his young life flash before his eyes. He'd gone with a friend to see his then girlfriend Barbara at a Presbyterian church camp. Coming home, they hit a vulture. There was an explosion of feathers and a large section of the prop plummeted to earth. With the engine dangerously unbalanced, the terrified boys had to no choice but to shut it down. Only then could they look for a place to land.

But even after that, Jack rarely gave a thought to the possible consequences of his obsession. He and his friends continued to get into anything with wings. 'If it was an old dawg, that was okay too if the alternative was that we couldn't fly.'

Jack had come hurrying into the world on 22 December 1933 when the doctor was held up by a train. Granny delivered him in the back of his father's convenience store. The third of four children, he was the great-grandson of Elijah Earle, the first Earle in Jacksonville. Elijah had migrated to East Texas from Scottsboro, Alabama, in 1840 with a wife and baby and a

4

yoke of oxen. Beneath the unforgiving sun he'd cleared the land by hand and the simple log chapel he constructed still stands today. Elijah intended the church to be a gathering place for the people of all faiths, with Methodist Episcopalians having preference, as well as a community school. Now rebuilt and painted white, it stands proudly amid a grove of trees, its neat wooden pews brushed by the humid Texas breezes.

In 1932, Elijah's son, Albert Franklin, died, leaving eight children. Jack's father, Albert Milton, was the youngest. Known simply as Booster, he grew up connected to the land as if by an umbilical cord. When all the other children had grown and moved on, he continued to reside on the family farm, just a mile or so down the road from Earle's Chapel. The homestead in which he lived was an unpainted five-bedroom frame house with no indoor plumbing. In time it underwent various renovations but it remained intact until a tornado levelled it in 1987. Booster himself had the heart of an adventurer and a healthy entrepreneurial spirit. He was still a youngster when he began running a hamburger and chilli stand during the oil boom, moving from field to field with the ebb and flow of black gold. Another money-making opportunity arose when he and his friends caught a massive alligator on a nearby river. They charged ten cents a time for viewings. Then somebody had the bright idea of touring the country with it. The friends put it on the back of a truck and set off across America to get rich from their portable zoo. In Colorado, the traumatized creature finally expired. Unwilling to let go of their meal ticket, Booster continued to pretend the alligator was alive for another couple of days. Few people noticed the difference.

When Booster married a vibrant girl named Jewel Wall from Indian Gap, Texas, he put his adventuring days behind him. He worked the farm for many years and later for the Railway Express. His mother, Ammie, known simply as Granny, lived with the couple and ruled the roost. Shortly before Jack was born, Booster ploughed his savings into a service station and convenience store in Jacksonville and he and his family moved into the apartment behind it. Their dream died with the Depression. They took their debts and returned to the land, which Booster knew and understood. Tomatoes were Jacksonville's biggest export, and for years the family farmed tomatoes, peanuts and Christmas trees. In the fifties Booster found success with peaches, pink and yellow and thick with juice. By the time Steve was old enough to pick them, there were over six thousand trees on the family farm.

Jack spent the first eight years of his education at a little country school in Ironton, Texas, where the soil was red with iron ore. When it came time to go to high school he went into Jacksonville, where he discovered girls. An intelligent, popular boy, he played bi-district championship football and sung in an all-state barbershop quartet. In his senior year in high school, the yearbook featured a caricature of him as a rock 'n' roll singer in the section about what people would do when they grew up. He became more and more musical as the years went on. He could play the ukulele and the piano by ear and people joked that his older brother Arlon was the best nine-fingered piano player in Texas (one finger had been crushed in an accident). At sixteen, Jack found himself a steady girlfriend. He was in the games room at her house one afternoon playing ping pong when some visitors came over to see her parents. Voices drifted up from downstairs. The visitors, who had only recently moved to Jacksonville, had a child. They were sending her upstairs to play.

Into the games room came a skinny thirteen-year-old girl. Her name was Barbara. Jack was having too much fun to be bothered trying to entertain a child. He gave her short shrift and sent her downstairs. The adults sent her back up again. Finally, she just sat on the stairs.

Barbara Thomas's upbringing had been very different from Jack's. Born in Nashville, Tennessee, to Helen and James Walter Groover, she knew insecurity from a young age. Her parents filed for divorce when she was barely six months old. When she was five, her mother remarried. Barbara spent a fragmented childhood journeying between her grandparents' house in Nashville, several warm-hearted aunts, and the famous Peabody Hotel in Memphis, where her stepfather Emmett Thomas was manager. At the Peabody, Barbara was raised in a world full of grown-ups. During World War II, the hotel was the social centre of Memphis and the Glenn Miller Orchestra could be found playing in the rooftop bar. Barbara's mother, Helen, a woman of tremendous poise and refinement, became the first civil service employee to be hired at the naval base.

Barbara was eight when her mother divorced again, this time turning to drink. 'It was an escape. She never did go out and party. She would just go into her room and close the door and drink.' They moved to Longview, Texas, where Helen, or Mudder, as Steve would later call her, sank into chronic alcoholism. The bottle had been her grandfather's best friend and in time his addiction would soon be passed on down the line – with shattering consequences. Barbara experienced that heartache first. By the time she was in the fifth or sixth grade, Mudder's drinking was out of control. Barbara found herself in the role of parent. After school, it was she who took care of her mother. Watching over Mudder's slender form during drunken stupors, Barbara often feared she was dead. Eventually the frightened girl was sent to live with her father. She was twelve when Alcoholics Anonymous and bachelor Sam Fain saved Mudder's life. A recovering alcoholic himself, Sam married her, adored her and was strong for both of them. Barbara and her mother moved to Jacksonville, Texas, where Sam owned a hardware store. Barbara was in her mid-teens when Helen Fain gave birth to a baby boy. He was named Nick.

In Jack Earle's senior year in high school, he took a summer job at the department store where Barbara's mother was a bookkeeper and office manager. Helen took a shine to him and invited him over for her maid Novella's beautiful lunches. Barbara had grown into a pretty young woman with elfin features and wavy brown hair and Jack saw her in a different light altogether. They started dating. She was in her junior year in high school; he had just graduated. Their romance was blossoming nicely when Jack went to Texas's A&M University to study architectural engineering. The following year, escalating fees sent Jack to Sam Houston in Huntsville for agricultural education. He told Barbara that it would be 'really civilized' if, while he was away at school, they both went out with other people. That worked well until Jack, cock-a-hoop with the new arrangement, arrived home from college to find Barbara and a friend on a double-date. A burly boy with quarterback shoulders, Jack stood foursquare in the yard and ran off both suitors. Barbara was incensed. 'And then it turned out that what he was home for was to pick up a tuxedo to take a girl to a dance at college. So I wrote him a really short letter. That was, I guess, the only break we've ever had.'

They were married on 19 July 1953, a month after seventeen-year-old Barbara had graduated from high school. Their plans of an Earle's Chapel wedding had been scuppered by the Korean War. It would be another year before the US Army was officially desegregated, and racial profiling was still in place. The draft board cast its net over the next lowliest group: poor white Southerners. 'They draft the white trash first 'round here anyway,' Steve Earle would write more than thirty years later about another war with the same immoral bias. Knowing that his number was up, Jack volunteered for the draft, cutting a year from his three-year service. The Korean War fizzled out in an uncomfortable stalemate the month he married Barbara, but by then Jack was already in basic training in El Paso.

In February 1954, Jack was dispatched to Fort Monroe, Virginia, to await the departure of his anti-artillery unit to Korea, where 33,629 Americans had already died and 103,284 were wounded or missing in action. In May, when spring flowers spread their rainbow hues across Virginia, Barbara became pregnant. The young couple's rejoicing was tempered by panic. Jack had just received orders that he was to be shipped to Korea as a radar technician. The army chaplain came to the rescue of the newlyweds. Knowing that Jack could type ninety words a minute and knowing too that he had an exemplary work ethic, he took pity on him. Jack spent the rest of his service as a company clerk on the base in Fort Monroe.

Safe in America, Jack and Barbara soon discovered that the future they'd chosen off-base meant life below the poverty line. Money came to them in tiny increments. On a rare visit home to the farm, Jewel loaded them up with canned green beans and they ate beans for breakfast, lunch and dinner until Jack vowed he would never touch a green bean again. Jack did most of the cooking. Barbara bought a cookbook and attempted to put a few meals together, but mostly the results were disastrous. Her one skill was baking. Novella had taught her to bake amazing cakes with sinful hot fudge frosting, but the rudiments of meat and three veg were beyond her. Jack had learned to cook to get out of field work, so he usually took over. Finally, Barbara just left the meals to him.

Treats were thin on the ground. At Christmas time they were unable to afford the luxury of turkey so they opted for chicken fried steaks, the most nourishing meal they could imagine. When Barbara spent the holiday in hospital with pre-eclampsia–toxaemia, Jack ate both steaks by himself, all two pounds of them.

Late at night on Saturday, 17 January 1955, Barbara went into labour. Jack rushed her to the Fort Monroe Army Hospital and stayed with her as the complications set in. The doctor was slow to get there and inexperienced when he came. He was also the bearer of bad news. It would be a breech birth. Night flowed into morning and then into night again. Jack suffered with his wife through the labour, afraid she wouldn't make it. At four in the morning on Monday, shortly before he was due to report for KP (kitchen police) duty, he contacted the base and explained the situation. His superiors were unsympathetic. He was to report for KP duty as usual and the hospital would send word when the baby was born. Jack was naïve and 'kinda dumb back then' and, to his everlasting regret, he just wrung his hands and 'washed pots and pans through most of it'.

At noon, they came to call him. Stephen Fain Earle had been born. Jack whooped and ran the whole two miles to the hospital.

There was earth on the new baby's feet, rich Texas loam, chasing the mists of Virginia from his bones and infusing them with sunshine and the cattle-scattered plains of the Lone Star State. His grandfather had sent it in a Prince Albert tobacco tin, determined that the first soil his grandson's feet ever touched would be Texan. Steve was a big happy baby, quick to talk and slow to walk. So slow, in fact, that his grandmother was convinced there was something sinister happening. For sixteen long months he sat in his crib like a little plump Buddha, watching the comings and goings in a knowing sort of way. Words rushed from him in scrambled torrents. He talked and talked and talked to anyone who would listen, so that little more than a year on he was communicating in full sentences. And still he just sat.

Music poured through the house. Barbara's torch songs and show tunes, Jack's Mills Brothers and Hank Williams and, of course, the new music sending rumbles through America. In the year that Steve was born Les Baxter was breaking hearts with 'Unchained Melody', Mitch Miller was crooning 'Yellow Rose of Texas', the Chordettes were singing the chirpy fifties soundtrack, 'Mr Sandman', and Bill Haley and his Comets ushered in what *Life* magazine described as a 'frenzied teenage music craze' with 'Rock Around the Clock'. That year, 1955, drew a line under the apple-pie ideal of the fifties and hinted at the revolution to come. It was the year that Disneyland opened in Anaheim, California, and Ray A Kroc opened his first McDonald's, selling hamburgers at fifteen cents a piece. Fourteen-year-old Emmett Till was kidnapped, shot dead and mutilated for allegedly whistling at a white woman in Money,

Mississippi. And Rosa Parks opened the door to the Civil Rights movement by refusing to give up her seat in the whites-only section of a bus in Montgomery, Alabama. Culturally and socially, America was reinventing itself and Steve, ears open, eyes darting, unknowingly soaked it all in.

Three months before he was discharged from the army, Jack sent Barbara on ahead to Jacksonville. She was expecting again. Jack's medical benefits were due to end as soon as he left the army and he wanted to ensure Barbara had the support she needed in the final stages of her pregnancy. She drove away with his brother Neil, taking her still stationary baby with her. Jack followed on 7 February and Mark Neil Earle was born eight days later. Jack and Barbara set up home in Palestine, Texas, some fifteen miles from Jacksonville. Jack took a temporary job with the Railway Express. He still dreamed of becoming a pilot, but flying opportunities were scarce. Many of the military pilots had returned from Korea with extensive flying experience, and America was still nine years away from the madness of Vietnam. Jack put in three applications to airlines and one to work in air traffic control at the Civil Aeronautics Administration, renamed the Federal Aviation Agency in 1958. The CAA called first. Jack would spend the next thirty years as an air traffic controller, never realizing his ambition of becoming a pilot. In at least one family member's view, that summed him up. He was all business. You did what you had to do.

It was in Palestine that Steve first walked – or at least, that his parents first saw him walk. He was sixteen months old. He never crawled or tottered or took a few tentative steps. He simply stood up and strolled the full length of the house. Jack and Barbara were dumbstruck. They could only imagine that he had been walking in secret. Jack scooped him up and they jumped in the car and raced over to his mother's house to prove that their son was healthy. When Jewel came out on to the porch Steve was waddling towards the steps, fat arms outstretched. He walked without looking back.

* * *

Jack's first air traffic control assignment was in the dusty border town of El Paso, Texas. There, he and Barbara found they had a different problem with Mark. He walked early but he rarely talked because Steve did it on his behalf. 'He wants a drink of water,' Steve would interrupt when people tried to coax a few words from his brother. A reticent child, Mark talked to Steve but to no one else. Steve talked for him for years. 'We were like twins.'

It was the tumbleweeds that Steve always remembered about El Paso, big spindly balls that he could kick into the wind; they came back at him like footballs. In a steady wind, you could do that for hours. Tumbleweeds aside, there wasn't much in Mesa Road. In later years the developers would move in and suburbs and malls would spread across the landscape, but in the fifties it was in the middle of nowhere, a quiet street in a subdivision close to the airport, the Mexican border and Fort Bliss. El Paso is the scene of Steve's earliest memories. He recalls lighted fountains (the 'dancing waters'), walks down to the border and the arrival of Katherine Kelly Earle, born on 11 October 1958. Steve was crushed to find that the baby sister he'd been promised was an actual baby. He'd imagined her fully grown. 'I didn't know where kids came from so I thought, you know, they go and get 'em at the hospital. I thought it was a gameshow or something . . . I was like, "This is not a sister, this is a baby."'

At three, Steve saw Elvis Presley on television for the first time and was transfixed by the curling lip and swivelling hips. In the past two years, America had been rudely awoken to the idea of music as aural sex. Church leaders, politicians, parents and journalists rushed to condemn Elvis for behaving, as the famous jazz guitarist and raconteur Eddie Condon put it, 'like a sex maniac in public . . .' In *The American Dream: The 50s*, one fan recalled asking his mother what was so horrible about Elvis. 'She snapped: "Because he's sleazy, is why! Calling a lady a hound dog! And using *ain't*. It's disgusting."' But in spite of their protests, sensuality poured as unstoppably from Elvis as it did from Brando and Jimmy Dean. There was the gleaming black hair and the big-collared shirts and then there were the records – 'Don't Be Cruel', 'Heartbreak Hotel' and 'All Shook Up' – flying out of stores in their millions. Steve was an instant convert.

Across the street from the Earles lived a father and son; the mother was nowhere in evidence. In the afternoons, the boy – an intense seven-year-old named John – was often on his own for a period of time, so he, Mark and Steve would play in the fields behind the house. Jack and Barbara worked during the day and the children were watched by Juanita the maid. Out of sight of the house, John would load his father's rifle and show off for the younger boys. One afternoon, the game changed. Instead of firing at cacti, he shot a hole in the Earles' wagon. Then he shot a hole in their house. Steve has no memory of the incident so it's unlikely it made an impression on him, but Mark recalls Juanita rushing out of the house in a panic. 'She's trying to get us away from this kid. The kid ends up holding us hostage. He captured us. It was kind of like a game to us all. He was playing army. The maid finally got us away from the kid and put us under the bed and called my father at work, speaking Spanish. She forgot the little bit of English she knew. My father couldn't keep up, couldn't figure out what was going on, but he knew something was wrong. And the kid had just basically gone nuts.'

When Steve was five, Jack was posted to a Strategic Air Command (SAC) base in Lake Charles, Louisiana. The Earles rented an apartment first and then moved across the river to Sulphur. This time they lived in a house on a bayou and the boys spent many happy days playing in the swampy shallows. Jack and Barbara began to think about putting down roots. Barbara was pregnant with her fourth child in five years and longed for a permanent home of her own. Their life since Steve's birth had been relentlessly nomadic. They bought a ranch house in an attractive suburb – their fifth move in as many years. Like most of the houses of Steve's youth, it had three bedrooms, a bathroom and a living room, all arranged in shotgun fashion off the main passage.

Stacey Carole was born on 25 September 1960. All four children were already quite distinct from one another. Stacey had small, pretty features and blonde hair and suffered from epilepsy until she was five. As a consequence, people tiptoed around her and over-protected her until she was in her teens. Kelly was a bubbly child with red cheeks and a mop of curly dark hair, forever frustrated that she had to wear dresses and white pinafores while Steve and Mark ran wild in ripped dungarees.

Barbara was the all-American mother, a peerless example of *Life* magazine's assertion that, 'Of all the accomplishments of the American woman, the one she brings off with the most spectacular success is having babies.' If she wasn't dyeing Easter eggs with the children, she was volunteering as a scout den mother (both Steve and Mark were angelic cub scouts) or in the kitchen baking cakes. Kelly remembers a Spanish señorita doll birthday cake, with every detail perfect, right down to her paper fan.

Steve was, in Jack's words, clumsy. 'He wasn't athletic. His feet would get in his way when he tried to run.' In years to come, many of the qualities Jack had exhibited as a young flyer – daring, a thirst for new horizons and an obstinate belief in his own invulnerability – would manifest themselves in his son, but as a child Steve was the last in the family to learn to swim or ride a bike. He was afraid of heights. 'I was always kind of fearful.' Self-conscious about his awkwardness, he was mortified when he accidentally knocked Mark off a railing at their apartment complex when they were playing aeroplane and snapped his leg in three places. 'Mark fell all the way down and landed on my back. I remember that well.' Steve was scared to death. All the parents came running out of the house and Jack hauled his brother off to hospital.

In spite of this, Barbara remembers Steve as a happy and

'real easygoing child', not disruptive at all. 'He *talks* about being a bad kid!'

The first indication that Steve was not like other boys came when he entered first grade at six and a half. A month after he started school, Barbara received a telephone call from his flustered teacher. 'She said, "You know, I'm going to have trouble finding enough for him to do." And that's the way it was all the time. He was already learning so fast and remembered everything immediately, and the school systems weren't as advanced then and there was nothing for gifted children.'

From the time he was seven years old, Steve absorbed books with a sponge-like ease. He had an ability to process information laterally and see through the machinations of grown-ups in a way that was almost eerie. History and politics made an impression on him at an age when most boys applied their minds to nothing more complicated than pinball. At six, he remembers being 'very, very afraid of the atomic bomb and Nikita Khrushchev', an understandable paranoia in an era when one in twenty Americans built bomb shelters in their backyard. The Red Threat preoccupied them. 'My generation grew up watching these ads on television which were all black and white in those days with Vaseline on the lens. They looked blurry and scary. They showed Nikita Khrushchev making that speech at the UN [in 1956] where he took his shoe off in the middle of it and banged it on the podium. But they were actually misquoting him. He's speaking Russian and, you know, I didn't know anybody who spoke Russian . . . The translation that they superimposed over it was, "We will bury you" – which actually was taken out of context from another speech. But I didn't know that at the time. It was scary. I was five, six, seven years old when it started and it was propaganda. I was totally convinced when I was six years old that if I ran into Nikita Khrushchev, he would totally eat me.'

To a sensitive, fearful boy with a fertile imagination, the blurred, dramatized violence imbued even mundane activities with a sense of urgency. Leaflets depicting mushroom clouds attested to the fragility of life and the nearness of death. In the midst of the Cuban Missile Crisis, Steve and his classmates were bussed out to the woods on evacuation drills three or four times a week. In the event of a nuclear attack, these drills were supposed to save their lives. Other boys obeyed orders unquestioningly but Steve was sceptical. 'All it meant was that a bunch of kids were going to die by themselves in a bus out in the middle of the woods. I remember thinking years later, They're not being honest. They should have just sent us home because if that happened we were all gonna fuckin' die so they might as well send us home to our parents to die. It was really weird. It was one of the weirdest things I've ever come across.'

By the age of seven, Steve was already deeply affected by the three things that came to define and influence his life: music, politics and the freedom of the road. Within a year, all would come together in an fateful collision, precipitated by a visit to Texas by the President of the United States. On 21 November 1963 John F. Kennedy visited San Antonio, Texas. By that time the Earle family had moved to the city and Jack took Steve and Mark out of school to watch the motorcade go by. Later that afternoon, Kennedy flew to Forth Worth and then on to Dallas. Mark was in class the next day when the principal knocked on the door. His conversation with the teacher was low, urgent and distressed and several times Mark caught the name of Kennedy. I remember sitting there and thinking, somebody shot the President. Somebody killed Kennedy.'

2
Someday

It was Barbara Earle who had decided that they should move again, though she hated to do it. Moving meant getting Steve and all his friends to hoist the piano and its obscenely heavy solid-brass interior on to the back of a truck. It meant packing and repacking things that had probably not been unpacked since the last move. It meant sweat, tears and, frequently, blood. 'Oh, no!' Barbara would cry when Jack came home to tell her that the FAA was transferring him to a new division. 'We're not going to move *again*? Oh, when are we going to have a home? When are we going to buy a home and live in the same home?' When little Stacey tried to comfort her, echoing a phrase her mother used in more cheerful moments, Barbara would say, 'Home *is* where the heart is but our friends are back *there*.'

This time, it was Barbara's decision to go. In April 1963, midway through Steve's second grade, Chenault Air Force Base had been closed and Jack reassigned to San Antonio. Steve completed the school year at East Terrell Hills Elementary while Jack and Barbara struggled to sell their house. The closure of the base had had a devastating effect on the economy in Lake Charles and the Earles, scraping to find the money for both mortgage and rent, had quickly become engulfed in debt. Desperate to save her family from ruin, Barbara searched San Antonio for a house with a tiny rent. Steve was eight when they moved to a two-hundred-acre Quarter Horse ranch bordering a drag-racing strip in Converse, Texas. The house was decrepit but it was a bargain. The rancher had four other tenants on his property and charged a token $75 a month.

To the Earle children, it was as if they had stumbled into paradise. Horses filled the landscape, their thick gleaming flanks heaving as they flashed down the practice track – greys, duns and chestnuts. Over the fence were the noisy cars of the San Antonio Drag Raceway. The children were expressly banned from ever going there and, as a consequence, they were there most weekends, wheedling free soda from the concession stand owners. Kelly and Stacey weren't even supposed to go out of the yard without their brothers. Every afternoon, they'd sit on the porch with Steve's collie-cross dog, Penny, listening for the sound of the bus bringing the boys home from Kirby Elementary so they could escape into the greater freedom of the ranch.

The Earles lived in Converse for a little over a year, but at the time it seemed to Steve as if they lived there for ever. He fished for bream in the lakes that served as cattle tanks on the property, warily avoiding the rattlesnakes. 'Rattlesnakes are something you just grew up co-existing with in Texas. Tornadoes and rattlesnakes.' The only other kid on the property was the drag strip owner's son, 'the meanest little motherfucker I ever met in my life', who was the bane of Steve's existence. He threw rocks constantly. 'There's lots of rocks in South Texas and I hated the little fucker but I played with him because he was the only other kid around besides my brother.' During the summer, the family would go to Jacksonville on weekends to help Booster on the farm and return exhausted and happy, smeared in peach juice. Sometimes Steve went up by himself on the train. He adored his grandfather, with whom he had the magical bond that forms between very young children and the elderly. 'It's one of the most special relationships in the world. In some ways, my grandfather, who died [in 1964], was more of an influence on me than my father.'

With Jack's help, the boys built kites. As time went on they became increasingly elaborate until eventually the three produced a twelve-foot box kite, weighing some thirty pounds. Kelly and Stacey could fit comfortably in the corners. The kite had a 900-foot nylon cord, which itself was so long and heavy that it had several smaller kites attached to it to decrease the drag. One afternoon when the wind was high enough, Jack, Mark and Steve took it down to Randolph Air Force Base and let it loose. Jack was having so much fun that it never occurred to him to wonder why one aeroplane was flying round and round the field in a holding pattern. A rescue helicopter hove into view. High above them, a voice on a megaphone ordered sternly: 'WOULD YOU BRING THE KITE IN PLEASE, BRING THE KITE IN PLEASE, YOU'RE IN A TRAFFIC PATTERN.'

One day, Steve was on the school playground at recess when the ground shook so hard that he fell to his knees. A giant brown cloud bubbled slowly into the sky. Jack, who was patrolling air traffic, also saw it. It was reported on the local news as an accidental TNT warhead explosion at Medina airbase, a missile site, but the Earles were convinced it was a nuclear explosion. On the national news there was a deafening silence. No word of it crept outside San Antonio.

A month later, John F. Kennedy was dead.

To Steve, eight years old and impressionable, Nick Fain's visit was almost more momentous than the assassination of the US President. Both he and Mark worshipped Barbara's younger brother and always looked forward to seeing him. Nick was young enough for them to relate to (just five years separated him and Steve) and old enough to have a coolness to which they could only aspire. A really brilliant cat, Steve thought. A skinny blond boy with a glint in his eye, Nick had a bold, confident charm that masked the insecurity of his childhood. At five, he'd contracted polio and spent nearly two years in hospital. His left arm had withered away. Since then, he'd been spoiled rotten. His status as a polio survivor made him a minor celebrity in Jacksonville and from time to time feature writers would do stories on him. His recovering addict parents indulged his every whim. Kelly watched them give him 'every single solitary thing he ever wanted and we all know what that does to children'.

It was Nick's talent for music that appealed to Steve – as well, perhaps, as his outsider status. He had something of Elvis's rebel heart. Far from being an inhibiting factor, Nick's crippled arm had driven him to learn guitar, piano and even trombone. He'd built a little transistor radio from a kit and it was through that and his record collection that he introduced Steve to the pop music surging like a tidal wave over the last lingering traces of fifties apathy – notably Bob Dylan and the Beatles. On 9 February 1964, the biggest audience in the history of American television sat down to watch the Beatles perform live on the *Ed Sullivan Show*. They sang 'All My Loving', 'Till There Was You', 'She Loves You', 'I Saw Her Standing There' and 'I Want to Hold Your Hand' and the reverberations were felt across the nation. They were featured on the *Ed Sullivan* three times in successive weeks, making one more live appearance the day before Steve's ninth birthday. The impact on Steve was huge.

'I just remember being absolutely stunned . . . I was a big Elvis fan from the time I was really little but the Beatles was when I started getting in front of the mirror with a tennis racket and pretending it was a guitar and all that stuff.'

But as America was already discovering, the Beatles' appeal went far beyond music. They were masters of the droll put-down, the self-deprecating one-liner. When fight promoter Harold Conrad arranged for them to meet Cassius Clay, he told them: 'You guys ain't as dumb as you look.'

'No,' said John Lennon, 'but you are.'

An 11 February 1964 press conference in Washington DC, transcribed in Geoffrey Giuliano's *The Lost Beatles Interviews*, contained the following lines:

QUESTION: Do you have any formal musical training?
JOHN: You're joking.
QUESTION: What do you think of President Johnson?
PAUL: Does he buy our records?
QUESTION: Do you have any plans to meet the Johnson girls?
PAUL: No. We heard they didn't like our concerts.
QUESTION: You and the snow came to Washington today. Which do you think will have the greatest impact?
JOHN: The snow will probably last longer.

Dylan went into raptures about their outrageous chords and harmonies, Leonard Bernstein called them the best songwriters since Gershwin. Steve, razor-sharp and in love with language, drank it all in – the Beatles' throwaway lines about drugs and politics included. He and his siblings were constantly singing along to a Beatles and Tony Sheridan recording of 'My Bonnie Lies Over the Ocean'. There was a butane tank beside the house and Steve would climb on top of it and pretend it was a stage. With Mark watching from down below, he would belt out Elvis and Johnny Cash numbers, singing 'Ring of Fire' over and over again. For the first time he began to feel that the spotlight he had first recognized, aged three, watching Elvis perform, was available to him through music.

It was a wrench to leave the ranch and move again, this time to Schertz, further out of San Antonio. To Stacey, it was always she and Steve who adjusted best. 'We'd go, "Okay! Pack some boxes and let's go."' But for the first time in years Schertz brought a measure of stability into the family's lives and in fact, Steve would live there from the fourth grade till the eighth. He was a tall lanky boy with a Buddy Holly buzz cut, as athletically hopeless as he had been as a toddler. Mark, on the other hand, was a natural sportsman. When the school introduced a physical fitness award programme, based on President Kennedy's drive to make America more active, Mark was one of the first to pass. Steve tried to keep up and failed. He simply wasn't as aggressive as his brother.

Steve also hated maths. He spent hours and hours wrestling with multiplication tables. At eight he scored his first poor grade: a D. But when it came to reading, he was far ahead of his age group. He started with Mark Twain and was barely in his teens when he discovered the Beats, William Burroughs and Tom Wolfe. In later years, it would be Hemingway and Graham Greene whom he most admired. 'One day, you're going to write something like this,' Barbara would tell Steve and Kelly as she read to them in their infancy, and it stuck with them. Kelly had read through all of Louisa May Alcott by the second grade. There was a strong storytelling tradition in the family. Evenings in the Earle household were a time for intense dinner table debates about writing, music or even politics. On visits to Jacksonville, the older children would sit up until the small hours listening to Uncle Arlon and Aunt Puella, their grandmother's saltier sister, tell riveting stories of the Old South. Even at those gatherings, Kelly noted that when Steve talked everyone listened. 'Steve would go out to the deer woods with these crazy old deer hunters and listen to the tales they told and the difference is, he listened *and* he saw it. He doesn't just listen, he sees things. I really believe that when he writes a song, the reason why you feel the song is because he sees it like a movie. He just lives it.'

The Quarter Horse ranch had given the boys a taste for freedom and adventure. All summer long, Steve would go barefoot and bare-chested, his worn jeans cut into ragged shorts. He and Mark spent whole days down at Cibolo Creek, a strip of wilderness between Schertz and Universal City, Texas. They'd crawl in and out of the caves that were hidden in the bluffs. Thick forests of mesquite and white oak flanked the wide bottomland of the creek, a tributary of the San Antonio River. 'It was real Tom Sawyer. It was great.' Steve began to spend more and more time alone there. He would take his bicycle and strike out on his own, riding for ten or twelve miles in every direction. Kelly claims she 'never saw anybody could ride a bike like he could – standing on the seat or one foot in the air'.

In their neighbourhood in Schertz all the local kids turned out for street games. They played baseball, football, free tag, army and cowboys and Indians. Money being tight, Jack and Barbara were continually devising new ways to entertain the children at weekends. Often they'd take a barbecue to Brackenridge Park or go to see the baby animals at the zoo (a favourite pastime of Steve's to this day). Then somebody dreamed up 'Pick-a-Road'. 'Pick-a-Road' was a brilliant real-life board game. The whole family would pile into the station wagon – usually accompanied by Penny the dog – and they'd drive out of San Antonio in any direction they took a shine to. According to Kelly, 'Literally, Dad would say, "Okay, your turn," and you'd say, "Turn right here," and we'd drive for a while and Dad would say, "Okay, let me know the next person in line," and the next one would say, "Turn left here." And then we'd get to a certain time of the day and he'd stop, depending on how far we were from San Antonio, get his bearings and take us back.'

Music was a big feature of these drives. To keep the kids from killing each other *en route*, Jack and Barbara encouraged them to sing. They travelled hundreds of miles on perfect five-part harmonies. Sometimes Jack and Barbara would sing alone, Jack's barbershop quartet training and Barbara's perfect pitch enabling them to sing beautiful duets. So enjoyable were these outings that they travelled further and further afield, sometimes spending the night in an interesting town. Once they took a wrong turn and went barrelling through the front gates of the governor's mansion and the security guards rushed out like anxious rottweilers. Another time they found themselves, as if by magic, in Mexico. While Barbara took advantage of the cheap dentistry, Jack and the kids went in search of picnic food.

They loaded the station wagon with multi-coloured sodas and oily treats from cheerful street vendors. When Barbara returned, they went in search of a picnic spot. They drove and drove but there didn't seem to be one. The houses thinned and the land became flat and barren. Dust plumed behind them.

Kelly hung out the window and tried to catch the breeze. The sun beamed down white-hot, bleaching out the landscape. A little park came into view. They bumped down the track and through the trees. The vision that greeted them was, to Kelly, 'like a Technicolor movie, with everything in lights'. The houses ringing the park were as vibrant as art – brilliant splashes of fuchsia, pastel pink, red, yellow and cobalt blue. There was no one around. Jack parked the car in a patch of shade, and silence, broken only by the chirrups of the cicadas, enveloped them. They laid out the picnic lunch and the kids dived in hungrily. All of a sudden, first one vendor cart came down the track, then another and then another. People appeared as if from nowhere. The Earle kids jumped up and began shyly to play with the Mexican children. They didn't speak Spanish and their playmates didn't speak English. Then the ice man arrived. As Kelly remembers it, 'It's a brutally hot day and he's shaving by hand all of this wonderful ice in all these colourful bottles, every colour of the rainbow. Another vendor comes in and he's got these big huge glass jars and they're filled with water and fresh fruit. Then the pork skin vendor comes in and everything's fresh and hot and he put the hot sauce in it. Then the music starts – the mariachis and this old man playing all this wonderful old music. Next thing you know, it's like a carnival. There had to be a hundred people there . . . And it was probably one of the best days of our lives. We were covered with different-coloured stuff from all these ices, stuffed with all kinds of Mexican food and cotton candy, coming down from a horrible sugar high, all in the back of the station wagon. It was one of the few times that we were totally silent on the way home.'

*　　*　　*

This idyll came to an abrupt end when Daddy Sam Fain suffered a major stroke. Steve was eleven. When Daddy Sam came out of hospital, he was confused and slurring his words and it didn't take long for Jacksonville's gossipmongers to start speculating that he was drinking again. Barbara's mother was a gracious, intellectual woman, the very picture of a Southern belle, but her psyche was as fragile as glass. Years of AA meetings had not steeled her to the viciousness of public opinion. The tittering tore her apart. She stopped going to work. Jack and Barbara persuaded her and Daddy Sam to move to Schertz so that he could be near the Veterans' Association Hospital and they could help keep an eye on Nick. In Schertz, Daddy Sam fell victim to another stroke and was admitted to the hospital. He would never leave.

In the fifth grade, Steve brought home an F for the first time. It marked the end of his interest in maths and the beginning of a bitterly fought battle to escape from class. One of his teachers told Jack and Barbara that he absorbed everything he ever read, he just couldn't learn by rote. School bored him. So did most sport. Having struggled by on baseball in the early grades, he suddenly found his athletic deficiencies glaringly highlighted in the jock culture of Texas schools. Everyone else in the family was activity-oriented. Jack was a weebolos (a junior good citizenship troop) leader, Kelly was a cheerleader, Stacey was a brownie and Barbara was a girl scout leader, a brownie leader and coach of the football cheerleading squad. Mark made the high school football squad the first time he tried out for it; Steve gave up after several attempts. Jack felt for him. 'He was never good at sports, and Mark, who was thirteen months younger and coming behind, he was good at everything. He could hit every ball they threw at him and run fast. Steve wanted to do that. He tried. You could see he was frustrated because he'd get up and try to run and he'd trip over his own feet. He was real sort of stiff. He wasn't agile.'

Mark, who alternately envied and defended his brother, worried sometimes that his parents put too much pressure on

Steve. 'I always thought that my parents would over-praise the things that I did, trying to get Steve to improve.' Handsome, courteous and physically and academically gifted, Mark would hold his breath when Steve tried to match his achievements in sport. 'I felt like it was kind of a sore point for him and I hated to see him fail at something. At *anything*.'

Unable to make progress in football and maths, Steve joined the school band programme. Jack bought him an old cornet and his oldest son spent two years attempting to learn it under the direction of Mr Philippus, before being kicked out of the class in grade seven. One of them hit the other over the head. As Steve's brother, Mark was hated by Mr Philippus and almost every other teacher before he ever enrolled in a class. He would spend most of his school days trying to prove to teachers that he wasn't Steve or – worse still – Nick, perpetrator of numerous, still shuddered-over, acts of ill-discipline.

Although Mark maintains that there weren't many shy people in the Earle family, Kelly noticed that Steve retreated into his own world after his failures on the football field. Inwardly if not always outwardly, she felt he was shy and awkward. In fact, Steve's reasons for withdrawing were different from those she imagined. 'I talked a lot but what I discovered is it bothered people when I talked.'

In 1967, the course of Steve's life was drastically altered by several events. The first was that Sam Fain died and Nick moved in with the Earles – specifically, into the bedroom Steve shared with Mark. Nick was playing in a garage band, rode a scooter and was, in Kelly's words, 'wilder than a shithouse rat'. The windows rattled with the music of the Rolling Stones and Nick and his band held noisy rehearsals in the Earles' carport. He presented Steve with a guitar. Nick was left-handed so Steve had to turn the strings over, but the guitar changed the whole focus of his existence in a matter of days. As Mark put it, 'It was clear he had found something. He played the guitar constantly. Everywhere he went, he carried it.'

The combination of Nick's arrival and the onset of puberty ended Steve's closeness with Mark overnight. 'I kinda got pushed to one side because Nick was teaching Steve guitar.' After years of being inseparable, Steve suddenly found he had absolutely nothing in common with his brother. 'You know, me and Nick were talking about girls and cars and guitars, and Mark couldn't understand why we didn't want to go on a hike.' It was a distance that would last for years, 'mainly because, later on, when I got into high school, Mark and Kelly had to follow me into a high school where I had wreaked absolute havoc. They were pretty good kids and they got tortured because they were related to me.'

Meanwhile, Mudder had gone into a decline. For years, Steve's grandfather had been the key to her sobriety. Now she was alone again, with an out-of-control teenage son. Agonizingly, deliberately, she started drinking again.

Barbara was devastated. Throughout Steve's childhood she had been an invincible figure. Now she was flayed by ghosts. The most excruciating memories of her childhood – changing trains twice by herself, aged six, as she was shunted off to yet another relative – returned to sap her spirit. Drunk, her mother was rarely gracious; just vicious, bitter and manipulative. Within a year, Steve and Kelly would be going on search and destroy missions at Mudder's house, telling themselves that they would never be like that, that alcohol would never control their lives. There were other worries. The house in Lake Charles had been repossessed by the bank when Jack and Barbara were unable to make the notes on it. The financial fallout from it would dog them for years to come.

Another big event in Steve's life that year was the release of *In Cold Blood*, the movie based on Truman Capote's non-fiction novel about the 1959 slayings of Herbert and Bonnie Clutter and their children. While researching it, Capote and Harper Lee, who'd finished *To Kill a Mockingbird* but not yet published it, roamed the bleak, flat landscape around Holcomb, Kansas, trying to understand the community that could foster such apparently motiveless violence. 'It was always bitterly cold, really so incredibly cold on the plains,' Capote recalled in Gerald Clark's biography. 'We would drive out to some lonely ranch or farmhouse to interview the people who lived there, and almost invariably they had a television set on. They seemed to keep it on twenty-four hours a day. They would sit there talking – and never look at us. They would go on looking straight at the TV screen, even if there was just a station break or an advertisement. If the television wasn't on, if the light wasn't flickering, they began to get the shakes. I guess television had become an extension of people's nervous systems.'

It was not the first time Steve had given thought to the death penalty. In 1963, his father had written to the governor of Texas pleading for a stay of execution for Ralph Carl Powers, who'd shot a boy named Dicky Renfro. In court Powers had never had a chance. Texas law still allowed the families of victims to hire their own prosecuting attorneys, so Renfro's family hired a top-dollar prosecutor and district attorney. Powers had a public defender. In that particular case, Jack was incensed at the unfairness of the trial, but he still believed on some level that certain people were bad enough to kill. Barbara was opposed to capital punishment for any reason. She held all-night vigils if an execution was due to take place in Huntsville, Texas. The year after it was published, *In Cold Blood* was released as a movie, and it was its portrayal of killers Dick Hickock and Perry Smith, given five stays of execution before being hanged on 14 April 1965, that brought Steve round to his mother's point of view.

Hickock and Smith were kept in the State Penitentiary on Death Row, a medieval structure built in 1864. It consisted of twelve seven-by-ten-foot cells lit by a dim bulb and a narrow window covered in a black wire grille. Once a week they were let out for a three-minute shower and a change of clothing. In the summer, temperatures in the cells could reach 110 degrees. 'Forty-two months without exercise, radio, movies, sunshine, or any physical means of occupation, is a steady strain on a man's nervous system,' Hickock said at the time. 'Add the mental strain of facing a death sentence and you have a man – or men – who slowly becomes an animal – or a human vegetable.'

Years later, Steve would tell *The Nation* that the scene that made the biggest impression on him was when the Robert Blake character is 'harnessed up to be hanged. And there's an argument about whether to let him go to the bathroom. And a guard says, "Don't worry about messing yourself, everyone does it." So I'm against the death penalty on every level. It is nothing more than about pain.'

From then on, Steve began to identify more with outsiders. While Mark and Kelly showed every sign of growing into wholesome, all-American kids, Steve and Stacey had trouble socializing with their classmates. Stacey worried her parents by spending what they considered to be an unhealthy amount of time mowing the lawns and carrying the shopping of elderly people in the neighbourhood, some of whose motives they suspected, and Steve hung out with underdogs and misfits. To Mark, 'Steve very early on . . . started going a different route altogether. He was treated as an outcast, he kind of saw himself as not succeeding in some ways that were considered normal, I guess . . . and that probably was something that pushed him out seeking something else.'

The catalyst for all of this was, of course, their young uncle. Nick came to live with them at that pivotal age when Steve was making his first life and career choices. Nick's arrival made Steve very certain of what he wanted to do. He wanted music to be his life. In 1966, San Francisco celebrated psychedelia with the Love Pageant, hippies flocked to Haight-Ashbury in the wake of Jefferson Airplane, Country Joe and the Fish, Janis Joplin and Big Brother, and the counterculture kicked into overdrive with the aid of free sex and freely available wonder drugs like speed, amphetamines, LSD, heroin and acid. Steve's grades plummeted as he spent every waking hour trying to recreate the acoustic songs of Dylan, Elvis, Tim Buckley, Johnny Cash and the Beatles on his guitar. Jack finally lost his patience and decided to lock the guitar in the cupboard until schoolwork resumed its place as a priority in Steve's mind.

Steve took the cupboard door off its hinges, put the guitar over his shoulder and ran away.

3

Acid Tests

Steve and Nick lay in the disabled Hillman convertible at the bottom of the Earles' garden watching the stars blur over San Antonio. They talked softly so as not to alert Steve's babysitter who, if she'd peeked between the curtains, would have seen the faint orange glow of Steve's first joint. He was thirteen years old. With Nick as his charismatic guide, he had already travelled much further from the smalltown dreams of Texas than his parents could have imagined or even feared.

Steve first became aware that there were artists who wrote their own material when he noticed the names of Lennon and McCartney beneath the titles of his favourite songs. Almost as soon as he'd mastered the basics of guitar, he became obsessed with doing the same. His first four or five songs were all about girls, with girls' names for titles. None of them survives, although Kelly maintains to this day that the most beautiful song he ever wrote was about his high school girl-friend, Joanie. When it came to performing music in public Steve was still very shy. He seldom practised in the living room, preferring to shut himself away in his own room. Kelly was aware that 'he was playing pretty well and we knew he could sing beautifully but nobody took it really seriously until he decided he was going to be in the talent show'.

It was Steve and Kelly's music teacher, Miss Mode, who organized the district-wide show. The proliferation of military bases in and around San Antonio meant that military music dominated the curriculum, but Miss Mode was a fan of songs like 'Georgy Girl'. She taught at several schools and she encouraged her students to explore music they loved. The week before the talent show tryouts, Steve emerged from his bedroom with his guitar and sang 'As Tears Go By' for the family. Kelly listened open-mouthed. 'We didn't know where it came from. It was unbelievable. It was really amazing. And back then his voice – before all the years – it was a very, very sweet, very rich voice. It was a folk voice.'

Both Steve and Kelly, now in the fourth grade, made it to the finals. Kelly did a hula. Grandmother was almost more excited than they were. She'd been working at the college designing costumes for all the shows and with her help Steve was transformed into a rock star. At the talent show, he walked on stage in a gold satin troubadour shirt, ankle-length black jeans, white socks and loafers. He had a Buddy Holly brush cut and slung his guitar over his shoulder. He finished third.

Steve's shyness seemed to vanish overnight. He'd sing anywhere and for anyone. Mark felt from then on that Steve would be a star. 'He always thought of himself as being a star. And always acted like it. There was never any doubt that that was what he was going to do. You didn't see any plans, like, "I'm going to be successful, I'm going to do this." He was just going to drive there and do it.'

On 4 April 1967, Barbara gave birth to Patrick Collins Earle and post-natal depression closed in on her like a fog. Overnight, the forcefield that was Steve's mother was gone. The light around which the entire household had revolved – the smiling den mother, the baker of elaborate cakes, the passionate advocate of music and literature – shut down in a matter of days with no apology or explanation. She was burnt out. She'd spent so long trying to be everything to everybody that when the source of her worst nightmares, her mother's alcoholism, returned, she had no reserves left to cope.

'I can't believe it's happening again,' she said to Kelly. 'It happened to me too many times and it's all back.'

By the time the family moved for the ninth time, in Steve's eighth grade, Barbara was in the grip of a full-blown depression. She'd spend entire days at their Bella Vista Street home sitting on the couch with the curtains drawn or sleep all day and be up all night. Kelly remembers coming back from school to find the house in total darkness. 'The TV would have been on all day and she'd have been eating ice incessantly all day long. That's about all she lived on. She'd just chew ice. She ruined her teeth chewing ice and just trying to cope. And back then depression had a great stigma attached to it. Horrible. And the family in East Texas didn't really understand.'

The effect on the family was catastrophic. Steve, particularly, found it difficult. American health insurance did not extend to psychiatric care in those days and Jack's meagre income was quickly swallowed by medical bills. Barbara went into hospital for months at a stretch and had three series of electro-shock treatments. There was no Prozac in sixties East Texas. If you were depressed, Barbara remembers, you were crazy. She endured blinding migraines and debilitating surgical procedures to remove her gall bladder and appendix. Jack worked double shifts to try to make ends meet but the bill collectors hounded him constantly. It was still legal for them to call a creditor's place of work so even the FAA was inundated with calls. A stellar employee, Jack was nevertheless forced to beg for his job several times. His life, in many ways, was an unimaginable hell.

All of the Earle children felt varying degrees of anger, guilt, resentment and sadness at the storm that came over their house at that time (mingled with brief bouts of sunshine whenever Barbara returned from the hospital), but each had his or her own method of dealing with the crisis. Kelly retreated into poetry and writing and chose to view the world with what she describes as an 'altered reality'. Steve threw himself into music with a defiant passion. At fourteen, he started playing solo at coffeehouses around San Antonio. Jack drove him willingly from gig to gig, perhaps hoping that if he supported his eldest son's music, more energy might go into his schoolwork. Money was tight and Steve broke a lot of strings so Jack kept a packet in his pocket and dispensed them one by one.

It was in the coffeehouses that Steve first got a taste of the politics that would inform his music for the rest of his life. The irresistible forces and immovable objects that were Vietnam and the Anti-War movement, the Civil Rights movement and the entrenched racism of the Old South, swirled like oil and water until April 1968 when Martin Luther King was gunned down in Memphis. America exploded. Racial equality had just joined pacifism and the counterculture at the frontline of the revolution.

Steve had been raised to be tolerant and fair. 'I *heard* people say nigger, including, once in a while, my father when he was around his brothers. And his brothers certainly said it. But he tore us out if we ever said it to a black person. There really wasn't any hate attached to it. A lot of black people worked for my granddad whenever he was having a good year with the peaches. They would come and pick for him. There were years when he didn't have any money to hire anybody and people would come and help him out anyway. Not everybody but some people. There were a lot of black people at his funeral.'

Meanwhile, US television broadcast grainy images of riot police beating back black protesters and men in white hoods holding torches aloft. Then Bobby Kennedy was shot in Los Angeles on 6 June. The nation was shaken to its core. Nothing seemed sacred any more, nothing seemed secure.

Coffeehouse politics 'radicalized' Steve at an early age. The 'CID' (United States Army Criminal Investigation Command) shut down at least one of his places of work due to the activities of the Anti-War movement and the FBI opened a file on him – something he confirmed himself when the Freedom of Information Act came into being. 'If your picture got taken at [an Anti-War] rally, you got a jacket in those days.' Surrounded by activists, radicals and hippies, he became a passionate advocate of many of their causes. *The Communist Manifesto* had an almost biblical impact on him. Marxism won him over. It imbued him with 'the idea that songs should be about something – that there were more things to write about than girls – although I still write about girls'.

The bohemian culture of the coffeehouses also encouraged Steve to experiment further with drugs. Babysitting nine-year-old Stacey one evening, he began tripping badly on LSD. It was not the first time he'd had an adventure babysitting. Once he'd ordered little Stacey to cook him a bacon sandwich and she'd set the kitchen on fire. This, though, was something infinitely more dangerous. Tormented by hallucinations, he drifted in and out of reality. Stacey became more and more distressed. Both were terrified that Jack and Barbara would return. In the end, Steve was frightened enough to beg Stacey to call an ambulance. He was in the emergency room in the hospital when his parents came rushing in. Steve was hidden behind a wall of screens and white coats.

'Mom, mom!' he screamed frantically.

Barbara went rushing forward but the doctor stopped her. 'Don't go back there,' he instructed. 'Let him be scared.'

It was an incident that would have repercussions for the rest of Steve's life, largely because the innocence of the early sixties and its manifestation in Steve's parents meant a vital lesson went unlearned. Shortly afterwards, they had an almost identical experience with Mark and LSD. Jack and Barbara were shaken but couldn't see any evidence that drugs were a problem with either boy. It was only when the family doctor advised Barbara to get her brother out of the house that she become alarmed. 'Everybody knows with Nick being into drugs, he's passing it on to Steve,' he told the Earles. Jack, who had never even heard of marijuana until he was in high school, could hardly take it in. 'We just couldn't deal with the concept that our kid might be doing this.'

Nick moved out of the house when he graduated high school that year and relocated to a series of run-down houses in San Antonio. He had become a fine pianist and played in rock bands around town. Slowly but surely he slipped into heroin addiction. Steve got into trouble several times buying him groceries on his parents' charge account. Jack and Barbara pushed the problem of Nick's influence over their son to their back of their minds. They admit they were in denial. Submerged in medical bills and health worries, they thought nothing of it when Steve and Nick took a ride in to San Antonio one evening to visit a couple of Nick's friends. They had no idea that Nick, who had introduced his nephew to guitar, pot and LSD, was about to sow the seeds of Steve's destruction. At the edge of Brackenridge Park, Steve followed Nick through the doorway of a 'ratty-assed' hotel. Inside, Nick's friends were shooting heroin. So little was known about the long-term effects of heroin then that when an actor died of an overdose in 1969, Janis Joplin told a friend: 'Well, some people die and some people are survivors. I'm a survivor.' In *Scars of Sweet Paradise: The Life and Times of Janis Joplin*, her one-time boyfriend Milan Melvin describes heroin's 'best effect, the dreamy, warm, safe return to your mother's womb'. High on junk, Nick's friends offered some to Steve.

'I couldn't inject myself – Nick had to do it for me. I didn't throw up, which most people do. I should have known I was in trouble right then. It kind of really agreed with me.'

A month after the sixties reached their apotheosis in the drug-fuelled madness and musical glory that was Woodstock, Steve enrolled in his freshman year at Holmes High School. By now he had embraced the hippie aesthetic with a conviction that was life-endangering in Texas. His grandmother sewed his clothes. Stacey claims that while she was the only girl in school wearing home-made underwear with ruffles, Steve had shirts with mirrors on them. 'Picture Steve standing in the living room, my dad hollering at him to straighten up and fly right, he's got this David Cassidy haircut, pink hip-hugger pants, a midriff shirt with mirrors on and clogs . . . He wouldn't wear any underwear. He was very hippie. I remember my dad saying, "You don't have to be such a hippie. You *can* take a shower. It's been ten days."'

At school, Steve was the kind of pupil teachers' nightmares are made of. He launched an underground newspaper with a caricature of the vice-principal on the cover of the first issue. He was forever being disciplined for smoking or playing truant. The school board in San Antonio had strong military connections and they were so preoccupied with hair length and skirt length that Jack and Barbara called a parents' meeting to protest that dress was taking precedence over teaching standards. Steve registered his own protest by growing his hair. At Holmes, there were three groups of kids: the Cowboys, the Kickers and the Freaks. The Kickers listened to pop music and dressed in San Antonio's version of the latest fashion. The Cowboys wore hats and boots and belonged to the school rodeo club. They regarded it as their sworn duty in life to uphold the values of the Old South. Steve was a member of the third fraternity, the Freaks.

'It was a real division and it got violent. Kids fought about it. I got my hair cut with a pocket knife three or four times on my way home from school. I got beat half to death just because I had long hair. It just happened in Texas in those days. And it didn't really change until Willie Nelson moved back to Texas. I'm serious as a heart attack. In 1973, when Willie Nelson started having the Fourth of July picnics and these big gigs, all of a sudden Texas became, at least on that level, more tolerant.'

Steve's response to having a short haircut enforced on him was typically contrary. He took to wearing a hippie shoulder bag and was beaten up for his trouble. The south side of San Antonio, where he'd attended Rogers Junior High, was redneck country and Steve knew that there were times when his father was literally afraid for his son's life. But Steve couldn't help himself. At O. Henry, in Schertz, he wore a really long gold brocade Nehru to school one day and was sent home. 'It actually belonged to Nick. And I wore a fringe jacket and they sent me home for that. It was stupid. I got singled out because I was really loud and really called attention to myself. By the time I went to Holmes I was in a very weird position socially.'

In junior high, Steve had taken to prowling around the city at night, telling his parents he was staying over with a friend. It is the first real evidence of the wanderlust that would later consume him and become an integral part of his songs. Alone with his restless, insatiable energy, he would walk the silent streets, planning and dreaming, lyrics and music unfurling like banners in his head. 'If there were girls that were having a sleepover, that was always an attraction. But if there was nothing else going on, I'd just wander the streets all night and if I got sleepy I'd go to a Laundromat inside an apartment complex or something because it would be warm in there, and I'd sleep. I started doing that mainly to be by myself. A lot of people lived in my house, you know. But that's when I started writing, that's when I started getting fairly serious about it.'

Midway through Steve's eighth grade, the Earles moved to North-West San Antonio and life settled down a little. At Holmes, Steve had three close friends, Cary Houston, C.W. Weddington and Charlie Mullins, all misfits in their own way. Steve had met Charlie at an off-campus party and they'd bonded when they worked behind the scenes on *The World of Carl Sandburg*, a play based on the works of the renowned American poet, novelist, historian and musicologist (1878–1967). Theatre was the one subject Steve took any interest in. He liked his drama teacher, Vernon Caroll, and was happy to run lights, build sets or play music. He refused to read for parts. 'I just could never bring myself to do it.'

By the time the play was over, Charlie and Steve were close friends. A bright, awkward boy with the fire lit twenty-four hours a day, Charlie was fascinated by Steve's gift for music and the first of numerous people in Steve's life to be drawn in by his Pied Piper charisma. 'I kind of gravitated towards him because he was intelligent and insightful in a way I wasn't.'

Steve was fascinated with Charlie's ingenuity. The son of a scientist at South West Research, Charlie had a rare gift for physics and electronics. At weekends, they'd build car engines that would hardly stay on the ground, and Charlie would follow Steve around to tiny coffeehouses to help him set up his Fender Twin amp and microphone. Once they 'liberated' a set of speakers from the local football stadium and built a PA Steve could use when he played in short-lived rock bands. Their notoriety soon spread. When a set of microphones was stolen from their high school, Steve was accused. 'It wasn't me. I stole my microphones from a completely different high school that I didn't go to. And stealing wasn't something that I did. Liberating gear from the top of a pole was one thing. But I didn't break into people's cars or do any of that shit. I knew people that did but I didn't hang out with them.'

Charlie was not the only person Steve brought home. Playing the coffeehouses, he developed a reputation in the Earle household for collecting waifs and strays that lasted long after he was married. There was always a table full of extras. Jody Fletcher, a sixteen-year-old American who had grown up in Australia and was now travelling round the world, actually moved in with the family for eighteen months after Steve brought him home. Now living in Perth, Australia, he still regularly corresponds with Steve's parents. Next to arrive was Doug King, a local boy. Barbara called his mother. 'I really don't want him,' Mrs King said flatly, so Doug stayed too. Barbara still has his high school diploma. Next Steve arrived with a Spaniard in tow. The boy's father was a Spanish envoy to Mexico City and he had run away from home, catching two buses and somehow managing to hitch across the border to San Antonio. On that occasion, Jack intervened: 'I started questioning him. I worked for the federal government and it kinda scared the hell out of me that his father was a diplomat. We were getting into territory that might get me into trouble so I insisted he go home. I finally talked him into letting us call his parents.'

In the meantime, Steve had outgrown school. To Kelly and the other siblings it was clear that it had nothing to offer him. 'We always just assumed when he was younger that he was a genius.' Steve was wired, restless and ready to move on. In October 1969, the month *Abbey Road* marked a milestone in musical development, Steve's chair was empty when the Earles gathered for dinner. After a few hours went by, they began to panic. Steve was missing. More tellingly, so was his guitar.

Seventy miles away, Steve and another schoolfriend, David, were sitting on the roadside half-laughing, half-cursing at the smoking engine of the scooter. The strain of carrying two big boys to Houston had proved too much for it. They hitched a ride for the last hundred and thirty or so miles of the journey. Steve had his guitar on his shoulder, Nick's adventures in his head, and a mission.

'I was going to Nashville. That was the plan.'

In Houston, Steve found work in a pizza place. After a week, his aunt and uncle came into the restaurant by chance and he was forced to escape out the back. Bored, the boys bought some speed and a syringe and took turns to shoot it in a gas station bathroom. When the police arrived, Steve tried to flush the rig. It didn't go down. Hauled away to the station, both claimed to be seventeen. His friend, who was six feet four and could grow a full beard, might have got away with it but he had his ID in his shoe. They sent him home on the next plane. Steve stuck to his story and that afternoon an officer hit him so hard he flew out of a chair. To teach him a lesson, he was put into the adult jail overnight to think it over.

He was 'at large' for another five days, which he spent in a makeshift camp down on Buffalo Bayou. A variety of local kids brought him food until he made the mistake of taking an underage girl down there. At that stage, her parents became involved. Steve's food supply dried up. He went hungry for three days until the girl persuaded a friend to feed him. 'I remember eating two big huge bowls of Rice Krispies with ice-cold milk and almost getting sick because I ate it so fast. I was starving. And then I stole a salmon croquette that was in the refrigerator.' By now, the running-away-with-the-circus romance of it all was wearing thin. Hitchhiking around the next night trying to find the house of a girl who'd promised to leave a window open, he had his guitar stolen by a band of larking boys. They drove away with his precious guitar, laughing at his misfortune.

Back in San Antonio, his schoolfriend, David, had confessed that Steve might be found in a pizza place in the Memorial area. Jack and Barbara loaded all the kids into the station wagon and drove straight there. After two days and two nights of searching, they found him. The first thing he said was, 'Oh Mom, I've lost my guitar.' As it turned out, one of the young thieves bragged about the guitar to someone Steve happened to know and in time he managed to recover it, but the hurt caused by his escapade was not so easily fixed. 'I didn't run away from home, I ran away from school,' Steve told his parents, but still they blamed themselves. 'It broke my parents' hearts because they didn't understand it.'

In spite of these sentiments, Steve ran away again. This time Jack and Barbara, who was fresh out of the hospital and not in good shape, rounded him up in a day. They guessed he would go to a rock festival in Bass Rock, near Austin. As they were leaving the house, they were contacted by the parents of his girlfriend, Joanie. She was also missing. When the Earles reached Austin, the festival had been halted by legal wrangling and it was Barbara who surmised that Steve's next port of call would be the area close to the University of Texas. They turned off the highway and headed down Guadalupe Street, hippie central in Austin. Steve was walking down the road with Joanie.

'Huh!' Steve grunted when he saw them and heaved a big

sigh. He climbed into the car with a slightly wounded glance at Barbara, as if her sixth sense had somehow guided her to him. 'He thought it was magic.'

Bribed by his grandmother, who bought him a Gibson guitar, Steve made one more abortive attempt to start the ninth grade at Holmes High School. By the end of October, he had been dropped from every class bar theatre and biology for failing to hand in a single piece of work. He was expelled. Compulsory school age was seventeen in Texas, but the teachers were glad to be shot of him. 'If you don't come back, we won't file on you,' they assured him. Steve neglected to mention it to his parents. For several weeks, he went out the door each morning as if he was going to school, peeling off at the gates to spend the day getting into trouble with other truants and miscreants. The police began to feature more regularly in his life. He and four other boys were smoking up a storm in a vacant lot, shielded from the road by a grove of trees, when a police car came rolling by. Naturally, they were all innocent. They couldn't imagine how a bag of pot had come to be lying on the ground between them. Protesting vigorously, they were arrested and cautioned.

A week after the first marijuana incident, Steve was playing pinball at Wonderland when a familiar reflection loomed into view. 'Hi, Dad,' he said resignedly. The officer who'd cautioned him had informed Jack that Steve had been caught smoking pot during school hours. Jack had made some enquiries and found, to his horror, that Steve had been kicked out. In the end, he tried to make the best of a bad situation. 'If you're going to stay home, you're going to take care of Patrick,' he told Steve. But the pressure on him was close to unbearable. By day there was the stress of air traffic, with thousands of lives hanging in the balance, by night there were six mouths to feed and the bill collectors calling. And now there was Steve, going rapidly off the rails. Stacey still remembers the anguish at home over Steve's future. 'He was ready to go and Mom and Dad weren't ready to let him go, so there were some pretty heavy-duty arguments.'

Out of the blue, Nick, in his first year at college, was arrested for selling a matchboxful of marijuana to a federal narcotics agent. He was sent to prison for ninety days with five years' probation. With Nick out of the picture, Steve began secretly experimenting with heroin again. On a couple of occasions he did it often enough that he felt sick when he woke up in the morning and the waves of withdrawal kicked in. His parents sent him to Dr Kleck, Barbara's highly regarded psychiatrist, hoping that at the very least he'd persuade Steve to go back to school. Six months later, Dr Kleck asked to see Jack. 'He finally told us, "Steve knows what he wants to do and I think he has the talent to do it, and he's going to do it one way or the other. Either you can oppose it and read about it, or you can help him out and he'll tell you about it and he'll always come home." And that's basically the way it went.'

Towards the end of 1970, as Barbara began finally to recover and Jack retrained as a data systems officer, Jack helped Steve rent his first apartment in San Antonio. At sixteen, Steve was still too young to play at places that served liquor, but his voice and confidence made him seem older than he was and several of the bars near the river were willing to overlook his age. Steve still played coffeehouses and in bands around town, but he performed solo at Kelly's Pub, Kangaroo Court and a slightly seedy bar called the Cellar. Jack and Barbara, who had calmed down somewhat since the psychiatrist had delivered his verdict, were blissfully unaware that the Cellar was a favourite after-hours hangout for strippers. Nor had they any clue that their fresh-faced boy was actually living with a twenty-year-old exotic dancer called Karen, in whose car he would get his driver's licence. 'Very talented young lady. She could get both tassles going in opposite directions.'

Years later, when an appalled girlfriend came to him to report that his own seventeen-year-old son was sleeping with a twenty-year-old girl, Steve just laughed. I said, 'Honey, twenty-year-old girls are the only reason seventeen-year-old boys ever learn how to fuck.'

Nick emerged from jail when Steve was seventeen and started a band called Hammer, which played Allman Brothers and Steely Dan songs and some original material. Steve went to see them at the Cellar. The jail term had not dulled Nick's lethal appeal. He was still as charismatic as ever, full of dreams and plans and promises. When the gig was over, Steve spontaneously decided to move to Houston. He simply packed up and rode off into the velvety darkness with Nick, stopping at his parents' house so he could pick up some clothes. In Houston, Steve stayed at his uncle's house for a month. Prison had cured Nick's heroin addiction but not his taste for alcohol. Barely in his twenties, he was already in thrall to the drug that had killed his stepfather and would come close to killing his mother before AA and a halfway house saved her. She would spend the rest of her life working as an addiction counsellor.

Steve found work at a car wash in the midst of one of the worst gas crises ever to hit the USA. Passions ran so high among disaffected motorists that the manager handed him a .25 automatic and told him to put it in the pocket of his coveralls. Steve wasn't alarmed. It appealed to his sense of drama. He settled in the Montrose District, which was gradually becoming home to Houston's still closeted gay and bohemian community. Houston was, after all, the city which had banned Janis Joplin two years earlier 'for her attitude in general'. Gay- and hippie-bashing was a local sport. But art galleries, restaurants and little interior design or clothing stores were springing up all over the area and doctors and lawyers from the nearby medical centre were frequenting it.

Music obsessed Steve. He searched out gigs with untiring energy, haunting the popular gathering places of the burgeoning Texas songwriter scene until his songs won people over if his high-speed chatter didn't wear them down first. He wrote furiously, finding inspiration everywhere. Even the

44

venues seemed soaked in musical history, as if art clung to the smoky air. Jerry Jeff Walker had written 'Mr Bojangles' in the poky flat above a club named Sand Mountain, inspired by a man he met after being jailed for a night for intoxication. Four years after its release it had become part of the lexicon. It transcended music. Steve was a huge fan of Jerry Jeff, principally because he was larger than life. 'But he was drunk all the time. He was famous for falling into the drum kit in the middle of shows.' Listening to Jerry Jeff's best-selling album, *Viva Terlingua!*, he was also impressed by the spare elegance of a couple of Guy Clark songs. At Sand Mountain, Steve played looking at a mural of some of the icons of the new Texas songwriter scene. Guy Clark was one of them, along with Townes Van Zandt, Jerry Jeff and Mickey Newbury who wrote scores of hits, including 'Just Dropped in (to See What Condition My Condition was in)'.

It was in Houston that Steve rediscovered Sandra Jean Henderson, a pretty blonde girl who had nurtured the runaway on his first flight from home. Now sixteen and single, she and Steve started dating, but it was a year or more before Steve stopped travelling. He hitchhiked back and forth between Houston, San Antonio and Austin, where the Cosmic Cowboy scene was in full swing, playing wherever he could. He even performed for two hours at Kelly's eighth grade graduation party, something Kelly has never forgotten. 'It was the best party of the year . . . All the way through my freshman year, people were talking about it.' He went to New Mexico and Colorado for three months with a carnival after a 'carnie' Steve had fixed up with a couple of kilos of marijuana offered him a job running the grease joint. 'It was cool. But you're never really an insider there. There are people who have been with it for generations. It's very weird. It's a completely different language. They call what they do, "winning money". 'Cause all the games are rigged. So every night they go, "Let's go out and win some money."'

Steve returned to settle in Houston, as much to be with

Sandy Henderson as anything else. By now, Sandy's wealthy father had taken an intense dislike to him. He had no prospects and was a musician to boot. Steve suspected that the only reason Mr Henderson allowed his daughter to move in with him just after her seventeenth birthday was because he thought Steve's ruffian ways might put her off marrying him for good. The young couple moved into a second-storey apartment in a scruffy area near the Astrodome and Sandy got a job at Fox Fotos. Steve supplemented his income with the odd shift at the car wash.

Country music was in a strange place. At the height of the Vietnam War, President Nixon had latched on to it as the epitome of middle American values. He regularly invited the likes of Johnny Cash and Merle Haggard to the White House. In the middle of the Watergate Crisis, he travelled to Nashville to attend the official opening of the new Grand Ole Opry. As Bill Malone observed in *Country Music USA*: 'The Nixon–country music linkage seemed ominous to some liberal observers and one writer was moved to describe the music as "the perfect musical extension of the Nixon administration."'

The Texas singer-songwriters with whom Steve identified were as far from being an extension of the Nixon adminis-tration as Janis Joplin was. Like Steve, they were as influenced by the Who, Hendrix and Texas bluesman Mance Lipscomb as they were by Merle Haggard or Dylan. But no one was melding country and rock with the effectiveness of Gram Parsons. Born into a family of Florida citrus millionaires Parsons, like Steve a teenage runaway, was singing protest songs in New York's Greenwich Village at the height of the folk boom. A musical visionary, he dropped out of Harvard University in 1967 to leave an indelible impression on first the Byrds, then the Flying Burrito Brothers, which he formed with the Byrds' Chris Hillman. His fascination with both country music and the Rolling Stones resulted in a series of pioneering country-rock albums: the Byrds' *Sweetheart of the Rodeo*, the Burritos' *Gilded Palace of Sin* and his solo album *GP*, and

'Grievous Angel'. In 1973, Steve saw him play Houston's Liberty Hall with Emmylou Harris and was captivated by both the music and the ethereal loveliness of Harris, Parsons's muse and protégée. Just a few months later, Parsons was dead, his beautiful, rebellious spirit snuffed out by drugs. He was twenty-seven years old.

Throughout the early seventies Steve hitchhiked far and wide to listen to music. At a Jerry Jeff Walker show in Austin one night he overheard a band member telling someone where the after-show party was going to be. It was Jerry Jeff's thirty-third birthday and there were rumours that it was going to be the party to end all parties. Steve hitched a ride there and talked his way inside. He pulled his stetson down low over his eyes and tried to act as if he belonged. He introduced himself to a couple of songwriters he admired and puffed knowingly on a joint someone handed him.

At three in the morning, Townes Van Zandt blew in like a whirlwind. Steve noticed that when Van Zandt came through the front door, everything stopped. 'He had on this gorgeous white buckskin jacket with beadwork on it that Jerry Jeff had given him for his birthday two weeks earlier. It was Jerry Jeff's own jacket. He gave it to him literally off his back. And Townes started a crap game on the floor in the kitchen and lost every dime he had and that jacket within forty-five minutes of arriving and then left an hour after that. I thought: "My hero!" I was really impressed.'

As heroes went, Townes Van Zandt made Nick Fain look like a choirboy. He was a beautiful heathen, charming and deadly in equal measures. Born in Fort Worth, Texas, to a wealthy oil magnate, he'd led a nomadic childhood, which included a two-year stint at a private military school. At eighteen, he made a brief but dramatic appearance at the University of Colorado, where he was intending to study law. Automatically accepted into his father's fraternity in his first semester, he was invited to a mixer in the second and told to bring alcohol. He turned up drunk, hours late, with a near-empty bottle of cheap flavoured wine. Snow lay heavy on the ground, but he was barefoot and clad only in jeans. His pledge pin was threaded through his skin and two streams of blood ran down his chest.

Music was Townes's saviour and his demon. It was said that he learned his first chord at fifteen and his second at twenty-one. When he realized that Dylan wrote his own songs, he knew he wanted to write regardless of whether he made a living. By the time Steve met him he'd released six albums, the most recent of which was presciently entitled, *The Late, Great Townes Van Zandt*. Townes saw life as a 'veil of tears'. Beneath his graceful melodies and intricate blues, his lyrics were as barbed as they were lovely, full of death and codeine and the heartbreak of yellow-headed women who took all you gave them and left only shame. Guy Clark, who met Townes in the mid-sixties at the Jester Lounge and would become his closest friend, thought his songs were 'just drop dead beautiful'. But Townes valued art above business. After half a dozen albums he was known only by word of mouth beyond Texas.

The more Steve heard about Townes, the more fascinated he became. Banned from Sand Mountain for reasons now lost to history, Townes hung around at the Old Quarter. Steve started playing and socializing there too. He liked its mellow ambience. There was a pool table upstairs and it was always fun to go out on to the rooftop and smoke pot while looking at the Houston Police car pool across the street. His audience at the Old Quarter rarely exceeded five people. 'The most exciting thing that happened during a gig usually when I played there was that some dog would wander in and [the owner's] dog would get laid right in front of the stage. It happened a couple of times and I got totally upstaged.'

One night, Townes himself walked in and sat so close to the stage that his feet were resting on it. Between every song he shouted out: 'Play the "Wabash Cannonball"!' Steve played on doggedly, wondering what he'd done to deserve the dubious honour of being heckled by Townes Van Zandt. At last, he admitted that he didn't know the song. 'Call yourself a fuckin' folk singer and you don't know the "Wabash Cannonball"!' jeered Townes. Steve flushed with anger. Without a word he began to play 'Mr Mudd and Mr Gold', a Townes song with so many lyrics that he'd worn out his vinyl copy of it picking the needle up and putting it down again. Townes was silenced for the rest of the show.

They were twin souls, Townes and Steve, fiercely bright and drawn to danger, obsessed with music, politics and writers – literary as well as musical. Within weeks of meeting him, Steve was hitchhiking to Austin and other Texas venues to open for him. He also began playing at the University of Houston coffeehouse and Anderson Fair, a now legendary vegetarian restaurant in the Montrose District. Both were popular hangouts of a whole host of fledgling Texas songwriters; Nanci Griffith, Lyle Lovett and Richard Dobson all got their start there.

Townes, Steve discovered, lived from gig to gig. He never had any money. At the end of one night at Castle Creek in Austin, he paid his band members $30 a piece, gave Steve $20 and kept $50 for himself. 'That's mine, I'll eat that,' Townes declared and he put the $50 bill in his mouth and swallowed it. Drunk, the shock value was worth every cent to him.

Flirting with disaster was Townes's favourite hobby. According to Steve, 'one element of his masochism' was to go down to a hardcore gay leather bar in the Montrose District in the early seventies and sit there and drink. 'He got the living shit beat out of him, got his tooth knocked out and his Martin stolen. He never had a decent guitar after that.'

After 1976 or so, Townes never cared much for any other drug except alcohol, which was well suited to his lifestyle and, Steve came to believe, gave him a better excuse for behaving badly, but in the early seventies he was not averse to shooting heroin. He was twice declared DOA in Houston after overdosing on it. Steve no longer had enough money to experiment with heroin himself so he drank a great deal and did cocaine whenever Townes saved him a few lines. Despite this,

Townes, he says, was very protective of him. 'He wouldn't stop me from drinking but he'd lecture me about not putting the cap back on the bottle because it can get kicked over and you can lose a whole bottle of whisky after the liquor store is closed.' Spellbound by the contrast between Townes's manic thrill-seeking and his gentle, poetic integrity, Steve savoured his newfound friendship. In art and in life, Townes was everything that he aspired to be. 'I was still a child when I left home so my upbringing was completed by Townes and Guy. Well, first a lot of strippers and then Townes and Guy.'

4

Nashville Skyline

The night before Steve married Sandy Henderson, her father offered him $5,000 to leave town and never come back again. Steve put it down to an excess of alcohol. 'You don't think much of your daughter, do you?' he said sarcastically. 'That's pretty cheap.'

It was not the first time that Sandy's affluent parents had attempted to postpone the inevitable. In Houston, they'd persuaded Steve and Sandy to go to a family counsellor in a bid to talk them out of getting married so young. They knew nothing of Steve's extracurricular activities with Townes, but they had him down as a boy from the wrong side of the tracks. He wouldn't fit in at the country club. Much to Steve's amusement, the counsellor failed to play the game. 'He said we were all right but they should maybe think about getting a divorce.'

Steve and Sandy were married in June 1974 at Earle's Chapel under an electric-blue Texas sky. Despite the bad feeling between Steve and his father-in-law, it was a magical wedding. Grandmother made all the gowns and nineteen-year-old Steve was beaming in a suit. As Mark put it, 'Steve and Sandy were in love for sure.' Siblings, cousins, aunts and uncles came from all over the country and Elijah's Chapel resounded with the rich voices of the family singers. Afterwards there were photographs amid the shady trees and walks through the little cemetery, where Steve's great-great-grandparents lay buried. Along the track, a feast was laid on at the Earle family farm.

In one respect, the Hendersons' fears were not entirely groundless. Steve and Sandy were innocents, with no way of knowing or preparing for what lay ahead. All they felt they needed was love. But Steve was not about to forgive Mr Henderson for trying to buy him off and within a month of the wedding he and Sandy had moved to Cibolo, Texas, near San Antonio, where they could stake a claim on their independence. It would be easier for Steve to earn good money there. He would play the coffeehouse circuit and hitchhike to Houston and Austin whenever Townes needed an opening act.

In Cibolo, the newlyweds rented a little house for $50 a month and travelled around in Sandy's ailing car. Steve got a regular spot at a restaurant called the Roth Baren. On Fridays and Saturdays he sang 'Help Me Make It Through the Night', a handful of Jerry Jeff Walker songs and some original material, and for that he received $25 and all the free food he could manage. Most weekends, he made around $200 with tips. Sandy worked part-time. But beneath the surface everything was not as rosy as it seemed. Caught up in the excitement of being the new Mrs Earle, Sandy was unaware that Steve was wrestling with his emotions. His safe, middle-class background had left him feeling compelled to create tension in his life in order to have something to write about. Now he found himself in suburbia. In more ways than one, he was beginning to sympathize with Marlon Brando's character in *The Wild One*, who in reply to the question: 'What are you rebelling against?' drawls: 'What have you got?'

Steve's siblings had gone through puberty and Barbara's depression and emerged the other end with only one thing in common: they were fanatically driven. Mark, particularly, was almost obsessively focused. A fine athlete and A-student, he'd had to fight throughout his school years to live down Steve's reputation and be accepted on his own merits, and a degree of rivalry and resentment had sprung up between the two brothers. They were polar opposites. While Steve was playing in coffeehouses and reading William Burroughs's *Junky*, Mark's teens were spent drawing and playing trombone in a twenty-piece big band. Even a brief flirtation with drugs smacked less of rebellion than a conscious protest. Mark's gift for music had earned him a scholarship offer for North Texas State University but he knew without asking that his parents couldn't afford to send him. Instead, he applied to join the air force for four years on a programme guaranteed to get him into air traffic control. To Kelly, it was 'almost like he had a shield up during that period'. The family were concerned that Mark was smothering his artistic side, but Mark had made up his mind that he wanted to follow in Jack's footsteps and succeed in what he called 'an organized environment'.

Towards the end of Mark's last year in high school, Barbara and Jack moved to Houston, where Barbara, her health and vigour restored, would build a thriving career as an apartment manager. At that point, Mark moved in with Steve and Sandy. According to Steve, that didn't go down too well with his new wife of only thirty days. In fact they rarely saw each other. With Mark working during the day, Sandy in the afternoon and Steve at night, there wasn't much time left for socializing.

In October, Mark was admitted to Lackland air force base in San Antonio for six weeks of basic training. Steve came to visit him on his only day off. The first thing Mark knew about it was when the phone rang and the desk sergeant barked: 'You need to get up here right away.'

Steve was standing cheerfully in the orderly room looking like a passenger on Ken Kesey's bus in *The Electric Kool-Aid Acid Test*. He wore his favourite white clogs and his hair cascaded over his collar. Behind his desk, the sergeant was boiling. Steve's very existence was an affront to everything he stood for. 'I'm tempted not to let you go,' he snapped at Mark.

53

Mark feigned a look of innocence. Was there, he asked, anything in the regulations that said he couldn't leave the premises because of the way his brother looked? Huffily, the sergeant signed him out. He flounced out from behind his desk and marched towards the office door, wrenching it open. Steve walked through it in front of him.

'Thanks,' Steve grinned.

In November, it was Steve's turn to feel aggrieved. Sandy's sister took a student teaching position in Mexico and the Hendersons organized a family vacation to help her settle. They invited Sandy but neglected to ask Steve. 'I was pretty hurt by the deal.' He was even more hurt when Sandy actually went to Mexico. Every time he pictured his pretty young wife drinking margaritas in the sunshine, he fumed. Alone in the still, empty house, he picked at his guitar and paced about. The nameless restlessness that had caused him to wander the midnight streets and run away from home repeatedly in his early teens still nagged at him, marriage or no marriage. The week stretched invitingly before him. He'd played his two gigs at the Roth Baron and his $200 earnings were still unspent. His thoughts turned to Nashville, the city made vivid by the stories of songwriters like Townes, David Olney and Richard Dobson. On the spur of the moment, he decided to hitchhike to Tennessee. He made a couple of calls to recruit a replacement act for the Roth Baron and left behind $50 to pay the rent but no note for Sandy. Pausing only to pick up his guitar he took off.

It took Steve two long days to get to Nashville. He spent the first night with his grandmother in Jacksonville, buying a bag of pot from one of the students at the college where she was a den mother, and the second at a motel in Memphis when he couldn't get a ride. Add food and a fair amount of alcohol and it wasn't long before he had only $6 to his name.

Steve finally rolled into Nashville at ten o'clock in the evening. Broadway had been suffering from urban decay even before the Grand Ole Opry had moved from the Ryman the previous March and now, eight months on, was shabby and forlorn, as if the heart had been ripped right out of it, but Steve was elated simply to be in Nashville. At Limeballs, a pre-Opry all-night diner, he ordered a grilled cheese sandwich and a coffee and settled into a booth and drank refills and read *The Tennessean* until sunrise. His eye was caught by an ad for movie extras for a crowd scene being filmed in Centennial Park. No money was involved, but they were offering dime hotdogs and nickel Cokes. That sounded like breakfast, lunch and dinner to Steve. When the streets began to hum, he made his way past the dismal souvenir shops, grubby bars and adult movie theatres of Broadway, and along West End to Centennial Park.

The movie turned out to be *Nashville*, Robert Altman's sly, sardonic commentary on Music City, which used the business of country music as a metaphor for American society. It was critically and commercially successful but, as Bill Malone noted in *Country Music USA*, 'Many country fans perceived the movie not as a fable of a society that had lost its direction and purpose but as a frontal attack on their music and the culture that embodies it.' Steve spent the day hanging around Centennial Park with a bunch of friendly local kids. When he asked them if they knew where he might play for tips, they pointed him in the direction of Bishop's Pub on West End.

Rodney Crowell, a hot young songwriter who would become one of the key figures in the alternative country movement, still remembers Steve's arrival at Bishop's Pub: a 'skinny kid in a big black hat' with 'pin ball machine energy'. To Steve's surprise and relief, his songwriter friend Richard Dobson was working behind the bar and offered him a place to stay. That was lucky but not as important in the long term as a chance meeting on the second night. He was leaning over the pool table at Bishop's in a swirl of cigarette smoke when Guy Clark came over and complimented him on his hat. Hats and boots were important in those days. The hyperactive kid and laconic, craggy-faced songwriter liked each other on sight, and not just because they had Townes Van Zandt in common. Much more than by Steve's hat, Guy was 'knocked out' by his songs. 'They were really outstanding. They were stark and really not self-conscious or cloying or trying to get in the music business. They were pretty real songs. Imaginative. He has a really nice way with the language.'

Guy also warmed to Steve himself – his quick intelligence and fizzing energy – although on the whole he preferred him when he drank because 'he didn't talk so much.'

Unknowingly, Steve had stumbled into what Rodney calls, 'the heart and soul of Nashville in that day'. Bishop's was a lively musicians' haunt, not dissimilar to many others in town, but it had the distinction of being the second home of a now legendary group of writers: Guy and Susanna Clark, Townes, Robin and Linda Williams, Johnny Rodriguez, Richard and Rodney and, of course, Mickey Newbury. That night, Richard had a blazing row with his wife and Steve moved in with another Texas songwriter, Hugh Moffatt, now best known for the Dolly Parton hit, 'Old Flames (Can't Hold a Candle to You)'. After ten days in the buzzing, creative vibe of Bishop's Pub, Nashville was in Steve's blood. Although he needed to return home to Texas he was also planning to come back. Motorists glancing at the young cowboy hitching a ride on the city limits, sweat-stained t-shirt pulled taut by his guitar, dark hair flopping across his face, had no idea that they were witnessing the birth of a revolution in country music: Steve Earle had just begun the most tempestuous journey of his life.

Steve arrived home the day after Sandy returned from Mexico. 'I'm moving to Nashville,' he informed her. Within a week, Sandy was living with his parents and Steve was packing his bags for Tennessee. Barbara was vehemently opposed to the idea, heartsore that her brilliant son was squandering his intelligence on a dream that might never be realized. 'It wasn't that I didn't want him to do that, I just thought he could do so much more than that.' A lawyer or doctor was what she had in mind. But Steve was nineteen and on fire and nothing she said or did could stop him. Jack combed the house for all the loose change they had left after paying the electricity bill and came up with $17. Steve's grandmother gave him another $20. Steve stopped in at the Kerrville Folk Festival on his way out of town. Folk singer Nanci Griffith recalls him rushing up to her and her songwriter husband Eric Taylor, with whom Steve had become friendly through the Houston circuit, and asking if they would look after his belongings because he was moving to Nashville. They still had them two years later. Nanci had never met Steve before and thought him a beguiling, vital presence. 'He was incredibly handsome, incredibly handsome. Just a lovely, lovely person. From that point of meeting him until today, he's still the same Steve Earle.'

As female singer-songwriters, Griffith and Lucinda Williams were something of an anomaly in Texas in those days and were regularly confronted with the sexist attitudes of male writers like Guy Clark, Townes and even Eric Taylor. But from early on, Nanci found that Steve was different. He adored women in general, always had women friends, and consistently appreciated and encouraged the music of gifted female writers – Nanci in particular. 'He still treats me with the greatest of respect, just as he treated me with respect when I was nineteen. And I think that says a lot for Steve Earle.'

Years later, Steve's country classic 'Guitar Town' would reflect the youthful optimism he felt as he finally set off for Nashville.

> *Everybody told me you can't get far*
> *On thirty-seven dollars and a Jap guitar.*

The plan was that he would go on ahead and find work and Sandy would stay with his parents until he could afford to send for her. In fact, she lasted just a night with Jack and Barbara before deciding to go home to her own family. Steve was already halfway to Nashville. It was December and he was confident that he could get a job framing houses while he shopped his songs and tried to make a name for himself. He hadn't counted on Nashville being at the tail end of a recession. In some ways, country performers were more high-profile than ever; Loretta Lynn and Merle Haggard had both appeared on the covers of *Newsweek* and *Time* in the preceding two years. But the industry had lost its way. Historically, country music had had many flirtations with commercial popular culture – rockabilly being just one of them. Each had resulted in a further attempt by Nashville itself to slough off country's rough edges and distance itself from its hillbilly origins. By the seventies, country music was well established in the public mind as white music. More particularly, it was seen as the music of white Southerners, conservative and steeped in religion. In fact, the music that had crossed the Atlantic with the early Anglo-Celtic immigrants evolved into 'hillbilly' or early country music only after a process of filtration through other, predominantly black musical forms, such as Negro spirituals, the blues and a whole host of African-American vocal and instrumental techniques. It was in the isolated Southern mountain regions – the Ozarks and Appalachians – that the music first took hold. It's ironic that white Southerners borrowed most heavily from the music of immigrants and the black people they helped enslave or discriminated against, but the purity, grit and aching longing of the songs spoke to the rural poor. They themselves were among the most dispossessed people in America.

Ensuing generations of hillbilly singers – Jimmie Rodgers and Hank Williams being among the most influential – would acknowledge the debt they owed to black music, but that contribution was one of many to be erased or glossed over as the rise of rock 'n' roll and rhythm and blues forced country to smother its impoverished rural beginnings in a bid to retain commercial appeal. The word 'hillbilly' itself became anathema. By the early seventies, these tactics were proving a resounding success, although traditionalists felt that they came at the expense of country as a musical form. When the Country Music Association named Australian pop singer Olivia Newton-John as its 1974 Female Vocalist of the Year, outraged country stars Tammy Wynette, George Jones, Loretta Lynn, Dolly Parton, Tanya Tucker and others formed a rival organization called the Association of Country Entertainers (ACE) to preserve the heritage of country music. Funnily enough, it was Barbara Mandrell – of all people – who described the controversy as 'the worst crisis country music as an art form has faced in twenty years'.

With the construction industry at a standstill, Steve's minimal building skills were of little use, and it seemed an age before he found work in a pizza place. Unable to afford to go back to Texas, he spent Christmas alone and it was January before he had saved enough money to send for his wife. Sandy rode up on a bus by herself. 'Her parents were horrified, but they weren't going to buy her a plane ticket because they weren't going to help. That's the latest thing the counsellor had told them.'

Sandy stepped off the bus to find a very different scenario in Nashville from the one she had imagined. Her handsome young husband had found a niche for himself and a channel for his songs in Guy and Susanna Clark's home. If he wasn't at their house making tapes, he was at picking parties (song-writer jams) or playing for tips in bars. He was caught up in a whirl of musical mavericks to whom boundaries (artistic and legal) were for smashing and nothing else mattered but the integrity of the songs. Except, of course, poker. Steve lost his jacket to Mickey Newbury on a visit to Guy and Susanna's house and almost froze to death.

'We drank a lot. *I* drank a lot. And we took speed because it was cheap and it allowed us to stay awake and drink longer. You could stay awake for two or three days at a time. And cocaine was beginning to happen, but with us it was still pretty democratic and nobody could really afford it that we really knew directly.'

None of this necessarily included Sandy unless Steve made a point of taking her along, as he did to a going-away party for Rodney Crowell, who was leaving for the West Coast to join Emmylou Harris's Hot Band. The apartment building where Rodney had, to all intents and purposes, been squatting, had been condemned and was to be razed to the ground the next day, so the party had a hedonistic, apocalyptic vibe. Steve and his friends went out and bought four gallons of pure-grain alcohol and several litres of Kool Aid and 'made this big huge No. 2 washtub full of punch. We bought two grocery sacks full of different colour markers and everybody wrote or drew on the walls all night . . .' It was, Rodney recalls, 'a blast of a party . . . We practically burned the place down.' A painter friend of theirs devoted the evening to creating a giant mural and a woman Steve uncharitably viewed as 'probably the person I'd least wanted to see unclothed in the whole world', stripped off and spent the rest of the evening wandering around naked. Sandy was wide-eyed. Even Steve had to acknowledge it was weird. The building was torn down the next day. 'Rodney moved out in the morning, got on a plane, and as he was doing that they were levelling the building. I went by the next night and it was just a pile of bricks. Now that's art!'

Steve's lodgings since leaving San Antonio had largely comprised of floors and couches, but that January Townes and Guy introduced him to Texan John Lomax III, who needed someone to housesit for him for three weeks. John was the grandson of John Avery Lomax and nephew of Alan Lomax both renowned American folklorists and musicologists. His father, John Avery Lomax Jr, had been in real estate but he also ran the Houston Folklore Society. It was through the society that Lomax had met Guy Clark and Lightnin' Hopkins in the fifties. Raised on rock 'n' roll, he'd tended for the most part to shy away from the folk music associated with his family until he saw Townes play the 11th Door in Austin in '67 or '68. Lomax was 'floored, absolutely floored. I thought he was as good as Dylan or any of those guys back then. Should have been huge.'

After moving to Nashville to work as a writer and publicist, Lomax had stayed in touch with Townes and Guy Clark, and it was Guy who recommended Steve and Sandy. Lomax was married but he was reluctant to leave his wife in charge of his house and three-year-old son for fear that she would wreck the place. 'Nutso', was his term for her. Later he claims, 'Steve . . . actually carried on with her quite a bit.'

Lomax had been hearing about Steve's songwriting skills for a year or so from Townes and he was intrigued to meet him. 'This is Steve Earle,' he remembers someone saying and in came a force of nature. His overwhelming impression of the young man who would change his life's course was one of pure, uncontained energy. 'Just somebody that couldn't sit still and was just so full of what he was doing and the "life". You know, he was sort of living the Townes/Hank Williams life absolutely full on, pedal to the metal at all times. No pause for reflection or anything. I mean, he might pause in his talking because his mouth got dry and take a drink!'

Through it all Sandy sat there quietly, never really volunteering a word. Whenever Steve did quit talking, it was only to pick up his guitar and sing. Lomax thought he was terrific, but more of a folk singer than a country singer, at least with the way country music was at that time.

'But good enough. He could have cut a record back then. And his goal was to cut an album before he was twenty-one. 'Course that didn't happen.'

It's not clear if Steve actually features in any of the crowd scenes in *Nashville*, released in 1975, but one thing is sure: even as Altman's view of Music City was winning over pop fans to the three-chords-and-the-truth sensibility of country music, so country music was beginning its own courtship of pop. For all their righteous anger at the dilution of traditional country music, many ACE members were quick to recognize the opportunities offered by the country–pop merger. Within a couple of years of the Newton-John outcry, Dolly Parton, the CMA's Female Vocalist of the Year in 1975 and 1976, was actively reinventing herself as a pop singer, scoring pop hits with 'Here You Come Again' and '9–5', and Mandrell was proceeding along a route where she would eventually out-Vegas Vegas. 'Nash Trash' was the term disparagingly used to describe some of the music at that time. Still, there was no denying the appeal of artists like Anne Murray and John Denver, who courted both audiences with songs like 'Snowbird', 'Tennessee Waltz' and 'Thank God I'm a Country Boy'. Kenny Rogers, too, sold $250 million worth of records between 1977 and 1984, thanks to hits like 'Lucille', 'The Gambler' and 'Ruby, Don't Take Your Love to Town'. The Bellamy Brothers raked in royalties from the crossover smashes 'Let Your Love Flow' and 'If I Said You Had a Beautiful Body (Would You Hold It Against Me)'.

The world inhabited by Steve and the Bishop's Pub songwriters was a million miles away from the soul-searching going on in the area known as Music Row, home to Nashville's country music business. They were inspired as often by Robert Johnson or Gram Parsons, as they were by Hank Williams. Experimentation was their watchword. They were drunk on music and life and cheap bourbon or, in the case of Rodney, the dregs of drinks brought to him in the kitchens of TGI Friday, where he worked as a dishwasher.

Steve was the youngest person in the group and he watched and learned hungrily. The charts were full of saccharine but the substance was making itself felt. *Red Headed Stranger*, Willie Nelson's concept album about love and death in the Old West, broke that year and his cover of 'Blue Eyes Crying in the Rain' was the biggest-selling country song. Nelson was a member of the so-called Outlaws, a group of artists who, in looks, behaviour and music, had more in common with rock 'n' roll musicians or the gunfighters of the Old West than mainstream country artists. They included men like Waylon

Jennings, a protégé of Buddy Holly, and David Allan Coe, who sported 365 tattoos and who, between the ages of nine and twenty-nine, had never been out of reform school or prison longer than six months. As a group, the Outlaws existed largely as a product of the Nashville publicity machine, but their anti-hero status and the harder, more adventurous edge to their music was very real. It was that stream of country music which spoke loudest to Steve at the time. He spent as much time as he could at the studio of the legendary producer, publisher and musician, Pete Drake, where Outlaws like Coe could often be found.

But it was Guy and Susanna's house out on Old Hickory Lake which was the main gathering place for songwriters. Susanna remembers musicians turning up twenty-four hours a day, never phoning ahead, much less knocking. 'Anybody who walked in the door just knew it was going to be fun all the time. It was wonderful.' Wine flowed constantly. It was an environment every bit as decadent and exhilaratingly creative as that inhabited by the Beats who had captivated Steve in his youth. One high – whether induced by drugs, alcohol or music – inspired another. On any given night, you could see John Hiatt, Mickey Newbury, Billy Joe Shaver or renowned finger-picker Dick Velour or Jim Stafford. And Steve, long skinny limbs clad in denim and flannel shirts, would be right in the thick of it all.

To Susanna, the artistic electricity in the house was 'like Paris in the Twenties. The most brilliant people came by to show us new songs or we'd show them new songs. There was always a guitar going and I was painting in the background and listening to all this wonderful music, or I was out there trying to sing songs with them and writing a few of my own at that point too . . . I do remember that if anyone brought in a new, surprisingly wonderful song back then, we'd all say, "Let's kill him." And that was the highest compliment you could give anybody.'

* * *

To the twenty-year-old singer-songwriter all of these experiences were invaluable, but it was Townes and Guy who were Steve's real mentors. Guy included him in everything, every chance he got. When Neil Young came to town, Guy and Jerry Jeff Walker drove to Steve's apartment at three in the morning and hauled him out of bed to play Dave Olney's song 'Illegal Cargo'. Steve couldn't get over the fact that they'd 'drug' him out of bed to play somebody else's song for Neil Young. Townes, too, never lost an opportunity to say, 'Hey, Steve, play that song,' if there was a newcomer in the group. Steve saw himself as Townes's apprentice. 'He was genuinely interested in what I did and wanted to hear my songs every time he saw me. He made me feel really good. He made me feel important.'

Watching them together, it occurred to Rodney that Steve emulated Townes the way he himself emulated Guy. 'Townes was so dreamily poetic and Guy was so possessed with this self-editorship – like this jeweller's eye.' But Townes's mentorship came at a price. While Rodney was very wary of Townes, discomfited by the man's searing criticism of his songs, Townes could be even more cruel to Steve. Steve did everything he could to try to earn Townes's approval, but the older man rarely – if ever – praised his music directly. His approval of Steve was strictly tacit: he let him hang around. As Guy put it, 'what Townes was trying to show Steve was, you've got to be yourself, not me. Because the minute you try to be me, I'll beat you every time, because you can't compete with me.'

In Guy's opinion, Townes was hard on everybody. When an acolyte brought a song to Townes for his approval, he had a habit of going, 'Mmm, that's nice,' somewhat patronizingly, then picking up a guitar and playing the song considered his masterpiece, 'Pancho and Lefty'. Guy saw that as honest rather than hard. 'The one thing you couldn't do is blow smoke up Townes's dress about quality work.' Like him or loathe him, most people acknowledged that Townes's intellect was breathtaking. The class and refinement of his background were as evident in his work as they were in his personality. It was hardly surprising people aspired to be him. But Rodney felt that Townes's 'free-wheeling decadence belied the fact there was an extremely wise man there. He was an enigma, Townes. While he was real scary and kept you off balance, he was also very courtly and sweet and gentlemanly and well bred.'

Like Rodney, Steve felt Guy was much more pragmatic and patient when it came to the mechanics of songwriting. 'Townes talked in sound effects. But being in his presence, it became obvious what he was doing and I just got it. I understood that I'd met people who had decided that doing something was so important that they were going to do it whether they made money or not.'

Lomax was struck by the difference between Townes and his protégé. 'Steve had ten times the ambition or maybe a hundred times the ambition of Townes to *succeed*. I mean, Townes just wanted to write songs and play 'em, that was the end of it. Steve wanted sort of a Bob Dylan-sized success. He wanted it all . . . He'd certainly paid the dues and he could entertain by himself which, if you find an act like that, especially nowadays, you've really got something because most of them are a construct of one sort or another . . . I thought, this guy's going to make it if he doesn't explode or spontaneously combust.'

A record of that time still exists in the form of a video called *Heartworn Highways*. A beautiful evocation of the songwriter scene in mid-seventies Nashville, it tells their story through a series of offbeat encounters with people like Townes, Guy and David Allan Coe. Steve himself appears in the scenes shot at Guy and Susanna's house on Christmas Eve. He sits around a table with the Clarks, Richard, Rodney and photographer Jim McGuire singing Christmas carols and drinking whisky and wine. When the group strikes up a spontaneous version of 'Silent Night' ('Shhi-i-lent Night'), Steve plays his guitar and sings along. Despite his youth and shyness there is something compelling about him.

Townes's magnetism comes off the screen like a tangible entity. A handsome and engaging character, it's not difficult to see why Steve was so drawn to him. But Steve was attracted to the dark side of Townes as much as he was to the poetic side. Townes revelled in head-games. Every time he saw Rodney he'd intimidate him into a duel to see who could slap the other's hand first. Rodney's hands would turn 'blistery-red on either side' and tears would burn the back of his eyes. Townes would just laugh at his distress. There came a day when he stole Rodney's girlfriend without him even realizing it, took her upstairs at the studio, had sex with her and sent her back down. Susanna told Rodney later: 'You didn't even know it but Townes fucked your girlfriend!'

Leaving Guy and Susanna's house late one night, Rodney offered to give everyone a ride back to downtown Nashville in his van. He drove an ancient red bakery-type truck, with a seat for the driver and a mottled selection of lawn chairs in the back. His one-time housemates, Dobson and Skinny Dennis Sanchez, a six-foot-seven bass player weighing about 120 pounds, piled in, along with Townes, who was so drunk he appeared to be in a stupor. The chairs rocked loosely around in the back. None of them was bolted down. If Rodney had had an accident, everyone would have flown through the front windscreen. Driving into town that night, Rodney kept looking in his mirror. He had a feeling something was up. Skinny kept poking Townes. 'Wake up, man,' he teased him. 'Can't you hold your liquor?'

In Hillsboro Village, Rodney pulled up outside the house where Townes was staying. Without warning, Townes sprang out of the vehicle and smashed his beer bottle against the wall. He threw Sanchez on to the pavement and leapt on him amid the broken glass. Dobson tried to tackle him and Rodney was yelling, but Townes wouldn't let go of Sanchez. 'He's going, "I'm going to cut your goddamn throat." He goes down like he's going to cut his throat and I said, "STOP!" And he looks up at me and gives me the old wink. He was having us on.

Skinny Dennis thought for sure he was dead.'

Somehow, Steve kept up with them all. To this day, Susanna's not entirely sure what made her and Guy take Steve under their wing, except that they liked the fact that he wasn't ambitious in a hard way but simply wanted to learn everything he could possibly learn and do everything he could possibly do. He just had so much raw energy and nerve. 'He hung with everybody and after he started, do you know he sprouted wings and flew faster than anybody I've ever known in this business. He went, in my eyes, from a little kid to an incredible, incredible talent once he was allowed to let his light show . . . Every time I heard a new song of Steve's I was just amazed because I always thought of him as the Kid.'

In October, Guy persuaded Pat Carter of Sunbury Dunbar, a division of RCA, to sign Steve on a publishing deal and put him on a $75-a-week draw. Steve was so determined to write songs that lived up to the art aspired to by his new friends that he threw away every song he'd written before he came to Nashville, except one, which he sold to Sunbury for a $100 advance. It was the most money he'd ever made. In that golden fall, writing songs like 'Darling Commit Me' (in which a man appeals to his lover to put him in the looney bin so he can play Parchese with his looney friends) and making his first multi-track recordings, it began to seem as if Steve's path to success in Nashville would be smooth and uninterrupted, as if cutting his first album at twenty-one was not such an ambitious proposition after all. He couldn't know then that it would be eight years before he got a record deal and ten before he made his first album. Or that there'd be many terrifying rivers to cross before then.

He settled down to write, adopting the philosophy that he would live on his draw and anything else that he could make from music, but would absolutely not do a regular job. Sandy worked at J.C. Penney's until she became convinced that standing behind the candy counter all day would make her fat. Then she gave waitressing a try. Money was tight. When Susanna ran into Steve at Sunbury Dunbar and he told her he was fretting about how to raise the money to rent a new apartment, she loaned him $100, telling him to pay her back when he was rich and famous. Twenty years later, he paid her back in spades, donating a 'large' sum of money to her favourite charity, a Nashville dental clinic for the working poor.

Steve's progress was largely due to Guy, who invited him to sing backing vocals with Rodney, Sammy Smith and Emmylou Harris on his classic song, 'Desperados Waiting for a Train'. It appeared on his first album, *Old No.1*, released in 1975. Steve had adored Emmy ever since he was sixteen and saw her play Liberty Hall in Houston with Gram Parsons, so he was thrilled to meet her. 'She gave me half of her cheeseburger. I wasn't the same for weeks.'

Planning a little New Year tour to follow the release of *Old No.1*, Guy had the idea that Steve should play bass for him. 'I figured if he could play the guitar, he could play the bottom four strings. How hard can it be? I learned later.'

Steve could hardly believe his good fortune. 'Oh, wait till I tell my friends back home I'm playing bass for Guy Clark,' he raved to Susanna.

By any reasonable standard, the gains he had made in under a year, barely out of his teens and in a strange town, were enormous.

They left for the tour in a blinding snowstorm, their rented van restricted to fifteen miles an hour all the way to Arkansas. Guy, Susanna, Steve, guitarist Champ Hood and drummer Chris Laird were headed for Austin and Houston with a few pit stops along the way. Steve had worked hard on his bass parts but concedes, 'I wasn't the best bass player in the world.' Guy loaned him a bass, which he managed to lose: 'Don't know what happened there.' Guy, who had always performed as a traditional folk singer and had never played with drums or bass before, just laughs when he thinks of that tour. 'We were *horrible*! I mean, I'm not a great guitar player, Steve's not a bass player and Champ was learning to play the fiddle so he played it every chance he got . . .'

Out on the road Steve was 'sorta in charge' of Susanna. 'One time, Susanna was really on a rip. This is when cocaine had sort of become the drug of choice whenever anybody could afford it and they were starting to spend money on it. She came and got me. She hired me. She paid me $50 to follow her round and apologize for her as she left every room. I dutifully did it all night. "She's sorry, see you later!" She behaved really horribly and I'd follow her round and apologize.'

In some ways, Steve felt closer to Susanna than he did to Guy, just because Susanna communicated more. Steve, on the other hand, was never quiet. Susanna still teases him about the long drive back from that tour when he sat in the back seat and delivered a stream-of-consciousness chatter from Houston to Nashville. 'I finally turned around and said, "STEVE! You have *got* to get your one-liners down!" And he and I have never forgotten it. I knew there was brightness there but it was just so anxious and scattered and going in a thousand different directions that hadn't been harnessed yet, you know, and once it got harnessed and he had a direction, he grew into one of the finest people I have ever known.'

It was Nick who phoned Steve to tell him that fifteen-year-old Stacey was pregnant. Afterwards, Steve wondered why it had been his uncle and not his parents who called to say that his sister had just discovered she'd been expecting a baby for five months. She was going into the Methodist Mission Home in San Antonio. She would give the baby up for adoption at the end of her term.

Back in Texas, the Earle family was in shock. Steve felt only compassion for his sister. The late diagnosis had left Stacey ill, and Steve wrote to her and went to see her as often as he could muster up shows in Texas. To Stacey, isolated and sick with self-loathing, those visits were literally life-saving. 'He never let me down, that was the thing about it. I had to look forward to someone coming to see me. I was in there with thirty other pregnant women and we were all just sitting there like ovens baking. I had to be there [four] months. But Steve would come and see me – "spring" me, he called it – and he was very sympathetic. He always managed to calm Mom and Dad down because anything that I did could not be as bad as what he was doing. He could always top me.'

In her early teens, Stacey had become something of a wild child. She had not had an epileptic fit since she was five, but she continued to be treated with kid gloves for years afterwards. Barbara's depression and Steve's early exit, leaving Stacey in charge of little Patrick, highlighted two traits in her: a strong mothering instinct and a restless rebelliousness similar to Steve's. She had blonde hair, big eyes and olive limbs, and boys flocked around. School bored her. She and her oldest brother were the most alike of all the siblings. When Steve came home from Nashville, Stacey would sit at his feet and listen to him, feeling as if he was the only one in the world who understood her. Watching them, their mother realized, with a little jolt of fear, that they shared a self-destructive streak. Steve himself recognized his own tenaciousness and independence in his little sister. 'We both started out at a really early age deciding that we knew what was best for us. And as far as the big things go, I think we both did. We both have had to deal with mistakes that we've made that are just human and make the best of what went on around them.'

Increasingly, Kelly was left out of the circle. Mark had taken on a military demeanour and Steve and Stacey were always off smoking pot under the pretext of going out for Dr Peppers. Ever since Kelly had been caught shoplifting in her mid-teens – a schoolgirl prank in which her only part had been agreeing to pocket an eyeshadow her friend stole – she'd resolved to be as good and sweet as she possibly could. If there was tension in the house, she made it her mission to get rid of it. At high school, she shone. 'I decided I wasn't going to have sex, wasn't going to do drugs and I wasn't going to do a lot of drinking.' She was relentlessly cheerful. Steve, meanwhile, had taken Susanna's advice and honed his one-liners. Kelly's perfectionist agenda included trying to make herself beautiful and she found herself constantly the butt of his cynicism. 'He just treated me like I was this piece of fluff. "Oh, you look like the lead singer from Kiss." Or I'd say something and it would be, "You don't know what you're talking about." All the things that make you feel stupid.'

The most sensitive of all the Earle kids, Kelly became progressively more defensive. She put a wall up around her emotions. When Steve came home and was welcomed like the prodigal son, she made a point of avoiding him.

Steve and Sandy were also growing further and further apart. Steve was moving ahead so furiously that his wife of two years was already part of his old life, a symbol of the inertia, banality and pain of everyday existence he'd left far behind. Steve was on the road for days and weeks at a time, at the Clarks' house or playing music with Townes. When Guy's short tour was over he had formed his own band with guitarist Larry Chaney, a 'lunatic' drummer named Leland Waddell, keyboard player John Salem and Dwight Harrad on bass. It was the sort of band that played a bit of everything. Steve sang his own songs but also those of Bob Wills, Bob Marley and Bob Dylan ('All those Bobs'), and he and the band developed a little four-state tour, starting in Texas and moving on to the Carolinas and Georgia.

For the most part, Sandy was either left out or left behind, unable to keep up with the whirlwind of music, musicians and intoxicating substances. 'Sandy put up with a lot of shit and she did not deserve any of the crap that she got. I still feel really guilty about it. But I met somebody.'

That somebody was Cynthia Hailey Dunn, born in Davidson County, Tennessee on 16 December 1951. She was four years older than Steve and had one prior marriage. Steve was having the time of his life at a party on Music Row in mid-1976 when their eyes met across a crowded sidewalk.

'I was balancing on a wall about twelve foot above Seventeenth Avenue in front of this house. I had a dispenser of nitrous oxide in one hand and a bottle of tequila with sixteen hits of LSD dissolved in it in the other, and a joint about [a foot] long in my mouth and everybody was sort of out there cheering me on and Cynthia got out of this cab and looked up and it was love at first sight. And she could match me hit for hit and drink for drink and suck the chrome off a trailer hitch, and I was twenty-one years old, how the hell was I supposed to know it wasn't love?'

5

Weddings and Shotguns

The wedding was held in the Take 5 Bar at the old Metropolitan Airport in Nashville, an unromantic venue but a convenient one: Steve was on his way to catch a plane. There was no white lace and no angelic bridesmaids and the presiding 'clergyman' was a mutual friend who had obtained a minister's licence in the mail. Lyricism was not his strong suit. When it came to the vows, he turned to Cynthia during a break in airport announcements and queried: 'Do you?'

'Yeah,' she responded.

'D'you?' he asked Steve.

'Yeah.'

'Well, you are.'

And with that, he signed the marriage certificate and dropped it in the mail the next day.

It was 21 January 1977. Steve and Cynthia had known each other for about nine months – 'It's a blur' – and had been living together since Sandy's tearful departure from Nashville in the summer of 1976. As Barbara put it, 'Her daddy kept trying to get her to come home and finally one day she did.' Steve and Cynthia's relationship was, to put it mildly, tempestuous. 'God, you talk about a nightmare. We *fought* – I mean, fist fights occasionally. I tried to run her over in my truck in the middle of the parking lot next to the Goldrush one time, chased her round until I finally hit someone else's car. Then I gave up.'

Their worst row had in fact happened *before* they decided to get married. Steve had been scheduled to play a gig in Athens, Georgia, but his band had been fired shortly before they were due to perform. Fortunately, Cynthia was there with her car. Steve sent the band home in the van and he and Cynthia continued on to Rosa's Cantina in Atlanta, which was holding a fifty-cent tequila night. Both Steve and Cynthia had a lot of affection for Rosa's. Steve had spent several memorable nights playing there and Cynthia, who'd lived in Atlanta when she first left home, still had friends who hung out there. That evening, they got stuck into the fifty-cent shots of tequila. Next thing Steve knew Cynthia 'turned up missing'. She was in the back seat of a Volkswagen with a biker. Steve 'shot up the whole parking lot. The only reason I didn't kill him, her and somebody else is, I couldn't hit anything. I was just too drunk. I was really lucky. I did manage to murder a Toyota Tercel that I'm pretty sure never ran again because I hit it three times in the bonnet. Pow, pow, pow! It was the closest car to the Volkswagen.'

They left in a hurry, before the cops arrived. Tearing through the midnight streets, screaming at each other at the top of their lungs, they had a small accident. Steve drove up on to the median, collided with a broken signpost which had been the victim of another hit-and-run driver and flattened two tyres. They were forced to leave the car there. When they woke up in a motel the next morning, the worse for wear, Steve telephoned the cops and told them he'd lost his car.

'You mean, your car was stolen?'

'No, I lost it.'

It took them two days to find the car and then another day to round up the money to replace the stolen distributor cap. Steve still shudders at the memory. 'It was a nightmare.'

By a curious coincidence, their wedding took place on the

very day that the biggest break of Steve's career so far was due to materialize. Elvis was planning to record his song, 'Mustang Wine', and was scheduled to appear in Buzz Cason's Creative Workshop, a modern Nashville studio, on 21 January. But on the day of the session, Elvis cancelled due to a 'throat condition'. By now his handsome, smiling, baby-blue-eyed looks had given way to a sagging belly and heavy-lidded frown, leading the *Memphis Commercial Appeal* to describe him as a fat 'sensuous clown'. There was open speculation that he was depressed and using drugs. When he returned to Memphis without recording a single note, the *Nashville Banner* suggested that he was 'paranoid' and 'afraid to record'.

Scarcely had Steve recovered from that disappointment than RCA announced that it was selling Sunbury Dunbar to an LA-based company. It wasn't clear what was going to become of writers like Steve and Guy. Steve was on tenterhooks until it was established that he hadn't been released from his contract and would continue to receive his weekly draw $150. His relief was short-lived. Within weeks it became apparent that the LA office had no interest in his songs and considered them too country. Telephoning them to discuss the situation, he found he couldn't get past the receptionist. Disillusioned, Steve sat around the house getting high and watching TV. He was restless. He and Cynthia owed back rent on Cynthia's apartment while the house Steve had shared with Sandy just stood abandoned until the sheriff came and took away all the furniture. 'I went and tried to pack it up but I ran across a picture of Sandy in her wedding dress and just absolutely broke down for the first time.'

As an interim measure, Steve made tentative plans to fix up a cabin on a property in Williamson County, North East of Franklin. Nobody had ever lived there and there was no indoor plumbing but the rent was only $45 a month. Steve had just had the electricity hooked up when, overnight, he and Cynthia suddenly had the idea of moving to San Miguel de Allende in Central Mexico. They were spurred on by the notion that they could just pack everything up and go.

For Steve, at least, it wasn't just a whim, it was an obsession. Growing up in San Antonio, a city infused with the art, culture and history of Mexico, he had always been fascinated by the romance of life across the border. His family's musical road trips, with Mexican treats and a riotous border town at the end of them, were among the most fondly remembered days of his childhood. Two years previously, Sandy's parents had grudgingly paid for him to go to San Miguel with his wife to help her sister move some belongings. Steve had fallen head over heels in love with the town. Founded in 1542 by a Franciscan brother, it had become a thriving artists' community, with cobbled streets and the ambience of a Tuscan village. Steve had dreamed about it ever since. Now with Sunbury Dunbar gone and his band winding down, there was no longer any pressing reason for him to be in Nashville. It stood to reason that life would be much cheaper in Mexico. Besides, Steve thought, he needed a change of scene.

They left for Mexico in the middle of the night. Cynthia had put everything but a few clothes in storage at her parents' house and she loaded the rest into Steve's white Ford van, on which his dad had co-signed a loan at the Credit Union in San Antonio. Late the next afternoon they rolled into Jacksonville.

Steve's plan was to wait for 1 April when he was due to receive a $600 cheque from his publishers and then his old schoolfriend Charlie Mullins would drive him and Cynthia to the border town of Laredo so that they could catch a train to San Miguel. That was the plan. In the end, about eight or nine friends decided to give the couple a big send-off in Corpus Christi on the Gulf Coast, which was not exactly on the way. On the beach, after much revelry, Steve fell asleep in the sun. Normally encased in jeans and cowboy boots, his bare legs and feet burned and blistered so badly he could hardly walk. The impromptu vacation was expensive and by the time he reached Laredo, Steve had $300 remaining. He was forced to pay a $20 commission charge to cash another $100 travellers' cheque.

Red, aching and considerably lighter in the wallet, Steve boarded the train with Cynthia.

Over two hundred years ago, San Miguel was formally charged by the Crown for having 'an excess of fiestas'. It was a criminal charge which the citizens defeated and, by 1977, when the young couple climbed off the train, the locals used any excuse for a carnival. Even on the most ordinary days San Miguel was ablaze with colour. Perched on a hillside, with church spires and plazas sprawled below, every available space was alive with bougainvillaea, lilies, marigolds and yellow roses. There were street-sellers and rainbow-hued salsa bands and the air was scented with jasmine. And everywhere there was legend and exotic history. It was on the tracks at the foot of the town that Neal Cassady, Kerouac's exuberant muse for *On the Road*, was found face down in 1968. He had, so the story goes, set out on an amphetamine-driven mission to count every railroad tie between San Miguel and Celaya.

In *On Mexican Time: A New Life in San Miguel*, Tony Cohan describes the city as a verdant paradise: 'Nature is still strong here: extravagant birds of eye-popping colour, insects of surreal size. Weather is vivid, immediate: fervid sun, steep cooling shadows. Intense daily rains cool the town. When the first fat drops hit the stones, vendors break down their displays or drape them in plastic and scurry for cover. Disdaining umbrellas, people hover cheerily beneath arches or in doorways while the savage downpour hammers roofs, smashes foliage, turns streets into impassable creeks. Just as quickly the clouds pass on, leaving the land cleansed, the sky released into blazing sunsets and star-flung nights.'

In San Miguel, Steve and Cynthia went straight to La Cucaracha, a bar named after a folk song which uses marijuana-smoking cockroaches as a metaphor for Pancho Villa's army. When they asked about cheap accommodation they were directed to the Hidalgo. It wasn't the Hilton but it was close to the centre of town and its clean, spartan rooms had hot water and access to a courtyard. To celebrate their arrival they went on a tequila and marijuana binge. When Steve woke up the next morning, he was lying in a pile of glass. Cynthia was watching him from the bed.

'Let's go,' she said.

Steve pulled himself groggily upright. 'What do you mean, "Let's go"? We just got here.'

'Oh, no,' said Cynthia. 'We got kicked out. We've got to leave. He told me, soon as you woke up we had to be out of here."

Irritated and hungover, Steve paid out about $80 in damages – anything breakable in the room was in pieces and the sink was off the wall – and they dragged their bags back over the cobbled streets to La Cucaracha. There, they ran into Steve's friend, 'Pancho', the black sheep of an old Castilian family, whom he had met on his first visit to San Miguel.

'We got kicked out of the Hidalgo,' Steve told him.

'Fuck,' marvelled Pancho, 'you might as well go home. That's the pits. There's nowhere else to go. You started at the bottom and got kicked out.'

The Corpus Christi episode, the hotel fiasco and assorted indulgences had left Steve close to broke and, within a few days of arriving in San Miguel, he was penniless. But Steve was too bright and made friends too easily ever to be left completely in the lurch. He went in search of a guitarist friend, Eric, whom he'd met on his first trip to the town and discovered that his mother, Sidell, was taking in boarders. She offered to let the Earles stay for free until Steve could arrange for money to be wired to him. Hers was an eccentric household, not dissimilar to Mrs Madrigal's in *Tales of the City*. A gay English antiques dealer, who played chess, smoked a huge amount of pot and was generally adored shared the residence with an alcoholic from California, who was whiling away his twilight years by drinking a litre of tequila every single day.

The latter was generally loathed. Steve put a litre of tequila away himself most days, but he felt he was fairly good-natured. 'I mainly was a danger to property and myself, not to people. I didn't start fights. I got into them but it was usually running into somebody that was a bigger asshole than I was.'

The other occupant of the house was Steve's drinking buddy Pancho, Sidell's live-in lover. When he wasn't downing tequila, much of Pancho's energies went into going out of his way to horrify his traditionalist, moneyed family. Steve was a willing collaborator in these endeavours and it was with that in mind that he, Cynthia and Pancho set off to a party at the family ranch on the outskirts of town. Outside the hacienda, guests were dotted in elegant cliques on the emerald lawn, sipping politely at Pepsi and El Presidente. The new arrivals were soon bored. Steve wandered over to a little compound where the hired staff were roasting a pig and spent several pleasurable hours smoking, eating and drinking tequila in the sunshine.

By two o'clock in the afternoon, he could hardly see. It was then that the guests relocated to the bullring. The ranch was renowned for the fighting bulls it bred and matadors came from miles around to hone their skills in its practice arena. The idea behind the party was to give some of the local young bucks an opportunity to test their manhood against the young bulls. Steve tottered over to the arena and sat on the wall with the cowboys on the opposite side to the guests. A bull trotted into the ring. Steve's neighbour looked at him with a huge grin. '¿Esta banito, Stevie?' he cried. 'You want to go for it?' And with that, he slapped him on the back and shoved him off the wall.

Steve landed hard on the ground, the muleta over his head. When he stood up, the bull was in front of him. He performed an awkward pass, making sure the cape was as far away from his body as humanly possible. When this ploy worked, he grew bolder, fortified by the tequila. The next pass was conducted with a flourish, drawing a loud 'Ahhh!' from the crowd. But when he looked up for a third time, the bull was staring directly at him. Ignoring the cape, it came at him like an express train.

'About four feet away, I go, "Uhh-oh!" I dropped the cape and, in three-inch-heel cowboy boots, ran up a fuckin' adobe wall six foot tall and somehow was sitting on top of it. I don't know how I did it. And then I went back to the party and fell in the food. That's the last thing I remember. I woke up with guacamole all over me.'

After more than a month of waiting it became obvious that the money wired to Steve had gone astray. He and Cynthia managed to get a lift to the border, some 700 miles away, and Charlie brought him two cheques; until Steve had a fixed address, his mail was being sent to Charlie's. He and Cynthia had been fighting like cat and dog, so she went home to Nashville and Steve went to Houston for Kelly's high school graduation. Nobody in the family knew what to think about his marriage to Cynthia. Kelly considered her a 'perfectly lovely woman' but wondered whether Steve had met her on the rebound. 'I don't think he's ever gotten the fact that you can live with a woman and not marry her.'

Steve went back to San Miguel on his own. It was the beginning of a two-year spell where he spent much of his time in Mexico, renting accommodation for two or three months at a time and moving on when the mood took him. Cynthia came and went, depending on the state of their marriage. On that first occasion they were apart for three or four months. A 'mutual interest in drug abuse', as Steve has always referred to it, meant their relationship was a tempestuous one, exacerbated by the amount of tequila they consumed. Steve claims to have forgotten everything that happened after six p.m. between 1977 and 1979 when he was in San Miguel.

In August 1977, Steve went to Nashville to try to persuade Cynthia to return to Mexico with him. As a temporary measure, he moved in with Townes, who was camped out in the ramshackle cabin Steve had begun to fix up before Mexico had lured him down south. After several migratory years Townes had finally settled in Nashville. His 1976 double album, *Live at the Old Quarter*, had at last earned him some measure of the attention his exquisite songs merited and Emmylou Harris and Hoyt Axton would both record 'Pancho and Lefty' in 1977. But despite these gains his behaviour was becoming increasingly self-destructive. To Steve's mind, Townes was always a nightmare when he drank. 'And he knew it. He really had a gift for sabotaging himself.'

The problem was that alcohol didn't merely cause Townes to become rude. More often than not, he became childlike and out of control, actively courting disaster or even death. He had been known to jump off bridges and catch himself by his hands at the very last second, fling himself from third-storey windows or balance on railings ten storeys above the street. That August Steve saw him play Russian roulette in Nashville. He walked into the house to find Townes in a chair with his old .357 single-action revolver in his hand. What happened next chilled him to the bone. 'I don't even remember how it started because we were both pretty drunk, but he started loading one chamber with a shell, spinning it, and putting it to his head and pulling the trigger. And every time I'd reach for him to try to get it, he'd pull the hammer back and I was afraid that I'd cause the gun to go off if I grabbed it. I watched him do it about three times. But that's all it was: stupid drunken behaviour.'

On 16 August, Steve and Townes were sitting idly listening to Paul Harvey, an ultra-conservative commentator to whom, to Steve's bemusement, Townes listened religiously every morning and noon on a Nashville rock station. They had decided that they weren't going to drink that day. Suddenly an announcer cut across Harvey's latest invective and said the unthinkable: the King was dead. 'It was weird,' Steve recalls. 'We both heard it at the same time but we both went: "What? What did they say?" We had to hear it a second time. Both of us heard it but neither of us would say it to the other one.'

It was surreal to be in Tennessee on the day that Elvis Presley died. He had passed away in his bathroom at Graceland in the early afternoon, his gold pyjama bottoms around his ankles, his face in a puddle of his own vomit. Before any autopsy was completed, Shelby County medical examiner Dr Jerry Francisco had told a press conference that his death was due to 'cardiac arrhythmia due to undetermined heartbeat'. The medical examiner's office would cling to that original diagnosis from that day forward, even after the two main laboratory reports concurred that the primary cause of death had probably been polypharmacy. In *Careless Love*, Elvis's biographer Peter Guralnick found that one report indicated the 'detection of fourteen drugs in Elvis's system, ten in significant quantity. Codeine appeared at ten times the therapeutic level, methaqualone (Quaalude) in an inarguably toxic amount, three other drugs appeared to be on the borderline of toxicity taken in and of themselves, and "the combined effect of the central nervous system depressants and the codeine" had to be given heavy consideration.'

Stunned and emotional, Steve and Townes went out on a drinking binge. In Franklin, it took them a while to find anyone to wait on them in the liquor store. The whole town was at a standstill. People were standing frozen beside televisions and radios, transfixed by the terrible news. When they eventually headed down the rutted dirt road that led back to the cabin, Townes was drunk. Without warning, he suddenly swung out of the passenger seat and shoved his foot hard against Steve's on the accelerator pedal. They careered crazily off the road, with Steve shouting and wrestling with the wheel, before Townes laughingly relented. His arm was still in a cast following a car accident two weeks earlier.

Steve had always been intrigued by the macabre romance of genius cut down in its prime. Brilliant, vibrant, seemingly unstoppable figures who'd all but impaled themselves on the altar of their art. Hank Williams, for instance, or James Dean.

His association with Townes and the death of Elvis, his boyhood idol, fuelled that fascination further. He wanted to know every detail of the mysterious events that followed the death of Gram Parsons, whose body had been kidnapped from Los Angeles airport by his road manager and an accomplice posing as undertakers, and later found ablaze in California's Joshua Tree National Park (in accordance with Parsons' wishes). One of Steve's favourite books was *Lust for Life*, a graphic account of Vincent Van Gogh's tortured artistry. He recognized that Van Gogh had taken things to their furthest extreme but he liked the idea of 'art at all costs'. Still he maintains, 'I didn't go out and become a heroin addict thinking that I could write better songs if I was a heroin addict.'

The live fast, die young ethos of bands like the Sex Pistols also appealed to Steve and on 8 January 1978, he would see them live at Randy's Rodeo in San Antonio. As he later told *Q Magazine*: 'It was one of the shows on that last tour, the one where Sid got hit by a bottle and probably lost half a pint of blood. If it hadn't been such a shitty, short show he probably would have died! Ha ha! I didn't think they were very good but I thought it was kinda cool. And it had a big effect on me, and this is the point of it all: hey this is supposed to be fucking *fun*.'

Listening to Steve talk, Pam Lewis had the impression that he didn't expect to live beyond thirty. 'But part of that is you die a legend.' Staggering out of a bar at two o'clock in the morning, he would scare Charlie Mullins half to death by climbing on top of the roof of Charlie's truck and insisting on riding down the interstate at eighty miles an hour. With the wind tugging at his clothes and only an alcohol-loosened grip on the luggage rack between him and the flashing blacktop, he would, like Townes, laugh in the face of disaster; living fast, unafraid of the hereafter.

New Year 1978 had found Steve and Cynthia back in San Miguel. They rented a little apartment on the hill above the square. Its name translated as 'the place where doves live', which Steve considered apt 'because it was a long goddamn walk up there when you were drunk'. He started a little three-piece band with a harmonica player and a guitarist and played acoustic shows of his own material.

But Steve could never stay still for long. The rootlessness of his childhood was nothing compared with the nomadic life he led now. He was in constant motion. If he wasn't in Mexico or Nashville, he and Cynthia were living with Charlie and his new wife in San Antonio. Charlie and Cynthia were constantly at each other's throats, however, and in the summer of 1978 the Earles found themselves in a trailer in Wimberley, Texas. Steve's newest idea was to base himself in the Austin area and try to become involved in the latest attempts to create a music industry there. He soon discovered that work fell by the wayside with so many temptations on offer in the town. 'It was too close to the border and the dope was too cheap and the girls were too pretty.'

In Wimberley, Stacey came to live with the couple. Her experience in the Mission Home and the anguish of giving up her baby for adoption had left her traumatized, caught somewhere between childhood and a very adult rebellion. She quit school and was waiting tables and living with her parents in Houston. She felt desperate. As always, it was Steve to whom she turned and it was Steve who suggested she come to Wimberley. It was a wild few months. Once Steve collapsed with alcohol poisoning and had to be resuscitated by Charlie's sister, Peggy Mullins. But Stacey stayed. 'He always took good care of me.'

Guns – specifically cap 'n' ball pistols – were Steve's new obsession. At weekends, he and Stacey would sit on the porch in a haze of pot smoke and shoot cans off the fence. If Charlie, Michael Mimms and friends came calling, the trailer park would resemble a scene from *Butch Cassidy and the Sundance Kid*. There'd be guns blasting, bullets zinging crazily and the acrid smell of gunpowder hovering over upturned whisky bottles. One memorable afternoon, they pulled all the spare tyres out of their cars, rolled them down the trail and tried to shoot them. Ricocheting bullets twice hit the trailer behind them. As a life-saving measure, Cynthia confiscated the guns, but not before the idea was born for 'The Devil's Right Hand', arguably the best song Steve had written to date.

Guns and experiences with guns would crop up more and more regularly in Steve's life. Guns were synonymous with outlaws. They appealed to the revolutionary in Steve. Like millions of other Americans, his attitude was, if they take away handguns, other freedoms will be next. It would be years before he'd come to realize that attitude sat strangely with his stance against the death penalty. Guns too were an integral part of the live fast, die young ethos. Gram Parsons had been photographed in a Cadillac bedecked with ornamental revolvers. Townes played fast and loose with weaponry. And in Nashville, Wild West imagery and lawlessness in general cropped up regularly in both the music and personal lives of the Outlaw movement, to which Steve felt he was apprenticed. 'Whiskey Bent and Hell Bound', Hank Williams Jr sang gleefully and tattooed Outlaw David Allan Coe claimed to have actually killed an inmate during his spell in Ohio State Prison. Steve, as yet, was still experimenting with weapons. In the first of literally dozens of close calls with guns, he was shot with a .22 at the Triple A Icehouse in San Antonio. Drunk on tequila, it had slipped his mind that Mexican etiquette required him to check with a woman's date before asking her to dance. Steve found the whole episode comic: 'Broke the fuck out of my rib but the bullet barely broke the skin. Couldn't hardly breathe for two weeks.'

While Steve and Stacey were blazing a trail through Wimberley and Mark was between air force postings, their sister Kelly's life had become a waking nightmare. In November 1977 Steve had received a shock announcement. His nineteen-year-old college-bound sister was getting married. Steve went to

Houston for the wedding but he, like the rest of the family, had reservations about it. Kelly walked up the aisle on her father's arm knowing that she should have taken Jack's advice and run.

Within months of the wedding, Kelly's handsome upper-middle-class husband had dropped out of college, joined a motorcycle club and started undulging heavily in drugs and alcohol. Life quickly became unbearable. David developed a violent streak. Soon his problems spilled over into Kelly's job as a leasing agent and she was fired. Terrified that her parents would discover the truth about her marriage, Kelly encouraged David to move with her to his hometown of Oklahoma City. They moved in with Kelly's mother-in-law, the most eccentric woman Kelly had ever met in her life. Bright, bubbly Kelly, who had dreamed of going to college and becoming a writer, suddenly found herself waiting tables at 5.30 in the morning.

It was the Waffle House that saved her life. 'I would have gone completely insane living in that house and, when he'd get mad, beaten up . . . I worked in three Waffle Houses and four Steak & Eggs and there wasn't a person there who didn't have a worse story than mine growing up. But they were the most hopeful people I ever met in my life. They're the ones who told me, "It's okay to be whoever you want to be. It's okay to tell your parents 'I screwed up' and they're not going to tell you 'I told you so.' It's okay to leave this loser."'

Throughout her ordeal the person whose judgement she feared most was Steve. 'Because he was the only one that would come up to my face and say, "You've done a lot of stupid things but this is the absolute stupidest thing and I can't wait to tell you 'I told you so.'"' And at that point I'd lost sight of who he really was . . .' When Stacey became the latest Earle to take a rapid-fire trip up the aisle, marrying Michael Mimms and giving birth to their son Christopher, in February 1979, Kelly finally found the courage to escape her hellish existence. She went home to Texas to see the baby and never left. Steve arrived for a visit to find the family all aghast at Kelly's story. Steeling herself for his sneering condemnation, Kelly, who'd piled on weight and was a withdrawn imitation of her former self, received only unconditional love and support from him. 'He and Mark wanted to go and kill [my husband]. My poor parents. *I* was moving back in with them, Stacey, Michael and the baby were living with them and Mark was living with them – all in a three-bedroom apartment.'

The principal appeal of Cynthia as 'somebody as interested in destroying themselves as I was . . .' began to wear thin when Steve's publishing contract ran out in the spring of 1979 and the couple moved back to Nashville. Cynthia was a talented dressmaker with visions of running her own business, but she had plenty of distractions – cocaine, for instance. According to Steve, 'Cynthia's circle of friends were completely and totally about that. All they did was sit around and snort cocaine.'

Steve's introduction to coke had been as a class-A narcotic that people injected, but he was always very wary of it and preferred to inhale it. However, it had become trendy. The in-joke was that cocaine should be declared a vegetable. 'People who were almost health-conscious otherwise went around saying that all that stuff about cocaine being addictive is a myth. And it's not a myth. It's one of the most addictive substances known to mankind. The physical withdrawal symptoms are much more subtle than heroin but they do exist and the emotional part of it is devastating. It instantly changes your brain chemistry, it instantly creates a demand for itself.'

Steve's first adverse reaction to cocaine happened out of the blue. Since returning to Nashville, Steve had been performing at writers' nights around town and had put together a couple of short-lived bands which opened for bigger acts at a venue called the Exit/Inn. There was very little money about. On this particular night, Steve was playing a benefit for the National Organization to Reform Marijuana Laws (NORMAL) when he suddenly 'melted down', losing co-ordination and forgetting lyrics. Dizzy and disoriented, he stood on stage feeling as if he was about to pass out. For a man to whom performing had become an integral part of his life, the experience was shattering. A fortnight later it happened again. For the most part, the attacks were performance-related. They would strike without warning and leave him paralysed and debilitated, his chest clamped tight. He was forced to stop playing live altogether. When he visited the doctor, he was told he was simply wound too tight. He should get some exercise, cut down on the junk food and eat a balanced diet.

It would be nearly two years before Steve could perform again. The fact that he was unable to play live was a massive blow to his pride and to his self-esteem. Depression gripped him. The panic attacks didn't stop him writing songs, but they seemed to steal the froth off the joy of his existence. They put his career on hold. Nothing was the same, not even the songwriter evenings. He felt very alone. Broke, he had no choice but to get the first day job he'd had in years, hanging billboards for an outdoor advertising firm. Working at dizzy heights with a collection of unreconstructed rednecks for company, he felt further than ever from his dream.

In a last-ditch attempt to free himself from the horrific attacks, Steve gave up cocaine, marijuana and alcohol completely. He simply eliminated them one by one. Effectively, he realized, he also had to give up Cynthia. She was determined to continue to enjoy a hedonistic lifestyle; Steve couldn't and wouldn't participate. It's hard to say which of them was more impossible to live with during that period. The elimination of virtually everything pleasurable and desirable from Steve's life left a huge, all but unfillable void in him. It was four or five months before he began to feel better physically and longer still until he started to get to grips with the situation emotionally. The combination of looming debt, Cynthia's affection for the high life and Steve's lingering depression put a huge strain on their marriage.

'I don't think things were ever the same between us. I mean, it was a very volatile relationship. It was fuck or fight. 'Cept we always fucked more than we fought.'

That changed when a new factor entered the equation. Bored by Steve's attempts at clean living, Cynthia started staying out all night, sometimes at the house of a coke dealer friend. According to Steve, there were always fifty or sixty people there. To begin with Steve went with her but then he stopped doing coke. 'For several months I hung out there for a while and it's kinda boring sitting watching a bunch of people eat their own teeth. And then a couple of different men dropped her off at the house at five or six o'clock in the morning. We rowed about that and then finally I was out someplace and I came home and caught her in bed with somebody.'

It was Christmas Eve. Cynthia had already planned to spend Christmas Day over at the dealer's house, where they had what Steve viewed as an evil celebration every year where 'they passed out gifts, half of which were electric dildos and shit like that'. Steve decided to give it a miss. 'It was the only time I ever called my dad and had him send me a plane ticket. I went home for Christmas.'

6

Ringside Seats

Carol-Ann Hunter sat on a bar stool at the Villager with her back to the stage where Steve was setting up. It was a shotgun room so there wasn't a lot of choice in the matter, but in truth she was enjoying the attention of her friends. They were envious that *she* was there with Steve. Sipping at her beer, Carol barely paid attention to his preparations until the first languid notes stole into her heart. 'He was in the middle of a song – the first song – and it just hit me so hard. I turned around and looked at him and I thought, "My God." I got chills to my bones. I thought, "You are going to be a star."'

Carol was utterly in love with Steve. They had met two summers previously at the Villager, in Hillsboro Village, where Carol was working behind the bar. A gregarious college dropout, with the high cheekbones and the glossy dark hair of a young Emmylou Harris, Steve took one look at her and decided she was 'drop dead beautiful'. Carol-Ann thought Steve was the most handsome man she'd ever seen. 'He's a Capricorn, so he's winning, he's charming, intelligent and just very friendly.' Despite this mutual admiration, they started as friends and nothing more. Steve was still roaming between Nashville and Mexico and Carol didn't believe in playing around with married men. Besides, Steve made her nervous.

'I liked him – my God, I thought he was cute. But I was afraid of guys like him. They would come running into your life, take over and just dump you. And I didn't know Steve that well. I just knew that he and Cynthia were having trouble. I did *not* want to get caught up in that.'

Towards the end of 1979, with his marriage collapsing and depression threatening to consume him, Steve went to the Villager more often and found comfort in his friendship with Carol. At that stage in his life, comfort was in short supply. Years later, his liner notes for 'Hometown Blues' ('Went home to Texas and no one remembered me but the cops') would read like an amusing aside, but the late seventies when the song was written it was a harsh truth. In 1975, his youthful declaration that he would record an album by the time he was twenty-one had seemed a realistic probability when he was at the centre of all that was daring and decadent and brilliant in Nashville music. Half a decade on, after scores of tequila-laced road trips in the tradition of the Beats or *Easy Rider*, Steve could not even be said to be back where he started. He had, in fact, regressed.

For Steve, it was his inability to perform live that was hardest to bear. Even the set at the Villager had ended prematurely when he felt the pressure in his chest build up and the lyrics dissipate. With music gone, Steve's only salve was Carol, whom he had started dating on his return from Texas at Christmas. In December, he had visited her at the print shop where she worked part-time, seeming distracted. 'Miss Carol, do you want to do something or go somewhere?' he asked.

'You're married,' Carol said reproachfully.

'We're getting a divorce,' Steve burst out, and emotion welled up inside her. Still, she kept her distance until he and Cynthia were officially separated. When Steve's divorce came through on 10 March 1980, he and Carol moved into an apartment.

With two marriages behind him, Steve tried hard to make this new relationship work. Carol was outgoing and bohemian and so kind that – as her son would later put it – 'it almost makes you mad'. It bothered her for a week if she was mean to anyone. But Carol was also very vulnerable emotionally. An abusive childhood had left her with traumatic scars. At twenty-one, she was working two or three jobs, drinking beer and 'acting crazy', as she puts it. She had no goals besides having babies. Her weekends were spent at the Springwater bar in Nashville. Steve had practically eliminated drugs and alcohol from his life so he wasn't a big fan of it. 'They had a pool table and that's what she did on Friday and Saturday nights and that was non-negotiable.'

In the summer months, Steve found a part-time job building tennis courts. He started at seven and sweated over the tram-lines until noon, at which point the Tennessee heat made the material too difficult to spread. His afternoons were spent knocking on the doors of publishing companies and pitching his songs. It was disheartening work. None of the mainstream publishers had any interest in signing him. This situation might have continued indefinitely had Steve not become reacquainted with his old Sunbury Dunbar publisher, Pat Carter, towards the end of 1980. Carter was now a producer at RCA, where he had befriended staff producer Roy Dea. Soon they were talking about starting their own company. At RCA, Dea had been responsible for Gary Stewart's honky-tonk classics 'She's Actin' Single (I'm Drinking Doubles)', 'Drinking Thing' and 'Out of Hand', all cut on the same afternoon. Steve consid-ered them some of the coolest records ever made in Nashville in the seventies. He was strongly tempted to forget any attempt to get a record contract of his own when Carter suddenly turned to him one day and said: 'Why don't we cut a demo on you and see if we can get you a deal?'

And it was that simple.

The songs that Steve chose for the demo tape were 'Lucy Dee', later recorded by country star Vince Gill, and 'All the Kind Young Strangers', which was straight out of Tennessee Williams. To Steve, the resulting tape was passable but nothing special. When he returned the next morning to do the over-dubs and a few vocals, there was no sign of Dea at the studio. Steve was put out. 'It was Roy that I really trusted musically. It was Roy that got me excited. Pat believed in me and I probably wouldn't be making records if it weren't for Pat Carter, but Roy was the one I was learning from and we finished these without him.'

Dea, it transpired, had been fired by RCA. That night, Dea and Carter took Steve for a meal at the Peddler, a popular steakhouse and music business drinking hole. They told him that they were launching their own publishing company. Would he consider being their first staff songwriter?

High Chaparral was up and running early in 1981. Pat and Roy set up an office on 16th Avenue and Pat bought LSI studios. Steve was the only employee. He received a $100 per week to write songs, make demos of them on a little porta-studio and pitch them to the record labels. If he felt isolated he'd walk over to Combine Music, Bob Beckham's legendary publishing house, where several of his friends worked. For the first and only time in his life, he co-wrote regularly – most often with John Scott Scherrill. It was in this way that the longed-for miracle finally happened. Johnny Lee, who was riding high on the *Urban Cowboy* craze sweeping the US ('Looking for Love' had been a smash hit on the soundtrack of the John Travolta movie) recorded Steve's song 'When You Fall in Love'. At twenty-six, thirteen years after he wrote his first love song on Nick's hand-me-down guitar, Steve had a top-ten cut.

Steve and Carol-Ann were married on 22 March 1981 at the Church of God on Eighteenth Avenue. It was a simple, beautiful ceremony. Carol wore a gown she had paid for herself and flowers spilled from a vase in front of the altar. Their family and friends were invited and Steve's brother Patrick was his best man. Carol thought Steve was just wonderful. 'He was perfect. He was so happy. It was very sweet.'

For sentimental reasons their reception was held at the Springwater, which one family member describes as 'the dirtiest bar in Nashville'. Carol fell pregnant that very week. She and Steve were elated, particularly since Carol had miscarried a short-term baby three months earlier. They'd wanted another baby, planned another baby and now, Carol thought, it was as if it was meant to be. It was only with hindsight that Steve realized that a baby was the main motivation for their marriage. 'We weren't in love. We were just looking for someone to have kids with.'

With the pressure of a baby on the way Steve began to panic about money. The tennis court job, which was seasonal, had started up again. Steve laid tramlines in the morning with the sun boiling down and at night entered the twilight world of a restaurant called the Ringside Seat, where he worked as a dishwasher. Diners downed their dinners to the grunts and thuds of live boxing. 'It didn't last very long. I mean, people don't want to eat next to the spit bucket. It was pretty horrible. Bad Mexican food and bad boxing.'

He began for the first time to try to write songs to fit the market – to be a 'briefcase songwriter', as Nashville contemptuously referred to nine-to-five writers. 'Sometimes She Forgets' was as commercial as his songs ever became and even that, ironically, would later feature on the most determinedly noncommercial album of Steve's career, *Train A Comin'*. But now he ran into an unexpected hurdle. His songs were 'too country'. Nobody would cut them. Dea could easily have recorded Steve's songs himself, as he and Carter had planned, but when it came time to make the decision, he couldn't bring himself to do it. Steve sensed that Dea felt like he was cheating on someone if he cut songs in which he had an interest.

Steve redoubled his efforts to earn money in other ways. When Carol gave up her job at the print shop because she was worried about the effects of the chemicals on her unborn child, Steve was working four jobs. Apart from songwriting, washing dishes and laying tennis courts, he had inherited a job collecting master copies of records from Nashville's mastering labs and taking them over to the plating plant in the industrial area. He did that twice a day for almost two years and he went to pre-natal classes with his wife. It didn't alter Carol's perception that Steve was having a hard time adjusting to the idea of becoming a family man. 'He wanted children but he was scared. He misbehaved the whole time I was pregnant. He would run around. He was trying to find himself in the middle of the music business. He was playing all sorts of crazy games just to try to fit in.'

Justin Townes Earle was born on 4 January 1982 at Baptist Hospital in Nashville, just as Steve's mother Barbara had been before him. 'The proudest moment of my life,' Carol called it. With Steve determinedly coaching her through her breathing exercises, she'd endured a fourteen-hour labour. Steve carried the son he'd named after his hero from the delivery room to the nursery, his heart threatening to burst from his chest. 'After the nurse wrestled him away from me and made me leave, I thought, "Fuck, I'd better call my dad." So I called my dad and I immediately apologized for every shitty thing I'd ever done. It was really instantly obvious to me, "Oh, *now* I get it." It's funny, parenting changes everything . . . How much you take that seriously, how much you rise to it, is up to the individual.'

Steve was forced to rise to it within days of Justin's birth when Carol slumped into a post-natal depression. The miscarriage, the new baby and the insecurities inherent in her marriage to Steve had brought the memories of her own violent, insecure childhood to the surface and for three weeks after she came out of hospital she lay in bed and cried. Steve had always been partial to babies and frequently babysat for his friends, so he fared better than most new fathers would, but inevitably it brought back memories of his mother's depression after the birth of Patrick. He had run from the situation then and there were times when he wanted to run from it now.

But there were compensations. Steve absolutely doted on his new son. Jack Earle had sent him a container of red Texas dirt, just as his own father had done when Steve was born, so that the first soil Justin's feet touched was Texan. Steve made a resolution to honour the tradition again in the future. He had already decided that there would be more children. He spent so much time playing with Justin that the boy barely had time to sleep. Justin's earliest memories are looking down at his father from atop a big yellow pillow as Steve lay on his back and hoisted him into the air, and being swung around in a pillow case.

'And I remember using the stove for a house for my little Alvin and the Chipmunks doll and Dad coming in and deciding he was going to cook dinner and cooking Alvin.'

Justin was five months old when Steve took him to Texas to meet his grandparents, and 'When You Fall in Love', was playing on the radio as he drove. It didn't bring him any of the pleasure he'd hoped it would, perhaps because he imagined how Townes might measure it, perhaps because it was deeply irritating that Nashville chose one of his more commercial, co-written songs over 'Devil's Right Hand' or 'Ben McCulloch'. It wasn't even as though he was financially compensated for the frustration. Over the years he'd make $100,000 from the record, but he received no meaningful money at the time. For the first two years of his life, Justin was brought up on food stamps.

In August 1982, Steve's sister Kelly married Ron Meers, a neat, likeable man as quietly-spoken as she was ebullient. They moved from Massachusetts, Meers's home state, to Texas a month later, routing their journey via Nashville so they could see baby Justin. Steve and Carol were living in a homely old apartment steeped in atmosphere and Carol had renounced alcohol and toxins of any kind and was a glowing testimony to the benefits of health food and herbal medicine. Kelly saw her as an 'earth mother type. Steve was the healthiest. He was just eating right and lean. I said, "Steve, what have you been doing? You look absolutely great." He said: "I've been playing tennis.""

The following morning, before Kelly's incredulous eyes, Steve donned an orange polo shirt and khaki shorts and set off to play tennis at the local country club. His in-laws had given him a course of lessons as a gift. Kelly couldn't believe it. 'He had this nice haircut and moustache and was clean. You'd have thought he was off to some kind of lawyer's office the next day.'

Kelly's impression was that Steve and Carol were happy together. There was a nice feeling of family in the house. Carol had cast off the depression and taken a year off work to look after Justin. She wanted nothing more in life than to make oatmeal for her son and put dinner on the table for Steve. That was a noble aim, but there was a sense that Steve was not being stimulated enough intellectually. It occurred to Kelly that after the madness of life with Cynthia, Steve had been drawn to Carol's qualities as a homemaker. 'Carol *was* all that to a point but she wasn't bright enough for him. There wasn't much conversation.'

Nevertheless, two years of good food, no stimulants and a relatively stable home life had made a big difference to Steve's peace of mind. The anxiety attacks went away. Nearly two years after he felt their first paralysing bite, he started performing in earnest again. He bought himself an electric guitar and wrote songs with a rockabilly groove. He was preoccupied with putting a record out. Socializing down at Franks & Steins, the local punk joint, he had got to know Jack Emerson, former bassist for Jason and the Scorchers. Emerson had enrolled at Vanderbilt University but he was putting together a four-track EP for the Scorchers, much of which had been recorded in his living room. Steve, who was sick of getting slapped in the face by the suits on Music Row, was struck by the notion that it was possible to bypass the major labels altogether. 'People were making their own records. They weren't waiting for someone to tell them it was time to make a record. They were just making them and putting them out.'

Steve resolved to do the same if it killed him. The return of his stage presence had restored some of his battered self-esteem and he used all of his persuasive powers to convince Carter and Dea to put some money behind a four-song EP. Once won over, Carter and Dea were sufficiently inspired to come up with the idea of launching their own label and capitalizing on the rockabilly sound that had become cool in Nashville with the success of the Stray Cats.

That winter, they went into the studio and cut four songs in one night – 'Nothing but You', 'Squeeze Me in', 'Continental Trailways Blues' and 'My Baby Worships Me'. Drummer Martin Parker and Reno Kling, who played bass in John Scott-Sherrill's band, backed Steve on guitar. All vocals were live. It was decided that the name of this outfit would be Steve Earle and the Dukes.

The plan was for Steve, Carter, Dea and a secretary to ship the new record to mom & pop stores across America, without employing a distributor. Steve would tour Texas, Georgia and the Carolinas in support of the album and they'd sell a few extra copies at shows. Steve rushed around exuberantly in search of a road band. Parker and Kling had not been prepared to tour at such a hand-to-mouth level. The second incarnation of the Dukes included twenty-one-year-old Zip Gibson on bass, Steve on guitar and drummer Bullet Harris Jr, whom Steve considered 'a pain in the ass and a really erratic drummer. He was really, really good but he drank a lot and there were nights when it was kinda all over the place. But we all sort of deserved each other at that point.'

Pink & Black was released shortly after Valentine's Day in 1983. Steve was mad with excitement. He went home to Texas to see his parents and there were champagne celebrations. Ron and Kelly and Steve's little brother Patrick was there. Kelly had taken up tarot reading and Steve asked her to look at his cards. The portents were not good. As loath as she was to bring him down, Kelly admitted to him that his cards predicted that this record would go nowhere but the next one would make him a star. Steve was furious. He made up his mind that he would never let her read for him again.

Back in Nashville, Steve set about packaging *Pink & Black* for distribution. One copy landed on the desk of John Lomax, the publicist and freelance writer whose house Steve and Sandy had tended in 1975. He listened to the record and loved its old Memphis rockabilly feel. It was 'really, really fresh and different and wonderful'. Steve had swept into Lomax's life like a tornado on several occasions over the last five or six years, even moving in with him briefly when he fell out with Cynthia. Lomax had a lot of affection for him. 'He was almost like my son. It went beyond music.'

Listening to *Pink & Black*, Lomax felt a surge of paternal pride. He was sure that if the record found its way to the right person, Steve would finally get a deal. Steve was less certain. *Pink & Black* had been sitting at CBS for a month, unwanted and, for all he knew, unheard. With Steve's permission, Lomax went to the label himself. In those days, Music Row was still relaxed enough that people on official business could walk unchallenged through record company offices. Rick Blackburn, CEO of CBS, was out but John left *Pink & Black* on his desk with a note: 'This is great.' He went away for two days and returned to find his phone ringing off the hook. 'It was like, "I want to sign this guy yesterday."'

In retrospect, it's perhaps no coincidence that it was Blackburn who gave Steve his first major-label deal. Many of the artists he signed (Ricky Skaggs and Rodney Crowell and his wife of four years, Johnny Cash's daughter, Rosanne) would go on to become stars of the alternative country movement. For Steve, however, Blackburn had nothing more adventurous than rockabilly on his mind. CBS was the umbrella company of Columbia and Epic and the home of

Johnny Cash and George Jones, then in the midst of what Blackburn terms 'his craziness' with cocaine and alcohol. 'Every time he'd wreck a truck, I'd sell another 100,000 records.' Another big seller for the record company was Ricky Skaggs, who for years had been cursed with the same label as Steve – the ludicrous 'too country'. Blackburn had taken a chance on him and Skaggs had gone on to collect the CMA's 1982 Male Vocalist of the Year Award. Blackburn decided that Steve Earle was the rockabilly act he needed to balance out his country roster.

'What I come to find out is that Steve Earle's attention span was about five minutes and he was in his rockabilly mode then.'

On 18 April 1983, CBS signed an agreement with Carter and Dea's company, LSI, licensing the use of Steve's songs and paying his old bosses $40,000 to produce another six tracks. In the seventies and early eighties, Nashville record contracts were in the main singles deals, with an option to record an album. But it seemed a foregone conclusion that Steve would go on to make an album. 'I'm going to make this guy the next Ricky Skaggs,' Blackburn raved. 'We're going to give him the push that we gave Rosanne Cash and Lacy J. Dalton and Ricky."

Lomax agreed to take the Epic contract to a lawyer on Steve's behalf but he was wary of getting roped into managing him. In 1976, he had begun managing Townes at a time when Townes was just drifting – burnt out because he had put out six albums on Kevin Eggars's Poppy label and nobody had paid any attention to them. Lomax had put a fan club ad in *Rolling Stone* – 'Townes Van Zandt, the World's Greatest Songwriter' – and received only 350 responses. After two and a half years of hard work, culminating in Townes's double album, *Live at the Old Quarter*, he was elbowed aside by what he calls 'evil forces of darkness' at the label. He resolved never to manage an artist again. Years later, he would tell a court that Steve 'induced' him to enter a five-year management agreement in June 1983 by promising him twenty per cent of his income plus expenses.

Blackburn encouraged the union. He had already discovered that Steve was 'left-brained . . . If I called a meeting for ten o' clock, he'd show up at 10.20, for no other reason than he abhorred authority.' Steve was a deep thinker and even a little shy, but from very early on Blackburn had the impression that responsibility of any kind was alien to Steve. 'He partied back then, so we'd have talks about that. I didn't know whether I was a label head or a parent. His wife would call the label looking for him.'

With 'Nothin' but You' and 'What'll You Do About Me' already recorded, Steve went into the studio with Carter and Dea to cut six more sides. But even as they were recording, there was a new development at Epic. Blackburn had signed the veteran group Exile, and it was Exile who were now receiving the big push. 'Girls don't want to buy records by people who look like their daddies,' Lomax told Blackburn, but already Exile were being hyped as the next Alabama. Steve's first single, 'Nothing but You', was released on 1 October, with limited support from the label. It barely climbed to No. 70. The second single, 'Squeeze Me In', didn't chart at all. Blackburn put the blame on Steve, who refused to schmooze with the radio people.

Following the death of the singles, Steve received a curt summons to CBS. 'I found myself sitting in Blackburn's office being told, "Well, we experimented with your little three-piece band. If you want a deal here you're going to have to take on a producer other than Pat and Roy and record with a bigger band and do something more conventional."' If truth be told, Steve himself was starting to feel that the rockabilly band was musically restricting, but he was so enraged about being told how to make records that he resisted every attempt Blackburn made to move him on. 'But it finally came down to, "Do you want to make records or not?" And no one else was offering me a record deal.'

Steve was given a list of CBS-approved producers. He chose Emory Gordy Jr, whom he knew only from his reputation as a bass player for Elvis and Emmylou Harris's incredible Hot Band. Together they began searching for a new collection of songs, choosing 'Cry Myself to Sleep', by Paul Kennerly, Emmy's first husband, Denis Lindy's 'What'll You Do About Me' and a John Hiatt song. But the track Steve most wanted to record was a rockabilly tune called 'The Whole Damn Hawg' by Colonel Jim Silvers. 'It had this incredible guitar on it and I was playing it for Emory and he goes, "Oh, I know who that is, it's Richard Bennett. He plays on all that stuff. He produced this. That's who I was thinking of getting to play guitar on all your tracks." And I remember [label executive] Mary Martin and Emory were living together at the time and she was kinda managing Emory as a producer. She goes: "Emory, isn't flying guitar players into Nashville a bit like flying hookers into Vegas?"'

Whatever Steve felt about Blackburn's bully tactics, he could not have complained about the weight of talent behind his prospective album. Virtually everyone who worked on the sessions, including Gordy Jr, would go on to become part of country music legend. Hank De Vito, another fine Hot Band player, was on steel guitar, Bobby Ogden on keyboards and the great Larrie Londin was on drums. Londin had not only revolutionized the use of drums in country music but had been the heart and soul of such Motown classics as 'Papa was a Rolling Stone'. Most importantly, perhaps, the band included Richard Bennett, a small, handsome man with wavy brown hair and a pleasant manner. He had a precise way of moving that was echoed in the lightning smoothness with which his fingers negotiated the fretboard of his guitar. That, combined with the kind of creative flair which saw him co-write the Neil Diamond classic, 'Forever in Blue Jeans', made him a favourite sideman of Diamond and later Dire Straits' guitarist Mark Knopfler. Bennett's inclusion in the band meant that Steve had all the talent he could possibly need on his side, and he went back into the studio for what he felt was 'this last-gasp recording session'. Without a perfect result, there would be no CBS album.

From mid-1983 onwards, Steve toured continually. Despite the continuing stalemate over the album's release date, his live shows in Arkansas, Louisiana and Texas were bringing him a cult following. 'Earle is certainly a personable frontman, with the sort of youthful good looks and raw energy that indicates star quality, but most telling is the fact that, virtually alone, he carries the show,' reported *American-Statesman* critic Ed Ward, after seeing him play in Austin.

Far from being distressed that Steve was on the road all the time, Carol actually preferred it. Even if she didn't know what he was doing, she knew at least where he was – which wasn't always the case when he was in Nashville.

Steve had started drinking again when he went back to playing in bars, although it was still pretty sedate by his standards – just four or five beers. Touring with the rockabilly band, however, he slowly but surely got into prescription narcotics: specifically Tylenol 3's, Percadans, Bercacets and Tussionex, a prescription cough syrup containing oxy-codeine that was a closely guarded secret among junkies. His friend Rick Steinberg introduced him to several of them. Steve and Rick Steinberg had bonded back in 1976 when Steinberg was supplementing his day job as a copy boy at *The Tennessean* newspaper with a sideline selling pot. At their first meeting, Steinberg had produced a bag of pot and rolled a joint.

'What's that?' Steve demanded.

'It's a joint.'

'*That's* not a joint,' Steve said. He pasted together six papers, rolled himself a sausage-sized spliff and put a match to it. '*This* is a joint!' he grinned.

Steinberg burst out laughing. 'You're my kinda guy!' he cried, and they were friends from that moment on. Steinberg shared any leftover pot with Steve at the end of every week and Steve in turn would take him along to the studio. 'He had just got a writing deal with Sunbury Dunbar and I thought that was pretty cool. He had this office and we would go in there and smoke pot and hang out and it was just a lot of fun.' Half a decade on, their association wasn't quite so innocent. Along with selling pot, Steinberg had a talent for working doctors for prescriptions and he passed some tips along to Steve. Visiting the dentist, Steve would try to get pain medication scripts refilled as often as possible. The drugs he liked all had opiates in common. 'The opiate thing was escapism and there was a part of me that knew it. I liked to get high and watch television. I mean, it was a total shut-down thing. I don't shut down very much. I run kind of wide open all the time. It's my natural tendency. And it did shut me down.'

Steve hadn't done heroin in years but he found that like junk, prescription medicine made him 'want to do it again and eventually you do it again because you're sick if you don't do it. You literally get flu-like symptoms, only ten times more intense – like really intense pain in your legs and your back and your head, and nauseousness and vomiting, *plus* a feeling of impending doom. You know, like really deep dark depression.'

Driving the van on some of Steve's rockabilly road trips, John Lomax was aware of none of this, only that Steve was captivated by Kerouac and the Woodie Guthrie lifestyle. 'He would take some barbiturates and lie in the back of the van on long trips when [the show] was done, but I figured I might do the same thing if I wanted to sleep in the van. But I didn't notice it becoming a problem.'

Steve's friend Bill Alsobrook, a sound engineer who once won Townes's gold tooth in a craps game (they used whisky as an anaesthetic but the wrong tooth was extracted by mistake), told *Newsweek* a story about a night in the studio with Steve and Jerry Jeff Walker. 'They were drunk and snorting . . . stuff. It started getting so crazy that I crawled underneath the piano in the studio, because if somebody started shooting the floor was a good place to be. Steve followed me under there, then I went to sleep, and that must have seemed like a good idea because we woke up in the morning at about the same time.'

Marijuana aside, Carol seems to have remained completely oblivious to Steve's drug use the entire time they were married. But she could hardly have missed the side-effects. Justin was still a toddler when Steve, Bill Alsobrook and another friend drove a brand-new Camero through the front wall of the house and into the living room. They were roaring drunk. Carol came flying into the room to find them all laughing hysterically. 'Get the fuck out of here!' she screamed. With some difficulty, Steve managed to heave himself out of the car. Dust and rubble was floating down on to the furniture. Steve's friends were pulling out of the living room and into the yard when there was an explosion. A bullet shot out of the roof of the car. Alsobrook was sitting playing with his new gun.

Carol got her own back. She and Steve were driving home from a show at the Bluebird Café when a row broke out over Steve's plan to go partying while Carol sat at home with Justin. Steve had had enough to drink for that to seem like a good idea. They were in downtown Nashville when Carol suddenly doubled up her fist and punched him in the face. 'Damn near killed both of us,' as Steve put it. 'We were not going very fast because we were in the alley behind the San Antonio Taco Company, but she just knocked the living fuck out of me. The doctor thought she'd detached my retina. I mean, it completely closed my eye. And Carol was six foot tall and had two or three inches of reach on me.'

Steve's reaction was largely philosophical. 'The only question was, whether violence was necessary and how smart it was to hit the operator of the vehicle!'

With his third marriage showing familiar signs of trouble, Steve took refuge in his music. Despite the failure of the singles, good things were starting to happen. 'Buddy Holly and Eddie

Cochran have got nothing on this guy,' raved renowned Nashville music critic Robert Oermann, 'and he's darn sure more authentic and *alive* than nouveau poseurs like the Stray Cats.' In the photograph that accompanied the article, Steve wore a denim shirt and looked fresh-faced and gentle. A Stratocaster was slung across his chest. He told journalist Patsi Bale Cox that artists often messed up their record deals because they expected more from the label than it was able to offer them. 'Record companies are in business to sell records. They aren't in business to create a career for someone. If artists really understood that, they'd be a lot better off. A chip on the shoulder just gets in the way. If you get a deal and you have a break, then it is up to you to use that break. You can make it whatever you want it to be.'

But as the months dragged on and Epic showed no inclination to put out Steve's album, his optimism dwindled. He had lost all confidence in his songwriting. Only two of the songs on the record were written by other songwriters, but the label had opposed him all the way. 'They really wanted me to do outside material.' To his mortification, Steve no longer had a publishing deal. Carter and Dea had withdrawn their long-term support after the CBS débâcle, and in May 1983 Steve was once again pounding the streets of Music Row, knocking on the doors of people who didn't want to hear from him.

Help came from the most unlikely of sources. The head of ASCAP, one of the biggest publishing companies in America, took it upon himself to telephone Noel Fox at the Oak Ridge Boys publishing company and tell him about Steve. 'You're crazy enough to understand him,' he said. Fox had been a tenor in the Oak Ridge Boys during their white gospel phase and had run the Oaks' company, Silverline/Goldline, since 1978. He took time out to listen to *Pink & Black* and thought it 'cool' but dated. Still, he agreed to meet Steve over at ASCAP. Steve played him 'The Devil's Right Hand' and 'Tom Ames Prayer'. Fox signed him on the spot, recognizing instantly that Steve was not 'just a songwriter, he's a *writer*. He's so driven to write and report his findings here on earth.'

Unlike Blackburn, who had recoiled from Steve's thirst for continual change in his music, Fox told him from the start that he could and should write anything he wanted to. He had already been on the phone to his friends in the record business, advising them to sign Steve while they could. 'Anyone as musically driven, with that much energy inside, he was naturally a star. There was no telling where he would go. That was the way I saw it.'

At Silverline/Goldline, Steve found a virtual re-creation of the halcyon days at Guy and Susanna Clark's house. There was the same chemistry and camaraderie, the same zeal for songs that exploded convention, the same sense of living for the music regardless of what was at the end of the rainbow. Every afternoon at around 4.30, Fox would send out for beer and the writers would gather around and play their new tunes. After years of being told that his songs were 'too this' and 'too that', Steve found that he had in Noel someone who appreciated his music for itself. In a burst of confidence, he wrote 'Fearless Heart' and 'Goodbye's All We Got Left'. At Silverline, he felt comfortable and valued. The Oak Ridge Boys didn't understand Steve or his music at all, but Fox liked all the qualities that comprised Steve Earle – the caffeine-fuelled chatter that disguised the thoughtful poet inside, the way that he could glance at a couple walking down the street and, off the top of his head, paint a believable scenario of their entire lives. And his songs, to Fox, were real songs.

'Steve's music was roots, unabashed, balls to the wall, get the fuck out of my way American music. That's exactly what it was to me. Still is.'

None of this altered the fact that Steve was still signed to Epic and still touring as a rockabilly artist. The new songs called for a bigger band, so Steve hired keyboard player Ken Moore – a man so thin he was unkindly nicknamed 'The

Cadaver', moved Zip Gibson over to bass, put his bass player on lead guitar, kept Bullet Harris Jr on drums and played rhythm guitar himself. The re-ordered Dukes performed a couple of showcases with the tracks Steve had cut with Gordy Jr, but nothing ever came of them. The band just fell apart. 'What'll You Do About Me' was released on 8 December, with 'The Crush' on the B-side. The fact that the single had a lurid pink and purple cover, with a cerise tinsel curtain cutting into one side and Steve pouting in the middle of it in a pink shirt, showed how determined CBS were to mould him into something he was not. It's a measure of Steve's charisma that he almost got away with it. 'What'll You Do About Me' entered the charts at No. 81 and died at 76. The next single, 'A Little Bit in Love', didn't chart at all. From that point on there was absolutely no doubt that CBS would drop him. There would be no album. Steve, who was earning $350 a week at Goldline Music Inc, didn't lose any sleep over it. 'I instinctively knew that I couldn't go any further down that road with Rick Blackburn, so it didn't make any difference to me.'

Years later, Steve would say that he reacted to the CBS failure by writing *Guitar Town*. He had made up his mind that he was going to write the record he wanted to write, whether or not he had a deal. 'I knew I could put a record out if I wanted to. It didn't turn out to be necessary but I was prepared to do it. So I was writing my record anyway.'

At home things were not going well at all. Steve had left Carol for a few weeks but had gone back to her because he couldn't bear being away from Justin. They rowed constantly. Carol was convinced Steve was having an affair with a woman friend who lived down the street from them. It drove her crazy the way everyone seemed to get the best of him – his generosity, his humour, his kindess – except her. But she tried to save the marriage because she didn't know what else to do. 'I was so out of it and so afraid and so scared. I was so mad because I'd gotten married and it flopped on me so badly. I was not strong. I was *not* strong . . . You know, I cried all the time. I was a nutcase. That's my own fault. I had done this and I did not know what to do. I did not know how to raise a little boy by myself.'

They went back to Texas for Christmas. Steve's head was a whirl of the hurts and highs of the past few months, but it felt good to be heading home. Steve always found moving healing. There was something hopeful about it. It was almost as if the physical act of crossing borders could erase the grim realities of life and replace them with some new and exotic horizon. His literary idols were always nomads or adventurers like Hemingway and Graham Greene, men who, like their characters, went boldly into romantic danger zones like Cuba or elephant territory in Africa, with scant thought for the life they'd left behind. Watching the tree-lined interstates of Tennessee give way to the wide open spaces of Texas, Steve found himself humming songs from *Born in the USA*, the album that had recently catapulted Springsteen into the mainstream. Experiencing Springsteen live and listening to the album had had a profound effect on him. 'I was intrigued by the fact that Springsteen opened the album with "Born in the USA", that it was really a theme and an overture and he opened the show with it.' Inspired, Steve wrote 'Guitar Town' on the drive home, specifically intending it to be the opening song of his album. When 'Down the Road' came to him, he knew it would close the record. And from that point on it was easy. Stacey's Christmas present that year was the Gibson Steve used to write 'Guitar Town'.

When Christmas was over, so was Steve and Carol's marriage. On Boxing Day, Steve announced that he was going to San Antonio and taking Justin. Carol was confused. 'You don't want *me* to go?' But Steve didn't. He drove away in Carol's mother's old car, leaving her alone with her in-laws in Houston. Carol was tearful and 'mad as hell'. She was sure he was going to see a woman. She telephoned Lyle Lovett, whom she'd got to know through Steve.

'Steve's gone to San Antonio and left me behind,' she said to Lovett.

'Well, what are you doing?'

A little desperately Carol asked: 'Can I just go out with you as a friend?'

'Sure,' Lovett told her. 'Love to have your company.'

He came over from Spring, Texas in a big Ford truck and took her to a jazz club. A close friend of his had just been killed and he was still shaken and upset. Carol spent a slightly subdued evening with him and after the show, he dropped her back at Jack and Barbara's apartment. Carol walked through the front door to find the household in a frenzy. As soon as she'd left, Jack had called Steve in San Antonio and told him his wife had gone to Spring, Texas with Lyle Lovett. Carol was in disgrace. 'To the Earles, blood is a whole lot thicker than water. That's how I felt. They had said they loved me. They didn't even think Steve was running around on me. I guess they didn't know.'

For Carol and Steve, it was a tense ride home to Nashville. Carol didn't confront him about what he'd been doing in San Antonio because she had no proof. 'I knew there had to be a woman involved because that was just his MO. There was a woman behind just about everything, and involved in just about everything, that he did back then.' It terrified her that they were beginning to ease into a divorce. Steve seemed to take every opportunity he could to be out of the house. Carol knew that her own mental frailty didn't help. She wished she could give Steve the comfort and understanding he clearly needed and she wished she could receive it from him. 'I was an abused child, you know, and I was looking for that strong male figure.' The more Steve withdrew, the more she clung to him. The more she clung to him, the more he withdrew.

A few weeks after they returned from Texas, Carol opened the mail to find a receipt from the bank. It was for a $5,000 transfer from their account to a Macayla Lohmann. 'I said, "Well, here it is. I don't know who you are, Macayla, but you've got $5,000 of [our] money and I haven't had a new pair of shoes in years . . .'" When Steve came home, she demanded an explanation. 'He said, "That was to help her open up her business." And I said, "Why didn't you talk to me?" He could care less how I felt. I'd like to say it's all water under the bridge but sometimes when I think of those things, I just want to cry.'

They were separated on New Year's Day 1985. Steve immediately started going back and forth to San Antonio to see Macayla Lohmann. His friend Charlie Mullins had introduced them earlier in the year. A pretty freelance writer, Macayla had worked with Charlie on the city's 1977 bicentennial celebrations and later became a 'spin doctor' for the mayor. According to Charlie, Steve met her at a bar called Los Padrinos, where she did part-time work in the evenings. 'She liked the music. She'd pick up empty bottles and dance all the way back to the bar. Steve just fell in love with her.'

That winter, Steve took Macayla to San Miguel, which he later decided was about as good an idea as taking Cynthia there. Their relationship was always a volatile one, but it is significant that it was very 'active' while Steve was writing the songs for *Guitar Town*.

It was in Mexico that Steve wrote 'My Old Friend the Blues'. He was heavily into bluegrass at the time and the 'High Lonesome' sound of the Louvin Brothers seeped like mist into the song. The lonely desolation of it would almost be unbearable if the narrator wasn't comforted by the nearness of music. It embraces him as warmly as a lover and is more constant than any friend. Significantly, it is the blues to which he turns. It consoles him because, far from being the clichéd refuge of the downhearted, the blues often cheers, motivates and stimulates with its darkly comedic take on life and love. The blues is self-deprecating rather than self-pitying. Its tongue-in-check use of sexual metaphor or repetition of harsh fact allows it to stare unflinchingly not only at the actions of faithless lovers or cruel twists of fate but at the narrator's own weakness with regard to temptation. 'South Nashville Blues', Steve's slice of autobiography on 1996's *I Feel Alright*, is a good example.

> *I took my pistol and a hundred dollar bill*
> *I took my pistol and a hundred dollar bill*
> *I had everything I need to get me killed.*

In 'My Old Friend the Blues' the narrator holds fast to the realism of blues because his own life seems so hollow and cold. In Mexico with Macayla, Steve felt much the same way. '"My Old Friend the Blues" was about me discovering that I was a little fascinated with my own pain and that I was capable of actually revelling in it, and that I was capable of seeing the way I dealt with pain as being something that separated me from other people – that I found some value in it and some sort of positive energy. You know, because I turned it into things like "My Old Friend the Blues" and "Little Rock 'n' Roller".'

With three marriages behind him, his career at a standstill and his little son back home in Nashville, emptiness threatened to engulf him. 'Little Rock 'n' Roller', written as a companion piece to 'My Old Friend the Blues', was testimony to his state of mind. 'You leave a child behind, you immediately feel incredibly guilty. And I'd done it twice and couldn't deal with the guilt the first time and went back to his mother strictly because I felt guilty about leaving him.'

This time Macayla left Steve. Or, at least, when he was packing to go back to Nashville, she announced that she was staying in Mexico. Steve decided she had a fear of commitment. Charlie Mullins maintains to this day that Steve wrote *Guitar Town* about her 'and then dumped her. Pretty much changed her life. She left town shortly after that. I introduced them and I'm so sorry I did, but anyway it's a great album.'

To Steve, Macayla Lohmann wasn't a casual relationship at all. Far from it. '"San Antonio Girl" is about Macayla. That was basically my "Fuck it" statement – "I've gotten myself into something I can't deal with." Macayla was very whirly-twirly, *didn't* want to be committed to anything and *then*, as soon as I was with someone else, Macayla was heartbroken.'

Steve went back to Nashville in a huff. Like a character in a blues song, he had lost his wife, his lover and his recording career. Some day soon his luck was bound to change.

7

Guitar Town

It was Noel Fox who came up with the idea of a songwriters' weekend. The Oak Ridge Boys were enjoying an unprecedented period of success and baritone singer William Lee Golden had bought a waterfront mansion on Ono Island in Gulf Shores, Alabama. As luck would have it he liked to loan it to his friends for free. Sitting in his office on a dank February day in 1985, Fox could think of nothing more edifying than a holiday on the coast with plenty of seafood, golf and beer. Steve was in enthusiastic agreement. Noel suggested that they borrow the house for a long weekend, invite his friends Jimbeau Hinson and Tony Brown, and combine some intensive songwriting with some intensive R&R.

As a former piano player for Elvis and Emmylou Harris and vice-president of A&R at MCA Nashville, Tony Brown was one of the most respected music men in Nashville and Fox had been trying for several months to interest him in signing Steve – so far without success. The weekend would give Brown a chance to get to know Steve and hear his music. Besides, they could use his input on one or two songs.

Brown was not exactly enthusiastic. Few people in Nashville had a better ear than he did for commercial music. At RCA, he had signed Vince Gill and country supergroup Alabama, and at MCA he'd been responsible for the phenomenal success of artists like George Strait and Reba McEntire. But Brown also had a passion for music that coloured outside the lines, music that challenged or healed or moved. He knew what he liked and, based on what he had seen and heard so far, Steve Earle wasn't it. His impression of Steve's rockabilly records, with their gaudy pink and black covers, was that he was a 'cheap Elvis'. When he caught a glimpse of Steve on the Ralph Emery show *Nashville Now*, his first thought was: 'What *is* this guy? What's going on here?' On the few occasions he had run across Steve at Silverline/Goldline, the singer's high-octane delivery had shaken him to the core. 'Gawdalmighty, Fox, he talks a lot,' he muttered to Noel. Still, he was happy to do a favour for his friend and thought the sea air and a few mind-altering substances would do him good. With those incentives, he signed up for the trip.

They left on a Friday for the 450-mile drive to Gulf Shores, piling into the van, loaded up with alcohol and pot. Less than an hour into the journey Tony began to realize that, far from being a pale imitation of somebody else, Steve was a Technicolor version of himself, all charm and candour and wild stories. By the time they crossed the Alabama state line, 'I pretty much knew all about Steve Earle.' Musically, too, Brown felt that he had made a major misjudgement. Steve sang and played guitar as they drove and Tony realized with a shock that Steve was more allied to folk singers like Dylan and Outlaws like Waylon than any rockabilly singer he had ever seen. 'It was a totally eye-opening experience.'

Jimbeau Hinson, with whom Steve had co-written the Connie Smith song, 'A Far Cry from You', remembers the drive as an 'eight-hour history lesson', during which Steve 'played every song he'd ever liked, told us who wrote it and what year it was recorded – just minute details – and where they came from and what they were doing when they wrote the song. And then he'd talk about their influences and he'd go off at another tangent!'

They were wobbly-legged by the time they pulled up to the house on Ono Island. 'My dream house,' Steve thought as he crunched over the path to the big A-frame beach house, the salted wind brushing his face. Behind the house was the silvery sweep of the intercoastal waterway. Steps led down to the pier where Bill Golden kept his boat but it was winter and still too cold to use it. Inside, there was an open-plan lounge and bar area with far-reaching views across the island. They unloaded their gear in the bedrooms and returned to the great room for a drink.

The idyll didn't last long. Away from the van and the spell cast by Steve's singing and storytelling, Steve and Tony circled each other like wary bantam cocks. Tony found Steve abrasive and nerve-racking; Steve viewed Brown as just another Music Row suit and the epitome of everything he had come to despise in Nashville. He started in on him about the business of country music, going on and on until even Brown, whose affable manner enables him to get along with just about anybody, was beside himself with rage. 'Nobody's going to remember these fluffy little ear-candy records you're making,' Steve said disparagingly. 'They'll be forgotten as soon as radio quits playin' 'em.'

Brown sat on the sofa, red-faced and sullen. 'And besides that,' Steve drawled insultingly, 'you're short.'

Unable to contain himself, Brown sprang at Steve and tried to punch him. Jimbeau pulled them apart. 'Cut it out,' he said curtly. The atmosphere in the house was so toxic that Noel took Tony out for a drive. Steve laughed it off and he and Hinson sat down to write. The result was 'A Country Song', which Steve thought later was 'one of the most contrived things I've ever written. It was really Jimbeau's idea but I helped him write it.' The historical theme of 'A Country Song' did however remind Steve of a passage in Loretta Lynn's biography, *Coal Miner's Daughter*, which had resonated with him. It described the so-called 'hillbilly highway' – the migratory pattern of country folk from Kentucky and Tennessee to cities like Detroit and Chicago, first to get defence jobs during the war and later to work in the factories. Based on this idea, Jimbeau crafted some lyrics and Steve played around with a riff. What came out of the session was the catchy, irrepressible 'Hillbilly Highway', the road stories of three generations, one of which could easily have been Steve's.

When Fox and Brown returned, they broke the ice over shrimp and beer. After dinner Fox and Hinson sat at the bar and watched with amusement as Steve and Tony began to find a little common ground. Steve talked, paced and fidgeted and finally picked up his guitar. Noel was always fascinated by the stillness that came over him when he played guitar almost as if 'the instrument handles his fidgeting. Then he looks at you and talks or sings or whatever – never lets you go, does he? – and he did that to Tony and he sang "My Old Friend the Blues". *Killed* Tony. Laid him out.'

It was 'My Old Friend the Blues' that finally won Tony over. Steve had to play the song again and again so Brown could take in every detail from the soulful opening slide to the final lyric when the narrator, exhausted by the trials of love and life, surrenders his heart to the tender embrace of music. From there, it didn't take much for Tony to fall for Steve himself. Jimbeau marvelled at the transformation. 'It's just amazing to make somebody so mad and then turn around and make them love you so much.'

In the end, there was not as much writing time as they'd anticipated. A day and a half into their trip, Bill Golden telephoned. He was bored. 'I think I'm going to head down that way,' he told Steve, ordering driver Harley Pinkerman to bring his tour bus around and filling it up with crazy hangers-on. Steve did manage to write one more song – a collaboration with Brown and Hinson called 'Down the Road', although Steve maintains that Brown's only contribution was the opening line: 'On the blue side of evening'. Tony couldn't have minded less. He was blown away by the other songs he'd heard. More than that, he was mesmerized by Steve himself.

At intervals Steve would sweep out of the living room and they could hear him going hammer and tongs at Carol-Ann or Macayla on the telephone in the kitchen. Then he would stride back in, issuing steam and expletives, and write a song about it. Personally and artistically, Brown had never experienced anything quite like it.

'I bought into it a hundred per cent and I wanted to sign this guy. 'Course Noel Fox is going, "I told you so." And of course, Steve's kinda scary too and that's intriguing to me. I've always been attracted to those kinds of people. But I got to experience his anger on the phone. I mean, I'm serious, these phone calls to his wife . . . were a moment in themselves. They took place in the kitchen and we were in this great big room – it's like he wanted us to hear these conversations. And smoking the cigarettes! It was just a scene out of a movie. Jimbeau Hinson is a great songwriter himself and between him and Steve there was enough cynicism to make a bomb. That was my first experience of Steve and I came back willing to lay in the highway in front of a semi to sign this guy.'

Back in Nashville, Brown faced an anxious wait. Contractually, Steve was still bound to CBS and Brown had begged him not to play his new songs for fear that they would never let him go. Steve just laughed and drawled, 'I ain't skeered,' adding: 'They won't get it, I promise.' In actuality, he kept very quiet about the existence of the new songs. He wanted a deal with MCA as badly as Brown wanted to sign him, not because he had bonded with Tony at Ono Island but because Emory Gordy Jr had been taken on by the label as a producer. Steve wasn't entirely convinced by the production on the Epic singles, but he felt it was a step in the right direction and he wanted to work with Gordy Jr again.

Throughout this period, John Lomax tried to stay very much in the background. He was aware that Fox had known Brown before either of them had got to Nashville, 'back in that weird gospel world', and that they were close friends. He felt that

Noel could get to Tony in a way he couldn't. 'I could get to Tony but I wasn't Tony's buddy. So I just stayed out of it. I let Noel be the person.'

Shortly before the trip to Ono Island, Lomax had persuaded Epic to cough up enough money for a showcase at SIR rehearsal studios. He and Steve wanted to see what, if any, interest remained at the label. In Lomax's memory, the Dukes played virtually every song that would eventually make up *Guitar Town*. Steve is certain they played only three: 'Goodbye's All We Got Left', 'The Devil's Right Hand' and 'Fearless Heart'. The rest of the thirty-minute set was taken up with 'Cry Myself to Sleep', 'The Crush', 'What Do You Do About Me' and an Elvis cover, 'You're So Square, Baby, I Don't Care'.

Either way, the CBS crowd didn't get it. Three weeks later, Rick Blackburn announced that he was letting Steve go. It was obvious Steve was moving away from rockabilly and rockabilly, Blackburn told him, was the whole reason he had been signed. Privately he was convinced that Steve would go on to become one of the great songwriters, but he wasn't in the business of publishing. Steve listened to Blackburn's speech impassively. He'd known for some time that what he couldn't afford to do was make any more records with Rick Blackburn on Blackburn's terms. 'I knew I would end up with a record I hated. And that's one thing I don't have.' Legend has it that Steve left the meeting and called to friends across the road: 'These sons of bitches just dropped me. I'll have a new deal within a week!'

Brown, meanwhile, was having one or two difficulties of his own. His passionate endorsement of Steve Earle and his music had not been greeted with anything like the same enthusiasm by Jimmy Bowen, president of MCA Nashville and executive vice-president of MCA proper. In 1985, Bowen's name already had the power to strike terror in the hearts of artists and fellow executives. In industry terms, his achievements were formidable. Born in Santa Rita, New Mexico in 1937, he'd started out as a bass player, singer and writer, cutting a couple of hit singles in the fifties and working alongside Glen Campbell at the American Music Publishing Company. After a stint running the LA division of Chancellor Records, he moved over to Reprise Records, where his production work with Dean Martin resulted in twenty-six hit singles, fifteen gold albums and five platinum. He also produced 'Strangers in the Night' for Frank Sinatra. He ended the sixties with his own company, where Glenn Frey and Don Henley, Kim Carnes and Kenny Rogers recorded, but by the mid-seventies he was back at the helm of the major labels. He moved from MGM to MCA, from Elektra/Asylum to Warner and lastly back to MCA, where he was when Steve entered his consciousness. Conway Twitty, the Bellamy Brothers, Waylon Jennings, Reba McEntire and Hank Williams Jr were just some of the artists he'd signed or produced.

At MCA Nashville, Bowen's style of operating was part Sherman tank, part marketing genius. A bearded grizzly of a man, he would bludgeon any door down if he believed in an artist or any artist down if he didn't. In the nineties, his titanic battles with similarly megalomaniacal Garth Brooks at Capitol Records were the source of endless gossip on Music Row. 'I think Jimmy Bowen is the single most insensitive person in Nashville,' producer George Massenburg told one journalist. 'He came along at a time when the town was ripe to pillage and he pillaged what was left. He did increase the recording activity; anyone will warrant that. But he's wrecked music. He's turned it into a commodity.'

Bowen had no use at all for Steve's music but Tony refused to be put off. Bowen's aggressive condescension didn't make him nervous, it made him angry. Emory Gordy Jr felt the same way. Pressurized by both men, Bowen relented. 'If you can make me understand a word Steve Earle says, you can sign him,' he told Tony.

Tony, Emory and Steve went out to the Oak Ridge Boys studio in Hendersonville, Tennessee and cut a demo of 'Good Ol' Boy (Gettin' Tough)', which Steve had co-written with Richard Bennett. Tony was upfront with Steve about Bowen's comments on his enunciation. 'Go back out there and just try to imagine that the whole world does not know what you're saying,' he told the singer. To Brown's surprise, Steve took it in his stride: 'As opposed to him going, "Well, screw him" – well, he might have said that as well – but the bottom line was we got a vocal . . . That's when I found out that Steve is also a good businessman. He actually has great business sense.'

Bowen had attached another condition to Steve's signing, which was that something be done about his image – specifically his teeth. At thirty, Steve's looks were still comparatively clean-cut, his wide, sensitive mouth, intelligent eyes and slender muscled frame blending well with his bad-boy charisma, but he had little or no interest in the daily maintenance of his appearance and his teeth had been ravaged by drug use. Pam Lewis, who worked as a publicity consultant on Steve's first two albums and performed an almost managerial role for him for a time, was aware that the conservative faction at MCA often reeled when he came through the door. 'He used to have body odour sometimes and people at the label were like, "Oh, my God!" And he has the straightest hair so if he doesn't wash it all the time it's just really limp and that just was not the image for a country music artist.'

Tony dreaded broaching the subject of dental work with Steve. 'I was actually scared. I didn't want to insult the guy. And Steve was like, "Cool, man! I've been wanted to get them fixed for a long time. If y'all are going to pay for it, it's fine with me." So we did that.'

At MCA, Bowen listened to the demo and was sufficiently impressed to give the okay. MCA drafted a contract and Lomax passed it along to a lawyer. All that was needed now was Steve's release papers from CBS, giving him the legal right to sign with another label. There was nothing to do but wait.

Throughout the spring and early summer, Steve to and fro'd between Nashville and the West Coast, riding through the big red skies and grapy dusks like a character out of Kerouac. The faith of men like Brown, Fox, and Gordy had had a liberating effect on him musically and, on a personal level, he was enjoying some of the most casual relationships of his life. He was happier than he had been in years. Once, he rode the Oak Ridge Boys empty bus out to their first gig in Fresno, California, with only Harley Pinkerman for company. Another time Noel flew him to LA so he could spend a week or ten days writing with guitarist Richard Bennett in Hollywood. Bennett has a clear memory of him getting off the plane, his young face lit up with excitement. He was holding a cassette tape in the air. 'I've got the album,' he cried. '*I've got the songs for the album.*'

Back at the house, Steve could hardly contain himself. 'Put this on, put this on,' he urged Bennett as they walked through the front door. His bags were still on his shoulder. Bennett pressed 'play' and the pure restless energy of 'Guitar Town', 'Hillbilly Highway', 'My Old Friend the Blues', 'Fearless Heart' and 'Little Rock 'n' Roller' flowed into the room. Bennett thought they were fantastic. 'They struck me as what country music used to be, and what it fuckin' well should be.'

Of the two songs they wrote for *Guitar Town*, 'Think It Over' was the more lightweight, a rockabilly song which Bennett had made a start on but hadn't been able to finish. A third song, 'Some Blue Moons Ago', was always intended for Brenda Lee. It was 'Good Ol' Boy' that gave notice of Steve's promise as a political songwriter. Conceived as an angry protest against Reagan's firing of Mark Earle and other striking air traffic controllers back in 1981, it was an eloquent commentary on the state of the nation. In 1986, Steve would tell *Rolling Stone* that his politics were 'real schizophrenic . . . I'm somewhat to the right of Attila the Hun in some areas', but his heart was on the left. Lines like 'I got a job and it ain't nearly enough/A twenty-thousand dollar pickup truck/Belongs to me and the bank and some funny talkin' man from Iran', or, 'I was born in the land of plenty/Now there ain't enough' were a searing indictment of an America which increasingly equated wealth with worth and told people what they needed while giving them none of the tools necessary for their survival.

The sheer irrepressibility of Steve's appetite for life and music was contagious. Sitting around the kitchen table one morning drinking coffee, Richard casually mentioned that he and his wife were thinking of leaving LA. Nashville wasn't on their itinerary at all. In spite of the fact that Richard had been commuting there to do studio gigs since 1982, he had never considered moving there and wasn't convinced that he'd even want to live in Nashville if the opportunity arose.

Suddenly Steve said: 'You know, you just need to move to Nashville. Just come to Nashville. We're going to do this album and you need to be there.'

'And we said, "Okay,"' Bennett recalls. 'And it was kinda that quick.'

The one thing they knew from the outset was that Richard was going to play guitar on the album. Tony and Emory were co-producing and it was agreed that Richard should be involved as an associate producer. With Emory on board as bass player, they approached Larrie Londin about playing drums again, but Londin was committed to the Everly Brothers reunion tour and wouldn't be available when Steve was in the studio. The steel player they chose was Bucky Baxter, a flamboyant, ambitious man Steve knew through friends. He was working out at the Opry with country legend Jean Shepherd. Original Dukes member Ken Moore was recruited to play the organ parts on the album.

It was June before they found the right drummer. Steve and Tony were backstage at Fan Fair, Nashville's annual lovefest for country fans and their idols, when they ran into Harry Stinson. Stinson had spent the past decade in LA playing with artists as diverse as Peter Frampton, Al Stewart and Etta James, but he was in the process of moving back to Nashville, his hometown. Brown, who had worked with him the previous year on a Jimmy Buffett album, rated him very highly, not least because Stinson was well groomed and professional to a fault. Stinson had the impression that Brown had already spoken to Steve about hiring him. Steve seemed very relaxed about things. 'Great,' he said, and Stinson was employed. Everything Stinson saw and heard regarding Steve and his music inspired respect in him.

'I didn't feel like the project was fake in any way, shape or form. I felt that Richard's talents were perfect for the project, I thought Tony and Emory were great, I thought Steve was writing the real stuff and I felt like he *was* the guy he was writing about. He *was* that kid. It felt like his experience.'

With the musicians assembled, Steve and Richard went into 'the Dungeon', the pocket-sized basement studio over at Silverline/Goldline, to start pre-production on the album. Every song was rehearsed. The musicians set up and played very much as a live band, without the detached precision more usually employed by session players. Brown drifted in and out and there was input from Gordy Jr but ninety per cent of the arrangements were worked out by Steve and Richard Bennett.

Steve was fairly certain that Tony would be a record executive first and foremost in the studio, and was relying on Emory to be his 'go to guy' if he wanted to go out on a limb musically. He was amazed to find the reverse was true. The conservative streaks in Gordy Jr that had shown up from time to time on the CBS sides seemed magnified on *Guitar Town*. It was always Tony who encouraged him to push the boundaries. But when all was said and done, bold mixes and country music were deemed incompatible. Several of the musicians felt that the roughs were even better than the final record. Steve found that on 'Fearless Heart' and 'Good Ol' Boy', which were as much rock songs as country songs, 'the mix got really timid trying to constrain it and keep it from being too rock. So as soon as you start thinking that way, keeping it from being anything, you're in trouble.'

Down in the Dungeon, left largely to their own devices, Steve and Richard didn't try to keep anything from being anything but simply went on gut feelings and a shared appreciation for real music. Bennett's background had exposed him to influences as diverse as pop and Motown, classical and bluegrass, and he and Steve did what they thought best for the songs and never gave a thought to the commercial constraints of country radio. Afterwards, Bennett thought his biggest contribution to the album was simply that in a town preoccupied with 'targeting and pigeon-holing and naming and putting [music] in its slot on the shelf, he had no preconceptions of what *Guitar Town* should be.

'There were the company guys and the guys sort of thinking it through, and then there was Steve and me sort of operating emotionally and honestly. In the end, whether it was the right thing to do doesn't matter. We just were going on the fly.'

On a sultry evening in July, John Lomax drove down West End, deep in thought. It was an exhilarating time. The MCA deal was close to being finalized and in recent weeks John had broached the subject of a more formal managerial arrangement with Steve. A contractual agreement rather than a handshake. No inroads had been made so far but he planned to raise the matter again in the meeting to which he'd been summoned by Steve at Silverline/Goldline. Pulling into the parking lot, Lomax found plenty of spaces. It was getting on for seven and most people had gone home. Steve was in Fox's office, reclining in his chair. Lomax sat down. Without preliminaries, Steve said: 'Well, John, I can't figure out what it is a manager does. I'm going to have to let you go.'

Lomax stared at him in stunned disbelief. 'It was like, "*What?*" Two record deals and a publishing deal in less than two and a half years! I thought I was doing a pretty good job, you know. And out the door. And I'd probably spent $50,000 of my own money, plus two years and a hundred per cent effort on his behalf and he just said: "I'm going to have to let you go." I just got up and stumbled out, said ["Thanks for the memories"] and that was the end.'

Even with the benefit of hindsight, Steve has no regrets. He felt strongly at the time that Lomax had sold him out, that he had become 'a Rick Blackburn yes man'. He wanted a manager who would be on *his* side, not the label's, if he had to oppose them for any reason. 'I was ambitious and I thought John was inept. I didn't think John was capable of dealing with a record label in any other way except to be on good terms with the record label. When Rick Blackburn [called us in], John brought me in and sat there in that meeting and Rick Blackburn suddenly turned on me and was awful to me. He wasn't smiling. He was looking at me: "You want to sell records or not?" I'd had similar experiences with police officers. And John sat there. And that's when I decided I was going to fire John Lomax, that day. You know, he wasn't there with me.'

The MCA contract was signed on 22 August and committed Steve to seven albums, one every twelve months. He received an advance of around $15,000 and went into the studio soon afterwards. Stinson had timed his move to Nashville to coincide with recording, and hauled his belongings from the sunny esplanades of LA to the mountains of Tennessee with the *Guitar Town* work tapes providing a soundtrack. The raw poetry of Steve's music reminded him of Springsteen's. He liked its honest intent. Its life and soul and willingness to stand up and be counted were a million miles from the big hair and Vegas sparkle of Barbara Mandrell and Reba McEntire, or the dying embers of the Urban Cowboy scene. Coming home to Nashville with an outsider's objectivity, he could tell the town was aching for a change.

'I sensed that something was going to happen and, to me, Steve was one of the things, if not *the* thing, that could happen. I felt that if that record company didn't get in the way . . . it could really work. And that was the only reason I decided to go on the road at all. I really believed in him.'

The feeling that they were on the verge of something magical was in the studio from the first day. Brown was aware of the energy in the room and Steve felt that, with the exception of Bowen, everyone down to Chuck Ainley, who recorded the album, knew that something cool was going on.

Bennett just enjoyed the ease of it all, the camaraderie and the unconscious electricity of the playing. It felt right. It didn't necessarily feel important but he liked the way it fell into place very naturally. 'After the fact, people started kinda oohing and ahhing and it's still, *Guitar Town* . . . evoked around here almost on a daily basis. It's amazing. Because I thought nothing of it other than, here's some cool tunes and I think we've done the right thing by 'em and it's fun and it feels good. And that's all you can do.'

In the fullness of time *Guitar Town* would become one of the greatest albums ever to come out of Nashville, the serendipitous marriage of Steve's timeless songs and the synergy of the musicians and studio technicians who worked on it. But it was Bennett's guitar playing which gave the album its signature sound. His big-note approach to the guitar sound, which manages to be cutting-edge cool and a gloriously old-fashioned tip of the hat to the legends of country and rockabilly simultaneously, propels the album forward in a joyous rush even as it binds it together. Who could ever forget the opening notes of 'Guitar Town', with Steve, full of youthful arrogance and optimism, asking:

Hey pretty baby are you ready for me
It's your good rockin' daddy down from Tennessee.

Bennett used an old Les Paul on licks many people believe were made by a Fender Telecaster, a Gretsch Chet Atkins 6120, a Danelectro six-string bass and, occasionally, a Telecaster. For the first and only time in his life, he played direct, plugging his guitars into the console without the buffer of an amp. He thought of it simply as rocking country music and was astounded when, after its release, Nashville caught its breath and people whispered about how renegade the album was.

'For fuck's sake, I'd come from LA. It was *nothing*. It was just country music and it was old country music to me, anyway.'

To Brown, Bennett's structured approach to guitar playing, quite different from the free-flowing styles of players like Albert Lee and Vince Gill, was perfect for Steve's music. 'Richard didn't copy the Duane Eddy kind of thing but he sort of drew from that low guitar sound, the Dano thing. I think the whole Dano sound in country re-emerged through Steve's sessions.'

All of the sessions had a structured but spontaneous feel. Keyboard player John Jarvis, who could rock out with Rod Stewart or play rollicking honky-tonk piano for George Strait or Hank Jr, knew enough to lace the notes delicately behind Bennett's guitar. Stinson was frustrated at the time because the perfect drum beat hovered irritatingly out of his reach on 'Guitar Town', but over the years he came to see that even that was just right. 'The more distance I get from it and the more time goes by and I see what's been made since then, I think it's a great record. It's a classic.'

Guitar Town was recorded in two weeks, including all over-dubs, at SoundStage and Emerald Studios. Despite the fact that he had an office upstairs at SoundStage, Bowen deigned to venture down to the control room only once during the sessions. He took the opportunity to regale Steve and the musi-cians with stories about Sinatra. Steve lent a cynical ear. He had his own views on Bowen's musical contributions. '*Anybody* could have made "Strangers in the Night" with Nelson Riddle and Frank Sinatra. What the fuck did Jimmy Bowen have to do? All he was was the guy who filled out the paperwork.'

To quieten Bowen down, Steve rolled him an especially potent joint. Bowen inhaled deeply and stopped dead in the middle of his sentence. 'SON . . . !' he exclaimed to Steve, who later decided it was the only occasion he ever impressed Bowen 'in the time I recorded for MCA under his auspices'.

Jimmy Bowen was the reason that *Guitar Town* and every other album that came out of MCA in that period was recorded digitally. In the mid-eighties he owned the only four Mitsubishi X-800 thirty-two-track digital recorders in Nashville, and rented them to MCA. Until the early eighties, analog had been the principal method of recording in the town and the introduction of digital ignited a debate that goes on every day in studios across the globe. DAT technology revolutionized the recording process by allowing studios to polish and manipulate up to forty-eight separate sounds. Not everyone was a fan of it. Bennett preferred the warmth of analog to the diamond-hard clarity of digital. In his opinion engineers had yet to learn to compensate for digital's brittleness, and he was disappointed in *Guitar Town* sonically for that reason. 'To me, it was never a warm-sounding album . . .'

But Steve was won over to digital and would use it on every one of his MCA albums. In October 1988 he would tell *The Gavin Report* that he had a 'real commitment to digital recording. Analog is dead. CDs are here. There are $200 CD players that are sonically a better piece of gear than a $150,000 analog tape recorder. I produced an analog record and it was a fucking nightmare. It was like going back to the stone age.'

It was during the *Guitar Town* sessions that Steve and Bucky Baxter started making regular pilgrimages to North Nashville to score heroin. They'd bonded over the drug soon after meeting because both had dabbled in it in their youth. Baxter knew how to cop heroin in Nashville ('Stop and Cop', he called it), and Steve was more than willing to go along and snort it. Already he was doing junk often enough to make withdrawal from it very painful. Staying with Richard Bennett in Hollywood, he'd doubled over suddenly after dinner. Richard thought it was indigestion. He suggested they go out for a stroll. 'We went out and had a little walk around the neighbourhoood and Steve kinda copped to me that he was coming off heroin. And I was shocked: I felt like a rube from the country or something.'

Brown claims not to have known Steve had a drug habit in

the first two years he was with the label: 'He says he was doing it back then? Had no idea, no idea.' But Steve was open about it with his publicist Pam Lewis from the start. Following a lunch at the San Antonio Taco Company, which consisted predominantly of shots of Jagermeister, his favourite tipple at the time, he asked her if she would mind helping him to run an errand in her red Honda hatchback. Lewis was still new to Nashville and unfamiliar with the streets. It was only when they turned into a grim street and a dealer approached the window that she realized Steve was scoring heroin.

'I'm like, "Oh, my God, OH, MY GOD." I'm in this red car. I mean, *red*. I'm going, "We're going to get busted. You fuckin' son of a bitch, what are you *doing*?!' He goes, "Oh, you love it. This'll be a story you'll tell your grandchildren." He thought it was the funniest thing.'

The record was mixed in fourteen straight days in November at the Castle. Steve's relationship with Bowen was too confrontational for him to learn anything from the man directly, but he learned a lot about his approach to the art of record making indirectly through Brown. Some of it was so valuable that he would use it for the rest of his career, some of it he discarded. Bowen, for instance, was a firm believer in multiple mixes – twenty-five versions or more of each song. It was a formula. There would be a mix with the vocal up one increment, another with it up two, another with it up three. Then there would a version with the mix down one, down two, down three. And so on, with each of the lead instruments. It was a money-saving tactic as much as anything but Steve found it a drag. 'You know, I never stayed around for any of that stuff but it was just a lot of bullshit and a lot of rules and there got to be more rules all the time, depending on how good the pot was. He smoked pot constantly.'

Ultimately, Bowen was a distant figure in the making of *Guitar Town*. Almost everybody else involved in the recording or mixing process believed wholeheartedly in the music. Pam

Lewis, who was present at several of the sessions, wondered if Steve had any idea what an important record he had written. In the sixties and seventies, country singers had regularly confronted the harsh realities of life, death, sex and social dysfunction through songs like Loretta Lynn's 'The Pill', but those days were long gone. Now Nashville's principal obsession was preserving its image as God-fearing and steeped in family values. It had reckoned without Steve Earle. *Guitar Town* put two fingers up to the establishment and its rebellion had weight because it wasn't rebellion for the sake of it. It was about real people and real values and it used real music to send home a message that was concealed beneath a layer of catchy tunes and Duane Eddy guitar licks but was ultimately too powerful to be denied.

Steve had travelled 77,000 miles in 1983 so the freedom of the road as well as its loneliness was bound to seep into the songs. But it was only a road album in the way that *On the Road* was a road book, because it used the landscape of America and the psyche of Americans as a basis for understanding the country and its people at a certain point in history. In 'Someday', written in August, Steve explored his theory that in the USA, interstate highways were like a tunnel running from one end of the country to the other. 'You're not really in Texas and you're not in Ohio. It's like federal property and you don't see the towns.' One image had stuck in his mind. At two in the morning, nearly two years earlier, he and his rockabilly band had stopped at a gas station in Jackson, Tennessee. The forecourt was deserted. Moths whirled in the white lights over the pumps but nobody came to help them. They honked the horn three times before a reluctant youth appeared. He'd been out the back, working under his car. Driving away, Steve wondered why it was that he had taken such an obvious dislike to them. It occurred to him that it was possible the boy resented them because they were passing through and he was just stuck there.

Of all of Steve's songs, 'Someday' most perfectly showcases

his ability to embody a character and breathe life into it with the smallest of phrases. The power of the song lies in the spareness of the prose, which evokes the isolation and frustration of a young gas station attendant almost in sketch form:

> They ask me how far into Memphis son and where's the
>   nearest beer
> They don't even know that there's a town around here.

His fear that this is all he is destined for is present throughout the song, as is his instinctive realization that he has been fucked by the system from the outset:

> You go to school and you learn to read and write
> So you can walk into the county bank and sign away
>   your life.

The only song Steve had any reservations about was 'Goodbye's All We Got Left', which he saw as an 'odd duck' because it was lighter than the rest, but he was proud of all of them. He had achieved what he set out to do: make an album that 'when I finished it I could die'.

At MCA, Tony handed in the completed album and waited for the reaction. There was none. 'What are the singles?' he asked enthusiastically. 'There are none,' someone said. The few people at the label who liked *Guitar Town* tended to be those in the publicity department who could see the potential for promotion in areas of the media not traditionally interested in country artists. Some people actively disliked it. Sheila Shipley, head of promotion at MCA, hated the album. She told Brown that it was going to be a nightmare to sell to radio. Her antipathy towards Steve was blatant. According to Pam Lewis, she 'never understood Steve, never got along with him, never approved of him. Probably, if she had run the label, [it] never would have signed him.'

If Shipley had been Steve's only opponent at the label, life would have been relatively simple. But the label staff divided swiftly into two camps: those who saw *Guitar Town* as a ground-breaking work and Steve as an attractive renegade, and those who, like Bowen and Bruce Hinton, Tony Brown's counterpart in A&R, saw him as an ill-mannered, chain-smoking rebel with no regard for the realities of commercial radio. Ultimately, Steve would be caught in between. 'My relationship with MCA was war from beginning to end.'

8

Year of Living Dangerously

Guitar Town hit the shelves on 5 March 1986, the same week as Randy Travis's debut album, *Storms of Life*. Tony Brown handed Steve the first album to come off the presses and he tore all the way home with it and thrust it at Rick Steinberg. 'Ta da!' he had scrawled on it in triumphant black ink. Inside, he felt rather more exposed than he let on. 'My experience so far was failing in that arena so I was very nervous about it.' But with *Guitar Town*, Steve Earle finally, at the age of thirty-one, had delivered. 'I could be taken seriously as an artist for the first time.'

Had Steve known then what Tony Brown already knew, that thought would have provided little comfort. Apart from a few mavericks in the publicity department, the weight of negative opinion at the label about *Guitar Town* was growing daily. Brown shrugged it off. Listening to Steve's album or the music of his other risky new signings, Nanci Griffith and Lyle Lovett, he felt the same rush he'd experienced when he heard the first haunting crackle of a Gram Parsons track. Music was cyclical. If there was one thing Brown had learned in his journey through gospel, Elvis, Emmy and now Reba, was that every decade or so something magical and even primal happened – particularly when music was the spent force that country had become in the mid-eighties. Five years after the crossover smashes of 'Stand by Me' and Johnny Lee's 'Looking for Love', the life had all but drained from Nashville. For a while country had been the next big thing, but when the pop industry came calling it found Mickey Gilley – a nice enough man but no Elton John. It had occurred to Brown that most of the artists he saw were middle-aged or past middle-aged. They thought small. Social and political issues didn't concern them.

Everything changed in 1985. In one of those near-miraculous alignments of the stars, most of the artists who came to represent 'new country' were all signed within a year of one another. 'The great credibility scare of the mid-1980s', Steve would laughingly call it. At MCA, Brown added Nanci Griffith and 'tall-haired' angular Texan Lyle Lovett to his roster just months after signing Steve. Like other artists perceived as 'new country', they sprinkled liberal quantities of folk, jazz, big band and blues through a traditional country base. In retrospect, it was Randy Travis, the most purely country of them all, who often seemed the odd one out. To Steve's mind, there were two schools of derivative country singers – the Merle Haggard school and the George Jones school – and Travis 'was just the latest and the *youngest* Merle Haggard derivative country singer. The difference between him and a really great singer, to me, was, he had great chops, but you heard every single lick that he knew, every little trick that he'd ever heard Merle Haggard do with his voice on a record; he'd do it in every song.'

In some ways, Travis's position at the vanguard of neo-traditionalists had as much to do with timing (he had after all got in first with the 1985 singles '1982' and 'On the Other Hand') as traditionalism, otherwise he might simply have been lumped in with the Judds and George Strait. But the emergence of a whole gaggle of young, hungry, socially aware artists marked the return to country's roots, to sincerity, to music for its own sake. It was country, but not as anyone knew it. It was retro, but it reached beyond Haggard and Jones to invoke Duane Eddy, Buddy Holly, Gram Parsons, Dylan, Guthrie and Bob Willis, or all of them simultaneously. The only thing its protagonists had in common was their individuality. Lyle Lovett had weird hair and degrees in German and journalism. Dwight Yoakam sang honky-tonk songs that were cool enough to be embraced by California rockers. kd lang came later – big-boned, spiky-haired and, Nashville thought sourly at the time, probably lesbian – with the biggest, lushest voice on the planet, aggravating the radio folks and sending Opry members reeling with her pronouncements that she was Patsy Cline reincarnated.

And in the mix with all of them was Steve, waiting to see if his music would hold its own, if the album he'd written so that when he finished it he could die could ever live up to the attainments of his heroes – Twain, Hemingway, Greene and, of course, Townes and Guy.

The critical response to *Guitar Town* was almost instant. The *Houston Chronicle* called it 'compassionate heartfelt music' and Earl (sic) a cross between Joe Ely, Bruce Springsteen and T-Bone Burnett. 'This is folkabilly at its finest, a rich lyrical mixture of country and spare Texas rock delivered with a folk singer's immediacy.' Steve was cautiously optimistic but no more than that. 'Hillbilly Highway', the first single, was hardly racing up the charts and at least one of his heroes' reactions to the album had been muted. Guy Clark 'didn't quite get it' at the time, although he later changed his mind. 'I came to really appreciate that recording. I mean, it's really fine. Some of the songs from that period are just breathtaking.'

When he needed it most, fate dealt Steve an ace. In April, the industry bible *Billboard* reported that Bruce Springsteen had been seen buying *Guitar Town* in a Westwood, California, record store. It transpired that Bucky Baxter had given a copy of the album to his old friend Garry Tallent, the Boss's bassist, and Tallent had played it for Bruce. It was sheer luck that Bruce's purchase had made it into print. Out of that came a

20 May review in *Village Voice* by Springsteen biographer Dave Marsh, who named *Guitar Town* as one of the best albums of the year. That in turn precipitated glowing articles in *Time*, the *LA Times*, the *Washington Post* and *Rolling Stone*: 'Not since the Everly Brothers – I'm talking about tough stuff like "Claudette" not teen drivel like "Ebony Eyes" – has anybody been so successful at melding their purest, rawest elements'. *Time* was fascinated by the fact that Steve looked like the guy on the next stool at a truck stop, with a 'Peterbilt cap and waistline that has seen a little too much barbecue', yet he read Faulkner. His songs had older echoes – 'the scarred spirit and lonesome heart of Hank Williams, the grittiness of Johnny Cash, the Bull Run rhythmic charge of another Texas boy, Buddy Holly . . .'

All acknowledged the potentially unwinnable struggle Steve faced if he tried to conquer both rock and country radio from a Nashville base. 'Part of the reason *Guitar Town* seems closer to rock than country is the bitterly humorous spirit in which it's sung,' Marsh said. 'That and the fact that its riffs and rhythms are raging. Where this combination takes Earle is beyond my power to guess. "Everybody told me you can't get far/On thirty-seven dollars and a Jap guitar," he sings by way of introduction and as long as he's sold by Nashville's hide-bound entrepreneurs, they might be right. On the other hand, if his secret allegiance to getting the facts straight and smoking everybody within earshot carries him through, Steve Earle might just wind up where he belongs, in that long country tradition kicked off by Elvis Presley.'

And with that, *Guitar Town* exploded.

The MCA deal, Macayla Lohmann and the making of *Guitar Town* had helped Steve move on from the ruins of his third marriage much quicker than he otherwise might have the previous year. Everywhere he had looked there was opportunity. Even his home life was shambolic but enjoyable. After he'd left Carol, he went to live with fellow Texan and singer-songwriter,

Robert Jetton, who had a two-bedroom apartment on Blair Boulevard. When Robert met a girl and moved out, Rick Steinberg, newly released from jail after a three-year stint for selling marijuana to a cop, had moved in. Steinberg had been clean since 1984 and now had other enterprises apart from drugs. One of them was cutting pictures of celebrities out of magazines and using a button press to make them into badges he could sell at festivals and fairs. The apartment was bachelor chaos. When four-year-old Justin Earle came to visit his father, all he saw was 'buttons and pieces of buttons laying all over the house, and then the rest of it was just trashed'.

Steinberg loved to spend time with Steve down at the studio and listen to him talk about music. 'There'll be girls everywhere when I'm a star,' Steve would tell him and Steinberg, self-conscious about his looks, would say: 'Maybe for you but not for me.'

'If they want me, they're going to have to take you too,' Steve would reassure him.

For his own part, Steve thought more and more about an encounter he'd had with a tall, flame-haired woman in the music industry hangout, Close Quarters, in the winter of 1984. A popular local singer by the name of Billy Squire was chatting with her. Lou-Anne Gill 'saw this guy stand up – there was a light behind him – and I looked over and there was Steve and I have to tell you he was the most beautiful thing I'd ever seen in my life. He came over and kinda ran Billy off. I don't think it was love at first sight but an overwhelming attraction was definitely there.'

Apart from an intense conversation, nothing happened for several months. Steve was still married to Carol and Lou-Anne was married to drummer Greg Dotson. In the spring Steve was having lunch with record executive and friend Mary Martin at Tavern on the Row when Lou walked up to the table and handed him her number. With an abrupt, 'My husband left me', she vanished into the afternoon.

Steve took his time calling her and by then she'd got cold

feet. She sensed he was trouble. His interest piqued, Steve showered her with roses at the William Morris Talent Agency where she was assistant to the vice-president. He'd talked Fox into helping to fund them through Silverline/Goldline. 'I'm going to do this every day until you go out with me,' he told Lou on the phone.

By June 1985, they were involved in a smouldering, unstoppable affair. Steve was 'really strongly physically attracted to Lou in a really primal way . . .' and Lou could hardly keep her hands off him. A twenty-four-year-old Nashvillian with a four-year-old daughter, she knew she was playing with fire but she was powerless to resist. Lou's brother-in-law John Dotson, a William Morris agent, could understand too why Steve was so attracted to her. She was ambitious, headstrong and passionate about all that she did. 'Very independent, very outspoken. All of the things that appeal to him.'

On one of their first dates, Lou went with Steve to an ASCAP party and was dismayed when Carol Earle showed up. Steve had told Lou he was separated and she wasn't prepared to see the woman who was still his wife. Perhaps because he didn't want to frighten her off, he had led her, Lou says, to believe that he'd been married only twice. Every instinct in her body screamed at her to get away from him, but his wholehearted focus on her made her feel as if making a home with him was a possibility. He was a romantic outlaw. He charmed her and terrified her simultaneously. 'I was looking at Steve as if he were marriage material. He frightened me and he knew it. He just knew it instinctively and adapted to it and became whatever I wanted. And I know that makes him sound like a predator – so be it. You do not get to where Steve is without having some of those instincts in spades.'

Chemistry aside, one of the things that Steve found most appealing about Lou was her large comfortable family. He adored Lou's father, a retired fireman. On their second date, Lou invited Steve to a Fourth of July pool party and picnic at her parents' house. Steve was in his element. Sitting in the sunshine, washing down barbecued steaks with clinking glasses of amber liquid, he felt very much at home.

Lou's father nudged her mother. 'There's your future son-in-law,' he said.

Mrs Gill cast her eyes over Steve's frenetic form and rock star grunge. 'Oh,' she said, 'surely not.'

When it was the furthest thing possible from Steve's mind, his girlfriend Lou-Anne Gill announced she was pregnant. Steve was shaken to the core. He'd thought she was on the pill like every other woman he knew. 'I was in love with Lou but also my life had become this thing that was very much out of control in every respect. The last thing I needed was to have another kid. I was still married to Carol.'

Steve had moved in with Lou very soon after they started dating, but on the advice of his lawyer he kept the address on Blair and shared the rent with Steinberg for more than a year. Unaccustomed to the landslide that was Steve's life, Lou was seldom sure what was happening until it had happened to her. 'His intensity scared me. He immediately wanted to take the relationship from right here to moving in with me. I mean, that's the way he works. I remember when he first moved in with me, I thought, "How can I get this guy out of my house? How *did* he end up in my house?"'

Despite her reservations, their relationship went from strength to strength. They complemented each other. Steve brought out the wildness in Lou; she gave him a calmness and serenity that he seemed to be lacking. Lou had travelled extensively through William Morris; Steve had seen worlds Lou could hardly have imagined existed. Even their blue-eyed, fair-headed four-year-olds took to each other as if they were siblings. But neither Lou nor Steve was ready for another baby.

Carol-Ann reacted with furious tears to the news that Lou was pregnant. Steve broke it to her one morning when he came over to take Justin to daycare. 'Get out!' she screamed at him.

'Get out! I can't take it any more.' After that the divorce turned nasty. Steve suspected that Carol's lawyers were telling her he was rolling in money – 'I was making $100,000 a year but I wasn't rich.' In fact she had decided on her own that Steve was not going to leave her and Justin high and dry.

Lou was fairly frightened about the future herself. She was pregnant and living with a married man and her conservative, old-fashioned father was deeply distressed about it. She felt as if she was defying and turning away from her beloved family. 'And here was Steve who was starting to spin out of control . . . I told him, "I *cannot* go through this pregnancy by my-self . . ."' But Lou was in love and in denial about the changes fame would bring. 'Okay, I'm pregnant, this is where we'll slow down,' she told herself.

Instead, Steve put his foot on the accelerator.

MCA's plan was to send Steve out on a series of short promotional tours rather than the extended grassroots trawl favoured by most country artists – starting with a ten-day radio tour in May. Like the protagonists in 'Hillbilly Highway', it would follow the old US Highway from the South to the industrial cities of the North, thereby giving the publicity department a hook on which to sell it.

The single, meanwhile, was running into difficulties at country radio stations. In pockets of the South the word 'hill-billy' was as derogatory as 'nigger' and some stations were reluctant to be associated with it. George Jones made the comment that his generation of country singers had spent years trying to stop people calling them hillbillies and Steve and Dwight had undone that in a matter of months. Steve believed that reappropriating the word was empowering. 'I agree with Dwight that we should start calling it "hillbilly music" again,' he told the *Chicago Tribune*. 'The word "country" now has a stigma of mediocrity, whereas "hillbilly" has a strength about it. It denotes being proud of twang.'

In the first week of May, Steve opened for MCA country

artist John Schneider at the Center Stage Theatre in Atlanta, which had played host to punk rockers the Replacements the previous evening. Emotionally, if not musically, Steve came as close as anyone in Nashville to bridging the gap between Hank Williams and Sid Vicious and his inner punk was amused to hear that the band had torn the dressing room to pieces. 'We had to hang out on our bus because the dressing room been completely and totally levelled. I don't mean just food thrown around the place. They tore the walls out. Literally.'

Steve's memories of his own show are sketchy, but he does have a clear recollection of the party afterwards. He, Noel Fox and Tony Brown were all drunk, and Fox and Brown were in possession of a nine-iron. In the early hours of the morning they decided to hit golf balls out of the window of Steve's thirty-second floor room at the Marriott Marquee, gradually closing the gap between the sliding glass panels to make things more interesting. Their judgement being somewhat impaired, more balls hit the glass than made it out on to the street. White missiles ricocheted around the room, endangering life and hotel property. Steve sat on the bed watching a movie. Every time a ball clacked against the thick glass, he simply raised an ottoman as a shield. When he awoke the next morning it was as if Tiger Woods had had a nervous breakdown in the room. Several hundred dollars' worth of room service was congealing on various surfaces and there were golf balls everywhere.

Steve had taken it for granted that the Dukes who had played on the album would be touring with him all year and was, Richard Bennett says, 'pissed off' when Bennett explained he couldn't go. He would do the ten-day radio run, but that was it. 'The truth be known, I had a great time playing with Steve. However, I was making $1,100 or $1,200 a night with Neil Diamond and I was making $75 or $100 a night with Steve. I couldn't sort of quit my Neil gig to go run around with Steve and I think he resented that, kinda thought I was a mercenary. And perhaps I was.'

Richard wasn't the only band member reluctant to go out on the road. Steve had no idea that Tony had had to coax Harry Stinson into the tour by promising him half of his one and a half producer's points – points being the system by which royalties are apportioned in music. Thus the *Guitar Town* tour Dukes were Stinson, Reno Kling, Ken Moore, Bucky Baxter and, from mid-May onwards, Baxter's old bandmate, guitarist Michael McAdam. Steve had hired his childhood friends, Charlie Mullins and Chip Phillips, as tour manager and guitar tech respectively.

Because the radio-run was built around the gimmick of the highway, it made no real sense in terms of geography. From Atlanta, the band backtracked to Chattanooga, where they played to thirty people in a car park, and then it was on to Kentucky, Ohio, Illinois, Pennsylvania and Tennessee. If the low point of the tour was Cleveland, where their opening act was a limbo dancer, the high points were two sold-out show-cases in Nashville, where Steve had overnight become the most desirable artist in town. Interviewing him for her book, *Behind Closed Doors: Talking with the Legends of Country Music*, Alanna Nash discovered he was hungover and 'industrial strength nauseous. He joked that he was doing his Keith Richards impersonation.' Like Gram Parsons before him, Steve's infatuation with hard-living rock stars such as The Rolling Stones' guitarist had always had as much to do with the myth-ical link between creativity and debauchery as it did with music. After a decade of struggle *Guitar Town* had opened the magic door. Steve was 'elated and behaving very badly in the process. You know, it was crazy, it was intoxicating. And it wasn't happening to me when I was twenty-one, it was happening to me when I was thirty-one.'

In Nashville, where country's wholesome image is as integral to sales as the music itself, media training is taken very seriously by the record labels. Each new artist is schooled in the art of the non-inflammatory interview and programmed to respond neutrally to questions on everything from drugs and marital indiscretions to homosexuality and tantrums. Unfortunately for MCA, Steve was never going to be a good soldier in that department. Advised by a media trainer, 'If, say, you're asked about why you slammed the door in those radio people's faces the other night, this is how you'll respond,' he'd say obligingly: 'I can do that.' Confronted with the question in real life he'd tell reporters: 'Because the assholes deserved it!' Pam Lewis made the mistake of trying to tell Steve to do something only once. Aware that his personal appearance was generally the lowest of his priorities, she asked him to put on a clean shirt for a television interview. 'He came in the next morning, he had a t-shirt on and he'd spilled coffee all down the front of it, and I just guarantee it was deliberate.'

Steve relished being contrary, but it was rarely in the ways people expected. He claims to have fired Lewis in an argument over a *Hustler* magazine piece – something she contradicts. 'I didn't want to do it and she had a hissy fit because I disagreed with her. I don't do *Hustler* magazine. It's not my kinda magazine.' He did, however, do a *Playboy* interview in August.

Perhaps because his experiences had made him less malleable than many new artists, and perhaps because of Rick Blackburn, who had tried to make him something he wasn't, Steve had a degree of self-conviction rare in Nashville. Within a very short period of time he became known for his enthusiasm for massacring sacred cows. 'Townes is probably the best songwriter in the whole world and I'll stand on Bob Dylan's coffee table in my cowboy boots and say that,' he declared to *Pulse*. He referred to his own songs as 'eighties hillbilly music'. He was preoccupied with issues that didn't traditionally occupy the minds of country singers and had a breadth of knowledge that was bewildering even to his parents. Brown found that he could hold intricate debates on every subject from environmentalism to nuclear physics and the band received daily history lessons on Ming vases, the Vietnam War and other more arcane fields. These fragments of knowledge and how they affected the man on the bar stool at the truckstop were responsible for the existence of 'Bubba', who appears for the first time on 'Good Ol' Boy' and later on songs like 'The Week of Living Dangerously' and 'No. 29'. Bubba had a blue collar and a good heart but persistent failures by the system had left him feeling helpless and somewhat embittered. As Steve told *Music Row*, 'Bubba works for a living . . . his view of the world is thirty minutes of TV news that he watches when he's very tired, and he doesn't understand why everything that's happening is happening to him. So he lashes out at the first thing he sees that's convenient. Bubba's probably a little prejudiced and narrow-minded about some things, but not everybody has time to sit around and drink wine and talk about politics like songwriters and journalists do.'

America even in the 1980s was overflowing with bleeding-heart liberal songwriters, but Steve consistently backed his rhetoric with action. After playing at Farm Aid, Willie Nelson's annual benefit for farmers paying a high price for America's love affair with corporations, he wrote 'The Rain Came Down', a heartbreaking song of such power and potent visual symbolism that one feared for the life of any 'auctioneer man' who dared to take the land of a farmer who'd listened to it. Steve told audiences that he wrote it to clear his conscience when he realized that Farm Aid did more to benefit him than it did for the farmers.

Watching from the sidelines, it became apparent to Brown that this was the road Steve intended to travel. 'He had a platform and he basically wanted to say the truth whether the truth was the thing to say or not . . . For him, success wasn't about money. I think he enjoyed what money could buy because he got more guitars and stuff but success gave him a platform to speak and he's a political activist. He used it. That's how it changed him.'

Brown intended to make 'Guitar Town' the next single. Steve had always seen it as an album component, written to begin his record, so he had doubts about how it would fare. It didn't have a chorus or any of the other things that singles were always supposed to have. Other people at MCA were concerned that the lyric, 'thirty-seven dollars and a Jap guitar', might raise more hackles at conservative radio stations. Steve agreed to change the phrase to 'cheap guitar' for the single, but he baulked at altering the line about the 'funny-talking' Iranian banker in 'Good Ol' Boy'. As he later remarked to the *LA Times*, 'That was *meant* to be derogatory because it was supposed to reflect the feelings of the character in the song. The guy is angry because he's falling behind economically. That's the whole theme of the song.'

'Guitar Town' debuted on *Billboard*'s country charts on 21 June. Its progress up the charts over the next three and a half months ignited a feud between Steve and MCA's head of promotion, Sheila Shipley, that he would take years to get over. In general country singles at the time had a life of around thirteen weeks. If, during that period, the label produced another single more likely to climb to the top of the charts, it would ask the radio stations to remove the previous one from their playlist and add the new one. It took 'Guitar Town' fourteen weeks to peak at No. 7 on the charts, and according to Steve, 'Sheila was literally de-promoting that record, telling them, "No, play this Reba McEntire record."'

Steve was always very careful to nurture what he thought of as the footsoldiers at the label – people capable of making small but vital decisions – but that didn't alter the fact that people like Shipley and Bowen made the big decisions. As a measure of protection, Steve had signed a two-year contract (later amended to three) with Rosanne Cash's manager Will Botwin, an easygoing man well-liked by everyone who knew him. Botwin's New York-based company, Side One Management, was looking to expand into Nashville and Botwin had agreed to represent Steve on a fifteen per cent commission basis. It was Botwin who had helped Steve to get the 'Guitar Town' video made. Bowen liked to tell people that if it was up to him 'all records would come out in plain brown wrappers' and this attitude extended to music videos. As a result, no MCA Nashville artist had ever been allowed to make one. Bowen had never warmed to Steve and was not about to start now, but he did change his mind about the video when he saw Steve on TNN's *On Show*, performing live at the Cannery in Nashville.

'Man, this guy is serious,' he enthused to Tony the next day. 'He's *good*! I watched him huffin' and puffin'. Man, there's something there.'

The video was shot predominantly at a soundcheck in Akron, Ohio, on the ten-day radio run and made for $16,000. Gerry Wenner, now a successful country video director, filmed without sound and edited it later so it appeared to have been shot especially for 'Guitar Town'. Tony thought it made Steve look like a personable, accessible-type rocker 'like Waylon', who, incidentally, had included 'Devil's Right Hand' on his MCA album, *Will the Wolf Survive*. But Steve added Bowen's initial resistance to the video to a growing list of grudges.

The tour rolled into Manhattan on the wings of a steaming hot summer. There was a buzz surrounding Steve's debut at the legendary Bottom Line club on 18 June, inspired as much by the reported admiration of Springsteen and John Mellencamp as it was by the album reviews. Steve was on an adrenalin high. He was playing three shows in five days in and around the New York area and doing huge amounts of press and his siblings were there to witness it. Stacey and Kelly had flown in for a visit and Patrick, now a political science major at South-West Texas, was on the road with him for the summer, drum tech-ing for Stinson. Pat had always had an image of Steve as his rock star big brother, but the reality of fame exceeded his most extravagant expectations. 'It was all of a sudden status and respect and things that we weren't used to, instantly, overnight.'

The Bottom Line show was nerve-racking and exhilarating in equal parts. The room was awash with industry people, critics, high expectations and no small degree of cynicism. Steve felt the pressure of fame as well as its seductive rush. 'This next song was written by a pretty good hillbilly singer from South Jersey,' he drawled and delivered a smoking version of Springsteen's dark masterpiece, 'State Trooper', knowing all the time that Garry Tallent was in the crowd. After the show, *Rolling Stone*'s Rob Tannebaum interviewed him on the roof of the Day's Inn, high above the sweating streets. Steve relaxed with a vodka and tonic. When the inevitable country versus rock question arose, he said country was the original source of songs that were strong and topical. 'There would have been no Bob Dylan had there been no Hank Williams. It's the portability of the music that gave it its character, the fact that you could travel. I'm not a piano player 'cause you can't hitchhike with a piano.'

The photograph accompanying the 29 December *Rolling Stone* article (which mentions a 'fondness for cocaine') shows Steve leaning against an old truck in jeans and a leather jacket. Far from adopting the combed and starched cowboy image usually required of fledgling Nashville artists, he looks significantly more like a biker than when he was first signed.

At the Ritz, Steve opened for the Replacements, standing foursquare on the stage and delivering country rock to an audience with rainbow-patterned Mohicans. Stinson remembers it well: 'The entire front of the audience was giving us the finger.' When Charlie Mullins expressed concern about the amount of debris hitting the stage, a Ritz staff member retorted, 'Yeah, I've seen cabbages thrown.'

'Bricks . . . what about bricks?'

'Nah, we check for bricks.'

Kelly watched from the safety of the balcony thinking, 'This is the big time.' She felt so proud of her brother as he converted head-bangers to country music. They were having a ball. When the Replacements came out and started slamming themselves against the walls it was all Kelly could do to stop her sister flinging herself into the mosh pit. 'Oh, that looks like fun!' Stacey cried.

Back at the hotel, the craziness continued. Stacey had two small boys at home in Texas and took motherhood very seriously, but the temptations of the rock 'n' roll lifestyle were too much to resist. Everywhere she looked, someone was into the crystal meth or doing a line. With Steve away doing publicity, there was nobody around to disapprove, so she entered into the spirit of things with abandon. After two days she'd done as much cocaine, crystal meth, alcohol and pot as an abusive user would do.

The partying was not exclusive to New York. According to Charlie, 'What was going on that week had been going on pretty much full tilt for quite some time, actually.' He himself did the occasional thumbful of heroin in order to relax or cocaine to help him sustain a twenty-three-hour working day, but he maintains that he soon quit even that and did nothing stronger than marijuana.

For Kelly, it was a surreal visit. After years of watching Steve at down-at-heel bars and clubs and living vicariously through the near-misses and disappointments of his career, it was a pleasure to hear his music on the radio and see him living his dream. Yet there was a simmering undercurrent, a sense that things were not exactly what they seemed. Walking into Steve's hotel room on her first morning in New York, Kelly had been startled to see Lou-Anne Gill propped up against the pillows. They'd never met and Kelly knew next to nothing about her. 'Then I find out about twenty minutes later that she's pregnant and they're going to get married . . . That kind of set the tone for the whole of the rest of the weekend.'

That weekend was the first time Kelly ever felt excluded from her siblings' lives because she didn't drink or take drugs. She knew in her heart that they were trying to protect her from what was going on, but there was more to it than that. Fame had entered the picture. Sometimes she felt that Steve was a virtual stranger to her. 'That's when I first saw the two personalities. "When I walked up to the roof garden when he was being interviewed, he and Stacey were sitting in chairs and talking and the only thing I could think was: "What is all this bullshit that he's saying?" And then I thought, "Oh, it's only PR bullshit." And then as the weekend went by and I heard a little bit more of it and people would come up, I heard him speaking in that same voice. It's like the other Steve. It was really chilling.'

Swept along in a blur of music and meet 'n' greets, Steve was oblivious to either Kelly's disenchantment or Stacey's enthusiastic conversion to the rock 'n' roll ethic. After playing Maxwells in Hoboken, he continued on to Boston, Washington DC, Virginia, North Carolina and Georgia. The first he heard of Stacey's adventures was when she went back to Texas and had her first full-blown epileptic seizure since she was five. It was back with a vengeance. Now she calls it her 'blessing in disguise', believing that it saved her from a rapid spiral into addiction, but at the time it destroyed her life. It took doctors three weeks to work out what was wrong with her and in the interim she had up to thirty seizures a day. The fits were so violent that it would be a year and a half before doctors found a drug that could control them and longer still before Stacey could leave the house. Depression and agoraphobia gripped her. 'I had to learn to live again. I had to learn to drive again. I was afraid that I'd get out somewhere and it was gonna happen.'

By the time they set off for the West Coast Steve was in no doubt that, with very few exceptions, traditional country venues did not have the sound systems or production capabilities to do justice to his show. In that respect country music was still very primitive. Hank Williams Jr was one of the few country stars to attempt rock-style arena concerts, but the whisky consumption on his Jim Beam-sponsored tour had a habit of interfering with quality control. To Steve, 'It was mainly really, really painfully loud and not good loud. But everybody on the crew was whacked out of their skulls and they couldn't hear anything.'

For Steve's first Los Angeles show on 23 July, MCA's Nashville office had suggested a country venue, the Palomino in North Hollywood. The LA office recommended Club Lingerie, a trendy rock showcase venue. Steve selected the Roxy, which was somewhere in between. It was an inspired choice. The Dukes had been slow to regain their early chemistry when Bennett left the band but at the Roxy they put on a blistering show. By the end of it, the glitzy California crowd was visibly moved. Steve had a way of reaching into people's hearts and dragging them forcibly into a world in which the guilt a father feels for the son he never sees can be the purest emotion of all; where counting licence plates heading for somewhere more interesting is the most extreme form of loneliness; where the 'trickle-down' economic philosophy of Reagan has simply failed to trickle down.

'The mood of the country as a whole is that things aren't as they are being advertised,' Steve told the *LA Times*. 'Lots of people are going hungry. Even more have had to downscale their expectations. They are confused. They remember everything they heard about this country in school and they wonder what happened to it.'

Two days later he awoke to find his picture on the front page of the *Los Angeles Herald Examiner*'s arts section. 'Look Out Bruce, Here Comes Steve Earle', was the headline. Underneath was a rave review of both the album and the show. *Guitar Town* had 'all the vitality of rock 'n' roll and all the grace and symmetry of country music', and Steve's colloquial vocal style was 'rife with the sort of leathery timbre and emotional immediacy that characterizes much of Bruce Springsteen's most revealing work'. Live, the 'superb' Dukes were 'virile and tuneful', and Steve, like Springsteen, was an 'artist rising to the occasion of our era – indeed, an artist who is likely to help define and enrich the era'.

Credible music reviews are seldom more unstinting in their praise for an artist, but to Steve it was the fact that it showed for the first time that he was starting to be perceived as a singer-songwriter and not as a country act that meant the most. He wasn't ashamed of being a country singer but he didn't want to be slotted into the country music box either. He wanted to be taken seriously as a writer and have his songs appeal to at least some of the people who liked Springsteen and John Fogerty.

When Steve went to MCA that afternoon for his first meeting with company head Irving Azoff, the *Herald Examiner* article was already blown up, framed and in the lobby. Azoff was all smiles, promises and effusive compliments. It was heady stuff and, almost against his will, Steve found himself getting sucked in. 'I didn't realize until much later that to some extent I was a pawn in a game that mainly had to do with the fact that Irving Azoff hated Jimmy Bowen. Bowen was making money on paper at the time – the country division was doing really well – so Azoff couldn't fire him so he decided he was going to use me to fuck with him – you know, fuck with his autonomy. So Azoff started paying a lot of attention to me, which at that time I was just flattered by and later on I used as leverage when I started having problems with Bowen, which happened pretty quickly after that.'

Back on the road, Steve and the Dukes were plagued by bus nightmares. Trying to travel on the cheap, they had hired a succession of dodgy buses and dodgier drivers. In the midst of the New York run, an overnight trip to play the Amber Cabaret in Philadelphia had almost ended in disaster when the equipment truck blew a tyre. Charlie, who was driving, clung to the wheel and sweated blood until the semi came to halt on the side of the New Jersey turnpike. He was still recovering when the band bus sailed by. The musicians waved. Nobody stopped to help, much less call for assistance.

It was Charlie who crashed the bus into a light pole in San

Antonio after he and Steve 'borrowed' it in the middle of the night go to a Mexican restaurant, and he was at the wheel again when the band were almost killed after the brakes failed on the slopes of the Pokono Mountains in Pennsylvania. The bus just went 'faster and faster and faster' until Charlie managed to wrench into a lower gear and bring the rickety monster to a stop. The whole band was nearly catapulted through the front windscreen.

Another time, the driveshaft disengaged from the bus in the middle of the freeway in San Diego and Steve and all the musicians – fresh from their triumph at the Roxy – had to hitchhike to the gig. Days afterwards the bus died by the side of the road again. The band clambered out and stood eyeing the broken husk like survivors of the *Marie Celeste*. They were debating their options when a tourist bus inscribed 'Last Chance Express' flashed by. Everyone laughed. The driver slowed, turned around and came back. Within half an hour they were aboard 'Last Chance Express' (recently vacated by a cargo of Korean tourists on a getaway to Vegas) and racing to the gig in Mercet, California.

As a measure of their appreciation, the band hired the bus driver and his 'Last Chance Express' to finish the run. It turned out he was the worst driver in the world. Stop signs were approached at breakneck speed and brakes applied at the last possible second. Bumps were treated similarly cavalierly. Several people were given near-lobotomies by the accessories on the bus ceiling. Gratitude went out the window. The 'Last Chance Express'-man had had his last chance.

Dan Gillis came into their lives almost by accident. A former music teacher from Maine, he'd arrived in Nashville in the early eighties with aspirations of being a country singer. He cut a few demos but nothing ever came of them. Soon he was driving trucks to make ends meet.

In the spring of 1986, his wife Rhonda called him at work and told him she had seen a tour bus for sale. Dan went to the auction and put an offer in on a somewhat dilapidated '63

Eagle. When they rang him to tell him the bus was his, he realized that he hadn't even figured out how to pay for it. It took three months just to get it roadworthy. Expecting business to be slow at first, he and Rhonda set off to Maine for a vacation. When they rang from the road to check their messages, the machine was full. It was July, the height of the touring season and buses were like hen's teeth in Nashville. The Gillises tore back home and Dan drove Sweethearts of the Rodeo to Minneapolis the week before they signed their first deal.

A couple of days later Will Botwin called. 'Do you know who Steve Earle is?' he asked.

'I've no idea who Steve Earle is,' Dan said.

'Well, he's going to come by to look at your bus. He had problems with his last bus driver and the last bus kept breaking down, so he wants an older operator.'

'Well, I'm that,' Gillis told him.

Steve came over for an inspection and fell in love with the faded glory of the forty-foot Eagle. It reminded him of Neil Young's bus. It weighed thirty per cent more than a forty-five-footer, was as solid as an ocean liner and one of the best sleeping buses he had ever ridden on, if a little flawed in other regards. He and the band christened it the 'Green Monster'.

Dan's first assignment was to take Steve and the Dukes out on a weekend run in mid-August to play a hillbilly bar in Columbus, Ohio, and a sold-out show at Park West in Chicago on 15 August. Thanks to Chicago rock station WXRT, which had put several *Guitar Town* songs on heavy rotation, Park West was packed to the rafters with frenzied Steve Earle fans. There were people up the stairs and spilling out the doors. 'Hey man, we're rock stars,' said an awed Ken Moore. At the end of the show, Steve played three encores to ecstatic applause and a version of 'State Trooper' so ferocious that bootleg copies still float around today. When the band ran out of material, he went out and played solo.

Standing on stage with the roar of the crowd in his ears, Steve felt an intensity of emotion that almost took his breath away. This was it. This was the culmination of everything he had ever worked for. 'There's not many people who know exactly what point in their life their dreams came true,' he told the crowd.

Dan Gillis knew then that Steve would be a star. 'Steve Earle was the type of guy that, if there were a hundred people in a room and he walked in, everybody would stop and look at him. That's the impression I got . . . And in those days he had long hair and he always wore a bandana and he was a rock-star-looking guy anyway. Of course, when he came into the room, he always took over the conversation and the conversation was always about him. That always amazed me.'

As characters, they were polar opposites. Gillis was calm, methodical and obsessed with golf; Steve was volatile, funny and wired. When they met, Dan thought to himself: 'Oh, my God, this guy's on ten all the time,' but the combination worked. With Chicago behind them, they went out for a twenty-eight-day tour. Dan loved the shows so much that he often worked the stage for free when he could have been sleeping, lending a hand to guitar tech Chip Phillips, who had thirty-odd instruments to fine tune every night. Steve had a soft spot for loyalty and he stuck with his new driver. More importantly, he stuck with the temperamental bus, which had a fold-down bed for Steve in the back room and nine bunks so compact that seven-foot Chip had to be squeezed into them. On the road Gillis concealed from the band how much maintenance the 'Green Monster' needed. Whenever they stopped to eat Gillis would excuse himself and crawl under the bus with a flashlight and a wrench. The air-conditioning was archaic. Driving through Barstow, California, on the West Coast run, the temperature in the bus was so off the charts that the musicians sat around playing cards in their underwear. Stinson and the others 'opened up whatever windows we could and everybody had these bandanas that we'd kinda wetted down and everything was shaking back and forth. It was like something out of *Mad Max and the Thunderdome*.'

There were plenty of high jinks. Bucky Baxter and Mike McAdam would snatch beer from gas stations after hours, leaving $20 on the counter to placate the angry attendants. And Baxter tortured Charlie Mullins continually. At the New Music Awards in New York in November, he kidnapped Marvin Gaye's full-size cut-out from the Apollo and put it in Charlie's bunk. But when all was said and done, it was as much fun as they'd ever had. Riding through Salinas, Mercedes, Las Vegas and Los Angeles, and then across to Texas, Louisiana, Tennessee and Virginia, there was something free, sweaty and adventurous about it all, something bonding. They were all in it together. There was a sense that some kind of musical revolution was unfolding and they were on the brink – right on its teetering, ragged edge – driving across America with no constraints, the impact of the music kicking up little whirlwinds everywhere they went.

The week after Steve appeared on the 30 September *Tonight Show* with Johnny Carson, *Guitar Town* sold 13,000 copies, a huge volume for a country record. Two months later, on 8 November, the album went to No. 1 and would go on to sell 300,000 units. On the back of this success, 'Someday' entered the top thirty, and Epic opportunistically brought out Steve's unreleased sides in the form of *Early Tracks*. The accolades came thick and fast. In December, *Rolling Stone* named Steve Country Artist of the Year and at the beginning of 1987 he was nominated for two Grammys: Best Male Country Vocal Performance and Best Country Song for 'Guitar Town'. Randy Travis and Dwight Yoakam would go on to sell millions more records in the course of their careers but Steve's passion and belief in his own music had been vindicated.

Along for the ride, Gillis felt as if something huge was happening and 'it was getting out of everybody's control. It just kept growing faster and faster and faster. And Steve could roll with it. He knew what was going on.'

*　　*　　*

There was rarely room for pregnant Lou on these adventures. Steve moved her and the kids out to a stylish apartment in Brentwood Oaks, but it was no compensation for the time he was gone. Lou would spend hours sitting out on the deck at three o'clock in the morning, waiting for the sound of his car. She'd imagined that his solid family background would keep him grounded, but now it seemed that he was changing daily. Like Carol, Lou was very naïve when it came to drugs. She had no idea that Steve was using until she came home unexpectedly and he told her that one of the band members was doing drugs in the bathroom. 'I was just horrified. But it's amazing how, when you're repeatedly exposed to certain things, the horror of it goes away. You become anaesthetized to it.'

But success also brought wonderful moments. Steve took Lou for a vacation on the stunning Yucatan Peninsula and to the CMA Awards, and when he did take her on the road she had a very good time. As Kelly got to know Lou, she could see why Steve was so attracted to her. 'She kept a very nice home. There were all those qualities. There was dinner on the table. With what money that they had, she managed to make the house look really interesting and pretty. There was a feeling of family in the house. Maybe that's what he was looking for. She was very maternal, she was very good with the kids . . . And she was striking. She's tall and . . . she has white skin and red hair and gorgeous eyes. If you think of the typical Irish lass, that's what she looked like.'

It was only on a later visit that Kelly could see the early signs of discontent. Sitting at the dining-room table drinking coffee laced with Kahlua, Lou became more and more worked up about the fact that Steve was on the road having fun and she was stuck in Nashville. She'd given up her job at William Morris and she was telling Kelly how she and Steve were going to co-author a book and do all sorts of other important things together, but *when*? 'I felt like telling her, "Oh, honey, that's not what he's looking for. He's looking for someone that's going to be there when he gets home and take care of the kids and make a nice home . . ." I could just see that it was already beginning to unravel.'

Lou clung hard to her hopes for their future, but she was not nearly as confident that Steve would remain the person she fell in love with as she was prior to the release of *Guitar Town*. 'I remember Steve coming to me one time when I was about eight months pregnant – and I had already been through a hellacious pregnancy because of him. He said, "You know, I could have any woman in the world that I wanted." And I said: "*What?*" And he said, "You know, because of where I'm at and my stardom and all that." And I was just floored. And to this day it makes me physically ill to think about it.'

It's true that success brought girls, even if they were often eccentric ones. On Steve's first trip to Winnipeg, Manitoba, he played a college auditorium with a low stage and minimal security. *Guitar Town* was going through the roof in Canada and a whole audience of hockey player-sized college kids were rocking in the aisles. In the middle of the set, he heard footsteps over the music. 'I look up and there's this huge fuckin' girl. She wasn't fat, she was really beautiful, but she was just a girl on a grander scale. Everything on her was big. Just as I turned around, she left her feet – I swear to God, like a fuckin' linebacker – and did this diving flying tackle. I tried to run but it was too late, she was already in the air. And it was a sliding tackle. Harry Stinson's back on drums. He sees this coming and just sidesteps it. Me and the girl go right through the drum kit. Just wiped it completely off the riser. Microphones and drums flying everywhere. It fuckin' hurt. We got up, finished the set. It took us a while to reorganize and put the drums back up. It was one of those things where they finally came to their senses and drug her off. And then I couldn't find her after the show!'

But it probably wasn't those types of girls Lou had in mind. Most likely she feared the type of woman who might hold his interest for more than a few hours, someone striking, intelligent and accomplished. Someone, perhaps, like the golden-skinned, dark-eyed A&R woman who accompanied his friend Kim Buie to the sessions for his second album.

Someone like Maria Teresa Ensenat.

9

Last Exit to Mayhem

Somewhere west of Albuquerque, in the high desert, Steve pulled out the magic mushrooms. They were crammed into a ziplock bag. A high school acquaintance who had elevated himself to the status of old friend when *Guitar Town* came out was attempting to exploit a loophole in the law by selling hallucinogens through the mail. At Liberty Lunch in Austin Steve had been the recipient of his largesse. After the gig, he pocketed the bag with its potent contents and kept it warm as the Eagle hummed through the night, past the flickering neon towns and farflung cattle spreads of Texas and up into the mountains of New Mexico, still and sharp-edged as a Navajo painting. Steve sat up front with Dan, getting high. Two days stretched before them until they were due in San Diego to open for Waylon Jennings. They had decided to take the scenic route, riding I-10 through Southern Arizona and alongside the spiky wilderness of Joshua Tree National Park rather than the more practical Route 66 and I-40. Steve had threatened to fire anyone who didn't partake in the mushrooms during the journey.

A green highway sign loomed out of the darkness. 'Pull over,' shouted Steve.

The bus swerved to a halt by the roadside, spitting up stones.

Steve and the band stumbled out and stood staring up at the sign – 'Exit 0.' They were just short of the Arizona state line and the sign was, in effect, a mile marker, but in that psychedelic moment it seemed to Steve there was something profound about it. He distributed more mushrooms and the band fanned out in the starlight, turning their faces to the warm desert wind. They stayed there for three or four hours.

That had been in the summer of 1986 but the moment had stayed with Steve. Preparing to go into the studio in December later that year, he was sure of two things: the second album was to be called *Exit 0* and it would have a green highway sign on the cover. There was no way he was going to go along with one of Nashville's hokey country singer head shots.

Their touring schedule was such that they literally loaded off the bus and into Emerald Studios down on Music Row. There was no room to breathe, no break. Steve's impression was that Bowen was almost counting on that being the case. 'You won't be able to write your next record because you'll be touring,' he had told Steve matter-of-factly before *Guitar Town* was even released, and warning bells had sounded in Steve's head. The trouble with artists who wrote their own material was that they had too much control. Bowen wasn't alone among record executives in preferring the other kind of artist – those who complied with anything as long as it meant stardom. Steve was, in Brown's words, starting to become very vocal. 'He became that artist that labels fear.'

Songwriting wasn't the only area in which Steve clung to his autonomy. A minor skirmish broke out over his insistence that, with the exception of Richard Bennett, he use his road band to record the album. As one of the country's best bass players, Emory was obviously a cut above Reno Kling, but Steve didn't want some of his band playing on the album and not others. He objected strongly to the unwritten Nashville rule which said that the same A-list session musicians played on virtually every album in town, so that every album had a uniform sound. In this, he had Brown's tacit support. Brown was a firm believer that music's soul came from its roughest edges; contemporary country was dedicated to smoothing them out. In the studio sometimes he'd tell musicians: 'You guys are playing too good. I want this like a Gram Parsons track. I want it to sound like you're all fucked up.' They knew what he meant but they couldn't do it. Indoctrinated with the goal of perfection, they had lost the ability to be natural.

Tired and a little punchy from the road, Steve Earle and the Dukes went into the studio and worked thirty straight days with almost no break. Richard Bennett had been brought in as a full producer, which meant there were three with Brown and Emory. Plus, Steve was asserting himself increasingly. Recording the album, Chuck Ainlay was driven almost mad by the warring egos. Tony would go home for dinner and Emory would take the opportunity to change all the mixes. Then Steve would arrive and argue for the mixes to be harder – more rock and less country. In a now notorious incident, he brought his gun to the studio one night and laid it casually on the console. 'Put that fuckin' thing away, man,' Richard snapped at him. 'I don't want to see it.' And Steve, he says, for once obliged.

The gun aside, Richard's memory of the making of *Exit o* is all positive, apart from his nagging suspicion that Steve was still 'bugged' at him over his refusal to go on the road. Richard found Steve 'a pussycat', a joy to work with in the studio. His ideas got shot down as much as anybody else's. The best idea won. It was very open, very enjoyable. There were no traumas. We kind of approached *Exit o* the same way we approached *Guitar Town*. You go work those tunes up. You don't come to 'em cold that morning and go and make a record.'

Harry Stinson, who had co-written 'It's All Up to You' with Steve, was surprised at how at variance with his headstrong reputation Steve was. 'Steve talked big, he always talked tough, but he was real soft. He had a real sweet heart.' This dichotomy permeates Steve's writing on *Exit o*. The armed robber on 'Angry Young Man' is not the stereotyped rebel without a cause, vengeful and bitter for the sake of being vengeful and bitter. Instead, like Steve himself, he is a figure of immense vulnerability. There is nothing boastful about his confessions. Compelled to run without knowing what he is running from, angry at who knows what, he pleads only that his mother not blame herself for his actions. This contrast between emotion and intent echoes through 'The Rain Came Down' – a Steinbeck scene set to music – and is an undertone in the seemingly carefree boy's own adventure, 'The Week of Living Dangerously'. But the standout song on the album is 'No. 29'. The only hint that the man reflecting on his days as a high school football hero suffers from the same hurts and frustrations as the other protagonists on *Exit o* comes in the first verse: 'Ever since the glass plant closed down/Things 'round here have never been the same.'

Increasingly, Steve's own worldview seemed to be that of the 'Angry Young Man' – 'I've got to live like I please or die trying.'

On 7 January, bang in the middle of recording, Lou gave birth to Ian Dublin Earle. She had been lax about attending pre-natal classes, confident that she could rely on her memory of them during her pregnancy with Amy, and Steve had been on the road too much to train as her coach. Consequently, she called Steve 'eighteen different kinds of motherfuckers' in the delivery room, yelling: 'I want an epidural now!' before Ian came squalling into the world in a three-hour rush. His first outing would be to the studio.

Ian's birth did little to alleviate the strain on Lou and Steve's relationship. Lou's first husband had been a musician who was perpetually on the road and Steve could not understand why that had not prepared her for his long absences. There was additional pressure from her parents, who were mystified as to why Steve's divorce was dragging on and concerned that he should do the right thing by their daughter. Steve, meanwhile, had found solace in the arms of several girls on the road, two of whom he saw fairly regularly in California. 'I was kinda in love with all of them, and it was stressful to say the least.'

At the forefront of his mind, towering over everything, was Maria Teresa Ensenat. Nothing had happened between them – not physically at least. But mentally and emotionally, they were already inextricably bound. What had started as a few telephone conversations and 'care' packages had become in effect a long-distance courtship, with every word weighted and charged. Teresa was totally different from anyone Steve had ever met. She was very beautiful, of course, but more than that she was 'really, really supersmart', with a life and career of her own. Steve had known he was in trouble the moment Teresa walked into the studio during the *Exit o* sessions the previous November. She was everything that appealed to him in one gorgeous package. She was Cuban, for instance, with an exotic history. Born in 1960, two years after Batista fell to Castro, she had stayed behind with her mother and sister when her father was given permission to emigrate to the USA. In Miami, Emilio Ensenat bussed tables until his family were granted leave to follow him. A talented chemical engineer, he soon found a professional position and would spend the next fourteen years moving between Virginia, Costa Rica, Aruba, Ohio, Minneapolis and North Carolina. It was in Louisville, Kentucky that the Ensenats finally settled. Teresa attended high school there before working her way, via student loans and scholarships, through the University of Louisville and Loyola Marymount in LA. While at Loyola, she had interned at Will Botwin's company, Side One. Now she was a fast-rising star in the A&R department at Geffen Records after signing heavy metal icons Guns N' Roses.

Steve had never fallen for a woman so hard or so fast. Torn between the smart sexiness of Teresa and the guilty responsibility he felt for Justin, Amy and Lou and the new baby, he opted increasingly for the space of the road, to which he had returned almost immediately after finishing in the studio. In truth, the only place Steve was really happy was on the bus: 'I got into a thing on the road where I was comfortably uncomfortable. There are parts of it that are lonely for anybody. I got separated from the band in the early days no matter how hard I tried because I had to do press and I was on a different schedule and so a lot of times the bus would roll and I'd end up staying and having to get on a plane because I had to get there early to do interviews or whatever. And, you know, the first few years I didn't go to soundchecks. I insist on going to them now. But the road was home. And it's my failure. It's not anybody else's failure. *I* failed to make the houses and apartments I lived in home. Consistently. Because for fourteen years, I didn't settle in. I settled in the night the bus rolled.'

A month after the completion of *Exit 0*, Tony Brown sat mulling over his dinner plans in the muffled elegance of MCA. Once again, he had been hung out to dry by Jimmy Bowen. His orders were simple: take Steve out for a meal and inform him that he couldn't call his new album *Exit 0* ('Truck drivers' Zen', was how Steve had explained it), he couldn't use a highway sign on the cover (a head shot or similar was required), and he couldn't include his band's name on the cover because that would put him in the 'band' rather than 'male artist' category at the Grammys and he'd be up against Alabama and wouldn't stand a chance. Plus, the band wasn't signed.

Tony had the highest regard for Bowen's business instincts, but his working methods were sometimes difficult to take. He was the most intimidating man Tony knew. He liked to summon people to his house for meetings, make them wait in the study for thirty minutes, regardless of who they were, then call them in and fix them with a hawk-like stare over the top of his glasses, the straps dangling down. He was not above toying with the nerves of artists. Nanci Griffith, who had made four independent records and won a Grammy before she signed with MCA, was scared to death of him. 'He would do tortuous things to me. He would wait until Tony Brown was out of town and he would call me and say that he wanted me to come in and try different microphones because he thought my voice hurt people's ears. He would make me stand there all day, singing the same song over and over again on these different microphones and when Tony would get back in town, Tony would say, "How dare you do that to my artist?" There was no purpose to it, it was just because he could. He did it because he could.'

Tony sensed that Bowen was well aware that Steve would not stand still to be toyed with, manipulated or shouted at, and that he was more likely to get his way if he used Tony's friendship with Steve to his advantage. Steeling himself for the inevitable confrontation ahead, Tony climbed into his car and drove to Steve's favourite restaurant. He had taken the precaution of asking for a side room so that Steve could rant and rave if he wanted to. Steve swaggered in and soon there were smiles all round and ice clinking in the glasses. When the steaks arrived, Tony took a deep breath and attempted to couch Bowen's demands in diplomatic language. Steve's fist came down on the edge of the plate and a steak came flying towards Tony. The air turned electric blue.

The answer was a resounding 'No.' When the album came out, the 'Exit o' sign was on the cover and the names of Steve Earle and the Dukes were prominently displayed.

Much to Lou's agitation, Steve's touring schedule in 1986 was nothing compared to the onslaught of '87. Steve was on the road so much he had trouble sleeping at home. Lou had no sympathy for him. 'I've tried to get her to go "brrrr" until I fall asleep,' he told the *Nashville Banner*. 'But she wouldn't do it. She thought it was undignified or something.'

One thorn was removed from Lou's side when Charlie

Mullins 'resigned', in his version of events, and resigned and was fired simultaneously, in Steve's. Lou-Anne and Charlie had never got along, but by the end of his tenure as tour manager they couldn't stand the sight of each other. Charlie was convinced Lou wanted his job for herself. 'She'd come up to me when Steve wasn't around and tell me straight to my face: "I want you out, I want your job, I want you to go home. I don't like the influence you have over Steve." She played a game and she won . . . And the fact that Steve let her do it destroyed me. The fact that Steve believed her over me on certain issues. Her influence was such that I knew that it was just a matter of time and I resigned. I said: "I really don't need this."'

Lou was not the only reason for Charlie's departure. For one thing, the adventures on the road were taking their toll on his marriage and the pay was such that he was struggling to keep his wife and kids afloat. For another, he was sick of the sleep deprivation, the drugs and babysitting the band. With the exception of the easy professionalism of Ken Moore and Stinson, he found their attitudes and temperaments exhausting. Bucky 'I'm not a homosexual, I just don't give a damn' Baxter, as Charlie sometimes referred to him, appeared to do everything possible to irritate him. Charlie estimated that the steel player required eighty per cent of his band attention. Bucky and Steve were party buddies and it was always interesting trying to round them up once they had their hearts set on a good time. But the hardest part of all was trying to reconcile his role as tour manager with his role as Steve's best friend. He was in constant conflict. 'I know part of it was the drugs, and that was a big problem, but it was the way he treated women, the way he did drugs, the way he treated band members. He could justify it all because he could show how it benefited him. And a lot of people got hurt. Let me just say that that wasn't Steve all the time. That was when I was working for him. He got very successful very quickly, he really did, and you could tell.'

Steve was philosophical about Charlie's early exit, believing that his tour manager had some drug issues of his own. And Charlie, for all his grievances, was grateful for the ride. 'It was a lot to do and I did parts of it very well and parts of it very poorly, but I wouldn't have missed it for the world.'

Amid a whirlwind of spring dates, the band flew to Europe for the first time on 19 March, playing at the Paradiso in Amsterdam on the 21st. When the show was over, Steve went for a drink with the promoter, wandering though the heaving, furtive streets of the red-light district. At a private members' club the doors were locked behind them. Steve hung his new leather jacket over the back of his chair, tucked his passport into the pocket and relaxed. The next time he looked, they were gone. There was instant pandemonium. Everyone shouted at once as they tried to decide who had left the bar or come in unnoticed but it was all to no avail. Steve's replacement passport looked like a pre-war document. When he returned to Nashville later in the month, he showed it off to friends. 'Yep,' he said, 'this jewel is guaranteed to get you strip-searched at any airport in the world.'

On their last night in Amsterdam, some of the band members hardly slept. A generous acquaintance had presented them with a hefty bag of cocaine and they'd stayed up until the small hours doing lines and playing Beatles songs on the hotel piano. When they caught the plane to Paris in the morning, they hid the bag in the toilet so that those who were so inclined could avail themselves of it during the flight. They flushed the remainder away before they landed.

In Paris, Christopher Runciman, who had been drafted in by ASGARD promoter Paul Fenn to road manage Steve for the tour, was intrigued by the raw intensity of his performance. To him, Steve didn't so much sing as *feel*. He presented himself as a man of the people and audiences bought into it because 'you didn't get the idea that Steve was riding around in a Cadillac'.

Budgets being tight, Steve and the Dukes did in fact do much of the tour in a VW van with aircraft seats, going eighty miles an hour with guitars in the back. For a new artist, Steve played an extraordinarily comprehensive London schedule, including appearances at Dingwalls, the Mean Fiddler and the recently opened Virgin Megastore. His London base was the Columbia Hotel on Lancaster Gate, West Kensington. In the days when it still had a certain Victorian grandeur, the Columbia had been leased to the US military for use as an officers' club, but since the mid-seventies acquired infamy as the British equivalent of West Hollywood's Hyatt House, the ultimate rock 'n' roll hotel. By the early eighties it played regular, if unwitting, host to numerous entry-level bands. Its military history meant it was a bizarre mix of Brylcreemed ex-servicemen taking a trip down memory lane and heavy metal bands with distressed hair and full-body tattoos. After a night or two Steve decided it was a madhouse.

'It was one of those things where you did anything to avoid sleeping because then you had to be in your room, which was really fuckin' depressing.'

In the event he spent next to no time in his room, which he christened 'The Three Stooges Suite' because it had three single beds in a row. The bar at the Columbia had a policy (long since revoked) of serving alcohol for as long as their customers could stay upright and Steve and Dan Stuart, lead singer of Californian psychedelic country-roots band, Green on Red, for whom Steve was opening in Edinburgh and at the Town & Country Club, took full advantage of their hospitality.

Staggering off to bed at six o'clock one morning, Steve was flagged down by the receptionist. Lou-Anne was on the phone and she had a bone to pick with him. Steve stood in the lobby while she chewed him out. Dan Stuart listened to his side of the conversation with intense interest. When Steve hung up, Stuart walked over to the house phone, asked the operator to connect him to his girlfriend and started a fight. He was, Steve speculated, trying to keep everyone on the same wavelength.

*   *   *

May came with a virtual blizzard of good news. Steve's publishing deal with Silverline/Goldline had expired the week *Guitar Town* reached No. 1 the previous year and had been renegotiated when the Oaks sold the company to Lorimar Publishing Inc, a division of Warner Bros. On May 1, Steve received the first half of an $80,000 advance, with the balance to be paid in monthly instalments of $3,333.33. 'Goodbye's All We Got Left' peaked at No. 8 the next day. There were plenty of deals in the offing. Hughes Films wanted Steve to sing the theme song for the Steve Martin movie, *Planes, Trains and Automobiles*. He heard it and hated it but did agree to do a cover of 'Six Days on the Road' and his own song 'Continental Trailways Blues'. Plans were also afoot for Steve to tour with Rosanne Cash, who was enjoying one of the most successful periods of her career.

With real money in the bank, Steve and Lou moved to Fairfax Avenue, near Music Row. Steve had been uncomfortable out in the suburbs. There were no army surplus stores and no weird people in the 7–11. 'I like cities. I like the country. It's the in-between I have trouble with,' he told people.

Exit 0 was released on 18 May, the same week as Randy Travis's *Always and Forever* and Dwight's *Hillbilly Deluxe*. The fact that Travis and Yoakam's albums entered the pop charts in the upper 50s and *Exit 0* was the most added album on adult-oriented rock radio (AOR) reignited the country/rock debate. It was as though the two were mutually exclusive terms. When Steve tossed off a line like 'I'll always be a country singer because I'll always talk like this [but] I'm not going to say this isn't rock 'n' roll because it is,' it was treated as controversy by country radio and Music Row. Steve himself felt he had more in common with Outlaws like Waylon Jennings than the 'new traditionalists' or 'new country' artists with whom he was continually lumped. He lost no opportunity to distance himself from Travis and Yoakam, telling everyone that his next album would be 'heavy-metal bluegrass'. And while their albums went straight into the top ten on the country charts, the *Exit o* singles ran into difficulties. MCA quickly found that country radio would stop playing 'Nowhere Road' if 'I Ain't Never Satisfied' was doing well at rock radio. In October, 'Sweet Little '66' stalled at No. 37 on the country charts after dealers of imported cars complained about the lyric, 'So when your Subaru is over and your Honda's history/I'll be blasting down some back road with my baby next to me/In my sweet little '66 [Chevelle].'

Steve made it clear that he couldn't care less. 'I hate Hondas and Subarus, that's why I wrote the song in the first place.'

It was comments like that which made Steve a media favourite. He had a knack for the bullshit-eliminating throwaway line – 'People don't want to hear you feeling sorry for yourself because you're riding around in a bus that cost more than their house' – and his biker looks contrasted starkly with his passion for literature and political radicalism. While Nashville debated what to do with him, the *New York Times* included him in an article headlined 'Heartland Rock: Bruce's Children'. The *Washington Post* had compared the Dukes to Springsteen's E-Street Band and the *New York Times* went further by aligning Steve with John Mellencamp as one of the main proponents of heartland rock in Springsteen's wake. In the analysis of reporter Jon Pareles, it was Springsteen who had established heartland rock's main topics – unemployment, small-town decline, disillusionment, limited opportunity, bitter nostalgia. Heartland rock had its roots in the return to 'gritty, back-to-basics Americana', as evidenced by films like *Country* and *Stand by Me* and the proliferation of TV commercials selling blue jeans and beer with three-chord country and rock. The Reagan campaign had tried and failed to buy the rights to Mellencamp's 'Pink Houses' with its 'Ain't That America' chorus. Hard times were the traditional province of country and blues, but rock recycled itself constantly and 'every burst of pop escapism or technological wizardry' brought a back to roots resurgence. All of heartland rock revolved around a central question, Pareles said: 'What happens to the people in a factory town when the factory closes down?'

Steve wasn't the only country artist to be preoccupied with that question, nor was he the only one to employ heartland rock's main topics in his songs; he just articulated the factory workers' stories better than most. His writing had the shade and depth of classic fiction. More than a year after its release 'Someday' was the song more people quoted from than any other, almost as if its lyrics transcended the music. As Steve pointed out, 'For a lot of people there is some truth to the statement that print is dead. Songwriting is literature that you can consume while you're driving.'

Steve and Carol were finally divorced on 6 July, citing irreconcilable differences. They'd officially been married more than six years, during which time Steve had had three major love affairs (one of which was yet to be consummated) and a second child. The court ordered him to pay a total of $60,000 in alimony – $1,500 a month until it was paid. But even as Lou-Anne was heaving a sigh of relief, Steve was arranging to meet Teresa during the New Music Seminar in New York the following week. Teresa was no more free than he was. At Geffen Records, she had been secretly dating Tom Zutaut, her boss in the A&R department, and although things weren't going too well, they were still seeing each other. Zutaut had risen to prominence in 1982 when he discovered Motley Crue while working in the marketing department of Electra Asylum Records. Teresa became his assistant and, shortly afterwards, his lover. When he was offered the position at Geffen in 1985, he took Teresa with him. The following year, she was made an A&R representative and paid a salary in excess of $200,000 over three years. As a scout, it was Teresa who trawled the midnight bars for that glimmer of magic that separated one skinny metalhead from another, Teresa whose gut instincts enabled her to sense the hateful charm of Axl Rose or the dark appeal of Tessler. But on a personal level, she wasn't happy.

In New York, Steve agreed to meet Teresa, her sister Grace and her best friend Anna for dinner at La Luna in Little Italy. He was an hour late, which didn't go down well. A heroin-buying expedition on the Lower East Side had taken longer than expected. After the meal, Teresa and Steve went to the Cat Club to see Australian punk band the Saints. One thing led to another and somehow they ended up back at Steve's hotel room. Their defences weakened by drink and chemistry, they made love for the first time.

Across the city, in another hotel, Grace was panicking. Zutaut kept ringing and quizzing her as to her sister's where-abouts. Every so often she would dial Steve's room and go: 'Teresa, goddamm! He's just called again. Teresa, goddamm!'

But Steve and Teresa weren't interested. Teresa was the first woman Steve had ever been with whom he found genuinely intellectually stimulating. 'She had a life of her own, she had a career of her own, she wasn't dependent on me for an iden-tity. You know, I'd created these situations where all the women I'd been with were sort of dependant on me for an identity. Which I contributed to as much as they did. I mean, I had these very traditional ideas about what a relationship was supposed to be that clashed with the way I lived. And I didn't mean for it. Politically, I don't have a sexist bone in my body. But the idea of even thinking of trying to co-exist with some-body that did something that wasn't as self-involving as what I did had never occurred to me until I met Teresa.'

Both were agreed that they wanted to see each other as often as they could, but neither was sure what shape the future would take, especially since Steve was now engaged to Lou. And at the back of Steve's mind was the question of what to do about his youngest son if he ended the relationship with Lou. 'Ian was . . . technically a bastard and I couldn't live with that.'

*　　*　　*

Steve married Lou barely three weeks later, coming off the road and falling into the wedding all in a crazy rush. Lou had planned everything while he was away. 'It was almost like he was ambushed,' his sister Kelly thought. Kelly had made Lou a headpiece and had it shipped. She couldn't bring herself to go. She'd visited the couple earlier in the summer and had had a bad feeling about the marriage. When the subject of the wedding had come up, Steve had always kept quiet. Now she wished he *had* said something to the family. She wished he had told them that sometimes he would just drive home and sit outside in his car, unable to bear the thought of going up to the apartment. Had Kelly known that, she would have been in her car that very day and on her way to Nashville to tell him: 'Are you *insane*? To get your name on a birth certificate you're going to marry somebody that you know you don't love and can't be with?' As someone who had lived through a bad marriage, she would have said to him, 'Don't do it. You won't be happy. You'll be miserable.'

But no one stopped him. No one stopped Lou either, although Rick Steinberg made a clumsy attempt to warn her off. The day before the wedding he took her aside and said: 'Do *not* marry this man.' He hinted darkly that Steve was potentially addicted to a variety of things, including drugs and women. Lou became slightly hysterical. 'You don't think I should marry this guy?' she cried. 'You think he's fooling around on me . . . ?' And Rick, regretting that he had been rash enough to open his mouth, made some excuse and calmed her down.

The wedding was held at a hotel in downtown Nashville where Steve had taken Lou on one of their first dates. The family members who did go told Kelly it was the 'weirdest situation they had ever been in because there was such tension in the air. They couldn't figure out what was going on. It was almost like it was Lou's wedding and Steve was absent.' Steve went through the motions of the ceremony – 'I was very much in love with Teresa but I married Lou anyway' – and afterwards he went down the street to a payphone and called Teresa. Lou was furious that he had disappeared. *Vanity Fair* was coming in to talk to them and Annie Leibowitz was doing the photographs.

'Nowhere Road', the first single from *Exit o*, peaked at No. 20 on the charts on 22 August. Steve was flying. Despite the uneasy atmosphere at home and a dawning conviction that MCA were going to do nothing to support his album, artistically, things were moving along nicely. Ticket sales for the tour were booming and he appeared to be gaining the respect of even those critics who weren't convinced about the album. He was living his dream and he was in love. 'I had my head down with what I was doing and I was running on a lot of adrenalin and I just thought everything was the way it was supposed to be. It didn't occur to me that my life wasn't supposed to be like that and that I couldn't do it for ever. You know, there was loose end after loose end after loose end, and they were accumulating. In a big way.'

One reason for his optimism was MCA supremo Irving Azoff, who continued to make him feel special by inviting him to his office at regular intervals and having lunch catered in. Steve nurtured the relationship. He had every intention of going over Bowen's head to Azoff if Bowen started to jerk him around. The only time he felt a twinge of doubt about Azoff's intentions was when he ran into Bernie Leadon, the Eagles' original guitar player, on a plane, shortly after *Exit o* came out, and Leadon warned him to watch his back. He seemed to feel that Azoff was an incarnation of Lucifer.

Lou and Steve had not been married long when Steve received a message that Bowen wanted to see him. At his office at Soundstage on Sixteenth Avenue, Bowen came right to the point. 'Irving Azoff's been calling me and he's been telling me to give you a free hand to make whatever kind of record you want to make,' he said unpleasantly. 'Now I'll tell you something. I know what you're doing. You're hanging

Irving Azoff over my head and you're trying to use Irving Azoff to control me.'

In Steve's memory of the conversation, Bowen went on to attack *Exit o*. Steve might have set out to make a rock record but, in Bowen's opinion, all he'd ended up with was an AC (Adult Contemporary) record. Watered-down rock. Bastardized country.

'No,' Steve said coldly. 'I tried to make a country record the way *I* make records.'

Bowen interrupted him. 'Yeah, well, what this label is about and what I'm about is redefining what country records are and how they sound. Now you've made the right decisions. You're recording digitally and you're doing the right things. If you concentrate on touring the way you've been doing, you could do what Hank Jr did.'

Steve listened with no small degree of scepticism. It was all going somewhere, the only question was where. Bowen paused in mid-flow. His eyes flickered over Steve with distaste.

'I hear you've got a dolly in California,' he said slyly.

Steve stared at him in total disbelief, the shock struck him like a blow. It was impossible that Bowen should know. Nobody in Nashville knew, so far as Steve was aware. But somehow Bowen had the information and he was letting Steve know that he was willing to use that as leverage in order to control him. It was the longest conversation Steve ever had with the man. 'I never had another conversation with him, I don't think, after that. But that's when the battle lines were drawn. And by that time I'd started to figure out . . . that Irving Azoff was evil and that became more apparent as the year went on. I was aware that I was dealing with people that weren't in the music business for the same reason I was and they were dangerous people. They were ruthless.'

Ruthless or not, Steve paid Jimmy Bowen's warning no heed. If Lou wasn't on the bus, Teresa was. Steve saw his Cuban lover as often as he could, finding the intensity of their relationship curiously at odds with his very real affection for Lou's family and the stability family life represented. He and Teresa were purely focused on each other – with inevitable repercussions. '[M]y children suffered to a certain extent in the course of that relationship.'

Their efforts to see each other were helped when Steve was asked to LA to oversee production of two sides for Charlie Sexton, an MCA artist who was experimenting with a rock sound. He was paid $1,000 a side with the understanding that he would receive an additional $2,000 if they were released. On 30 August, while he was there, John Lomax sued him for $40,160 – $13,829 in commission payments, $19,696 in expenses, plus $6,635 in interest in a Chancery Court lawsuit. Lomax had spent the past couple of years bombarding Steve with bills in an attempt to recover some of the money he felt he had outlaid while representing him. For a time he'd travelled with Steve as part of the road band and there were claims for accommodation, promotion, phone calls, petrol, clothes and equipment. Lomax claimed never to have taken a nickel of the money Steve earned on the road because there was so little of it. Instead he'd held on in the hope that the MCA money would come through and he'd finally get his money back.

Lomax was represented by David Maddox in Nashville and, perhaps unwisely, he paid him by the hour rather than on contingency. When the depositions were filed, Lomax found that all he was entitled to was documented expenses. His time and, as he put it, 'blood and tears' were not taken into account. Lomax eventually received a settlement of $20,000, half of which went to his lawyer. In recent years, Lomax has had success with the Australian-born alternative country artist, Kasey Chambers. When he sees Steve he greets him cordially but he remains bitter. 'I think the world of Steve's talent, still do. But I just think he missed a few lessons in common politeness and decency. He's never said thank you, ever, much less said anything to anyone for publication about what I did for him and that pisses me off because recognition is an invaluable thing when you're building a career as a manager . . . The deal I got him in '85 he kept for fifteen years.'

Steve's former publicist Pam Lewis was co-managing Garth Brooks by this time and could see both sides. An artist's life was much crueller than it looked from the outside. Along with the glamour and the money came the suitcase lifestyle and constant scrutiny But a manager's lot was a thankless one too. 'By and large management is working for free, unless you get very lucky. That's why I don't do it any more. And you know what, at the end of the day they hate you. They hate you and they resent you and they don't appreciate you. By and large. I mean, there are those stories where people have been together for twenty years and they're very happy and the artist and the manager get along great, but they're few and far between.'

Steve remains convinced that he made the right decision to part with Lomax. He firmly believes that at least some of the $20,000 he reimbursed his ex-manager was 'him going around chasing girls and buying marijuana. And those were all expenses that I paid for. I didn't smoke marijuana, not on any regular basis. It just wasn't important to me. The main thing that was important to me in those days, in terms of drugs, was alcohol.'

For Lou, life swung between heaven and hell. Everyone wanted a piece of them. She and Steve shared a vision of a traditional family life, with all the stability, monogamy and nurture that that implies, but the rebel spirit that had driven Steve since childhood tugged at him constantly. New horizons and new muses were as necessary to him as breathing. Without them, what would he write? While Lou wrestled with the challenges of her own new married life, Steve was more preoccupied with the disappointment that followed the 12 September announcement that he wasn't a finalist in any of the categories at the Country Music Awards, particularly since he had had ten nominations in the preliminaries. Even T. Graham Brown, who'd been nominated for the Horizon Award for best new artist, thought that Steve was more deserving of it. The fact that the Grand Ole Opry continued to snub him was a source of irritation too. Randy Travis had been a member since 1986.

As the year went on references to drugs and drink started to surface in Steve's interviews, although they were always in the past tense, as if they were the product of a misspent youth. He was, he told one reporter, relieved that success had been delayed for him. 'I managed to damage myself enough with no money in those days. If I had had any money it would have been awful.' Few people seemed to question his inclusion of 'Dead Flowers', the Rolling Stones' hymn to heroin addiction, in his set, and Steve was charming in his assertions that he didn't do drugs any more and rarely drank.

'I don't have time to have hangovers,' he would say with a grin.

He did, however, have time for drugs, a source of some tension on the band bus. Melvin Markham had taken over from Charlie as road manager and spent his days marshalling the various characters in the band. Between Steve, Bucky Baxter and guitarist Mike McAdam, it was a continual soap opera. McAdam had been arrested back in February for raiding five or six 7-11s and ripping the covers off *Time* magazine in protest at their story on John Lennon assassin Mark David Chapman. As Rick Steinberg put it, 'It was a wild ride. There was a lot of money, a lot of people and a lot of insanity.'

In defence against the excesses of the tour, Stinson and Kling roomed together. Stinson felt that Steve's drug use was rapidly getting out of hand. He seemed remote. He wasn't there any more. It wasn't that the band members ever actually witnessed him doing drugs, but drugs were evidently part of his life and, more and more insuperably, part of him.

The abundance of drugs meant there were constant dramas. On 28 September, Teresa was with Steve in Norfolk, Virginia when he ran into more trouble. They had decided that they wanted to spend the night in a bed that wasn't moving. The bus went on to Atlanta, where Steve was opening the next day for Rosanne Cash, and he and Teresa checked into a local hotel. Steve paused just long enough to grab his Gibson USA duffel bag, which he kept permanently packed with a change of clothes and a shaving kit in case he had to stay behind or travel ahead to do interviews. It saved time. He had another, almost identical Gibson USA duffel bag, which he called the 'Keith Richards kit. Everything illegal or dangerous was in it.' Steve decided to leave that one on the bus. He thought it would be safer.

The next morning he and Teresa checked in at the airport. Steve was going on to Atlanta, Teresa was flying to LA. At the security checkpoint, Steve put his bag on the conveyor belt. In that instant he realized that he had the wrong one. 'Stop!' he shouted, but it was too late. The security woman had pressed the button and Steve's .45 Colt Automatic had been sucked into the X-ray machine.

'Look, there's a gun in the bag,' Steve said helplessly. 'It's a mistake.'

His subsequent arrest and Teresa's application for bond on his behalf took some time and Rosanne was on stage when Steve arrived at the venue in Atlanta. She was hopping mad. The unacceptable delay had meant that she had been forced to go on in the opening act slot and he was now headlining. When she reached the part in her set where they did a duet on her 1979 hit 'No Memories Hangin' Round', Steve strolled on to the stage as if nothing had happened.

'You don't have to create drama in your life,' she told him sourly. 'You embody it.'

Will Botwin, meanwhile, had spent the day placating Lou, who was unable to understand why Steve was not travelling with the band and distressed about his arrest in Virginia.

* * *

The Virginia incident was not the first time Lou's suspicions were roused that Steve might be having an affair, but he was convincing in his denials. 'You see girlfriends behind every bush,' he told her.

Bowen excepted, Steve was confident he had done a good job of keeping his romance under wraps. Unbeknownst to him, Melvin Markham had taken it upon himself to mention Steve and Teresa's affair to his girlfriend. Under normal circumstances that might not have posed a problem, but Melvin's girlfriend happened to be the live-in nanny Steve had hired to keep Lou company while he was on the road. And she in turn mentioned it to Lou.

Teresa and Steve were having breakfast with Harry Stinson in Hollywood, the night Steve was due to play the Palace in early November, when Lou erupted into their hotel room. She had flown through the night from Nashville and was wild-eyed and exhausted. Throughout the journey she had been haunted by the thought that she would be the first person in her family to be divorced and the first to be divorced twice. That was bad enough, but her nanny had supplied her with nauseating details: 'You know that time Steve supposedly came home from the road and went on a writing trip?' Jennifer reminded her. 'Well, he drove to Louisville to see Teresa.' Lou was devastated. She couldn't believe a man could behave so disloyally to his family, especially with a new baby at home. 'He had no regard for what anyone else felt or was feeling at that point. Steve wanted what he wanted and that's all he saw.'

At LAX, she caught a cab to the Franklin Plaza in Hollywood. At the front desk, she showed her ID and told them Steve was expecting her. Botwin and several of the musicians were standing in the courtyard when she swept through. Their mouths fell open. 'Where's Steve?' asked Lou, but no one was capable of speech. She continued to his room. The door was ajar. When Lou burst in, Stinson beat a rapid retreat. Lou shot a poisonous glance at Teresa. 'What's she doing here?' she snapped.

'Uhh, she works here,' Steve managed.

'Right,' said Lou sarcastically. Turning to Teresa, she said: 'You've got five seconds to get out of here.'

'Let's talk about this,' Teresa pleaded.

'Sweetheart,' Lou drawled, 'the last thing I want to do is talk to you.'

She walked past the couple and into the bedroom, where the tangled sheets told their story. In the bathroom, Teresa's cosmetics sat familiarly beside the basin. Lou scooped them up and threw them into the hallway. 'Please leave,' she told Teresa. 'I want to talk to my husband.'

Unwisely, perhaps, Teresa continued to try to make her case. Lou snapped. Before Steve could move, she had attacked Teresa – 'I mean, literally got a handful of her hair and beat her head against the wall, and then got her down on the floor and beat her head against the floor and scratched her real bad with her fingernails. It was really a trip.'

When the horror was over, so was their marriage. Steve had plenty of excuses, but Lou didn't believe a word he said to her. When she returned to Nashville, she called in Justin and Amy and broke the news. Steve couldn't believe it. 'Fresh off the plane, she told them, "Your dad has a girlfriend in California and we're going to get divorced." Absolutely no attempt to shelter them from it whatsoever.'

Steve and Lou were officially separated the next day on Friday 13 November, three months and five days after their wedding. Lou initiated divorce proceedings at that time on the grounds of adultery, cruel and inhuman treatment and irreconcilable differences. She and Jennifer threw everything he owned into the Cadillac he had bought from Tony Brown – 'his black El Dorado pride and joy . . .' To punish him further, Lou mailed Steve her wedding dress.

Five days after the Hollywood nightmare, Steve sat in a Seattle hotel room in the early hours of a cool, grey morning feeling as low as he could possibly feel. In time-honoured tradition, the show had had to go on. Steve had called Teresa as soon as Lou left. 'You can come back now,' he said. 'She's gone.'

When the news circulated that Steve was embarking on yet another divorce, the proverbial hit the fan. Steve's parents were distressed that he was abandoning the mother of his baby, his lawyer was in a state because he had barely completed the paperwork on the last divorce, and his business manager quit. Melvin Markham, the inadvertent cause of this latest crisis, also left Steve's organization in a hurry. Steve was not aware then that Stinson, too, had called Tony Brown from Portland and told him that he couldn't do it any more. Alone in his hotel room in Seattle, Steve was gripped by the notion that people were abandoning him in his hour of need. When the phone rang, he snatched it up, grateful for an interruption to his thoughts.

It was Will Botwin. 'I've been thinking,' he told Steve. 'You know, your life is getting so out of control that I'm not sure whether I want to keep doing this or not.'

The upshot of the conversation was that he wanted three or four days to consider his position, something Steve resented deeply. He and Will had had their first serious argument just a week or so earlier when Steve refused to do a non-ID jingle worth around $80,000 for Budweiser. Early on in his career he'd decided he would never do jingles, even if he wasn't actually identified in the advertisement. In the first place it wasn't Art. In the second, he didn't have the time or the inclination to examine the corporate policies of the companies behind the jingles. Will could comprehend neither reason. 'Now you're fucking with my income,' he scolded Steve.

In Seattle, Steve played two sets at the Backstage on NW Market Street. He was beside himself with rage that Will had, effectively, put him on probation. Will phoned him in Vancouver a few days later to tell him that he would stay on after all, but Steve never got over it. 'You know, from that point on I don't think I ever really trusted Will again because I just felt like people were bailing out on me when I was in trouble. Several people had bailed out on me and for him to do it too . . . I can understand it on one hand but I kinda thought that's what managers were supposed to do, was deal with all that shit.'

Teresa met him in Vancouver and rode the bus to Idaho before catching the plane home. Steve went on to Kansas City alone. It was the last show of the tour but the end-of-term partying was somewhat muted. Afterwards, the crew loaded out and the band dispersed for Thanksgiving, leaving Steve on his own, a little downcast. He planned to hitchhike to LA to see Teresa. On the spur of the moment, he decided to take a side trip to the house of William Burroughs, the Beat writer who had captivated him with novels like *Junky* all those years before. In Lawrence, Kansas, he stood on Burroughs's doorstep politely explaining who he was, where he came from and how much Burroughs's books had affected him.

Burroughs heard him out. 'Fuck off,' he said to Steve. End of conversation.

Thanksgiving was spent at Teresa's house, amid a bevy of young music industry friends of hers from back East. They were all women apart from one – a token guy Steve surmised they kept around to pick on. 'They had a rule that you couldn't watch football. For me at that point in my life, not watching football at Thanksgiving was threatening on a cellular level.' Within a few years, he would cease watching American football altogether, but at that stage it was essential. And all of it added to the sense of dislocation he felt. The vast Earle gatherings of his youth seemed a long way away. 'It just wasn't a family Thanksgiving. It was an anti-family Thanksgiving and it was weird.'

When Steve could avoid it no more, he went home. Lou refused to let him in the house. She had issued a restraining order against him because, she says, he didn't want the relationship to be over. 'He kept coming over, he kept calling me.' In the divorce records she alleged that 'on more than one occasion subsequent to the marriage but prior to the parties' separation, the Defendant without provocation has struck the Plaintiff with his hands and choked her . . . Additionally since the separation of the parties the Defendant has harassed the Plaintiff by numerous phone calls to her residence during which the Defendant uses abusive and profane language and threatens the Plaintiff.'

At Fairfax Avenue, Steve tried and failed to start the crowded Cadillac. Lou watched from behind the screen door. 'There's this whole dramatic thing, and there's the dead Cadillac sitting there and I'm thinking, "Man, how am I going to get rid of this guy?" The thing that held me up at that point was that I was so angry that this human being had treated me like shit. He had treated me like dirt and disrespected me to the point where he had no respect for me and our children . . . I wanted him gone.'

Perhaps because he was, to all intents and purposes, homeless, Steve elected to do a little solo tour in December, along with a one-hour set at the Winter Peace Concert at Nashville's War Memorial Auditorium. Rosanne Cash and Rodney Crowell were headlining. Then he picked up his guitar and hit the road for club dates in Chicago, Boston, Washington DC, LA and Alexandria, Virginia. As so often happened, it was his acoustic shows that moved people most. The poignancy of songs like 'My Old Friend the Blues' was laid bare by the stripped-down arrangements and Steve's empathy with the characters. 'Sometimes the peak of your life doesn't conveniently occur near the end of it,' he said as he introduced 'No. 29'.

Reviewing the show at the Birchmere, Jeff Bleiel of the *Alexandria Gazette Packet* described Steve as 'perhaps the best distinctly American songwriter to emerge from any genre in the last couple of years'.

Struggling to balance the critical acclaim with the turmoil in his private life, Steve was totally unaware that an indiscretion on a bus at a Hank Jr show back in March had had far-reaching consequences. And so it was that, on 22 December, while Steve was going about his day as usual, a band groupie called Theresa Baker was giving birth to a little girl in Johnson City, East Tennessee. Her name was Jessica Montana Baker and she was Steve's third child.

10

State Trooper

'I've only been arrested about fifty or sixty
times in my whole life.'
Steve Earle, 1998

On New Year's Eve, 1987, guitar tech Chip Phillips made the
unwise but none the less forgivable error of flirting with a
security guard's girlfriend at a show in Dallas. Had he known
the chain of events that would ensue, he might have paused
for reflection following an initial altercation with the guard,
but backstage a party was in full swing and Chip, like everyone
else, had been drinking. In Dallas Alley, an area popular for
its nightclub clubs, bars and restaurants, Carl Perkins was
performing on an outdoor stage. Steve had already played. He
was unwinding with Justin, his parents and a few friends and
relatives from Jacksonville and San Antonio when Chip made
another play for the girl. She was serving food.

Steve was livid. Chip had been banned from drinking at gigs
because they had had trouble with him in the past and now
he was drunk and objecting to being told what to do. Steve
decided that there was no option but to go back to the hotel.
Cabs were ordered and he, Chip and Barbara and Jack Earle
squeezed into the service elevator at the Dallas Alley nightclub. Downstairs, Chip and Steve started to row. Chip wanted
to go back and find the guard. Steve lost his temper. He took
off his jacket and flung it on the ground – fortuitously, as it
turned out, because the inside pocket contained two and a half

grams of heroin. Charlie Mullins, who had come back to work for one evening, had brought it down from San Antonio. Steve shoved Chip roughly towards a waiting cab and a scuffle began. Jack and Barbara were slightly perturbed at the turn of events but not worried because, as Barbara put it, 'You have to understand, Chip belonged to him – they'd been friends since Junior High. Chip was family.'

Unbeknownst to anyone, the security guard, aka Sgt Lonnie R. Allen, an off-duty member of the Dallas Police Department, had come silently down the back stairs. Steve had not laid eyes on him during the evening and didn't see him now as the cop flew like a panther at his back and began choking him with his nightstick. Steve collapsed in a dead faint. The weight of his body as he slumped caused Allen to topple backwards over the pavement edge, bringing Steve crashing down on top of him. 'Well, hell, that hurt, I know that hurt him,' Jack later recalled, 'but when it did this guy just went ballistic.'

Lights and pain flashed through Steve's brain as he surged back into consciousness for a few seconds. Violent spasms shook his body. According to eyewitness accounts, Allen panicked and sawed at Steve's throat with the nightstick.

'Hey! Hey!' yelled Jack, rushing forward. Steve's eyes rolled back in his head and he began foaming at the mouth. 'I got down there and kicked and hit and bit and everything I could do, trying to get the guy to let go of Steve . . . I thought he was going to kill him.'

A club bouncer grabbed Jack from behind. 'They're going to arrest you, too, if you're not careful,' he said. Barbara was almost in tears, convinced that both her son and husband were going to jail.

'Arrest, heck,' protested Jack, who had no idea Allen was an off-duty policeman. Suddenly, rough hands were pulling him off Allen and two police cars were screaming to a halt. Steve was handcuffed and manhandled into one car, Chip into another. Moments later they were spirited into the night in a swirl of blue lights, leaving Jack, Barbara, Justin and everyone else standing dazed or slightly hysterical on the sidewalk. Steve jerked blearily back to consciousness to find himself manacled in the back of a police car. At the station he was held for several hours without being told why or with what he was being charged. Chip, he discovered, had already been released. It was four in the morning before Steve was finally arraigned on a felony charge of aggravated assault. In all, he spent more than twelve hours in a cell before he was able to post bond and go home. It was New Year's Day. Barely one lunchtime into 1988, he already had a whole sheaf of court orders to look forward to.

On 2 January Steve played a two-and-a-half-hour concert to a capacity crowd of nine hundred at the Cannery in Nashville. He apologized for the rawness of his voice, explaining that it came 'courtesy of the Dallas Police Department', but to the audience it could not have mattered less. Steve's brush with the law and battered appearance only added to his dangerous appeal, and the gravel in his tones lent his songs extra power. When he sang 'Copperhead Road', the title song of his forthcoming album, the crowd went berserk. At the end of the set, the walls shook with demands for a third encore.

Backstage Steve said: 'Okay, let's go again.'

'Oh shit, we've played for three fuckin' hours,' Harry Stinson replied.

Steve stopped in his tracks. He had always considered Harry something of a cold fish and a record label spy to boot. He was a great drummer and a beautiful singer but he rarely broke a sweat. This, though, was something different. As far as Steve was concerned, the moment Harry Stinson moaned about doing an encore, they were done with.

Steve did not yet know that behind the scenes Harry and Reno had approached Will Botwin for extra money for the Australian tour that was planned in late January. At the time they were receiving $125 a show. Will assured the media that, despite sustaining some vocal cord damage in the Dallas incident, the tour was going ahead. In truth, it had been thrown into jeopardy by what Steve refers to as Harry's 'insurrection'. But Stinson insists his departure had nothing to do with money.

'It was just that I couldn't take any more. And that was a dark time. For one thing, it kinda broke my heart . . . I just didn't feel like I mentally could handle it any more.'

What it boiled down to was semantics. According to guitarist Mike McAdam, Stinson, Kling and Baxter were not asking for *more* money, they were only asking for their usual amount. Budgets being tight for Australia, Will had, he says, asked them to accept half their usual pay. When it came time for the contracts to be signed and the situation was no closer to being resolved, Will brought the matter to Steve's attention. Steve got straight on the phone to Bucky Baxter.

'Bucky, what's going on here?' he demanded.

'I don't know, man,' hedged Baxter. 'Let me call you back.'

Steve then tried Reno and Harry. When he failed to reach them, he phoned Will. 'Okay, fire 'em,' he instructed. 'Cancel the fuckin' Australia dates.'

Twenty minutes later, Baxter phoned back. 'I'm with Reno and Harry,' he said.

'Are you sure?' asked Steve. 'Are you sure you're with Reno and Harry?'

'Yeah,' said Baxter uncertainly.

'Fine,' Steve told him. 'Then you're fired.'

It didn't take long for Bucky to change his mind.

The Australian tour was officially cancelled in the third week of January. As it turned out, Baxter and Ken Moore were the only members of the *Guitar Town* and *Exit o* Dukes to survive a third album, not counting an appearance by John Jarvis. Before Steve went into the studio in the spring, everybody else had either quit or been axed. Mike McAdam had walked out of the rehearsals because it seemed to him that Steve was bringing in every guitarist he knew to play on the album. Richard Bennett, for example, had been involved in pre-production for *Copperhead Road* with Steve. But Bennett's days were also numbered. Even as he prepared for the actual album, he was notified that his services were no longer required.

'I never got a good explanation. Steve kinda glossed off that it was Jimmy Bowen's decision but I never was pleased with that answer. And both Emory and I had been sacked. And you know, that happens. You produce a record and frankly, until it comes out and your name's on it, you're still never secure that you've produced that record . . . But be that as it may, there were no hard feelings about it, not on my end. Everybody moves on.'

With the Australian tour cancelled, Steve turned his attention to other projects. The sides he had produced for Charlie Sexton in 1987 had never been released, but the demos had attracted the attention of British record executive Nigel Grainge. Grainge ran Ensign Records, a division of Chrysalis, which had a roster of impressive acts such as Sinead O'Connor and the Waterboys. It was his idea to ask Steve to produce four sides of a British indie band called the Bible. When he discovered that Steve was a Waterboys fan, the possibility of doing something with them in the future was dangled in a vague way.

Steve spent most of January and part of Februrary in London, working on the Bible record. Boo Hewerdine, the band's lead singer, can still remember him blazing into the rehearsal room where their first meeting took place, all long hair and tattoos, his eyes still bloodshot from the Dallas beating. Hewerdine sat in his vortex feeling like a 'softy from Cambridge'. Guitarist Neil MacColl thought Steve was one of the scariest people he'd ever seen in his life. 'We were all nice boys with a cute sense of irony and he was a rock 'n' roller.'

The Bible had been signed to Chrysalis in a whirl of enthusiasm after their 1986 album, *Walking the Ghost Back Home*, acquired a cult following. But a year of working with a producer who took a divide and rule approach to the band had destroyed their confidence. Steve's first action was to build it up again. 'You're all really great players,' he told them. 'You just need to get inside the songs and *feel* them.'

Hewerdine and the others found themselves caught up in Steve's energy and convictions. He strode around the studio in a Motörhead t-shirt expounding on the state of British music, which he considered to have sunk to new lows in the late eighties. Drum machines and the songwriting partnership of Stock, Aitken and Waterman were in; rock music was out. Kylie Minogue and bands like Depeche Mode held sway. Steve, the band found out, was all about music with passion and depth. He loved the English Beat and Fine Young Cannibals, which was essentially the Beat with Roland Gift on vocals. He despised the reigning fetish in British music for synthesized drum beats and trawled the city for an engineer capable of recording the acoustic sound he wanted. Chris Birkett, who had worked with Alison Moyet and Dexy's Midnight Runners during their 'Come on Eileen' phase, was his favourite.

'This is not rocket science,' Steve told the band, 'but you do have to feel the music.'

It was MacColl, the son of folk singing parents and brother of Kirsty, who spent the most time with Steve, but he was popular with all of them. There were musical differences between Steve and keyboard player Tony Shepherd, whom he nicknamed 'The Jazz Fairy', but for the most part their banter was good-natured. Steve, MacColl found, was full of contradictions. Every now and then he would vanish and they would find him in another room at the Chiswick studio playing with Hewerdine's baby daughter. Boo found Steve's adoration of children intriguing. 'He was a really gentle man. He was so different from all of the other people we'd met in the industry, who were all really weaselly.'

When Steve finished the four sides he had been hired to produce, the label heads were so pleased they asked him to produce the whole album for a total fee of $22,000. Steve couldn't bear to be away from Teresa another day and gave them an ultimatum: either they paid for her to fly to London or he was going home. A friend of his told him it was the fastest he ever saw a cheque requisitioned at Chrysalis.

Teresa took a leave of absence from Geffen and came over. The month that Steve had come for turned into two, during which he and Teresa lived like vampires, recording all day and most of the night and grabbing sleep when they could. Tensions began to creep in at Livingstone Studios in Wood Green, where the Bible's album *Eureka* was being mixed. Steve and the A&R man from the label did not get along. There were disagreements over the mixes. MacColl remembers Steve disappearing twice a day, for hours at a stretch, into Shepherd's Bush, a notorious drug-dealing area. But it didn't matter to the band. They liked Steve and loved his mixes and Hewerdine, particularly, was upset when Steve returned to the USA and they were redone by another producer 'for political reasons'.

Steve was strung out when he arrived back in Nashville, aching and out of sorts. Heroin was hard to come by and dilaudids overpriced, so he attempted to lie down and detox. For years he'd been able to endure the agonizing three days that followed withdrawal and feel well again or get high again. But it was getting harder and harder. Still, there was lots to look forward to. When Lou had thrown him out of the house at the end of the *Exit o* tour he'd rented a quaint studio apartment in a twenties-era brownstone on West End. Now he loved it. Even the elevator appealed to him. Teresa would come and visit or he would go to LA to see her. For several weeks when she was in Memphis making a record with local singer-songwriter John Kilzer, Steve commuted back and forth.

It was around this time that the ex-partner of one of Steve's lovers tried to take out a contract on his life. 'He tried to have me killed. He wasn't asking the right people and it didn't even come close to happening, but he really was that megalomaniacal that he thought that was the way to deal with it.'

Steve made the shocking discovery when the Guns N' Roses roadie the man had allegedly approached came and told him. 'Guns N' Roses had this whole "street", dope dealer element that hung around them. [X] thought: "They can find someone to kill him." But the kid came straight to me. I'd shot dope with the guy two or three times. It was weird.'

Spurned suitors were not the only people having fantasies about Steve's early demise. His divorce from Lou was getting uglier by the day. Periodically, the phone would ring and it would be Lou in full flow, and Steve would hold the phone away from his ear as she launched a bitter tirade against him or his lawyer or the whole goddamn world. Once, Steve and Teresa ran into her in a video store. She let them have it with both barrels, screaming at them with baby Ian on her hip.

On 13 April, Teresa quit Geffen. According to court records filed in December 1988, Tom Zutaut had approached Geffen president Edwin Rosenblatt the previous fall and admitted that he and Teresa had been in a three-year relationship. He was distraught. He told the startled Rosenblatt that their affair had been terminated by Teresa when she fell in love with someone else. Following this conversation it had become apparent to Rosenblatt that the 'hard feelings engendered by their break-up would not go away', and he had separated the two of them, giving Teresa her own office and secretary. He had also separated the acts the two serviced, apportioning them according to their experience.

In spite of these changes life at Geffen became untenable for Teresa and she moved to Nashville to be with Steve. Her sister Grace had been working as a publicist at Slash records and was no longer able to afford their LA apartment on her own, so it was decided that she should come to Nashville too and work as Steve's PA. She would live in the third-floor studio Steve had been renting and Teresa and Steve would move into a larger one-bedroom corner apartment on the fifth floor. Settled at last, Steve sat down to write the final songs for *Copperhead Road*.

Vietnam and the imagery of war runs like a smoking thread through the first half of *Copperhead Road*. Even the love songs on the second half seem touched by the lingering malaise of

Vietnam, which, by the mid-eighties, had begun to surface with a vengeance in the USA. The appalling waste of war takes time to sink in. After years of comparative silence Vietnam art was everywhere. Springsteen's *Born in the USA* was followed by a stream of movies like *Platoon* and *Full Metal Jacket*. Books like Neil Sheehan's *A Bright Shining Lie: John Paul Vann and America in Vietnam* gave voice for the first time to horrific truths. This national catharsis had a ripple effect. Veterans who had kept their experiences in a locked box in their hearts, woke up, as if from a coma, and started speaking out. A friend of Steve's who had maintained a stoic silence for years broke down and poured out everything he had been through for the entire thirteen months he was stationed in Vietnam. After joining the navy in the hope that it would keep him off the mainland, he had found himself on boat patrols. At night he searched junks in total darkness or dodged bullets on terrifying waterways as explosions split the gloom. Now, he told Steve, he couldn't stand fireworks.

The impotent rage of veterans who returned maimed or inexorably altered to an uncaring America is as much a part of the title song on *Copperhead Road* as the marijuana growers at the heart of it. Almost a decade before Steve wrote the song in 1987, his imagination had been caught by a news story about a woman in her seventies who had been arrested for marijuana growing in East Tennessee. She had started, she said, when her sons brought back seed from Vietnam. Erstwhile moonshiners, they had turned to the rather more lucrative pot when they realized that the mountains of East Tennessee and Western North Carolina were perfect for it.

The bagpipes at the beginning of the song – created using a sampler and a synthesizer in the studio – were inspired by the musical relationship between the mountains of Appalachia and Scotland and Ireland. They evoke a sense of isolation that is key to the storyline. Their lonely, almost chilling sound lends a novelistic power to the lyrics from the moment John Lee Pettimore introduces himself as the son and grandson of moonshiners. To Noel Fox, there was no better example of Steve's ability to distil a story down to its essence. "'[Him] and my uncle tore that engine down/I still remember that rumbling sound . . ." I can *hear* that rumbling sound. And he captures that period of time. Compare "Copperhead Road" to "Devil's Right Hand" or "Tom Ames' Prayer" and he captured those periods of time as [Larry] McMurtry does with *Lonesome Dove*. That's what a great writer has to do to be a great writer. Steve doesn't write ditties.'

The Celtic influence on the album continued with 'Johnny Come Lately', a razor-sharp spin on the GI in London theme that Steve had written specifically because he wanted to work with Irish band the Pogues. He had met the band, once described as a cross between the Sex Pistols and the Chieftains, in London in 1987. They were recording *If I Should Fall from Grace with God* at the time. A mutual fascination with Celtic and Appalachian roots music, serious partying and each other meant that they soon became firm friends – hence, the reference in the song to drinking Camden Town dry. 'Johnny Come Lately' was recorded in mid-March at Livingstone Studios in London, with Chris Birkett engineering again and Neil MacColl on mandolin. Shane MacGowan turned up four hours late for the session. Touring with the Pogues a few months later in support of the album, Steve and the rest of the band would draw straws in the morning to see who would get the hard-living MacGowan out of his alcohol-fumed bunk. 'When you pulled back the curtain, your eyebrows melted.'

The one thing Steve feared was that *Copperhead Road* would meet the same fate as *Exit 0*, which had sold 110,000 copies before MCA dropped the ball. When Steve asked why they weren't pressing any more records, he was told: 'Because you don't have a top ten country single.' He was also instructed to ensure that his next record had two songs suitable for country radio. Steve told Nashville music writer Michael McCall that he'd retorted that if he couldn't let an album hang together as an album, without cramming unwanted songs in just for the sake of getting radio play, he'd just as soon not make records. If that was the case, he *wouldn't* make any more records. They could sue him. They could do whatever they wanted. He'd go to Mexico. With what he'd made on the first two records, he could live in Mexico for the rest of his life. 'People will say, "God, I can't believe he said that. It's going to mess up everything." But it doesn't mean that I don't have respect for the people there who deserve respect. It just means that art sometimes has to be fought for. It requires a certain amount of vigilance.'

David Simone had never heard of Steve Earle when Bill Bennett first mentioned him. Born in Britain, Simone had been managing director of Arista and Phonogram (now Mercury) before Irving Azoff brought him in to revive MCA UK's flagging fortunes. Six months later Azoff honoured a promise to Simone and made him head of UNI, which was being relaunched in New York. UNI had once been home to Neil Diamond and Elton John, but the label name hadn't been used in years. MCA was weak in the rock department and Azoff thought that UNI might give it a more credible presence.

Simone joined forces with Bill Bennett, a renowned rock promoter from Nashville who now headed up MCA's promotion department. It was Bennett who suggested they look at Steve, an edgy original who was making music country radio wouldn't play. Simone flew to Nashville and met Steve and Tony Brown. Simone thought Steve was an incredible talent and he liked him on sight, but Brown was frank about his position. 'Look, I love Steve Earle but I don't know how to break through this wall in Nashville,' he admitted. Simone became aware for the first time that Steve, Nanci Griffith, Lyle Lovett, kd lang and several other 'new country' artists were actively hated in Nashville, particularly by country radio. 'They were too renegade.'

Tony had already witnessed the loss of Lyle and Nanci, driven to pop because country radio didn't want to know about them, and he was prepared to let Steve switch to UNI if it would give him a better chance. But Simone made it clear that the transfer was conditional. 'I'm only going to do this if I believe that Steve is making the right record and we can do something with it,' he told Brown.

Steve was a hundred per cent certain that his record was going to be the right record, but it had to be made under the right conditions. Knowing that it was going to be hard for him to record in Nashville with the divorce raging, and knowing also that he didn't want to record in one of Bowen's studios, Steve raised the possibility of making the album at Ardent. He loved the idea of working in the famous Memphis studio where ZZ Top, B.B. King, Stevie Ray Vaughan and Lynyrd Skynard had all recorded. At MCA, Tony remained his biggest ally. Bowen openly loathed Steve for doing the very thing he had warned him not to and trying to use Irving to get his own way. He and Bruce Hinton were incensed to be told that until the record was completed and Simone had decided whether or not it should go to UNI, all recording and mixing expenses were coming out of the Nashville budget. But Steve was past the point of caring what any of his perceived opponents at MCA thought about anything. Even his appearance was a form of rebellion. He had not visited a barber since 1987 when Sheila Shipley suggested he get a haircut. Not that it hurt his image. In February, *Playgirl* had named him one of its ten sexiest country singers ('This is the guy your parents were always afraid you'd meet.') Sheila, Steve had decided, was 'a cunt. She did not like me from the very beginning. She was an absolutely disagreeable, stupid person with a tin ear . . .'

So in many ways, the new record was about much more than music that rocked. It was a message to all the unbelievers in Nashville. '*Copperhead Road* was "Fuck You", to an extent.'

The fact that 1 May found Steve in Ardent Studios, making a rock record, with Tony Brown as his co-producer, was testament to the sheer force of his personality and willpower.

Against all the odds, he had got everything he wanted and a star line-up of players to boot. Along with the Pogues, there was also Maria McKee, Radney Foster, John Cowan and the acoustic supergroup Telluride, which featured the cream of Nashville's bluegrass talent – Sam Bush, Jerry Douglas, Mark O'Connor and Edgar Meyer. Steve and Teresa rented an apartment in Memphis for the duration of recording and Teresa served as the unofficial A&R person. She had yet to disentangle herself from Geffen.

Steve stayed high for much of the making of *Copperhead Road*. Tony cared for Steve and revered his abilities almost to the point of hero-worship, but he was no longer blind to Steve's excesses. The departure of Harry Stinson and a conversation with another band member, who confided to him that he felt sucked into the craziness of the tour, almost against his will, had made it obvious that Steve's drug use went way beyond the recreational. And Steve himself positively flaunted it. When they were mixing the record, he pulled out a piece of paper with heroin in it and snorted it right in front of Tony. 'I'd never physically seen him do anything and there it was and it just sent chills up my spine. The fact that he'd just got that comfortable just to pull it out there in the studio, and there was the engineer . . .' But even then Tony found it impossible to judge him. He thought it would be hypocritical to condemn Steve when he himself smoked pot. Marijuana might have been small beer by comparison but it was still illegal. And in some ways, he was a moth chancing incineration. He was as drawn to the danger in Steve's character then as he had been on that first weekend on Ono Island. Through Steve, he could live the Gram Parsons/Hank Williams life vicariously, but at a distance that allowed him to say, 'I told you so,' when it all went horribly wrong.

'To me, rock 'n' roll represents being a maverick and being against whatever is normal. With Steve, I was in country music but I was in rock 'n' roll too. And it felt cool. It made me feel cool.'

It was during the *Copperhead* sessions that Steve first went to see Dr George Nichopolous, the Memphis physician who had been responsible for prescribing a good many of the pills and placebos Elvis had made daily cocktails of in the years leading up to his death. Dr Nick's role in Elvis's life and demise had made him a controversial figure in many people's eyes, but Steve saw his medical history as a recommendation. 'I literally thought: "To have a prescription from Dr Nick, how rock 'n' roll is that."' Besides, a dead junkie was not necessarily a bad recommendation for a dope source. When Andrew Wood, the twenty-year-old singer of Mother Love Bone, the band that evolved into Pearl Jam, died of a heroin overdose shortly before the release of their first album in 1990, Steve and many others in the music community were saddened. He was a good kid, a wonderful singer. Then a junkie friend of Steve's remarked: 'I know where he got it.'

Without missing a beat, Steve said: 'I've got $200.'

After visiting Dr Nick with a bad throat (he was still suffering the after-effects of Sgt Lonnie Allen's enthusiastic baton demonstration), Steve was pleased to discover that the good doctor was happy to supply him with Tussionex scripts even after he returned to Nashville. He enjoyed the theatre of going to Elvis's doctor, with his white hair, pompadour and sideburns. He dismissed as bullshit the popular notion that Dr Nick had been some kind of monster preying on Elvis. 'For one thing, Elvis Presley ruined George Nichopolous's life as much as George Nichopolous ruined Elvis Presley's life.'

None of it bothered Steve in the slightest. 'For me, going to see Dr Nick was just like going to Graceland. I went for the same reason. Then I got the cough mixture, too, which was a bonus. I was going to get dope from somewhere.'

The Tussionex served only to mask the fallout from Steve's rapidly unravelling surrounds. He was getting more out of control daily. The *Copperhead Road* sessions had gone as well as he could have hoped. As proof of his regard Tony had given

Steve a virtual free rein during recording and Steve had finished the album and overseen the mixing with the help of respected former Georgia Satellites engineer Joe Hardy. But far from being exhilarated when he came out of the studio in mid-June, Steve was weighed down by dread. The unimaginable had happened. After all the tears, bad blood and vengeful thoughts, the overpowering physical attraction between Steve and Lou had led to them becoming involved again within a couple of months of them splitting up. He found the chemical pull between them difficult to resist; she still loved him. 'When I kicked him out, it didn't quite stick. It didn't work. I have to take responsibility for that.' The divorce was undeniably acrimonious and Steve was undeniably living with Teresa, but Lou still took him in whenever he needed her. 'It seemed like we were either fighting or in bed. That was the nature of our relationship for the longest time.'

Now she was pregnant with what she was sure was Steve's baby. She knew that there was no chance of Steve coming back to her on any kind of permanent basis. He was so 'infatuated' with Teresa it sometimes frightened her. She felt like a lone parent, trying to take care of Amy, Ian and, occasionally, Justin, and she didn't think she could cope with a baby as well. 'I talked to Steve about it and we decided that it would be bad to bring another child into the world at that point. I'm sure he had his reasons . . . but we're both agreed that the worst thing that I did during that time is I had an abortion. He went with me to the hospital and afterwards I was inconsolable. And to this day it's hard for either of us to talk about it. It was probably the worst moment of my life.'

Their divorce came through a month later, on 22 July. Lou had paid her counsel, James L. Weatherly, $1,500 out of their joint account, and Steve was ordered to pay him a further $2,500 in fees, plus $7,533.52 'for additional attorney's fees and expenses incurred by Mrs Earle in the prosecution of the divorce proceedings'. That was just for starters. Along with $2,500 a month in alimony and child support, he was also compelled to pay the $1,800 still owing on Lou's car, the $1,604.02 balance on her Visa card, the $925 balance owed on the purchase and installation of her security system, and medical bills incurred during the 'hospitalization treatment and doctor's care of Mrs Earle from June 23 to June 25', including $400 to Dr Lewis Bonvesuto, $165 to Dr Brenda Dew, $25 to Dr James Head, $300 to Medicount and $82 to the neurologist.

With his lawsuit against the Dallas Police Department pending and the trial looming, more and more of Steve's income was going straight to the lawyers. 'I was supporting half the women and half the lawyers in Tennessee . . . it was bonkers.'

When Tony turned in *Copperhead Road* at MCA, Bowen described it as 'a piece of shit'. By contrast, David Simone, who had visited the studio with Bill Bennett during the sessions, was exhilarated by it.

'This is a record I truly believe we can do a lot with,' he told Irving Azoff. The next thing Tony knew, Azoff was on the line. 'He said, "I don't agree with Bowen but I'm going to do him a favour . . ." I said, "Really?" He said, "Yeah, I'm going to tell him that I agree with him that it's a piece of shit, but I'll take it because I love it." So I started learning how the business works.'

In the meanwhile, Steve had decided Will Botwin had to go. Things had not been right between them since Will had put him on probation the previous year. Steve was in the same frame of mind he had been when he fired Lomax just before *Guitar Town* was made. 'I wanted everything in place. I really saw *Copperhead* as a chance to do something. And it was about getting on rock radio. I felt we had to do that. I was just trying to be ready.'

It was Teresa who came up with the idea of asking Cliff Bernstein and Peter Mench of Q-Prime in New York to manage him. Q-Prime represented heavy metal acts like Metallica, Def Leppard and Tessler, who Teresa had helped sign, and she knew them superficially through Tom Zutaut. If rock was the direction Steve wanted to take, Cliff and Peter might be the best men for the job.

In September, Steve and Teresa flew out to New York for a meeting at Q-Prime. Steve and Botwin had, at least to Steve's mind, parted company amicably (officially winding down on 13 October), and Cliff and Peter were happy to take him on. On the evidence of *Copperhead Road*, they thought he was a fine artist and he came with the endorsement of Teresa, whom Zutatut had always told them was the greatest.

With the album release only weeks away, Cliff and Peter had to hit the ground running. Steve explained to them how angry he was with MCA Nashville and why the new album was being released through MCA's LA headquarters. He wanted, he explained, to be treated like a rock artist, not a country artist. But Cliff and Peter thought it would be a shame for Steve to lose his country base. They persuaded him to set up a meeting with MCA Nashville. As Cliff remembers it, 'We went in and met Sheila Shipley, Bruce Hinton and Tony Brown. Well, Tony Brown was fine. He's a very, very nice man. But between Bruce Hinton and Sheila Shipley it was basically the *Godfather* thing: "I have no son." It was kind of like, "Well, Steve basically told us to fuck off, so we don't acknowledge him any more. We might have sold records with him before but now he wants something else. He wants UNI Records. Fine. Fuck him." They didn't say "Fuck him" but we certainly knew after that that they weren't going to work the record.'

While Cliff and Peter pondered the problem of trying to sell Steve to an audience to whom he was still an undiscovered treasure at a time when there was no alternative country or Americana scene, Steve was extricating himself from a new legal dilemma. On 13 September, he was mistakenly arrested at the border on his way back from Canada. A Dallas bail bondsman had his dates mixed up and was under the impression Steve had jumped bail. Steve was hauled away and handcuffed to thirteen other prisoners. He spent six hours in the back of a Detroit police van as it did the rounds of the suburban jails, before he was able to contact his lawyer and clear his name.

Seven days later, he was on trial in Dallas for the assault of Sgt Allen. His parents, grandmother, siblings and the members of his band and crew who had witnessed the events of New Year's Eve accompanied him. Most had given depositions.

For all his bravado, Steve was scared to death. It was during jury selection that the full import of his predicament hit him. Asked whether or not they would believe a police officer's word over an ordinary citizen's, most potential jury members said yes. It hit Steve there was a very real danger that he could go to jail for ten years. When he returned to the court in the afternoon after a recess for the choosing of the jury, the District Attorney presented him with his options. If he pleaded 'No Contest', which didn't mean he was guilty but didn't mean he wasn't guilty either, it was likely that he would escape with a year's probation. Steve's defence attorney was confident that they could win their case. But the police were claiming that Allen had warned Steve to stop pushing Chip Phillips and Steve had responded by punching him in the face and kicking him in the groin. They also claimed that Allen's chokehold was applied with his arm and not with a nightstick – the latter being illegal in Texas. Steve wasn't taking any chances. As much as it galled him to enter a no contest plea to the charge of aggravated assault, it did mean that he walked free with a $500 fine and a year's probation – to be expunged from the record at the end of that time.

'We're relieved the criminal part of the proceedings are over, but this is far from over,' Steve told the assembled journalists. 'Sgt Allen has not heard the last of Steve Earle.'

After the trial, however, Sgt Allen dropped his civil suit and Steve, in turn, halted legal proceedings against the policeman. It terms of priorities in his life, Sgt Allen came rock bottom.

* * *

Copperhead Road was released on 17 October to rapturous reviews. *Musician* compared it to the Stones' *Let It Bleed* and *USA Today* put him on the front page of its Life section. The British press were unstinting in their praise. In the USA, Simone and Bennett knew they were about to hit the same walls Steve had been running into all his career – while Nashville wouldn't accept him, the rest of America saw him as country – and they were determined to batter them down. They went to an A&R convention and preached the gospel of *Copperhead*. As Simone put it, 'We really proselytized Steve Earle.'

Steve told the *Chicago Tribune* that a lot of *Copperhead Road* was traditional country from a melodic point of view. In truth he had moved so far into Springsteen's terrain that the country/rock debate was more or less redundant. Career-wise, every gamble he had taken appeared to be paying off. 'Copperhead Road' was the most requested song at rock stations in Nashville, Atlanta and Orlando, and in the top five in telephone requests at seventeen other rock stations across the USA. By the second week of January it was No. 22 on *Billboard*'s album rock tracks chart and it made it into the top twenty. UNI had shipped 500,000 copies of the album and it was leaping off the shelves. Simone had the feeling that there was a degree of disbelief at MCA that they were doing real business with Steve Earle.

Bennett and Simone had now become friends as well as fans of Steve's. Simone saw him as cerebral, finding him so clever it was almost scary. 'I remember having dinner with Steve one night when he spent two hours talking about why men have nipples. And I still don't know why but he spent two hours talking about it at Terra Sushi in the Valley. You know, he's amazing.'

Bennett told Steve he was the smartest uneducated man he'd ever met in his life. 'Ninety-nine per cent of the time it was complete bullshit but he was so good at it! I truly adored him.'

In the media and out of it, Steve was a passionate advocate for human rights. He told the *Gavin Report* that there was nothing wrong with some people having more than others because they worked harder or had more initiative. 'That part of capitalism makes perfect sense to me. But when it comes to people being allowed to just flat-out starve to death and go without medical attention in a country like the United States, that doesn't make sense to me.'

Asked about his affinity with farmers in his songs and at Farm Aid, he said the collapse of farming was 'the death of all the things that we've held dear to us, that we thought were important at one point. The farms were things that we protected because they were right, not because they were profitable. That never entered into it . . . Although it may be true that it may be more efficient for corporations to grow food, I don't like the idea of corporations controlling that industry. I don't trust what I'm eating if the only motive is profit . . . In a lot of ways, farmers don't have a chance. It's a rigged game. We're telling them that they can't live the way their families have lived from one generation to the next. For a country that's supposed to be about having those kind of options, we are eradicating an entire way of life.'

Aside from the odd assault on MCA Nashville and comments like, 'I'm the person rumours start about', Steve came across as the man who had everything. He and Teresa had just bought a house in Fairview, Tennessee, some thirty miles from Nashville. It was as much Steve's dream house as the house on Ono Island had been, all glass and cedar, with cows in the backyard.

Behind the scenes, Simone and Bennett were putting everything they had behind the album. Steve was getting plenty of airplay at alternative and rock radio, but the pot of gold at the end of the rainbow was to get a Steve Earle track at Top 40 radio because the chances were that he would then explode as an artist in the way John Mellencamp had before him. There was a real bubbling of interest of Top 40 radio, but there were two small obstacles in front of Simone and Bennett. The first was that, roughly three weeks after *Copperhead*'s release, UNI was downsized. Looking back, Steve now feels very bitter about what he considers a betrayal by Azoff, believing that the decision halted the momentum of *Copperhead Road*. Simone is positive that it made absolutely no difference. UNI stayed fully functional for another year before it was closed down – at Simone's request. The real problem was that Simone and Bennett needed the help of MCA's whole promotion team to make the record a smash hit. They didn't get it.

To Simone, the album went on to be an enormous success, in terms of where Steve had been. 'However, Steve did not *for years* get over the fact that MCA Records . . . did not and would not go to Top 40 radio and break "Copperhead Road". Whether or not it would have broken at Top 40 radio, I don't know, but they didn't bite. And it was devastating to him. I think it took him a long, long time to let go of that disappointment. He found it very difficult to move on.'

At home in Nashville, life was equally challenging. Shortly before *Copperhead* hit the stores, Grace broke the news to Steve that she was quitting her job as his PA and moving to Louisville to live with her mother. She was thinking of returning to college. Steve wasn't particularly surprised. 'Grace didn't like Nashville very much. She was pretty California-ized.' It's likely, however, that Grace's departure was hastened by her receipt of a shocking parcel: the medical records of Lou's abortion. Lou had sent them in an attempt to get Grace to convey to her sister what kind of man she was involved with. Why she felt the need to do that, Lou now has no idea except that part of it was selfish and part of was a genuine wish to save Teresa from her own fate.

'Teresa is a very smart, very warm, very wonderful person. There is nothing in the world wrong with Teresa. She definitely got caught up in mine and Steve's drama.'

But even without the machinations of Lou, Teresa's life was starting to become a shadowy parallel of Steve's. In the summer, Simone had offered her a job as head of A&R at

UNI. Bennett had introduced them and Simone thought she was terrific. Very talented and very pretty. She reminded him of the actress Barbara Hershey. Next thing he knew David Geffen was on the phone, 'going absolutely nuts. He said I was stealing Teresa from him and he was going to kill me, blah, blah, blah. And I explained to him how Lincoln freed the slaves . . . Then I called a very powerful lawyer and I said, "I've just had this conversation with David Geffen, who was a friend of mine, where he said he was going to kill me over Teresa Ensenat. Now does he mean that as a turn of phrase or is he actually going to send someone to kill me?" So the lawyer said, "Well, you're not going to have anyone kill you, but I would advise you that you don't want David Geffen as your enemy and somehow you'd better work this out."'

On 5 October, Geffen Records launched a $1 million lawsuit against Teresa for breach of contract. Teresa promptly hired Don Engel, one of the most formidable music business litigation attorneys in the USA, and contemplated counter-suing. On 15 July, Teresa had sent a letter to David Geffen appealing to him and Ed Rosenblatt to empathize with her problems. 'I believe that both of you . . . are reasonably familiar with the disabling results of the termination of my personal relationship with Tom Zutaut.' She also alleged that the company had made decisions favouring his position. 'As I reported to Ed Rosenblatt and you on several occasions I felt violated, ineffective and unable to continue work under the horrifying circumstances that I faced.'

However, in his court declaration, David Geffen alleged that 'at no time prior to Ms Ensenat's suspension in June 1988 for failure to report for work for more than six weeks, did she ever indicate that she was displeased because of something Geffen Records had done or had not done'. It was at that point that David Simone convinced Teresa that they couldn't have 'World War III with David Geffen'. Teresa went back to the label for meetings lasting many hours. Finally, Geffen called

Simone. 'David,' he said, 'it's not going to work with Teresa coming back here. You have my blessing.'

And with that Teresa was hired.

Over the years, Steve's mother had 'once or twice' entertained the notion that her son created chaos for himself because he thrived on chaos. And he had 'once or twice said that himself'. She was not alone. In interviews, Steve openly acknowledged that, coming from a middle-class background, he had felt compelled to go out and create tension in his life in order to have something to write about. It was no accident that his life was a series of belief-beggaring dramas; quite often he was the cause of them. Consciously or unconsciously, he cultivated his own legend. At one stage in 1988, his answering machine informed callers: 'This is Steve. I'm probably out shooting heroin, chasing thirteen-year-old girls and beatin' up cops. But I'm old and I tire easily so leave a message and I'll get back to you.'

He dramatized other people's lives as often as his own. Steve's propensity for living out the lives of the characters in his songs, both before and after he had created them, was the one thing Lou and Charlie Mullins agreed on. He had done it, Charlie thought, ever since they were teenagers. 'If you're not living on the edge, you're taking up entirely too much space,' Steve used to say. Charlie was certain that Steve actively enjoyed chaos and near-death experiences. In his teens and early twenties Steve had had a habit of putting himself in harm's way purely for the sake – Charlie believed – of experiencing it. 'He would challenge people to kick his ass, he'd have his ass kicked many, many times and he would take that as an experience that he would draw from . . . His stories for the most part are accurate except for how the hell he got there in the first place. He always seems to leave that off.'

But by the fall of 1988, Steve's penchant for flirting with disaster was catching up with him with frightening regularity. He was paying $4,000 a month in child support and alimony alone. Then, when he least expected it, his one-night stand Theresa Baker came out of the woodwork. The first time he knew there was even a possibility he had a third child was when he was served with papers requesting child support. 'I went down and took a DNA test, which was much less sophisticated than they are now. They did one screening and I failed that. I basically failed to exclude myself. And then I stopped taking tests on my lawyer's advice. At first, it was a gamble. I knew I could be the father but I also know that it . . . wasn't necessarily beyond this person for me not to be the father.'

He never told a soul. If anyone ever found out about it, he simply denied it.

Throughout this period Lou was, she acknowledges, the 'Queen of Mean' with Steve. She was determined to make him suffer for everything she felt he had put her through. When he called her to tell her Teresa wanted him to marry her, Lou hissed, 'Well, think of me when you say "I do,"' and hung up on him. She had entered therapy in an attempt to deal with the trauma of the abortion and the anger she still felt towards him. Even so, she continued to sleep with him sporadically. 'Steve and I, I think we were addicted to each other – addicted to the raw attraction between us.'

On 6 November 1988, when Steve and Teresa were undergoing a brief separation, Lou arrived at Fairview with a hot dinner and all the kids. 'Out of the blue. Uninvited,' according to Steve. In the middle of dinner, a row blew up over an apple pie. Lou's parents had never fought in front of her and when Steve had yelled at her she'd been completely flummoxed. As time went on and their on-again off-again affair started to take on the properties of an unstable missile, she'd learned to give as good as she got. Their fights, Steve says, 'got physical a lot'.

With her hormones still raging from the aftermath of the abortion, Lou was probably quicker to react on this particular evening than she otherwise might have. She ranted at him across the dinner table until he finally blew up. In a moment of pure madness, Lou claims that Steve dragged her into the guest bedroom and started banging her head against the wall. The children were screaming outside the door. Lou cowered away from him, too shocked to defend herself. She begged Steve to let her go so she could comfort the children, but he barred the way.

Steve admits that he pushed Lou on to the floor but denies banging her head against the wall. 'She *may* have banged her head on the floor but *I* didn't bang her head on the wall or the floor. That didn't happen. I mean, it was two people. Lou's 5'8". She's never been a frail girly girl. She's very, very strong and very, very determined and she's meaner than a rick of rattlesnakes. You know, Lou hits. Lou was hitting me and I was grabbing her hands and I hit her. I never hit her in the face, ever. I shoved her and grabbed her. She hit me in the face with her fist *several* fuckin' times during the time we were together. It's one of those things. I wasn't raised to hit girls but when you get into a physical confrontation with one that's trying to hurt you, all bets are off.

'So yeah, we got physical and I probably hurt her in the sense that I didn't turn the other cheek, but I never attacked her and I never hit her with my fist and I never banged her head against the wall or the floor or *anything*. Probably put my hands around her throat on *more* than one occasion and probably that day because it's just absolutely . . . you know, it's what you want to do in that situation. But I never choked her. In the assault charge she claimed that I choked her unconscious, which is just her basically spitting out shit that she heard from the assault case in Dallas. But it was not pretty.'

By the time Lou emerged bruised and shaking from the room, Justin had called his mother and she was on her way to Fairview. Carol drove Lou to the nearest CentraCare clinic, where she was treated by a doctor. After speaking to her attorney and her therapist, Lou filed assault charges against Steve, alleging that he had 'hit and kicked [her] repeatedly'.

She had come to the conclusion that to allow her daughter and stepson to see Steve attack her without doing anything about it would send the wrong message. The charges were eventually retired on condition that Steve pay her medical bills, but Lou felt she had done what she needed to do for her own sanity. 'That was really when I said to myself: "What are you doing? You've got these babies and this guy is out of control. If he wants to do this to himself, then you let him do that and you get away from him."'

Steve ended 1988 as he had started it, defending himself against assault charges.

11

The Hard Way

Ten days after putting his signature to an assault warrant in Williamson County, Steve married Teresa in a low-key ceremony at his attorney's office in Franklin. Rick Steinberg was his best man and his brother Patrick and a friend of Teresa's were the only other witnesses. Steve turned up late.

To the Earles, it was obvious Steve had met his match in Teresa, intellectually and emotionally. Teresa, Kelly sometimes thought, had a dark side. She was warm to Steve but she could be moody and even a little cold to the family. Kelly couldn't figure out what made Teresa tick. When she visited the couple, she could never shake the feeling she was in the way. Steve was more in love with Teresa than he had ever been with anyone, but Kelly, like everyone else in Steve's life, couldn't help but wonder what it was that compelled him to keep marrying.

'I'm not scared of commitment,' Steve told anyone who would listen, adding as a rider: 'I'm not anywhere near as scared of it as I should be.' But he had his own definition of what commitment meant. It involved trying to reconcile his idea of a traditional marriage with the temptations and inse-curities of the road. 'Okay, so you're in love, what's next? Well, you control that person, naturally, and don't give them any room to breathe and panic if they give *you* any room to breathe – until you're sick of it. And it's so unhealthy. And it's so wrong for me . . . I should have known that it wouldn't work for me, I should have known what was going to happen every time I went into it like that. It's totally contrary to the way I do every fuckin' thing. That doesn't mean that I don't believe in monogamy but I think monogamy will happen when it happens and you can't control people.'

As past wives had discovered, Steve was constantly in search of new muses. He was a 'sucker for the romance of the outlaw', but that compulsion clashed with his need to have someone at home to cling on to when his world spun out of control. In Lou's experience, Steve had this whole 'kinda Catholic Mexican mentality about his wife and kids that, I can sleep around if I want to but you have to stay home'. Reconciling the two desires was tricky. As Carol put it, 'He's a hard dog to keep under the porch.'

Regardless of her feelings for him, Teresa could hardly have been unaware that Steve had a long history of doing what he was going to do. Even his fans were left in little doubt about that. Increasingly Steve's appearance seemed calculated to advertise his contempt for the country music business. In December 1988, he had appeared before the country music faithful on TNN's *Crook and Chase* in a Guns N' Roses t-shirt. In January, *USA Today* photographed him in a biker's leather jacket emblazoned with the Dukes' logo: a skull and crossbones with 'Fear No Evil' scrawled underneath. An ox skull glowered from the back. Steve stared cynically out at the photographer, a beret covering his long greasy hair. Under the headline, 'Nashville was Never a Happy Home', he banged on about MCA Nashville's failings and talked with typical frankness about his personal life. Teresa was his 'best friend' but he had a 'very vindictive ex-wife' and had been forced to go to court three times to get orders to see Ian. George Dickel whisky was his pleasure and he liked to take it on stage.

'It's a big drink, basically bourbon and ice in a real tall glass. But it's the only drink I have all night. But then about four or five times a year I get, like, screaming drunk for one reason or another. The hangovers are so deadly as you get older, it takes a long time before you even want to think about doing that to yourself again.'

But fewer and fewer people were willing to believe that whisky was Steve's drug of choice. Even Rick Steinberg, once an enthusiastic collaborator in the search for alternative highs, was disturbed by some of Steve's adventures. On one memorable day, they went to the Harley Davidson dealership in Nashville to buy a pair of bikes and spent an enjoyable few hours rushing from machine to sleek machine and admiring the handsome accessories. Riding back to Fairview, Steve struggled to get to grips with the clutch on his new bike. He stalled several times. A mile down the road, he ran out of patience. He pulled over, took a bag of heroin out of his pocket and snorted up. Steinberg fixed his gaze on the highway and wondered how they'd get home when Steve was high. The risk was mind blowing: here was a man poised on the very brink of superstardom and yet he was riding a Harley with heroin in his pocket. If the police stopped him it was all over.

Day by day he felt Steve was changing. In the short period of time since the wedding they had fallen out over the running of Steve's fan club, a role Steinberg had taken on after the release of *Exit o*. While Steve and Dan Gillis were not always convinced that the numbers added up, Steinberg was frustrated by Steve's apparent unwillingness to honour his obligations to the fan club. On one level, he understood. As a recovering addict, he was aware that in Steve's case not signing autographs had little to do with ego and a lot to do with wanting to be alone. But Steve was also changing in ways that Steinberg didn't understand. 'Steve did what Steve wanted to do and it didn't matter who he hurt, and if anybody wasn't okay with that, they were gone. That was the way things were.'

Watching from the sidelines, he wasn't sure if it was the drugs or the stardom or the combination of both; he only knew it was progressive. 'The Steve that I met that first time when we had fun together was a different Steve Earle than the Steve Earle that eventually became a star and got into drugs. He became hard to get along with, hard to be around. He had a power. He could just throw you away and if it bothered you, if you were afraid of that happening, you would do anything that he said or wanted. Of course you'd resent him for it, but for some reason people wanted to stay around him.'

Although he believed that Steve went through wives and friends like water, Steinberg, like so many others, still loved him. On a good day, there was no feeling in the world to beat Steve turning his focus on you. The sheer warmth of him, the shining, funny, genius of him, was irresistible. Alienated to some degree over the fan club, Steinberg yearned to have adventures with Steve again and to be close to him, knowing all the while that they'd never be able to bond like the old days as long as only one of them was clean. 'Our relationship changed. Every time he looked at me he could see how unhappy he was.'

From February 1989 onwards, Steve toured flat out. Pat dropped out of college and worked for him full time, and Steve invited Stacey to bring her boys to Nashville and take care of the house while he was on the road; Teresa travelled almost as much as he did. For Stacey, it was a godsend. Michael had been transferred to Louisiana and their marriage was in trouble, dragged downhill by a mountain of debt. Steve seemed to have an unerring instinct for knowing when Stacey needed him and he had no hesitation in lending her the money to pay off the loan sharks. He told Stacey she could live in his house rent-free and he would take care of her. Being both proud and a workaholic, Stacey couldn't bring herself to take advantage of his generosity. She wanted his help but she would take only so much of it. She found a job at the local elementary school serving lunch. 'I was the lady with the hairnet.'

Family values: Mark, Kelly and Steve in their first studio picture.

(right) Bright beyond his years, Steve enters first grade.

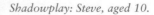
Shadowplay: Steve, aged 10.

(bottom left) Steve, wearing the Buddy Holly outfit his grandmother made him, smiles for the camera shortly before entering his first talent show. He went on to win.

(below) Steve, in full hippy regalia, takes the first steps along the road to becoming what he would call 'the world's loudest folk singer'.

American rebel: Steve, aged 16, shows off the bad boy charisma that would break hearts all over Texas and Tennessee in years to come.

Country roads: The youngest player in Nashville's burgeoning songwriter scene, Steve, barely 20, prepares to take on Music City.

(opposite top) Maestro: Townes Van Zandt, whom Steve would call a good teacher but a bad influence. (Photo: Tomato Records)

(opposite bottom) Guy and Susanna Clark, who were mentors to Steve in the early half of his career and remain heroes and friends to him to this day.

Southern bells: In a slightly surreal scene, Steve marries Carol Ann Hunter.

Steve and baby Justin. When his first son was born, Steve called his dad and 'apologized for every shitty thing I'd ever done'.

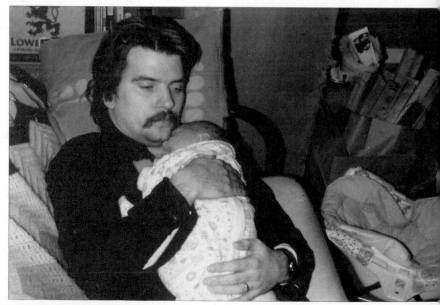

right) A clean cut Steve poses with a *Stratocaster during his rockabilly phase. He had no idea then that he would soon be dropped by Epic.*

below) Hailed as the new Bruce *Springsteen, Steve reinvents country music with Guitar Town, an instant classic.*

(above) Hell's Angel: Disillusioned with Nashville, Steve embraces rock 'n' roll and all that it implies.

Dark star: Steve's pale, haunted face reflects the toll drugs were taking by the late eighties.

Three eras:

(top) Steve, pre-jail, does a publicity shoot for Exit 0.

(bottom left) Post-jail and rehab: Steve hugs Justin who, by 1995, was already well on the way to following in his father's rebellious footsteps.

(bottom right) Clean, sober and Grammy-nominated, Steve prepares to face the music with the unapologetically autobiographical, I Feel Alright.

(top) Steve and The Dukes take on Europe during the Transcendental Blues Tour. In this incarnation, the band is (from left to right) Kelly Looney, Steve, Will Rigby and Eric 'Roscoe' Amble.

(right) Tony Brown, one of Steve's most loyal friends and supporters, watches the Guitar Town rehearsals in 2002 with Steve's dog, Beau.

(below) Steve and the Del McCoury band, with whom he would acrimoniously part company. They are no longer in communication.

(right) An eloquent history of Earle's Chapel, erected outside the church Elijah built.

EARLE'S CHAPEL METHODIST CHURCH

SETTLEMENT OF THE EARLE'S CHAPEL COMMUNITY BEGAN SEVERAL YEARS BEFORE THE ORGANIZATION OF CHEROKEE COUNTY. W. J. RAGSDALE (1811-1884), A VETERAN OF THE TEXAS WAR FOR INDEPENDENCE, AND HIS WIFE PATSY McADAMS (1816-1898) HAD SETTLED ON PRAIRIE BRANCH (MILL CREEK) IN 1838. ELIJAH EARLE (1804-1880), HIS WIFE MAXCEY BLANCHET (1811-1852), AND THEIR CHILDREN MIGRATED HERE FROM ALABAMA IN EARLY 1846. THEY CLEARED A FARM AND ELIJAH BUILT A MILL ON PRAIRIE BRANCH.

AS THE COMMUNITY GREW, ELIJAH EARLE AND HIS SECOND WIFE, MARY ELIZABETH JARRATT TATUM (1824-1904), SAW THE NEED FOR A SCHOOL AND CHURCH. THEY DONATED FOUR ACRES OF LAND, AND IN 1859 A LOG BUILDING WAS ERECTED AT THIS SITE. IT BURNED IN 1875 AND WAS IMMEDIATELY REBUILT. THAT SAME YEAR, THE EARLE'S CHAPEL SOCIETY, WITH TWENTY-FIVE CHARTER MEMBERS, WAS OFFICIALLY ORGANIZED BY THE REV. E. P. ROGERS OF THE EAST TEXAS CONFERENCE OF THE METHODIST CHURCH.

A NEW CHURCH BUILDING WAS CONSTRUCTED IN 1889 BY CHURCH MEMBERS T. J. SKELTON AND ROBERT TATUM. ALTHOUGH DAMAGED IN A 1987 TORNADO, THE BUILDING WAS RESTORED, AND AFTER MORE THAN A CENTURY OF SERVICE CONTINUES TO SERVE THE COMMUNITY, INCLUDING DESCENDANTS OF PIONEER FAMILIES.

(1993)

(below) Steve and his extended family gather outside their ancestral chapel during the Earle Family Homecoming in July 2000.

(top) The family home on the farm where Steve's grandfather Booster Earle grew peaches and Christmas trees and where Steve's aunt, Bettye, still resides.

(below) Watched over by their father, Jack Earle, Mark, Steve and Stacey Earle are reunited on the porch of the family homestead.

op) Jack Earle at the Earle Family Homecoming.

*bottom left) Steve and his mother, Barbara, watch his 95-year-old grandmother
nwrap her birthday present.*
bottom right) Steve shares a joke with his sister, Kelly.

Steve and his sons:
(top) Steve and Ian Dublin Earle, his youngest son.
(below) Steve and Justin, now a gifted musician in his own right.

True love: Steve vacations with his girlfriend, Sara Sharpe.

Steve performs at a rally in Memphis, Tennessee during the 1999 Journey of Hope, a state-wide campaign tour to protest against the death penalty.

(left) Mirror image: Steve, an uncanny reflection of his father at the same age, stands proudly beside Jack during the presentation of Gold discs for Guitar Town in 2002.

(bottom) Transcendental Bliss: After journeying to hell and back, Steve is happier than he has ever been in his life.

Out on the road, Steve's new managers, Cliff Bernstein and Peter Mench, were not coping terribly well with their new charge. Their usual method of breaking lesser-known artists was to send them out with the stars on their roster in the hope that they'd win over the audience themselves. Since Steve could hardly go out with Metallica they were at a loss as to how to proceed. Towards the end of 1988, they decided that the best thing to do was book a club tour for him. The first date was in Pittsburgh, and Cliff flew in for the show. He and Steve rode out to the venue together. Cliff warmed to Steve as they chatted while waiting in traffic. After soundcheck, Steve went missing. Cliff had some difficulty in locating him and when he did, Steve was bad-tempered and uncommunicative. Cliff felt very out of sorts. Naïvely, he wondered if he'd said something to upset Steve. 'I knew he'd had a drug problem but Teresa had gone out of her way to say that he was clean and when we met Steve originally, he said he was clean. Unfortunately, the first thing I usually do is take people at face value.'

That night, Cliff watched the concert and thought it odd that Steve started his set with 'Copperhead Road', his biggest song to date, at an hour when most people were still jostling for beer or hunting for their seats. He found it even more peculiar when Steve played thirty songs from his first three albums, a couple of covers and some material he'd written pre-MCA. 'In a show, you want to showcase your best and maybe leave them wanting a little bit more, but not Steve. He wanted to give them every single thing, and I believe he loved everything he'd ever written . . . Most of my musicians, they're not too precious about their songs. They're proud of what they've done but they've realized that some of them, in retrospect, didn't turn out as well as they should have. With Steve, every song was his baby.'

Bill Bennett had made a similar observation, noting that Steve's concerts had taken on the epic quality of Springsteen's performances – musically intense, up to four hours long, and laced with darkly funny asides and rants about the system. It was hard to know whether Steve was consciously emulating the Boss or whether he was purely drawing on the aspects of Springsteen that made him the perfect amalgamation of rock star and union activist, and one of the best live acts around. Either way, Bennett had a tendency to walk out of Steve's concerts after three hours. 'We used to have these insane arguments, he and I, about the length of his show and the set and how he always got hung up on the Springsteen thing . . .'

Cliff went back to New York and relayed his findings to Peter Mench, and in December they went to see Steve play at the Ritz. Steve turned up about a minute before he was due on stage. Afterwards, he gave them the silent treatment. Cliff put it down to nerves but Steve's publicist implied that there was something more to it. 'She just gave us the impression, hey, this is the way Steve is. Steve is a drug addict.' Cliff and Peter represented several heavy metal bands who looked as if eating the heads off bats was their favourite dining experience, but they were appalled at this latest development. It rapidly began to affect their relationship with their new client. When 1989 rolled around and David Simone suggested that 'Back to the Wall' should be the follow-up single to 'Copperhead Road', they disagreed. Steve sided with Simone. Cliff admits that that, plus the 'observance of what he was like on tour' meant 'the enthusiasm on our part started to die . . .'

Another bone of contention was 'Nothing but a Child', the last song on the album. Two years earlier, Steve had been approached after a show by Brad Durham, a Nashvillian who worked for Human Services in Cambridge, Massachusetts. Durham had persuaded Steve to perform at a benefit for a daycare centre and out of that came the idea to start the Fearless Hearts Fund, a daycare charity for the children of homeless families. The idea was that it broke the cycle of poverty by giving parents the freedom to go out to find work. In 1989, Steve assigned the publishing royalties of 'Nothing but a Child', originally written as a Christmas song for the Oak Ridge Boys, to the fund. He was determined to get it released as a single to raise more money. Cliff and Peter decided without consulting him that the song was weak and any attempt to do anything with it would be a waste of time. As Cliff remembers it, 'I'm sure we did not articulate that to him because, like I say, every song to him was so precious, it was his own baby, that to say something like that would be to deny his very existence. So we didn't want to go there. We just kind of avoided it and we didn't put any support behind it.'

On the surface Steve remained full of goals, plans and ideas. On 22 March, he told his old friend Jim Beal Jr, a reporter for the *San Antonio Express News*, that *Copperhead* had sold 340,000 units. Everything was going wonderfully for a change. He was finishing pre-production demos on a hard rock band called Guilt and there was a possibility he might tour with Bob Dylan later in the year.

Underneath, Steve was in turmoil. It was a time of extremes – extreme lows, extreme highs, extreme wealth, extreme excess. Two days before the *Express News* article appeared, Steinberg received a hysterical call from Teresa. She and Steve were in Houston, where Steve was scheduled to play the Xcess, and they'd had a vicious row about his drug use. Now Steve was on the bus with a gun to his temple. He was threatening to kill himself if she ever left him.

Thirteen years on, Steve has no idea where Teresa got the notion that he planned to do himself harm. He didn't, he says, ever have a 'suicidal second'. With the benefit of hindsight, Teresa is sceptical that he actually contemplated suicide: 'It was high drama.' Indeed the suicide drama itself paled beside the eruption that took place when Teresa confessed that she had taken the gun she had persuaded him to give up and tossed it into an undisclosed garbage can. For years afterwards, Steve was convinced that someone would find his licensed pistol and use it to murder someone and it would be Steve doing time on Death Row.

Some clue to Steve's state of mind would come in the liner

notes of his next album, *The Hard Way*, where he acknowl-edged that he'd spent the years since *Guitar Town* 'trying to figure out what one does with oneself once one's dreams have come true'. His sold-out show at the Palace in LA a week later was a case in point. In industry terms, playing the Palace meant an artist had well and truly arrived and on this particular night the audience glittered with stars. Springsteen, John Fogerty and Harry Dean Stanton had all turned out to see Steve. The energy in the room was overwhelming.

After the show, Simone headed downstairs to Steve's dressing room and was startled to see Bruce Springsteen waiting outside. He knocked on the door.

'Who is it?' Steve growled.

'David Simone.'

The door opened cautiously and Simone went in. 'Christ, Steve,' he said, 'Bruce Springsteen's waiting outside.'

'I can't see him,' Steve said instantly. He and Springsteen were mutual fans but somehow their paths had never crossed.

Simone was aghast. '*Why?*'

'I played "State Trooper".'

'It was great.'

'But I couldn't remember the words. I made up my own.'

'Steve,' David implored, 'Bruce Springsteen is waiting outside to pay homage to you. Let him in.'

'Do you think so?'

'Absolutely.'

'Well, okay, let him in.'

Springsteen and Fogerty came into the dressing room and a beaming Springsteen walked over to Steve and hugged him. 'Man, it was brilliant,' he said. 'It was incredible.'

Steve said: 'But I forgot the words to "State Trooper".'

Springsteen burst out laughing. 'Who cares,' he said. 'It was fantastic.'

The *Copperhead Road* tour was the first time Steve hadn't been able to lie down and get clean prior to going out on the road. Opiates have the same chemical make-up as the natural endorphins the brain manufactures to deal with pain. When those natural opiates are replaced by artificial ones, the body quickly stops making them. If the artificial source is withdrawn, the body goes into shock – a feeling Steve likened to 'being a toothpaste tube squeezed in the middle. I mean, the spasms are really hard and they last for a long time. So it can get pretty nightmarish pretty quickly.'

In William Burroughs's *Junky*, the 'junk sick' narrator describes a feeling of extreme weakness 'as if the life energy has been shut off so that all the cells in the body are suffocating. As I lay there on the bench I felt like I was subsiding into a pile of bones.' On the third day of withdrawal, he 'felt a cold burn over the whole surface of my body as though the skin was one solid hive. It seemed like ants were crawling around under the skin.' There was no detaching oneself from the pain. 'I was too weak to get out of bed. I could not lie still. In junk sickness, any conceivable line of action or inaction seems intolerable. A man might die simply because he could not stand to stay in his own body.'

Steinberg knew the feeling well. 'Different people react slightly differently but generally you'll start off with a headache and your nose will start running and your back will get real sore and you'll get sick to your stomach. You'll feel like throwing up. You won't be able to eat because you'll have diarrhoea. Every nerve ending in your body will be screaming. You won't want anybody to touch you. You'll want to curl up in a little ball and disappear. You just feel really bad. It's like a really bad flu, only worse. But the thing about it is you know if you can just get that narcotic in you – if you inject it, within thirty seconds it'll go away, if you drink Tussionex, within thirty minutes it'll go away.'

On his way to play the Royal Theatre in Victoria, British Columbia on 11 April, Steve was junk sick and aware that relief was as close as a bottle of cough syrup. No sooner had the band arrived than he called Dan Gillis over. 'We've got to fly in Rick Steinberg with a bottle of Tussionex,' he said.

Dan was flabbergasted. 'Jesus Christ, Steve,' he burst out, 'it'll cost $1,200 to fly him up here.'

'Fly him up here with a bottle of cough syrup,' Steve said flatly. 'Tell me when he's here.'

It was a freezing grey day in Chicago when Steinberg received the call. He was there with the Grateful Dead. The request put him in a quandary. After getting clean in 1984, he had been forced to undergo dental work he was ill able to afford and had agreed to give Steve his pain medication if Steve paid for the treatment. Further down the road to recovery, he'd felt very guilty about the transaction, and he did not feel good about being asked to perpetuate Steve's habit now. Still he agreed to do it. 'Even though I knew I shouldn't have done it, I did it anyway, because I was concerned about him. I knew he would get it anyway so I just said, "Well, this way at least I can be with him."'

Steve had already appealed to his personal assistant back in Nashville to bring the Tussionex to Canada, but she'd been terrified of crossing the border with it. He did manage to persuade her to fly with it as far as Chicago. Steinberg picked it up, boarded a plane and carried it to Vancouver. At the airport, his worst fears were realized. He was set upon by customs officers and subjected to a prolonged and embarrassing search. Amazingly, the Tussionex lay undiscovered. Although it was legal for Steve to have the cough syrup, it was illegal for Steinberg to be in possession of a restricted medicine with Steve's name on it. Shaken, Steinberg took a ferry to the venue and was rushed straight to the side of the stage where Steve was performing. Steve finished his song, walked over to the wings and gulped down the cough syrup as if his life depended on it. Which it probably did.

As an emergency measure Steve found a clinic in San Antonio prepared to let him pay a fee every ten days to collect a supply of methadone, a legal heroin substitute, and take it away with him. As tour manager, it was Gillis's job to bankroll these expeditions. It cost a fortune to fly Steve back and forth between Canada and San Antonio, but Gillis tried to save Steve from himself wherever he could by telling him they couldn't afford it. 'But he'd always find the money and find a way to do it and I'd just book him on the flights. If he couldn't find it in Canada, he'd go and get it.'

If the Tussionex incident represented a personal low point, professionally Steve had never done better. The Victoria show was the warm-up for a show at the PNE Concert Bowl in Vancouver the next night, where a hockey arena packed with fans responded rapturously to 'Copperhead Road' and every other song on the setlist. In stores across Canada, the album was flying out the door, already well on the way to the quadruple-platinum it would eventually sell. In the USA, the album was climbing to No. 7 on the country charts and 56 on the pop charts. Concert tickets were as popular as lottery tickets and on 14 April Steve played the biggest show of his career. Bathed in sweat, his guitar strings slipping in his fingers, he watched 8,000 people go mad to 'Copperhead Road' at the Saddledome in Calgary.

Watching him, Pat, now Steve's production manager, felt proud and afraid simultaneously. Steve was very secretive about his heroin use, especially around his little brother, and Pat idolized him so much he was reluctant to think the worst. But even he was starting to see that Steve's drug use was escalating dangerously. 'Once he became the really big star, everybody was pumping him up and all these people were telling him he was great, whether he was fucking up or not. That's when it got out of control.'

As the tour went on, Dan came under increasing pressure from Teresa to take part in an intervention, a radical form of addiction therapy. In it, a specially trained counsellor acts as mediator as friends and family members confront an addict with the consequences of their actions in a bid to shock them into entering treatment. Weary of being bystanders in Steve's daily courtship of impossible highs and possible death, Teresa, Steinberg and Patrick had decided to take matters into their own hands. For Teresa, the stakes were highest. She was desperate to save her five-month-old marriage.

Gillis, however, refused to be involved in any intervention.

'Well, you're the closest thing to a boss he's ever had,' Teresa pleaded.

'Don't give me that shit,' Dan said. 'Steve doesn't have a boss. Steve's his own person. He knows what's going on.'

The next thing he knew, the intervention counsellor was on the phone.

'Don't you love Steve?' he asked Dan.

'Yeah, I love him,' Dan replied. 'I love him more than I love many of my siblings because I know him better than my siblings. I'm around him all the time. Of course I do, and I keep him alive by controlling how much income he has, that kind of stuff, and staying with him and making sure he's okay. But if I get involved in an intervention he'll cast me out, just like he's going to cast all you people out.'

The intervention took weeks of planning. Teresa kept Steve's schedule clear for most of May and she and Pat attended special preparatory classes. But they had no idea what they were getting into. Later Pat realized how blindly they had blundered into the whole thing, how clueless they had been about 'how big the beast was'. No one agonized over the intervention more than Steve's mother, Barbara, who had suffered through the addictions of her own mother and her brother, Nick. As desperate as she was to save Steve, she knew in her heart that he was 'the wrong person for that to work on. Because he had to fall as far as he did. He had to have that happen and come to it himself.'

It was with heavy hearts that Jack and Barbara went to Nashville. 'How can we do this to our son?' Jack asked Kelly, knowing that the answer was a harder question still: 'Can we watch him die?'

Ultimately, Kelly chose to stay away. Her self-esteem had

yet to recover from past batterings and she didn't believe she had anything to offer. It was a decision she came to regret. Drugs and alcohol had never been part of her world, but she could have reminded Steve of those afternoons when they had crept around Mudder's house on search and destroy missions for booze bottles. She could have reminded him how, at ten and fourteen, they had sworn they would never be slaves to addiction. But she didn't. She couldn't bring herself to go. Some family members resented Teresa for her actions but Kelly couldn't condemn her. 'Teresa, really, honestly, it's a good thing she tried. Because isn't it the most horrible thing in the world if you see somebody sinking and you don't even try to save them?'

As a final measure, Teresa telephoned Lou and told her in confidence about their plans because she wanted to make sure that Steve's youngest son Ian was taken care of for the weekend. As incredible as it may seem, they had recently reached the stage where wives and ex-wives start talking. Teresa had either forgotten or forgiven Lou's past history of mad actions – the wedding dress incident, for instance, or the abortion records. Lou waited until Teresa hung up and called Steve. She found the very idea of people trying to throw a net over Steve, as if he were a wild animal, ridiculous.

'There's no way that would have worked with Steve. You just don't deal with Steve that way. You don't force Steve into anything. He's got to come to decisions by himself.'

Unaware of Lou's interference, Teresa, Steinberg and the Earles gathered in a hotel room and waited for Steve, afraid to imagine how he would feel about them ganging up on him, afraid to imagine where he might end if they didn't try. The phone trilled into the silence and everybody jumped. Teresa picked it up.

'There will be no intervention today,' drawled Steve.

Steve's reaction to the failed intervention was much as Dan Gillis predicted. He felt betrayed, particularly by Teresa and

Steinberg, each of whom blamed the other for initiating the intervention. When Teresa convinced him it was Steinberg's fault, Steinberg was excommunicated. The only person who fared well briefly was Lou, to whom Steve turned for support. He went to her house and hid. Jack Earle searched him out and tried to talk him into going into treatment. Steve convinced him that he didn't need to go. He told Teresa that he wasn't coming home. When it became clear that he meant it, she walked out of the house and went to LA. She moved into a hotel and started trying to piece together her life. She was devastated.

With Teresa gone and a fifth marriage apparently over, Steve went back to Fairview to lick his wounds. Stacey was still there with her boys. By now Nick Fain's fourteen-year-old son, Robert Collins, known to everyone as Cole, had moved in with them. At fourteen, Cole already carried deep scars from his upbringing. Nick was an alcoholic and his mother had been a heroin addict until she went missing one day, a suspected Jane Doe. Cole had been shuffled from relative to relative, at one time spending several years with Stacey and Michael. When money became tight, Stacey wrote letters to everyone in the family asking them to contribute $10 a month to his upbringing. Instead Cole was sent away to school. When he was expelled, Nick handed him on to Steve. He was incapable of looking after the boy himself. In retrospect, the very notion of Cole being sent to live with Steve even as the family gathered to plan an intervention, seems insane. And yet it shows that despite his fall from grace, Steve was the family's charismatic leader, the one they always turned to for support, especially financial. And perhaps they thought that there was no one more uniquely qualified to take care of Nick Fain's son than Steve.

Steve began writing songs for *The Hard Way*, his aptly named next album. 'Why do you always have to do everything the hard way?' his father was always asking him, but as Steve told one journalist, 'There isn't any way but the hard way. There isn't any way to get from point A to point B without taking some bumps.'

His mother believes he wrote the anthemic 'The Other Kind' in response to the intervention, and Steve admits there was an exorcism going on when he wrote it. The themes that would eventually make up *The Hard Way* – drugs, guns, suicide, capital punishment, injustice, prostitution and restless poor boys with razors in their pockets – are not nearly as far removed from *Guitar Town* as they seem at first glance. The road is a constant, as is social injustice and general disen-franchisement from the values of a wealth- and celebrity-obsessed America. But *The Hard Way* is written from the standpoint of considerable disillusionment – personal and political. The youthful optimism has gone. So has the humour. The characters in *Guitar Town* believe in the power of dreams, even if they know on a subconscious level that those dreams are out of reach or have already passed them by. Those in *The Hard Way* deal in the reality of the street. Drugs, guns and lying or being lied to are the watermarks of their existence. Song after song spells out the futility of life and the loneliness of death. In 'Have Mercy', which Steve wrote after the suicide of a close friend, the married man who takes whatever comfort his lover can offer him 'in that room at the top of the stairs' realizes only after she shoots herself that she might have needed comfort in return.

In *Guitar Town*, the road is a potent symbol of hope. Four albums later, it is a means to an end. Outlaw bikers use it to pursue their demons even as they flee from them.

Stacey did her best to screen the children from Steve's drug use at Fairview. She kept them from going down into the base-ment where Steve descended to be alone with his thoughts or his songs or his drugs. When Stacey ventured down there to clean up the debris, it was like going down into some hellish antechamber. It was in the basement that Steve wrote 'Billy Austin', the story of a twenty-nine-year-old half-breed in his last hour on Death Row. It was a work of fiction, based on the Clutter case in *In Cold Blood* and every murder story Steve had ever read, but it chilled like the truth. Stacey hovered in the shadows as he composed it, struck by its power. 'I remember the night it was being written. It was a high lonesome night and he was down there cooking his damn heroin. Every damn spoon in the house was black.'

Steve drove her crazy with his mess and his burnt-out spoons. The mere thought of feeding a child cereal off a spoon that had been stained by heroin made her sick to her stomach and she was always buying new ones. The mother in her enjoyed the challenge of maintaining cheerful domestic normalcy in the face of Steve's addiction – painted eggs at Easter and the like – but the little sister in her had never grown out of craving Steve's approval. In her own way, she needed Steve as much as he needed her. High or not, he was always by her side if she had an epileptic seizure. When they struck it was Steve's voice she found she most wanted to hear in the background. 'Just give her room,' he would tell people soothingly. 'Don't say anything. Just leave her alone and let her get through it.'

Steve himself depended on Stacey for 'continuity and for family and for anchor' in that chaotic time. 'Having her kids there meant a lot to me because all my attempts at trying to hold a family together were failing miserably.'

In the midst of this period Lou drove up with the kids and a carload of groceries and the apparent intention of camping out at the house. Even after the vengeful divorce, the abortion, the assault and thousands of dollars' worth of therapy, she was still addicted to the raw attraction between them, and in the emotional weeks after the intervention she'd embarked on an affair with him. That didn't mean Steve was prepared to live with her. 'Wait a minute. Time out,' he said when she walked through the front door. The subsequent row started another war between them. After that Steve just sat around the house for several weeks until he finally found the nerve to call Teresa. Heartsore and desperate to save her marriage, she agreed to take him back. Steve packed his bags and moved to LA, later wondering if he'd made a mistake because things were always on Teresa's terms from that point on. 'Because *I'd* fucked up, *I'd* left, *I* didn't come home.'

At Q-Prime in New York, Cliff and Peter were abuzz with good news. Following pressure from Steve and Teresa, Cliff had called in a favour and secured Steve a spot opening for Bob Dylan on the *Never Ending* Tour. There was considerable kudos to be had from touring with the great man, whose stock had been revived with the critical success of *Oh Mercy*, but despite his excitement Steve never thanked Cliff. Cliff's enthusiasm for him took another dive. He had found it was often the way with artists. 'They go: "Well, yeah, I deserve that."'

The Dukes had heard or been told that they would have next to no contact with Dylan, but Steve was put out that Dylan refused to speak to him. By all accounts, it was not uncommon. In *Bob Dylan: Behind the Shades*, bassist Kenny Aaronson describes him as distant and distracted on the '89 tour. 'I found rehearsals with him the second time very, very vague . . . He hardly said a word or even hardly looked at me at all for [the] two, three weeks I rehearsed with him in '89.' The Dukes had toured with Dylan for a month when he sent word that he disapproved of Steve's language on stage. 'They sorta said: "Bob said to tell you . . ."' Steve couldn't believe it. 'I said: "Fuck him." And that got back to him and it was okay. He started speaking to me after that.'

For Steve's band, unaccustomed to full-time stadium touring, it was a surreal existence. Not counting rest days, they lived almost exclusively on the bus. The towns changed but the scenery didn't. The bus would pull into the venue parking lot at three or five in the morning, the dew still heavy on the asphalt, and the musicians would sleep on into the waking day. They rose only to stumble into catering or find a bathroom.

Behind the scenes, Steve was deeply unhappy with Cliff and

Peter, who had failed to attend a single show. It was a legitimate grievance. Cliff and Peter had more or less given up on him. He had a habit of going missing for long periods of time and when he was around they felt completely estranged from him. They had been disgusted to hear that he'd had drugs flown into Canada. Cliff found it 'so unpleasant when he was the way he was on drugs, or when we thought he was on drugs, that we just didn't want to see him . . . So we just kind of avoided him.'

They weren't the only ones having difficulty communicating with Steve. Bill Bennett had been aware for some time that Steve was an addict. 'I used to argue with him and at the end I'd say, "Why am I arguing with you, you're a junkie." And he'd yell, "Well, I wrote *Guitar Town* on junk, so fuck you."'

On 17 July, Dan Gillis sat in the production trailer with Al Santos, Dylan's then production manager, in Stanhope, New Jersey, looking at the rain running in rivulets down the window. Outside, the backstage area was a quagmire. Waterloo Village was a field that had been fenced and transformed into a venue for the occasion and it wasn't bearing up well in the poor conditions. Buses and trucks were mired in the mud and bedraggled crew members were slipping and sliding as they went about their tasks. As Dan and Al watched, Steve came into view. He seemed to be searching for something. Dan thought nothing of it. Steve was always charging about as if he was looking for something but not really looking for anything. Suddenly, Steve changed direction and came over to the trailer. He wanted to know if Dan would come back to the bus and proofread something for him.

'That's cool,' Dan agreed, swelling a little with pride. Perhaps Steve needed his input on a song. At the bus, Steve presented him with a near-illegible letter. Dan struggled through it. 'Are you sure you want me to send this?' he asked when he finished.

'Yeah, I want you to send it.'

'Well,' said Dan, 'let's go and put it on Al's computer so we can read it.'

'No,' Steve told him. 'Send it like it is.'

So Dan returned to the production trailer and faxed the letter to Q-Prime telling them they were fired. Neither he nor Steve ever received another phone call on the subject from them. Cliff and Peter 'never called and said, "What the hell is this about?" We never heard a word, not a word.'

At Q-Prime, Cliff and Peter heaved a sigh of relief. Beyond a letter to Steve's lawyer asking for repayment of the money they had loaned him, which they received in due course, they were happy to sever all ties with him. They didn't even demand commission on dates they had already booked.

Unfortunately for Steve, the same was not true of Will Botwin, who was suing him for $56,544.76 in unpaid expenses and management fees. Steve believed the true amount was nearer $16,000. On Sunday, 20 August, he was handed a summons by Will's lawyers shortly before going on stage to open for Dylan at the Starwood Amphitheatre in Nashville. A hand-delivered letter from Levitan & Solomon to the Davidson County Deputy Sheriff noted that, 'he may be found for purposes of service of process at that location between 6:00 and 8:00pm, his performance being scheduled for 7:00pm. We also are informed and believe that he will make a rapid departure following his performance, for parts unknown . . .'

The tour ended in the second week of September, with two nights at the Greek Theatre in LA. Teresa had rented a house once belonging to Frances Farmer in Larchmont Village, the old Paramount backlot, between Hollywood and LA. Before Steve moved to LA, Teresa went with him to a hotel in San Antonio and stayed with him as he attempted to detox with the help of naltrexone, a narcotic antagonist. Where methadone works by decreasing the craving for heroin, eliminating abstinence symptoms and helping to promote normal functioning in society, narcotic antagonists only block the euphoriant effects of opiates. Since there are no rewards for taking them and no 'pharmacological consequences' for not, compliance with treatment programmes is quite low, according to the United Nations Office for Drug Control and Crime Prevention (UNODCCP). So it proved with Steve. He had always told Rick he would never use a needle, but the thirty-second release had recently become appealing when he used dilaudids – on an infrequent basis at least.

Within a very short period of time in LA, he fell in with a crowd of musician junkies and began using again. Specifically, he began shooting speedballs – a potent blend of cocaine and heroin which had been the death of *Blues Brothers* actor John Belushi in 1982. Steve had stayed completely away from cocaine for years, believing that heroin was a much more sensible drug. It was possible to maintain some semblance of a normal lifestyle for much longer with heroin, simply because you did heroin and you were okay for a number of hours and then as long as you did more heroin, you were okay again. But now he found that his addiction was not so easily satis-fied. 'I finally got to where heroin didn't do it for me any more, so I started doing cocaine *and* heroin. I couldn't not do heroin because not doing heroin means sitting on the toilet and throwing up in the sink. You become really desperately physically ill.'

It was in this climate that he started working on *The Hard Way* in earnest. He was heavily influenced by *Nebraska*, which had been one of his favourite records for several years and was often included in his concerts. It showed in the Springsteen-like 'Other Kind' and 'Hopeless Romantics'. Steve thought then that 'Have Mercy' and 'Close Your Eyes' were as good as 'My Old Friend the Blues', the benchmark by which all his songs were measured. 'Promise You Anything' was taken from some writing sessions he'd done with Maria McKee, and 'Esmeralda's Hollywood' was based on an idea they had worked on at the same time. Steve was determined that *The Hard Way* was going to rock harder than any of his previous albums. If it was going to be literature to drive to, it would be *The Sound and the Fury* not *The Old Curiosity Shop*.

In between, Steve commuted back and forth to Nashville. Teresa rarely accompanied him these days. For one thing, Fairview was always full of people. Stacey and her boys were joined occasionally by Justin and Ian. Then there was Cole, of whom a judge had inexplicably awarded Steve custody. By June 1990, Steve was having to make $8,000 a month before he saw a dime. The rest of it went on alimony and child support. Steve was also very busy preparing to produce both Guilt and a British Band called Energy Orchard as soon as he was done with *The Hard Way*. The former project already had disaster written all over it. Guilt 'were just as fucked up as I was and scammed me out of money constantly. I found 'em, Teresa signed 'em, and boy was she pissed at me about it because they really were a pain in the ass. Their record never came out.'

The other thing on Teresa's mind was that UNI Records was shutting down and she would then be working for MCA proper. Her colleague, Bill Bennett, stayed on at MCA until 1990 when he joined Geffen, eventually becoming president of the company. David Simone quit MCA and went back into law, his original profession. Steve and Teresa were his first clients.

Steve went into the studio in the New Year with *Copperhead Road* engineer Joe Hardy, now co producing. They had decided to record the album at Sound Emporium in Nashville and mix it at Ardent in Memphis, so that Joe could be in the control room he was used to. At home and on the bus Steve had made a comprehensive demo using a drum machine and a porta-studio and given it to the Dukes to study. For the purposes of the record, the Dukes would be Bucky, Ken Moore, Kelley Looney, Craig Wright on drums and Zip Gibson on guitar. Mike McAdam had been let go. Steve himself played both acoustic and electric guitar, mandolin, six-string bass and Mandoblaster. Steve told Britain's *Independent* newspaper that in the past 'my producers grossly underestimated my abilities as a guitar player and I bought that and I think that was the only essential mistake I was making'.

In the dead time, he disassembled his motorcycle in the studio lounge. There were greasy parts strewn everywhere and nowhere for anyone to sit down. He had four bikes in all. As a teenager he had lived in a motorcycle-intensive part of San Antonio – the local Bandidos clubhouse was in his neighbourhood. Somewhere along the line Steve had caught the bug. Simone's impression was that there were two things that were important to Steve by the time he made *The Hard Way*: motorbikes and guns. He'd shot two holes in the floor of the bus during the Dylan tour. Being English, Simone didn't know the first thing about guns, nor did he have any interest in them, but on a business trip to Nashville he found himself getting a guided tour of Steve's gun collection at Fairview.

'I said, "Steve, I don't like playing with these guns. Put them away. I'd rather hear some music." And it was just him and me in the kitchen and he was cocking the guns and pulling the trigger. I said, "What if one of these guns has a bullet in it?" "Oh no, none of these guns has a bullet in it." And then one of these fucking guns went off. I'll be honest, I'm a big guy but I was really shaken. I said, "You know what, Steve, I've had enough. I've got to go to the hotel." They drove me back and I was fairly freaked out.'

Steve admits that it was a 'really intense' period of time for him – 'I changed a lot.' To Bennett, whose office Steve liked to visit, his decline was visible. 'He'd come in, he'd have on that stupid Harley Davidson shirt with the sleeves cut off, the big engineer boots . . . He would smell so bad.'

Both men were in Simone's words, fairly freaked out, but not enough to lose faith in him. Steve's fascination with life's ugliest underbelly – the themes, in fact, that make up *The Hard Way* – made those years 'the darkest, scariest' time of his life, but in music and in life his intelligence and humanity shone though continually. Instead of asking any one of a dozen famous singers to sing Maria McKee's part on 'Promise You Anything' (Maria wouldn't do it because, Steve said ungraciously, 'she's a monumental flake'), he asked Stacey, knowing once again that she just needed something good to happen. 'I think it came straight from his heart. I wouldn't be [an artist] now if it wasn't for that. So that's a very special thing. Because the itinerary of an addict is not a giving one. It doesn't happen. They're very selfish.'

Steve was seldom selfish when it came to good causes. He still played regular benefits for the Fearless Hearts fund and now he had another cause: Native American rights and justice in Ontario. Soon after the release of *The Hard Way* on 26 June, Steve crossed Canada's St Lawrence River and was taken by Mohawk Warriors to Kahnawake via a secret trail through the woods. In Quebec, there were two main issues raging: one involved the planned expansion of a golf course built on disputed tribal land, and the other involved a series of police raids on stands selling tax-free cigarettes on several reservations. Mohawk Warriors had blockaded the interstate bisecting one reservation in protest but there seemed to be a news blackout and they were hoping Steve's presence would attract some national coverage. It didn't. The three journalists who did show up were already converts to their cause.

The Satan's Choice Motorcycle Club members who were the subject of 'Justice in Ontario' were rather more controversial. In 1987, an SCMC biker by the name of Wally High with whom Steve had become friends presented him with a book called *Conspiracy of Brothers*. On the flyleaf he wrote: 'Steve, just because you ain't paranoid, don't mean that they ain't out to get you.' The author of the book was Canadian crime reporter Mick Lowe, who argued that Gary Comeau and Rick Sauve, SCMC members convicted of killing a rival biker in Port Hope, Ontario, in 1978, would not have been convicted on the evidence provided had they not been members of a motorcycle gang. Steve became convinced that these men and three other bikers charged with conspiracy were innocent.

'The truth of the matter was, it was a very spur of the moment shooting in a bar and none of the guys who were convicted committed the murder. The guy who did commit the murder, who I also know . . . during the trial got on the stand and admitted that he did it.'

Reviewing *The Hard Way* later in the year, *Stereo Review*'s Alanna Nash observed that the America seen from the back of Steve's tour bus was a disturbing one. 'When Earle peels back the curtain on his travelling stateroom, he sees a frightening canker, a raw and rotting America, festering to the bone.' His songs, though, were rooted in reality, a million miles from the 'empty, smarmy dreck' that country radio attempted to market to people as the Truth. 'The Other Kind' was 'rock as autobiography' and 'Billy Austin' created an intensity of involvement that rivalled Bob Dylan in his prime. Even the *Erie, Pennsylvania News* noted that Steve's most wretched characters managed to 'retain some hope and dignity; he captures the spark of life which flickers within them'.

Years later, *The Hard Way* would become Steve's favourite album just because it was, in many ways, 'the red-headed stepchild. The maligned kid. You love those more.' But it was the most difficult for him to listen to. It was, as Nash perceptively observed, rock as autobiography. When Steve flew to England in June to do press for the record, one reporter was intrigued to see that with his ponytail, stubble, tattoos, beer-gut and biker's rings, he had acquired all the trappings of the characters in his songs.

There the similarity stopped. Steve could relate to the people in his songs and frequently knew them or lived among them, but he had rather more means at his disposal. In London, he stayed at the flashy Halcyon Hotel in Holland Park and he took Concorde back to America. His record and publishing contracts had been renegotiated after *Copperhead Road* sold in excess of 460,000 copies (stopping, oddly enough, just short of the 500,000 that would have precipitated a royalty boost), and had been substantially increased.

Dangerously, success reinforced the idea that he was okay because people still thought he was worth more money. It was then that Steve made a fateful decision. He decided to try crack.

12

Into the Darkness

Stacey Earle stood under the steaming stage lights in Newcastle, Australia and stared out at the bright blur of faces with a kind of paralysed disbelief. Only the weight of the guitar was familiar. Not counting a few rehearsals and a police department benefit out in Fairview, Tennessee, it was the first time she had played the instrument outside of her bedroom. A month earlier, Steve had walked up to her and said casually: 'So you sang on that track pretty good.' Stacey, who had put everything she had into 'Promise You Anything' during the recording of *The Hard Way*, felt the sudden rush of happiness she always felt when Steve praised her. Then he added: 'Now you have to take it around the world.'

'What do you mean?' Stacey asked.

'You've got three weeks to learn four Steve Earle records,' her brother told her. 'We leave on tour in a month.'

So Stacey had had a crash course in Steve Earle tablature from guitarist Zip Gipson, working with him day and night for three weeks and, at the end of it, taking a long-haul flight Down Under in August 1990 for a fiery baptism in rock 'n' roll touring. Minutes before she stepped on to the stage that first night it occurred to Steve that she could freeze up. He took her aside, put his face so close to hers that she could smell the rancid odour of addiction and yelled against the white noise: 'When you get out there, it's going to be loud.'

'Okay,' said Stacey.

'No, you don't understand,' Steve shouted. 'When you get out there, it's going to be LOUD!'

But Stacey didn't freeze up. She stood on the stage and couldn't stop smiling. She let the lights and the applause wash over her and knew in that moment that she wanted to perform on stage for a living.

Ostensibly, her job was play rhythm guitar and sing backing vocals, but her other role was caretaker. It was Stacey who packed Steve's bags when it was time to move on, Stacey who braided his long hair each night and combed it out for him each morning, Stacey who did his laundry and saw that he had a clean shirt to wear on stage, Stacey who helped him round the world.

They had arrived in Australia in the first week of August, an eccentric family grouping made odder by the addition of Teresa, Justin and Cole. From Sydney, they travelled up the coast to Newcastle, Surfers' Paradise and Brisbane. Initially, Steve was kept going by Buprenex (Buprenorphine Chlorydrate) an anti-depressant which was also effective as a narcotic antagonist. It had been prescribed for him by a doctor in Los Angeles. He couldn't get high on it but it did keep him from withdrawing. Unfortunately, Buprenex had addictive properties of its own and a host of unpleasant side-effects and Steve was annoyed to find that he couldn't use any amphetamines, barbiturates or marijuana while he was taking it.

In Sydney, the band stayed at the Sebal Townhouse in Kings Cross, the city's eclectic, electric red-light district. Razed to the ground in 2001 to make way for a new apartment complex, it was then still the legendary haunt of celebrities across the globe. They stayed there, partied there and indulged in all manner of excesses there. Steve made himself at home in the Sebal's big old elegant rooms and kept his head down until Teresa, Cole and Justin flew back to the States. Hours afterwards, he and Bucky Baxter hit Kings Cross in earnest. They walked through streets packed with revellers, past flickering XXX signs advertising strip joints and peep shows. Soon a smartly dressed woman approached Steve. She had the groomed, straitlaced appearance of a bank teller.

'Are you Steve Earle?' she asked.

'Yeah,' he drawled. He knew immediately what she was doing. There was no other reason for a woman to be out there – not on that particular street, at that time of night. He could see that that was her hook, looking like Anne Murray, all wholesome and in a suit.

'What are you doing?' she asked him.

'I'm looking for dope.'

'Well, no problem.'

Baxter was startled. 'What are *you* doing?' he said to the woman.

'I'm a whore,' she told him cheerfully.

From that point on, they were sorted. Steve recruited her to cop for him (not, as Stacey put it, for social reasons) and she came to his room regularly with 'the best dope in the world', heroin so strong he almost died. 'God, I worry about you,' she told him one morning when she knocked on the door to find he had already gone through the A$50 bag she'd brought him the evening before.

Stacey, meanwhile, was in agony with an ingrown toenail so infected she could barely walk. Steve, the prostitute and Baxter, all high, decided to operate on her toe. The memory still gives her shivers. 'I'm dead sober, I'm laying there and this prostitute's holding my foot and Steve's digging in my toe, because that's what you do. Because if I don't let them do it, it might hurt their feelings. Is that screwed up or what?'

Stacey was not the only person feeling rattled by events in Australia. Gillis was fairly jittery about Steve's chances of survival himself. 'His addiction was out of control at that point. It was really, really bad. I'd go to bed at night wondering if I'd get a phone call from somebody saying they'd found him dead in his room. Because that's how he was . . . Then we'd go and do a show and he'd be nodding off in the van with a cigarette in his hand and everybody was worried about whether he'd burn us out of the van or what was going on. As fucked up as he was, he still did brilliant shows, which always amazed me. After the show, I'd just tell the band, "Guys, look, we're not going into the dressing room. When you come off the stage we'll give you a towel. Towel down, we're going to get right in the van and go back to the hotel, because we can't stay here." I mean, it was almost like a bad movie for a while.'

Dope procured, Steve did his best to enjoy himself. Bands love Australia, he likes to say, 'because it's an island populated by beautiful women and ugly, stupid men. All you have to do to impress girls is not hit 'em.' Cheap Trick, Anthrax and Depeche Mode were all staying at the Sebal Townhouse, and the lobby was a regular parade of tattooed, raven-haired musicians, the sweet smell of marijuana smoke clinging to their clothes. Steve and the metalheads took great delight in torturing the effete members of the British band, Depeche Mode. All took a dim view of Depeche Mode's synthesizer pop and penchant for 'playing tapes and stuff and calling it live performance'.

But for the most part, Steve hung out with Stacey or was isolated in his room. 'I was sick a lot of that tour. If there wasn't any dope, I was sick.'

They crisscrossed the country in an uneven fashion, going to Melbourne and back to Sydney and then on to Perth, where they had sold 6,000 tickets in the local arena. Johnny Diesel, a huge star in Australia, opened for them. In Melbourne and Perth, where drugs were difficult to come by, Steve was wracked by cramps and flu, but it was in New Zealand, where there were no drugs to be found at all, that he was sickest. He remembers the night they played the town hall in Auckland as one of the most miserable of his career. It was 27 August 1990. Across the world came the news that blues legend Stevie Ray Vaughan had been killed in a helicopter crash in Southern

Wisconsin after playing a concert with Eric Clapton, Buddy Guy and Robert Cray. Junk-sick and stunned by the news, Steve played his heart out for the crowd.

They returned to Sydney and Steve was able to get back on to the street during their one-day layover and find enough drugs to function. Then came the flight from Australia to London – an entire day and night of stale air, miniature peanuts and glutinous food, made even longer because the Gulf War was raging. Steve took the precaution of pre-loading six syringes of heroin to last him for the journey. He was relatively unconcerned that the airport security personnel in Australia would discover them, reasoning that they were looking for metal rather than drugs, and he planned to use all of the heroin before he got to London. When the plane stopped to refuel in Bangkok, Thailand, he took the precaution of leaving his bag in the overhead locker when he went into the airport for a smoke. He might once have taken a gun through customs but he'd never taken drugs and he wasn't about to start.

When they landed in London, Steve was whisked straight from the airport to the flat of a friend who had promised to have some dope waiting for him. But he couldn't get high. The drugs in Australia had been so strong that not even heroin could keep the withdrawal sickness at bay.

It was a time of dread and trepidation. In between shows, everyone walked on eggshells. Dan was so preoccupied with keeping Steve alive that he felt his work was beginning to suffer – that shows weren't being advanced properly because there simply weren't enough hours in the day. He was a nervous wreck. 'I was convinced he was going to die of an overdose. I've never seen anybody do as much dope as he did in that time.' Since Steve wasn't exactly someone you could take aside and say, 'Look, buddy . . .' Dan and everyone else were helpless. Dan felt sorriest for Pat and Stacey. Pat, in particular, found it mind-boggling how slowly the addiction had seemed to come on until one day, like an evil vision, it was staring them all in the face. More than anything, it hurt him that his brother continued to claim that he only snorted heroin, didn't inject it. 'He'd go out of his way to convince me of that.' But Steve's bathroom visits were twenty minutes long and needles turned up everywhere. 'Steve, as things got further and further downhill, became less and less human . . . It got to a point where I hadn't had a real conversation with him in years.'

In the middle of it all, Steve's parents arrived from America. Jack had been embroiled in a new outrage at the FAA. He and his colleagues were informed that the present pension structure of the department was to be discontinued. The fund that they had been paying into for their entire careers would cease to exist the following year and anyone wishing to receive a full payout would have to retire immediately. Steve, who viewed the policy as beneath contempt and a poor excuse for trapping people into redundancy, was on the phone to Jack the moment he heard about it. He asked Jack how much he needed to clear all his debts and sent him that amount in cash, plus two air tickets to London.

As grateful as they were for Steve's generosity, the trip to the UK was a sobering experience for Jack and Barbara. For the first time they could see for themselves how much their son's addiction had progressed. Pat was too loyal to Steve to betray what he knew and Stacey, who Barbara later found out was 'doctoring his tracks – you know, putting make-up on his arms for the shows', was tight-lipped. But Barbara's experiences as an apartment manager had taught her how to recognize the symptoms of junkies. 'Touring with Steve, that's when we began to realize.'

The band played a comprehensive British tour. Their opening show was at the Civic Hall in Wolverhampton on 5 September, and they played Manchester, Liverpool, Nottingham, Cambridge, Leeds and Edinburgh in rapid succession before heading south again for three successive nights at the Town & Country Club in London. Boo Hewerdine, who saw Steve at the Corn Exchange in Cambridge, popped up to his hotel room to say hello. He walked in to find Steve 'chasing the dragon'.

'What are you soldering?' asked Hewerdine. Naïve in the ways of addicts, he imagined Steve was welding a piece of musical equipment, when he was actually 'hunched over a bit of gear'.

Nevertheless, the shows, as Dan said, were brilliant. Watching him play the Town & Country Club, sepia shots of the Old South behind him, the *Times* reviewer commented on how quickly the audience were put straight by the wall of five guitars that they had come to see a rock show, not a country one. Steve's voice completed the picture. 'Pitched somewhere between a snarl, a sneer, a grunt and a growl, it is truly one of the great rock vocals, the authentic sound of hard-bitten survival.'

In Ireland, Steve again found it impossible to lay his hands on any dope and had no choice but to detox. Sick and shaky, he did his best to get through the shows in Dublin and Belfast while playing tour guide to his parents during the day. Weaving through the emerald lanes, he fought down a mounting sense of panic. The day of reckoning was fast approaching. *The Hard Way* was not selling well at all. Outside of Canada, where sales would soon pass 115,000, most people didn't get it. Four short years on from the glory days of *Guitar Town*, *The Hard Way* never made it into the top 100 on *Billboard*'s pop album charts. 'Back to the Wall' had entered the rock charts at No. 49 in July and just barely limped to 37. And in the background, ever present, were the smoking ruins of past relationships – both personal and professional.

'When you have that much shit happen, you look up one day and go, "Goddamn, what did I do?"' Steve told one British journalist. '"What am I being punished for?" You start to develop a complex about it, and I was getting to that point.'

Even bassist Kelley Looney, who loved Steve and enjoyed the shows too much ever to be critical of him, realized there was something badly wrong at the first show in Canada in September when Steve arrived at the venue roaring drunk. 'He couldn't find any dope, from what I was told.' Kelly, who had rarely seen Steve drink let alone loaded up on whisky, was surprised but not overly concerned. 'He sort of had a rough night, I remember that . . . We still did the show but I remember, in particular, him saying, "Fuck God," into the mike and we were somewhere like New Brunswick, Nova Scotia.'

After that one wretched night, Steve seemed to find his equilibrium. He made it most of the way across Canada without using again. But the mood was set. At times it seemed as if a darkness had descended on the tour, almost as if some shadowy presence followed them, blighting their path. In Saskatoon, Saskatchewan, Dan had US$12,500 and Canadian $2,500 stolen from his room by two fourteen-year-old kids running a scam. They'd hang around the pool waiting for unsuspecting hotel guests to take a swim, steal their keys from underneath their towels or shoes, run upstairs and ransack their rooms. This particular hotel still had room numbers on the keys. When Dan realized he had been taken, he was absolutely devastated. Not only did it happen on his birthday, but the Royal Canadian Mounted Police immediately cast suspicion on the band and crew.

'It had to have been one of your people,' they told Dan, who knew beyond doubt that it was not one of his people.

When they had gone, Steve sat on the sofa in Dan's room trying to comfort him. Where another man might have reacted with anger, questioning his tour manager's actions and demanding to know how it could have happened in the first place, Steve was just sore on Dan's behalf. Dan vowed to come up with the money. 'It's my job, it's my responsibility,' he told Steve, but Steve wouldn't hear of it. 'Man, I do more dope than that in a week,' he said, only half joking. 'Don't worry about it.'

But Dan did worry about it. He pleaded with the RCMP to call the local schools and tell them to report back if any of their kids suddenly appeared with new bikes, clothes and other expensive treats. Two weeks later, the police phoned. They had caught the boys and recovered some of the money. Dan called Steve and told him he wanted to press charges.

'Don't prosecute those kids, Dan,' Steve told him gently. 'They're just kids.'

'Steve, this is a scam that they run,' Dan said. 'They did it the other week on a businessman. They stole $900 from the guy. This is a scam that they do with the pool and the key and the whole thing.'

'They did it last week and they did it the week before?' Steve asked.

'Yeah.'

'Burn 'em,' said Steve.

It amused Dan, Steve's natural inclination to side with the underdog versus the street-smart part of him that understood the dark side of human nature. 'Once he realized that these are just bad kids, these aren't kids that just happened on to something, these are kids that were doing this, scamming people, then he was okay about the fact that something should be done about them.'

But still the shadow followed them, looming over them, inserting its sinister tentacles into everything. It gave Dan the creeps when Steve and one of the other musicians played games, telephoning 'croakers' – the *Junky* term for doctors known by drug addicts to be a soft touch or open to persuasion for a price – and pretending to have kidney stones in order to get prescriptions. To the *Ottawa Citizen*, Steve admitted that it was becoming more and more of a stretch to be the regular guy people wanted him to be. 'I know that's why some people come to see me, they figure some of their hopes and concerns are in the music. But I was never too regular in the first place.'

Perhaps recognizing that their chances of getting a satisfactory studio album were greatly reduced at the present time, MCA had decided on a live album. A hits package had been shelved the previous year. *Shut Up and Die Like an Aviator* was recorded live on 5 and 6 October in Ontario at shows in London and Kitchener. The title came from the autobiography of aviation legend Chuck Yeager who, on his first combat mission in World War II, had witnessed a fellow member of his squadron being shot down. When the downed pilot saw death approaching, he started screaming hysterically. 'Shut up and die like an aviator,' the wing commander instructed him grimly over the radio. Nearly half a century later, political alienation, dissatisfaction and scorn for the Grim Reaper pervaded the choice of songs on Steve's album. They included 'Good Ol' Boy (Gettin' Tough)', 'Devil's Right Hand', 'West Nashville Boogie', 'Billy Austin', 'Copperhead Road' and a cover of 'Dead Flowers'. He dedicated the album to Gary Comeau, Rick Sauve, Tee Hee Hoffman, Gordy Van Haarlem, Merv Blaker, Jeff McLeod and Lorne Campbell of Satan's Choice Motorcycle Club 'for teaching me the meaning of the word solid'. References to Satan, death and drugs dominated his setlists. Standing on stage each night, Steve would grin malevolently as he growled his way through the autobiographical lyrics, savouring the idea of being in his 'basement room with a needle and spoon'.

Dan thought his voice was just horrible. 'You know, you do that much drugs, it affects your throat. He was sick and he'd been singing a lot. He didn't really have time to recover and his immune system was down. He was a mess. And trying to record the shows, it was brutal. It was a hard thing. And that record is not very good. It kills me, some people will say, "God, that's my favourite record." Because Steve will tell you, the band played good but his voice was shot.'

The days when Tony Brown politely suggested a headshot on the cover were long gone. *Shut Up and Die Like an Aviator* featured another skull and crossbones, this one superimposed over the burnt-out shell of a tour bus. It looked and felt like a death wish. Or a premonition.

*　　*　　*

In Canada, where the record was selling well, 'Justice in Ontario' had been released as a single and another video was planned for 'When the People Find Out'. 'In Canada, I'm Springsteen,' Steve told *NME*. But the Americans hadn't taken to the album at all and his manager Danny Heaps was struggling to find a way for Steve to keep touring. Since touring was Steve's lifeblood, relations soon became strained. Dan Gillis acted as mediator, communicating Steve's displeasure to Heaps via fax. 'Steve is one of those guys that if you show any kind of weakness, he can be predatory at times. If you show weakness, he'll pounce on that if he has to. And usually he's right when he does it.'

At the last minute, Heaps came up with a short Christmas tour with Los Lobos, where they would open for the band but receive co-bill money and play a three-hour set. They were in Vancouver when Los Lobos cancelled several of the dates for personal reasons. Bucky Baxter was enraged. He was counting on the *per diem* (the cash payment band and crew are given daily when they're on the road for food and incidentals) to make up his monthly budget. At nine a.m., he woke Steve up with an angry lecture about how the singer was fucking with his finances. When Steve could get a word in edgeways, he said: 'It's *per diem*, Bucky. It stands for *per day*.'

'I thought it stood for Pussy and Dope,' Baxter responded, incorrigible to the last.

Steve started to slam the door on him but thought the better of it. Baxter claims that Steve merely kicked at him 'like a girl' but Steve says he laid Bucky out with a couple of punches. Then he called Dan. 'Bucky's outside my door,' he said. 'Please come and get him.'

When the tour was over, several things happened that were to have lasting repercussions. First, Bucky Baxter, the longest-serving member of the Dukes, departed. The Dukes had been through several incarnations since their formation in 1983 for Steve's rockabilly phase, the best line-up being, arguably, the

Guitar Town Dukes with Richard Bennett. Nobody shed too many tears for the hedonistic Bucky Baxter (who would go on to work for Dylan and Ryan Adams), but it marked the end of an era. Baxter's eruption had been a symptom of the simmering discontent among band members, and most must have suspected, if not actually been convinced, that Steve's performing days were numbered.

The second thing that happened is that Stacey fled from Steve's house, too scared to go on another day. 'Everybody in my family was making me feel guilty. "No, you stay there, you've got a grand situation." I was like: "You really don't understand."'

Steve understood Stacey's abrupt departure least of all. 'Believe me, I have absolutely no problems with anybody washing their hands of me at that point. Everybody did and I totally understand why everybody did, but there's some other stuff that went on with Stacey caused a little distance between us for quite a few years. You know, she just called me one day and said she was moving out and all of a sudden I didn't have a base and the house just sat empty.'

Stacey's dreams had always been very different from Steve's. He had recognized her love of music by giving her the guitar he wrote *Guitar Town* on back in the Christmas of 1985, but her dreams of singing were only vague then and much smaller than the more immediate ones of a picket fence and food in the fridge. The *Hard Way* tour had changed that. Now she dreamed of standing on stage and of writing songs that moved strangers in the way her brother's did. How that went down is a matter of some dispute. What Steve remembers is that 'Stacey came back from the tour really driven and really obsessed with trying to get something going, which I totally understood. She basically went to some members of my band and said, "You know what, Steve's over with, he's never going to work again," and she basically tried to steal my band at a time when I thought I was going to get my shit together any minute and make a record, and there were some hard feelings about that.'

At least half of Steve's rage and disappointment in Stacey stemmed from the fact that he needed her and Patrick around, even if he had trouble communicating that to them. He missed the warm familiarity and unconditional love of his extended family. As a boy, he'd needed that security even as he'd run from it. Even after he moved to Nashville and was gone for months on end without so much as a forwarding address, he'd panic if any of the family did the same. After one such relocation, Kelly remembers him showing up wild-eyed at the door: 'You didn't tell me you were moving,' he kept saying. 'I didn't know where to find you.' Steve's visits to Jacksonville or to his parents' house in Houston were rare these days – he found it difficult to face them – but he needed Pat and Stacey more than ever.

Stacey, though, knew that she couldn't stay at Fairview any longer and keep her sanity. She had fallen in love with Mark Stuart, a Nashvillian singer-songwriter she had met at a writers' night, and she wanted to live her own life and pursue her own music. Being around Steve was too hard. 'Everyone loves Steve Earle but the true Steve Earle, and he knows it, was not a good person . . . So what he'd turn around and do, after he'd said something shitty, he'd go and buy you something or do something. Maybe *The Hard Way* was part of it, his way of saying sorry.'

Stacey wasn't the only sibling going through a crisis of confidence over their relationship with Steve. Pat had never lost the fear that the intervention had destroyed his relationship with Steve for ever. The New Year's Eve gig he did with Steve in San Francisco (where Jerry Lee Lewis refused to go on stage because he found out Steve was playing after him) was his last for five years. When it became obvious that there wasn't going to be any work coming up, he went back to Houston, which he still considered home. 'I finally got to a point where – I'll never say I gave up – but I pretty much left it up to powers bigger than me. We'd pretty much done all that we could and we were just killing ourselves. So I finally got married, got a straight job, went to work at the power company. I pretty much resigned myself to living a pretty normal life in Houston from here on out.'

While his family agonized over his addiction, guilt was eating Steve alive. Pain was a constant in his life, internal and external. He ached with drugs and ached without them. He ached with Teresa and ached without her. He ached for his children all the time. When he showed up at Lou's door after a nine-month absence, three-year-old Ian didn't recognize him and just burst into tears. Steve's heart nearly broke. He sat down on Lou's front porch and cried. 'He doesn't even remember me,' he said.

Lou was blunt: 'Steve, you haven't seen him in nine months,' she snapped. 'What do you expect?'

Carol saw even less of Steve. Her little boy hardly knew he had a dad. 'Steve gave us money but the money made no difference when it came to the emotional well-being of a child. I mean, I didn't know what to say to him. This is what I did say: "Your dad is making music and your dad provides money for you."

'"Where is my dad?"

'I said: "Son, I do not know. He's on the road somewhere, but he's doing the best he can."'

By 1991, each passing day lent further credence to Stacey's theory that his marriage to Teresa could have survived even crack if there hadn't been a third party in the relationship – Lou-Anne Gill. It was years before Steve realized that what really destroyed his marriage was the guilt he felt about being with Teresa when he had abandoned Lou and his children. Having children, he thought, was like 'somebody breaking off a piece of you and turning it loose in the world, and if it hurts, you hurt. You're forever altered once you have children, in one way or another.'

The opiates he turned to for relief were painkillers with euphoria thrown in. He reached for them to deal with the pain and guilt and then pain and guilt made him reach for them again. It was an endless cycle. In those harrowing days, there was only one place he found release. He had found it once, almost by accident, on a pilgrimage to see the bleakly beautiful wilderness where Gram Parsons died. Unexpectedly, perhaps, for a man so wedded to the temptations only a city could offer, Steve found peace in the emptiness of Joshua Tree's 794,000 acres. He would ride out there on his motorbike and watch the sun set over Key's View or Cap Rock. Alone in the creased, silent mountains, with only the roadrunners and twisted, fearless trees for company, the insanity seemed to stop for a while.

In Larchmont Village, Steve was writing the darkest songs of his career – when he could muster the energy to write at all. Songs like 'Hurtin' Me, Hurtin' You' and 'The Unrepentant' were shot through with pain and defiance and images of encroaching death and the hell that lay beyond it. In 'Hurtin' Me, Hurtin' You', the narrator loathes himself for being 'cruel and untrue' to the woman he loves, but knows himself well enough to admit that he'll do it time and time again. It is a naked plea for understanding. Since understanding is much more than he deserves, his only hope is to lay his weakness on the line and convince her that every time he hurts her, he hurts himself.

That same vulnerability and self-loathing is evident in the cold honesty of 'CCKMP' (Cocaine Cannot Kill My Pain). It is a song reminiscent of something the author William Gass once said: 'I write because I hate. A lot. Hard.' 'CCKMP' is 'My Old Friend the Blues' with the beauty and subtlety taken out. The pain that Steve discovered he was capable of revelling in when he wrote the latter has been taken to its ultimate extreme. By refusing to use lyrical subterfuge to disguise from the listener what he has become – a faithless lover, a hellbound outlaw, an unrepentant junkie – the protagonist in all three songs is giving us permission to hate him because he knows that we couldn't despise him as much as he despises himself.

Recording 'CCKMP' in the front room at Larchmont Village,

out of his mind on drugs, the natural echo in the house threw the words back at Steve spookily.

> Heroin is the only thing
> The only gift the darkness brings
> Heroin is the only thing.

He saw himself as a tortured artist, but art didn't bring him release. '"CCKMP" didn't exorcize any demons for me. I continued trying to kill myself for several years.'

Those three songs were the last Steve would write for nearly four years. Apart from the odd solo date at McCabe's Guitar Shop in Santa Monica, California, Poor David's Pub in Dallas or the Kerrville Folk Festival in Texas, he spent his time hanging around with other musician junkies. Teresa could hardly bear the sight of them. He still talked a good game but mostly it was only talk. When his management company put together a solo tour for him in England, he complied because he needed the money. There was no other reason for him to do it. He and Teresa had, at one stage, been making over $1 million a year between them. But Steve was in the grip of a habit that would ultimately cost him at least $200 in heroin and up to $400 in cocaine to get through a day.

At the height of summer, Steve and Dan Gillis set off in a rented Cadillac to do a few acoustic dates in the USA before catching the plane to London. On 21 June, the night Steve remembers as one of the most surreal he had ever spent, Dan dropped him in downtown Manhattan after a gig at Maxwell's in Hoboken, New Jersey. Steve was looking for Popeye – a cocaine addict prematurely aged by junk, his world-weary face as easily fifty-six as twenty-six. Popeye was on the slow side, but he was useful to an out-of-towner because he always had a handle on the heroin spots that moved like quicksilver ahead of the law. Steve wanted to buy crack off the street. Popeye suggested they buy cocaine and cook it. Steve confessed he didn't know how. 'I don't either,' Popeye said, 'but I can take you to someone who does.'

The night closed in with an inky finality. Popeye led the way to Alphabet City, a funky, down-at-heel mesh of streets on the Lower East Side that, until property started to boom in the neighbourhood, had always been the first refuge of the poorer sections of predominantly Eastern European and Puerto Rican immigrants. It was also the first port of call for white dope seekers who hadn't yet learned to cop higher-grade heroin on the meaner streets of Harlem. Eventually, Steve would. He and Popeye walked down Third St, between Avenue B and Avenue C, and stopped in front of a tenement building that had been condemned for as long as anyone could remember and certainly since the mid-eighties. Around the back were more condemned signs and a ladder that rose like Jacob's through a hole in the second floor before vanishing into the blackness. Upstairs was a gothic city of the dispossessed. They moved like wraiths through the catacomb of occupied rooms, witnesses to the feast. Steve and Popeye sat in the half-light before an old Jamaican woman with a moustache and watched her begin the elaborate business of cooking cocaine. First, she rolled the coke and baking soda in a dollar bill, then she dunked it in a test tube with a little water. Even before she heated it up, it snapped, crackled and popped like a dozen Alka Seltzers. The Jamaican woman held it up to Steve's ear. 'Ahh,' she said, 'listen ta the speeech!!' He stayed in that eerie netherworld until 5.30 in the morning.

Later that day, Dan saw him do drugs for the first and last time in their fifteen-year relationship. They were driving from New York to Boston when Steve deteriorated to the point where he could not last the journey without smoking crack. Dan had never judged him before and didn't judge him then. He wanted only to protect Steve and keep him alive. 'I never felt like I was part of his life to betray him . . . He's always taken care of me and I take care of him.'

*　　*　　*

Even as Steve's life disintegrated around his ears, his activism continued. In a way, it was particularly ironic that his daily courtship of death via drugs was set against a growing interest in the movement to save other people from death by abolishing capital punishment in the USA. As a boy, Steve had been strongly influenced by the execution of the young killers in Capote's *In Cold Blood* and by his mother's all-night vigils for Death Row inmates in Huntsville, Texas. His own involvement came much later. It began in 1989 when an acquaintance asked if he would consider corresponding with a Death Row inmate on Ellis Unit One in Texas. Steve agreed. Over the next three or four years, he wrote to several inmates. All were guilty of murder; one – Jonathan Nobles – became a regular pen pal.

When 'Billy Austin' was released in 1990, Amnesty International approached Steve about lending his name and music to the abolition movement. Steve went to Austin to march against the death penalty and played at the rally afterwards. In the shadow of the State Capitol, he lent a voice to the prisoners facing one of the most inhumane punishments on earth, asking their would-be executioners:

> Could you pull that switch yourself, sir
> With a sure and steady hand
> Could you still tell yourself
> That you're better than I am.

Since then, Steve's death penalty activism had continued at a low level. If anything, he was more focused on the fate of the jailed Satan's Choice motorcyclists. Performing at a 2 July rally in Ottawa, organized by Gary Comeau's sister, he spoke movingly to the 300-strong crowd, explaining that when another biker had confessed to the killing in the middle of the trial, the jury hadn't believed him. 'We have a responsibility to make our voice heard when we feel in our hearts something is wrong,' he said. He remains friends with all of the bikers to this day, including the man who actually pulled the trigger. 'He's actually a pretty nice guy. I don't agree with what he did but, given the culture he came up in . . . It basically was just he shot a guy who was holding a gun on two friends of his. And he had every reason to believe the guy was going to pull the trigger . . . It was the decision he made at the time and he's had a hard time living with it. He's been punished enough.'

In August, Steve and Dan flew to the UK, playing the Feile Festival in Thurles, Northern Ireland and then Leeds, Manchester, the Mean Fiddler in London and Norwich in rapid succession, accompanied only by Steve's guitars and a driver. All went relatively smoothly until the drug supply dwindled. With Steve too ill to perform, Dan arranged an unscheduled four-day break in Newcastle. 'Up until then, I don't think I'd ever cancelled a show. No matter how sick he was, whether from a cold or drugs, we always did the shows and the shows were always brilliant. I still loved the shows in 1991 as much as I did in 1986. I still do today. The shows, to me, never get tiring.'

Although the critics, for the most part, agreed, *The Times* thought he resembled Lemmy from Motörhead, with his moustache, sideburns and sallow complexion, and was a little bemused that someone who had enjoyed the acclaim Steve had should put on an 'unexpectedly rudimentary performance'. At one stage Steve told the audience that coughing was the only exercise he got. Still, critic John Street was captivated by Steve's voice, which was squeezed from his mouth and made the syllables elongate and the melody crack. 'It does not always work, but at its best Earle's voice gives a dignity to mundane experience and a sound to ordinary frustrations.'

They pulled into Leicester University on 15 August. When the opening act was on stage, Dan went back to the hotel to collect his charge. Steve was in his room, grey, weak and sweating.

'I can't do the show,' he said simply.

Dan took the news in his usual unflappable way. He called

a doctor – 'We had to have a doctor, otherwise we'd have been sued' – who confirmed what they already knew: there was no way on earth Steve could perform. In between sets, Dan went out and broke the news to the crowd and arranged for them to get their money back.

'There was a lot of disbelief in the sense that, how could it have got this far?' says Dave Howarth, who was entertainments manager at Leicester at the time. 'Is it just that he's had a bottle of Jack in his room or taken something that he shouldn't? But it was an older crowd so there was no riotous behaviour. They just had another drink and went home.' He received a doctor's note a couple of weeks later.

Dan cancelled their one remaining date, took Steve back to London and put him on a plane to LA, knowing intuitively that they had reached the end of a road.

'That's when he kind of started his downfall. At that point.'

It took Nick Wechsler Associates a little longer to arrive at the same conclusion. *Shut Up and Die Like an Aviator* was due to be released in September, and Danny Heaps was soon on the phone with another proposition. A big offer had come in from Prince Edward Island in Canada and another from the Winnipeg Folk Festival. Was Dan Gillis prepared to accompany Steve? Dan flew to Toronto and waited for Steve to arrive. But Steve wasn't on the plane. Nor was he on the next one or the next. Finally, Dan managed to get Teresa on the line.

'He's not going,' she said. 'He's got an ear infection.'

'Come on, Teresa,' Dan said wearily, 'I've been around a long time. Don't talk to me about ear infections.'

'He's not going to get on the plane,' she said.

Dan suspected that the real reason he wouldn't get on the plane was because Steve couldn't find drugs in Canada, but he knew Teresa would never admit that to him. 'So the day of the show I had to call the promoter on Prince Edward Island and go, "He's sick. He can't come." At that point, we cancelled the Winnipeg Folk Festival and it was over.'

*   *   *

At home in Larchmont Village, Steve had reached the stage where he was virtually unable to get on aeroplanes because he was unwilling to leave his neighbourhood and his dope source. He felt uncomfortable leaving LA. 'I literally got the O.J. Simpson award for arriving late for the limousines and planes that I did catch. I'd come back from getting dope and the limo would be sitting there and I'd have barely enough time to make the plane.' His failure even to get as far as the airport for the Canada dates was a shattering blow to what remained of his pride. Throughout the worst moments of sickness, the most nightmarish events in his personal life, he had always been able to perform. Now even that was gone.

'After that I gave up. From that point on, I was never the same again.'

He and Teresa occupied separate spheres. The emergence of Nirvana and the grunge movement meant that Seattle was exploding and Teresa and every other A&R person in the country was in Washington State 'trying to sign everything in a flannel shirt'. Left to his own devices, Steve concentrated on killing himself slowly. He'd spend all the money he had access to on dope and have none left for food. He'd go for days without showering. Weight melted off his bones. He began pawning guitars or anything he could get his hands on for crack. Life was miserable; music was worse.

Steve found it more and more difficult to complete projects, even when they were in his own neighbourhood. One assignment that fell by the wayside was a score he was supposed to be writing for a Stephen Frears film called *The Wild East*. Set in London, it was about a group of Asian kids who start a country band, and had several of Steve's songs in the script. Steve had the best of intentions but somehow he could never get around to it. There were not enough hours in the day.

In the music industry, rumours abounded about his condition. Pam Lewis, who managed country star Trisha Yearwood after her relationship with Garth Brooks went south, claims to have arrived at Trisha's debut album Gold Party at MCA in 1991 to find the room abuzz because 'the marketing guy' or somebody had walked in on Steve shooting up in the bathroom.

'Everybody was really worried. They were like, "We're going to find him on a slab somewhere." He looked awful. He'd lost all this weight and his teeth were really bad. People said that he would sit in the lobby at MCA for hours and just play his guitar and wouldn't leave and just be a fixture there.'

Steve has no memory of the MCA incident ever happening. He can think of no reason in the world why he would have gone to a Trisha Yearwood party at MCA. 'Nobody ever saw me do dope in the bathroom. I mean, if I shot dope in the bathroom, for somebody to see that they would have had to be standing on a toilet in the stall next door, looking over the top of the stall. You know what I mean?'

There are another two variations of the story, one of which has Steve shooting dope in the bathroom at a Virgin party in 1990 and another which has him shooting dope in the limo on the way to the party.

'No one else was in the limo but me and Teresa and I didn't shoot dope in front of Teresa. Teresa never saw me shoot dope and I lived with her.'

But that situation was always unlikely to last. The tacit understanding the couple had where Teresa would tolerate Steve's dope use, provided he was only smoking or snorting it, was destroyed when she came home to find Steve sitting at the kitchen table with a junkie friend, cooking up a speedball. He didn't have a needle in his arm but there was a syringe lying in front of him, ready to be used. He knew he had crossed a line, but it was a line he had never really understood. 'Shooting dope was where everything seemed to change for her.' It was as though by agreeing to come as far as she had with him, she was sanctioning his drug habit – by her actions if not her words – and to condemn it at this late stage was hypocritical.

*   *   *

Steve made one more attempt to work in 1992. In November, he started production on an album he'd been commissioned to produce for Virgin with a band called the Immigrants. In essence it was a solo project for Michael Aston, who had found fame singing with his twin brother Jay in the British glam/goth band, Gene Loves Jezebel, but Steve had been asked to help him put a band together. Curiously, while Steve sums up Aston as a 'little fuck-you teabag shit', Aston's memories are largely good: 'It was a wonderful experience.' The music with which Aston was associated made Steve an unlikely choice as producer, but both he and Virgin A&R man Mark Williams believed in Steve's genius as a writer and musician and had fought hard for his appointment in the face of considerable opposition.

Over the next couple of months, Aston wrote with Steve regularly and liked him and his politics a great deal. It was only when they took a break in December and Steve reappeared seeming to have lost 100 pounds that Aston realized the extent of his drug addiction. He was shocked. From that point on Steve's behaviour grew increasingly erratic. At rehearsals, he would be unstintingly gung-ho one minute and incandescent with fury the next. There were murmurings of alarm at the label. Two days before they were due to start basic tracks, Virgin held a dinner party for the band and their partners at Le Dome, the Sunset Strip restaurant where Richard Gere works his mojo in *American Gigolo*. Eyewitness accounts have it that Steve turned up an hour late, wearing the dreamy, unconcerned look of an addict who has just shot up. He sat down and pitched face forward into his food.

According to Aston, he was fired the next day – 'Not by me, by Virgin, but it put me in a terrible predicament.' Steve says he quit the night before basic tracks started when he was told that the band he'd hired with promises of long-term work was to be laid off after recording. He told himself he was doing it out of principle but admits that his decisions were becoming 'much more radical and much more suspect because I was pretty loaded all the time'.

Aston, whose career was irreparably damaged by this episode, disputes this version utterly. 'He's in fantasy world. It was *my* band and the band would have continued with me.' As far as he was concerned, far from taking a stand on behalf of the musicians, most of whom toured with him for the next two years, Steve 'actually owes four or five people a major apology'.

By now, Steve was leaving a trail of unspoken apologies behind him every time he left the house. At Christmas, he had gone home to Nashville, mostly to see Justin. He avoided family gatherings as much as possible these days. Waiting at the house of his maternal grandmother, nine-year-old Justin heard him before he saw him. 'He shows up late, real real late, and he's drunk out of his mind and wearing a Santa Claus hat with a Malcolm X symbol on it. And the door comes open and I'm sitting here and I hear: "Ho, ho, ho, mutherfucker." And you know, my very Southern, very God-fearing, Church of God grandmother wasn't too happy about that. She wasn't happy about it in the least. I remember getting up off the couch and stepping around her and looking at him . . . and he was my size exactly. I was about six feet tall at that point and just wiry as hell. And I remember just looking at him and his arms were as big as mine and his waist was as big as mine.'

It was a short visit. Shortly after blustering in, Steve locked himself in the bathroom. When he eventually emerged, the entire family were clustered anxiously around the door. They made it clear he had worn out his welcome.

From there, it was a speedy slide to rock bottom. Debauchery, once a tool of creativity, had taken over from it. In the final days of 1992, Dan Gillis received a phone call from a Nashville club owner, T, who had dealt Steve drugs from time to time. 'What time are you coming in for sound-check?' T demanded. 'Steve Earle just called me and said that he and Teresa are driving cross country and you're going to come in and do soundcheck on New Years' Eve.'

'I don't know anything about a New Year's Eve show,' Dan said abruptly. The man made his skin crawl. 'I haven't seen Steve in however long. I don't know what you're talking about. He's never called me.'

'Well,' said T, 'he's playing New Year's Eve. He talked to me on the phone and said you were going to take care of it. We've found a couple of guitars.'

Not wanting to let Steve down, Dan went to the club in time for soundcheck on New Year's Eve. Steve and Teresa eventually showed up at two o'clock in the morning. New Year's Eve had come and gone and the fans were furious. Steve drove away into the frosty darkness, rail-thin, haggard and high. It was the last time Dan would see him for two years.

13

Vacation in the Ghetto

It was late evening when the Jehovah's Witnesses came calling. They had been out to Fairview before; their visits so frequent at one point that Steve had hoisted a Jolly Roger on the flagpole in the front yard in the hope of scaring them away. It had worked very well for a while but now, with impeccable timing, they were back again. They climbed the steps like scruffy angels and appeared at the front door.

Steve was not in good shape. He had been awake for eleven days. He had finally become so notorious with the local police that he'd decided to buy a quarter of a kilo of cocaine, put out a few ounces for people to sell and retire to Fairview for a while. On this particular evening, he had decided to indulge himself by cooking up a rock of crack in the microwave. He was preparing to smoke it when the electricity went off. When the Jehovah's Witnesses arrived, the only light in the room was a candle burning in a human skull on the coffee table. Steve was sitting cross-legged on the living-room floor in the flickering darkness, his back against the couch, contemplating his crack pipe.

'Y'all come on in. Have a seat,' Steve called cheerfully.

They came in fearfully and perched gingerly on the edge of a couple of chairs.

'Y'all are Jehovah's Witnesses, right?'

'Yeah.'

'Cool,' drawled Steve. He took a long, noisy drag at the pipe. 'So I heard from somebody that y'all think that there's only a finite number of people that are going to get into heaven.'

'That's right,' the man nodded eagerly. 'Only 144,000. That's the number.'

'Oh,' murmured Steve. He sucked and slurped at the pipe. 'So how come you're all out recruiting?'

They were, he laughed, 'off like a prom dress'.

Steve's self-described 'vacation in the ghetto' had been a long slow journey into hell which had started in the City of Angels and would, he was fairly confident, end in the grave. Teresa had helped him on his way. In the last gasps of the California winter in 1992, they had taken their last ride together. Steve hadn't known then that it was their last ride. Teresa had loved him and put up with his 'junkie shit', as he referred to it, for so long it hadn't occurred to him that she might want him back in Nashville, or at least in Texas, close to his parents, so she didn't have to watch him die on the streets of her town.

In 'Doghouse Roses', the opening story in Steve's book of the same name (Houghton & Mifflin, 2001), country-rock singer Bobby Charles is taken to Texas by his soon to be ex-wife, Kim. Whether written as confession or apologia to Teresa, the parallels between Bobby's and Steve's own life at the time are so close as to be almost identical. Steve concedes that the story is 'ninety per cent' autobiographical. Like Steve, Bobby lived in Larchmont Village in LA but felt most at home on the forty-foot eagle bus he shared with his band and crew. Like Steve, he had enrolled in a methadone programme and 'woke up early every morning to line up at the clinic with the other "clients" to take communion at the little window – a plastic cup of the bitter powder dissolved in an orange-flavoured liquid, chased by water from the cooler'. Freed from the need to go heroin shopping on Hoover Street every day, Bobby and Steve told themselves and anyone who would listen that they were back on track and ready to make the next record, even though they hadn't written a song in years.

The similarities don't end there. Kim – coincidentally the name of one of Teresa's closest friends – grew up in St Louis; Teresa grew up in Louisville. Like Teresa, Kim is a record executive, drives a BMW and has kept her last name after marrying for professional reasons. Both Steve and Bobby first tried heroin as teenagers in San Antonio and suspect that, when they first met their lovers, dope was part of their mystique.

> 'It made him seem more dangerous, and after all, she was slumming. It stopped being cute when money started turning up missing from *her* account, or when he called her at work, whacked out of his skull and thoroughly convinced that their little craftsman bungalow in Larchmont Village was surrounded by police. Kim, having little or no experience in such matters, immediately called her lawyer and rushed home to find Bobby hiding in the hall closet with a loaded shotgun and a crack pipe. When she opened the door and stood there in tears, Bobby only stared back and demanded, indignantly "What?"'

There was no fiction to screen Teresa or Steve from the reality of the situation as they headed out of LA in the BMW on that fateful evening in 1992. They may have made a detour to collect cigarettes, crack or even 'doghouse roses' (cheap roses bought as a late night apology or a sheepish 'I love you' at the only shop that's still open), but by and large Teresa was concerned with getting Steve as far away from LA as humanly possible. She had lost her job at MCA when it had been bought out by the Japanese. Steve had already been 'released' from his MCA contract. Within weeks, Teresa had closed down the house at Larchmont Village and told Steve that a break would do them good. Driving through the grey scrub of the California Desert, Steve suddenly decided that they should spend the night in Joshua Tree National Park. The infinite stillness of the desert always left him feeling as lonely and exposed as the character in his story, as if 'something out there could purge him of a life's collection of demons and leave them exposed and writhing on the sand'. But nothing ever did. In this latest clash of wills, Teresa, for once, won out. Perhaps her resolve to drive on was just stronger. When morning came, the crack pipe was still in Steve's hand and the guilt still in his heart and he and Teresa were in the BMW and on their way to Houston.

It was in Houston that Teresa finally left him. They had dinner with his parents and, when Steve went out for cigarettes, she packed her bags and drove away. He came back to find his parents sitting there, 'really hurt and scared and not understanding what was going on'. Steve borrowed his dad's car and went out to score crack.

Teresa's plan was to go to Nashville, gather her belongings and shut the house up, and return to Kentucky. But Steve was Teresa's addiction, just as he had been Lou's. He called her from Houston and 'begged and pleaded' for four or five days until she finally sent him an air ticket. The real end came within two months. It was Easter. Steve had gone downtown to his crack den and somehow Teresa figured out where he was. She parked outside and demanded that he come out or she was going to take his car and go.

'Okay,' Steve shouted, 'fuckin' leave me here.'

Not even the thought of losing her jolted sense into him. 'I was just so hard-headed by that time that whenever anybody did anything it just made me worse.'

Teresa filed for divorce on 28 April 1992 and packed up her possessions and moved out of Fairview. Steve had been living on the street since Easter. In a 'last-ditch attempt' to get him to stop using, she cancelled all his credit cards. Then she called Lou and Steve's parents and told them that she couldn't do it any more. She confided to Lou that she'd been seeing a therapist. 'Get your life together and get away from him,' Lou advised her.

Barbara was worried sick about her son but did her best to console Teresa. 'I told her that we understood. That we would never ever hold that against her. Nobody could do it. She had to save herself at that point.'

It was the beginning of the most horrific period of Steve's life. In the ensuing months he divided his time between the crack dens of South Nashville and the now defunct Travellers' Motel in Nashville, which he used as a base rather than a place to lay his head. Sleep had a tendency to cost guests their possessions. Most days Steve simply took the city's well-kept highways to Murfreesboro Road, every block taking him further from the Nashville of legend – churches and rhinestones and wholesome young cowboys in blue jeans – to country's equivalent of hell. Down in South Nashville, the streets resounded with a sullen silence. Hardly a soul moved and those who did cast strangers quick, shuttered glances and resumed their lethargic strides. Even in summer, the air had a coldness that had nothing to do with the weather. It hung above the streets like a winter fog, crept into the heart like hopelessness. Watching warily for police, Steve would ease his car past the white clapboard house of the dealer who features in 'South Nashville Blues' ('The devil sits on Lewis Street I swear/I seen him rockin' in his rockin' chair') and pull up outside a crack den. Inside he could spend days and even weeks in a state of suspended animation, poised between sleep and guilt and bleak, painful highs, too far gone to give any thought to the life he'd left behind, the family he'd abandoned, the Springsteen-sized career he had held in his hand and somehow contrived to throw away.

Often the house at Fairview just stood abandoned, the front door left open. Stacey and Mark Stuart were living on Benton Avenue in Nashville, close to what Steve liked to call the 'war zone', so he spent a great deal of time with them. How much time he spent there is again a matter of contention. According to Stacey: 'Steve basically just moved in with us, but I cannot tell you what an adventure that was.' Steve insists that he spent maybe 'three nights with them. *Ever*. I'd come and crash there sometimes. I came and borrowed money for dope. They *saw* a lot of me.'

It was one of the lowest times of Stacey's life too. Her marriage had drawn to a painful conclusion and she was raising two children on the money she made waiting tables. In the evenings, she pursued her dream, doing the rounds of Nashville's songwriters' nights. Steve gave her advice in the form of lengthy harangues. He worried that the endless writers' nights were too hard on her, that they sapped her creativity without rewarding her. Didn't she realize, he would lecture her, that playing less might be better? Stacey was wounded to the marrow by these criticisms. 'People always ask me, "Was Steve a big supporter and a reason that you're doing this?" Yes, because he took me on tour and gave me a taste of it, but there was no help there. If anything, I couldn't play my songs because he wasn't going to have anything nice to say.'

Eventually, Steve's old friend and guitar tech Chip Phillips pulled her aside and reminded her that Steve was a student of Townes Van Zandt's uncompromising vision. He wasn't capable of being lenient with his sister because he had learnt from the man he considered 'the best job God ever did of making a songwriter' that the art required blood, sweat and all the tears one was capable of crying. Added to which, Steve was incapable of encouragement because 'I was just in the process of dying. So I really didn't have anything to offer anybody.'

All the same, Stacey's ardent songwriting and efforts to get a career going continued to be a source of tension between them. It made Steve feel weird when Stacey started to talk about cutting some demos and contacted several of the members of the Dukes. She even talked to Dan Gillis about managing her. It was as if she was stepping into a dead man's shoes. Steve was still around and yet she was taking over his old life. He knew it was ridiculous to think that way, but it was a bitter pill to swallow – made worse because he no longer had a record deal himself. In May 1992, the multi-million-dollar offers from Virgin and Mercury had fallen by the wayside after Steve's non-appearance in New York. Even as the label executives gathered around a shiny boardroom table in Manhattan's elegant Essex Hotel, Steve was selling his ticket for $100 at Nashville airport and heading out to buy crack. Not that David Simone knew that at the time. Instead, he sat there distraught, fearing the worst. His own brother was a recovering heroin addict and he couldn't stand to think of Steve entering the same hopeless spiral. He wanted to plead with Steve to get himself help, but he never had the chance. Steve went back to Fairview and didn't answer the phone for three days. Not even crack could mask the devastation he'd felt when he reached the boarding gate at Nashville airport with one certainty in his mind: 'I knew I didn't have another record in me.'

Dying, and the energy it took to pursue death, consumed him. When Teresa left in April, she'd tied up his money in the hope that it would slow down his supply of drugs. But Steve simply hit the pawn shops again. When his guitars and motorbikes had gone, he turned once again to Lou. Lou was in fact engaged but she was especially vulnerable. Her beloved father had died in June 1991 after a gruelling battle with cancer and it had hit her very hard. After the funeral, she and the kids had moved into a little apartment attached to her mother's house in Whites Creek and tried to rebuild their lives. Steve had always been in the background, as a friend, foe or intermittent lover. He'd call her up from LA sometimes and leave songs he'd written on her answerphone. They still got mad at each other every now and then but they never really lost touch. Lou was the one person in Steve's life who had never tried to encourage him to quit drugs – perhaps because she knew it wouldn't work, or perhaps, as Steve would later suggest, because she loved the helpless junkie in him. But Lou had moved on and was sure she was over him.

When Steve telephoned her that spring, after a long silence, he had a request. Since he no longer had a bank account, would Lou mind if he had some money wired into her account so he could obtain it that way? Reluctantly, Lou agreed. Steve was elated. 'I had a whole car load of African-American criminals and I drive out to Whites Creek and I see Ian for the first time in two years. I was really upset that Lou had brought him without thinking what I might look like because I'd been on the street. I was getting cash to buy a relatively large quantity of drugs, most of which I gave away to these people. They *got* it, they procured it, but I paid for it. They did more of it than I did before it was over with.'

When Lou saw Steve's wasted frame and abscessed arms, she felt ill with sadness. 'I'd wished bad things on this man because of all the things he had done to me but I never would have wished anything that bad on him. He was tormented. He was the walking dead.'

On 29 September 1992, Steve was on his way out to Fairview after several days on the street when he was pulled over with a broken tail-light. He was at the wheel of a friend's car at the time, driving with a suspended licence. Much to his surprise, the police didn't book him but merely asked if he was on his way home. At dawn, they showed up at his door. A Williamson County Sheriff's deputy and a Fairview cop arrested him for failing to show up for jury duty in July. Steve was not amused. He'd had an hour and a half's sleep in six days. At five in the morning he was sitting at the station in handcuffs, waiting to be booked. 'Here comes this guy I've never seen before, acid washed jeans, white sneakers, black t-shirt with the sleeves rolled up, big pumped-up arms, the worst mullet you've ever seen – a real 'Achy-Breaky' haircut at the height of 'Achy-Breaky'. He's got a clipboard and a pistol in his belt. He says, "Steve, I'm so and so from the 21st Judicial

District Drug Taskforce. Just want you to sign this and we can go out to your house and pick up whatever drugs are out there." I said, "Fuck you . . . I'm a taxpayer. Go and earn your salary. Go to the judge at nine o'clock and get a warrant.'"

They did exactly that. When Steve was released from jail later that day, after Lou had paid the $1,000 bond, he found his house torn 'all to shit'. They confiscated some 'camping equipment' (records show that they found a butane burner, a burnt spoon, glass pipes and [traces] of cocaine) and a police shotgun, which had been given to Steve by a friend in the Fairview police department. The man later lost his job over the incident. Steve appeared in court on 12 October before Circuit Judge Cornelia Clark. His impression was that the law were a little miffed at not finding anything more damning.

'Judge,' Steve said, 'I can save the taxpayer a lot of money. If I'm home and I'm asleep, I'm out of dope, it's that simple.'

Nothing ever came of it but Steve decided to lay low for a while and he spent more and more time at Lou's. Lou tried to run him off – 'I didn't want to get sucked back into his craziness' – but somehow he always wormed his way back into her affections.

Teresa also lingered like a drug in his system. Steve still received the occasional royalty cheque from his business manager in LA and once, flush with cash, he checked into a motel and persuaded Teresa to drive down from Louisville, Kentucky, to see him. A few weeks later, he checked into the same motel and rang Teresa and begged her to come and stay with him once more. She refused. Steve told her that if she came back to him, he would go into treatment. 'I did put a condition on it. And originally she agreed. And then she called me back and said, No – if I was going to go into treatment, it needed to be for me. I wasn't willing to do that. That was the closest I ever came.'

But still Steve could not bring himself to let Teresa go. He was staying periodically at Lou's house but thoughts of golden-skinned Teresa, with her agile mind and loyal heart, could keep him pacing the rooms until dawn. When Steve could bear to be away from her no more, he borrowed Lou's truck and drove to Louisville. It would be the last time he ever laid eyes on Teresa. Driving home the next evening, he was in turmoil, his head a scarlet haze of pain, crack smoke and tiredness. Sleep taunted him. The drugs had kept it at bay for several days. Steve put his foot on the accelerator and shot through the night doing 80 m.p.h. The red mist swirled across his vision. Sleep finally overtook him. The truck left the road and Steve was dimly aware of flashing lights and the scream of collapsing metal. When he came to, he was unscathed. The truck was totalled. Steve had no choice but to telephone Lou and confess that he'd been to Kentucky. Lou immediately called Teresa and told her that Steve had been in an accident.

'So what,' retorted Teresa. She did ask whether he was still alive.

Their divorce came through on 17 November 1992. Teresa asked only that Steve give her the 1991 BMW M-5 and repay, through his business manager, Larry Einbund, the $25,000 she had put down on the house at Fairview. He was to pay three mortgage payments in advance and if he ever fell more than two payments behind, he was to put the house on the market immediately. If he sold it in the future, he was to give her half of the proceeds.

Stacey ached for her brother but she was torn. He had taken her last $13 after she had told him she needed it to feed the kids. She sent the kids to Texas to be with their father and talked to a couple who specialized in drug addiction and recovery. They were prepared to treat Steve privately if he wanted to be helped. Stacey was determined that Steve should have a loving Christmas, free of drugs.

'Why don't we go and spend Christmas out at Fairview?' she begged Steve. 'Let's go and get you clean. Let's go for broke, let's clean up.'

At first, Steve was unwilling to co-operate. He wanted to get clean but he didn't believe it was possible. Finally he agreed.

A couple of days before Christmas, Stacey and Steve set out for Fairview, stopping *en route* to get groceries. When Stacey came out of the store, Steve was in the driver's seat. 'We're going to get some rock,' he informed Stacey. They drove to crack alley, where a couple of dealers attempted to sell Steve soap in the guise of rock. A police car prowled up. Steve hit the gas. At Fairview, Stacey told him firmly: 'You agreed to do this and we're going to do it.'

The homestyle treatment was a disaster from beginning to end. One member of the assembled party felt sorry for Steve and somehow he ended up in town buying crack with his crackhead buddy Ty. A furious Stacey let the air out of everyone's tyres. There was a notable absence of Christmas cheer. On Christmas Eve, Stacey extracted solemn promises from everyone to continue with the treatment and flew to Houston to see her children. She spent four hours with them and caught another plane back to Nashville. At Fairview, the house was silent. Mark was by himself. 'Soon as you left it all fell apart,' he told her shamefacedly. Steve had decided to attempt the thirty-mile journey to Nashville on foot and everyone else had gone home. Steve spent Christmas Day alone.

The New Year came with no lifting of the gloom. There was no respite from the endless drama. Stacey was exhausted, sick of being everyone's mother. She wrote 'Show Me How' about that feeling – 'Just let me be weak for a change.' In February 1993, or thereabouts, she came home from work to find Steve smoking rock in the house. The previous day her epilepsy had reared its head and she was convinced that crack smoke had been a contributing factor.

'Let's tell Steve we're going to a movie,' she whispered to Mark, 'and let's go to a hotel and just take a twenty-four-hour break. I need some clean air and I need to make things stop.'

They checked in to the La Quinta Inn and tried to settle in for a quiet evening. But Stacey couldn't relax. She felt guilty about lying to Steve, guilty about leaving him on his own. She fretted that he was turning the house upside down. 'We're talking about someone who was completely unstable. He'd convulse sometimes, so I had to worry about that.'

An hour or so after checking into the hotel, she asked Mark to call the house.

'Hello,' Steve growled into the receiver.

'We're just checking up on you,' Mark said brightly. 'We're still at the movie.'

'Don't come home.'

'What?' said Mark in astonishment.

'Lou just called the police and they're coming to the house,' Steve reported. 'I have Lou's dad's gun.'

For Stacey, it was the opening scene in her worst nightmare. Agitated in the house by himself, Steve had decided to go and visit Lou, only to discover that her fiancé had had the same idea. An argument quickly brewed.

'You have to leave,' Lou told Steve. 'I have another life. I can't do this any more.'

Steve flew into a rage. According to Lou, he yelled at her fiancé: 'This is my wife, you're not marrying her. She's still my wife, she's the mother of my children.'

Then he slammed out of the house. Perhaps to get his own back, he took a gun belonging to Lou's father with him, intending, Lou believes, to hock it. The next thing Lou knew, Stacey was on the phone telling her Steve was going to kill himself. After that, events are blurred in Lou's mind. 'All I know is that I ended up on the phone with Steve when [the police] were knocking on the door.'

Mark was convinced that unless they intervened in the situation the police would just enter the house and shoot Steve. He and Stacey rang the station and pleaded with the police to meet them four blocks from the house so that they could explain the situation. At midnight, Texas time, Stacey called her parents and finally admitted to them the extent of Steve's addiction. Then she called Steve's attorney.

At an agreed time, she and Mark set off to meet the police. 'I would put my life ahead of his that he would never physically harm anybody,' Stacey told them. She asked them to consider taking him to Vanderbilt Hospital and putting him under twenty-four hours' observation, or to hold him for a day on a couple of minor charges so that her parents had time to fly to Nashville.

The police were full of polite reassurances. They popped the couple into the back of a squad car and drove them to the house. Once there, Stacey and Mark were outraged to discover they were locked in the car. There was nothing they could do but watch helplessly as several SWAT team officers, arranged around Stacey's yard in sinister gun stances, edged closer to the house, screaming at Steve to open the door. Steve was incapable. He had pulled out the key and managed to lose it. He yelled at the cops to come around to the back door, they yelled at him to open the front. The decibels rose. Inside the squad car, Mark shouted until he was hoarse that he had a spare key. The hysteria was such that he was convinced the police were about to start shooting.

All of a sudden it went quiet. Through the fogged-up windows of the squad car, Stacey and Mark could see the cops enter the house and start negotiating. It was freezing and they shivered as they waited. Moments later, Steve emerged from the house on his own. He walked away unchallenged down the road, a lonely figure breathing mist into the darkness.

A couple of deputies strolled up to the squad car window. 'Well, he's gone,' one announced.

'What do you mean, he's gone?' Stacey said incredulously.

'We told him you wanted him out of the house. That *is* what you wanted? He's gone. You don't have to worry any more.'

'We don't want him out of our house,' cried Stacey. 'He'll get hurt out there. He's got nowhere to go.'

'We had nothing to hold him on,' the deputy told her.

'What do you mean, you had nothing to hold him on?' Stacey said, suspecting, even as she said it, that they had let him go because he was Steve Earle. 'He's got a stolen gun, he's got drugs in there . . .'

The deputy gave her an icy stare. 'Ma'am, the guns and drugs are in *your* house,' he said warningly. 'You've got five minutes to get in there and dispose of all of them drugs before we put *you* under arrest.'

Much to her mother's dismay, Lou took Steve in now, at the worst stage of his addiction. According to her brother-in-law John Dotson, it caused a huge rift in the family and Lou and her mother didn't speak for months. Steve had hurt Lou more than anyone else in her life, but she still loved him and she wanted desperately to help him. She fed him and cut his matted hair and rubbed antibiotic cream on his arms. She also enlisted the aid of Dotson, who remained Steve's biggest fan. In 1986, during his time as an agent at William Morris, Dotson had taken Steve on as a client at a stage when no other agent would touch him and had done his best to book him into good venues. A spruce, impeccably groomed man, with a determined fiery streak, he loved Steve's music unreservedly. When *Guitar Town* went to No. 1, Dotson was elbowed aside within the organization and it was a crushing blow to his pride. A more senior agent took on Steve's account and Dotson fumed over the incident until he left William Morris three years later. At the beginning of 1993, he set up his own management company. When Lou approached him in February with a couple of Steve's unrecorded songs, he had just signed his first client, a football coach.

Steve was in a desperate state but he still managed to project confidence. He'd visited Tony Brown's office on South Street once or twice to make phone calls and Tony had been struck by his attitude. 'He was a rail. It was skin against skeleton. And he was still just as aggressive like, "I rule the world." It wasn't like he walked in like a frail old man. He was frail but he came in there to kick my ass.'

Steve and Dotson went back and forth over the question of management for some weeks, Steve testing Dotson to see how badly he wanted the job, Dotson wondering if he had lost his mind. He distinctly remembers the moment he decided to take Steve on. 'He was at my house and, as you know, he paces incessantly and he was just going around and around in a circle. And my son, who was three at the time, was sitting at the coffee table, colouring. Steve was upset about something and he was yelling. Max, in a really small voice, asked Steve to look at what he was colouring. Steve stopped in his tracks, got down on his knees and praised him and gave him very gentle encouragement and made a suggestion to him and waited till Max went back to doing his thing and picked up again in mid-sentence where he was and started yelling again. But what that told me is, there's a pretty significant crust here but the heart and soul is alive in there and that's where his artistry comes from. I thought, I've got to do this.'

With that, Dotson opened his door to the madness. One of his first actions was to give Steve an electric guitar. Steve no longer owned a guitar and it was Dotson's belief that, for a songwriter of Steve's stature, that was a crime against nature. Within three weeks the electric guitar had been hocked like all the rest, never to be seen again. It wasn't long before Dotson's wife began to lose patience with his new fixation. It was not unheard of for them to return home to find Steve sitting in the driveway, hoping, Dotson suspected, for cash to buy drugs. 'I was spending my money with no guarantee I'd ever see it again. My wife resented that. He and she really got at cross purposes. She did not like the way he treated me. She didn't want him around the house. I was presented with a choice: it's him or it's me. She and I were not in a happy place at the time and it was probably an exit looking for a scene.'

In May, Steve was arrested again, this time driving the car Lou had rented. He had gone with a cocaine addict friend to score heroin and was dropping him off on Murfreesboro Road in a known drug sale area when the police came round the corner. When they saw a black man standing at the window of a car driven by a white man, they put two and two together. Steve was given a misdemeanour charge for driving without a licence with a 'heroin-appearing substance in the ashtray' and a needle in the glove box.

Undeterred, Dotson set about booking a little acoustic tour. Steve was in dire need of money and Dotson felt it would be relatively straightforward to line up thirty or forty dates, fly in, rent a car and drive to the venue. Dotson would act as attorney, publicist, accountant and tour manager and together they would reconstruct Steve's tattered career. There were two small obstacles. The first was that Steve relished making trains and planes by the narrowest of possible margins and appeared to revel in actually missing them. It never seemed to occur to him that there was a price to pay for changing the tickets. He told Dotson that there would be severe consequences if he was tricked about the departure time. Dotson found that Steve's first action upon arriving at the airport terminal would be to check what the scheduled departure time was, 'because if it was really 11.30 and I had told him 11.00, we were going to have an unpleasant day. I was going to have an unpleasant day one way or the other, it just depended on what the unpleasantness was from – the cost of rebooking or him being unhappy about being tricked.'

The other problem was that Steve was having anxiety attacks again. On several occasions he called Dotson from the roadside after pulling over, convinced he was having a heart attack. He would be sure he was dying and insist that Dotson call an ambulance. When the tour began, the attacks occurred regularly. On 25 July, when Steve was due on stage at the Birchmere in Alexandria, Virginia, he refused to come out of his hotel room. Dotson pleaded with him through the door for forty-five minutes before he emerged and the show went on. In Los Angeles, they weren't so lucky. Steve never emerged at all.

August brought another charge for possession. Lou, who was living at Fairview again, was on tenterhooks. 'I don't want to make it sound like I was a victim. I wasn't. I chose that. And I don't know why . . . I think I felt sorry for him. I mean, I genuinely loved the man.'

Lou hadn't wanted to move in with him but Steve had 'begged and pleaded' until finally she had given in, like she almost always did. Steve admits that 'She was scared to do it. There were days when she had a lot better sense and did *not* want to do it.'

They were married for the second time on 13 September, Lou's birthday. Stacey found Steve a clean shirt and then she, Mark, Steve and Lou went down to Fourth Avenue to pick up Ty, Steve's crack buddy. He was standing on the street corner and he too needed a clean shirt. Eventually they made it to the courthouse, having first stowed a supply of rock so that Ty and Steve could get through the day. Stacey found the whole experience utterly bizarre. 'I'm the bridesmaid, I guess, Ty the crackhead is the [best man] and Mark is the third witness and we're sitting there at this crack wedding. God, Mark and I just laugh about it now.'

Deep down, Steve knew that it made as much sense to marry Lou then as it had the first time. 'I think we were just both fucked up. Her father had died, I was trying to work again, and it was a solution to my problems and her problems – we thought . . . It was just real dysfunction. It was incredibly sick.'

As much to prove something to himself as to Steve, Dotson continued to search out career-reviving deals. There was some good news. MCA had released *The Essential Steve Earle*, a Tony Brown-compiled greatest hits, and in October Steve played one of Nashville's most famous songwriters' venues: the Bluebird Café. He wore sunglasses throughout the performance. 'The rumours of my demise have been greatly exaggerated,' he quipped, borrowing a line from Mark Twain, his old hero.

Steve had bet Dotson money that he couldn't extricate him from his publishing contract with EMI, which had taken over

Virgin, his last publishing company. Under the terms of the contract, Steve's songs had to be commercially released within a specific period of time. Since Steve had taken the money and not delivered the songs, his contract had been suspended. EMI still owned the rights but Steve himself had been frozen in time. He was just a file in a folder in LA. Dotson had the greatest difficulty prising any money out of the new people, particularly since the woman with whom they were dealing seemed to have some long-held grudge against Steve. Dotson pleaded with her for a cheque. 'The guy was destitute. I was paying house notes, I was paying electric bills . . . He lived thirty miles out of town, he had to have a car, he had to have a phone. My niece was out there, there was a lot of stuff going on.'

It took Dotson six months to negotiate Steve out of the contract but he managed. Steve went back to Warner Chappell with his entire catalogue intact and a bigger annual advance that he'd ever had before. In a rare move, Warner Chappell put together a collection of seventeen of Steve's unreleased songs and three MCA-recorded tracks in the form of *Uncut Gems*, which produced the Travis Tritt hit, 'Sometimes She Forgets'. Steve was paid $130,000, of which he saw less than $7,000. The Will Botwin lawsuit, which had now been running for nearly five years, had heated up. After Steve failed to respond to numerous court summons and hired and fired at least four separate sets of lawyers, the court passed judgment against him in September 1992. By that time Botwin alleged that he was owed $76,548.85 in record royalties, management commissions and tour advances, along with attorney's fees of up to $30,000. In a bid to obtain the money, his attorneys sued Warner Chappell Music Inc for songwriting royalties owed to Steve. Court records show that Steve contacted Botwin personally in March 1993 and tried to get him to agree to some other form of payment. Botwin filed a contempt order against Warner Chappell instead and the company was instructed to hand over $110,971.62 of Steve's royalty money as and when it became due.

Luckily, there were other deals in the offing, one of which was a duet with Joe Walsh on *The Beverly Hillbillies* movie soundtrack. In May, Steve had enrolled on a methadone programme in Chattanooga and Lou would spend an entire year driving him two and a half hours there and two and a half hours back every single day so he could get his quota. Because his continued crack use prevented him from getting a clean urine sample for cocaine, he wasn't allowed to take any methadone away with him. When the LA trip came up, Steve decided that his only option was to use heroin for the time they were there. When they landed at LAX, he made Dotson drive him directly to his spot at Hoover and El Dorado and bought $100 worth of dope. It was the first time he'd been there for almost two years, but the same guy was on the same corner. Like fuckin' McDonald's, Steve thought. He went to get heroin and cocaine twice during the night and suffered a massive overdose as a consequence, regaining consciousness by a sheer miracle two hours later. But it was only his first brush with death that week. Handing his money to a dealer on another expedition with Dotson, Steve heard the click of a switchblade. In the split second before the blade shot out of the dealer's coat sleeve, he put his foot on the accelerator and the knife carved a line down the side of the car. Dotson was shaken. Steve glossed it off, not altogether convincingly: 'Comes with the territory, hoss.'

The studio was in Encino, out in the Valley, and Steve was annoyed to find that they were staying nearby. That far out in the Valley, he complained, he got the bends. They recorded 'Honey Don't' in two days. On the second day, a session in Hollywood, Steve had an altercation with the producer and walked out of the studio. He was gone for some time before he called Dotson and told him he was at a burger joint nearby. Back at the Radisson in Sherman Oaks Dotson tried, as gingerly as possibly, to encourage Steve to check out of his room in good time so they could make their flight.

'I can't go home,' Steve announced. 'Lou's too mad at me.'

'Better to go home and face the music,' Dotson said in an attempt at light-heartedness. Steve started to yell. Dotson ignored him. He was determined to make the plane. The movie company stopped paying for their hotel that day. He made the mistake of mentioning that detail to Steve, but it seemed to incense him further. 'He grabbed my collar and threatened to kick my ass if he didn't get the keys to the car. I'm not going to lose teeth and get ribs broken over that.'

Steve could usually intimidate Dotson into doing whatever he wanted. 'I probably told him I was going to beat the living shit out of him if he didn't give me the keys. I probably wouldn't have hit him but I probably could have held John Dotson with one hand and taken the keys away from him even at that point in my life.'

The last thing Dotson saw was Steve, revoked licence and all, disappearing with his keys. He went up to his room and prepared to dig in for a long wait. 'I didn't know if I was going to be bringing him back sitting next to me or in a body bag in the luggage compartment, and I was equally prepared for both.' He was a nervous wreck. It had been pointed out to him that, under California law, he would share criminal liability if Steve hurt or killed anybody while at the wheel of the rental car. Not knowing what else to do, he telephoned Steve's parents with the bad news. Jack and Barbara were aghast. They imagined Steve lying maimed by the roadside or dead in some anonymous crack den. Kelly flew up from Boston to be with them and they took it in turns to call a long list of California hospitals and morgues. Barbara aged ten years when a body matching Steve's description, tattoo and all, came in. 'We were scared to death.'

Three days later, the phone rang in Dotson's hotel room. 'Thank God, you're alive!' he cried when he heard Steve's familiar growl. 'Did you hit anything? Have you hurt anyone?'

'No, man, I went up to Joshua Tree,' Steve said calmly, as if he was surprised Dotson didn't know.

'Stay where you are,' Dotson ordered. 'I'll come and get you.'

'I'll call you in a little while,' Steve said and hung up. The next three hours were the longest of Dotson's life. He was drained when Steve finally called back. 'Man, you're not going to believe what happened,' he told Dotson. 'I had a wreck.'

Dotson was thunderstruck. 'Is anybody hurt?' he said weakly.

'Well, *I* am, thanks for asking.'

'Are *you* hurt, Steve?'

'I hit the steering wheel. I'm bleeding.'

'Okay, is anybody else hurt?'

'I don't think so . . . I'm not at the car.'

'Where are you?'

'I don't know. I got out of the car and ran.'

Dotson took a deep breath. 'What did you leave in the car?'

'Everything . . . Don't worry, I've done all the drugs.'

'Great. Did any of the equipment to consume these substances get left in the car?'

'Fuckin' everything, man. What, are you not listening to me? I'M BLEEDING, why are you asking me all these questions?'

'Well, knowing where you are would really help me come and find you.'

Steve eventually managed to locate a street name and Dotson checked out of the hotel and drove out to look for him. Steve was curled up on the sidewalk like a homeless person, passed out cold. He was completely incoherent. 'I tried to get him to give me an indication of where he'd left the car. No idea. We drove around looking for the car, couldn't find it, so I came up with this whole story about the car being stolen. We went back to a restaurant in Hollywood where people had seen us and did this whole flustered, freaked-out thing about the car being stolen and got names and cards and went to the airport and booked us on the red-eye.'

At the airport, there were further problems because Steve looked like a corpse and FAA regulations prohibit anyone under the influence of drugs boarding an aeroplane. Dotson convinced the flight staff that Steve had been up for three days working on a record and had taken too many sleeping pills. Fifteen minutes before the flight took off, he telephoned the rental car company and reported the car stolen.

It was a decision that precipitated a long legal tussle. Steve had rear-ended a truck that delivered dispensing machines for a soft drink company. There was very little damage to the truck, but when the driver found he'd been rammed by a star, he scented money. Lou recalls receiving a threatening phone call where a man warned her he'd reveal what was found in the car unless they paid $15,000, and Dotson claims that Steve refused to sign the indemnification form which would have released him from liability. He was particularly upset that Steve's mother, who'd phoned him in Hollywood and thanked him profusely for not deserting Steve when he was missing, gave him a tongue-lashing for trying to get Steve to sign the form. Dotson paid $400 for the damage to the rental car but the truck driver got nasty. It was only when Dotson persuaded the rental car company to instal several of his company's dispensing machines in their offices that he agreed to sign the execution of waiver document releasing Dotson from any future liability or prosecution. Dotson was furious with Steve.

'At that point I was thinking, What am I doing?' In all, the Hollywood débâcle had cost $6,000 in drugs, accommodation, car hire, etc. and Steve had refused to stand between him and a potentially ruinous lawsuit. It was hard to forgive. The only reason Dotson continued managing Steve was, he says, out of a sense of obligation to Warner Chappell, who were close to finishing *Uncut Gems*, and for his niece's sake. He claims that in the back of his mind was the thought that if he could keep the money flowing for Steve, some of it might filter through to Lou and his niece Amy.

If Steve had been capable of enjoying his accomplishments, he would have found much to be proud of in *Uncut Gems* or in the number of artists – Shawn Colvin, Eddie Reader and Kathy

Mattea among them – who were covering his songs. But he wasn't. There was a large degree of truth in Dotson's assessment that apart from Steve's immediate family 'there were only two people in Nashville who gave a rat's ass whether he was alive or dead. Me and Lou.'

By 1994, almost every one of Steve's friends and former colleagues had given him up for dead. Townes Van Zandt made one attempt to get through to him, riding his bike out to Fairview, but he could tell that Steve was too in thrall to crack to seek help; Steve just laughed at him. 'I must be bad if they're sending you,' he kidded. Susanna Clark was immersed in her own problems with alcohol at the time. 'I prayed for him but I left him to his own devices as he did me mine.' Guy Clark took a tough love approach to Steve's habit. ''Course it concerns you but it's like, well, I sure hope you get through this. It would be a waste if you didn't . . . Townes was always more worried about Steve and drugs than I was. I was kinda like, "Hey, man, it's your problem. Take care of it." But Townes, having kinda been through the same thing, was concerned about Steve . . . In that respect, Townes was a gentle, good friend. I mean, the real deal.'

Few of Steve's friends and colleagues are as honest as Guy about why they turned a blind eye during the worst years of his addiction. Some are uncomfortable being asked about it and some, like Richard Bennett, admit they were simply at a loss as to what to do. 'There'd be these Steve Earle sightings . . . "Oh, you know, I saw Steve. He was down there at the pawn shop on Nolensville Road pawning all of his guitars and he weighed 120lbs . . ." I felt bad for him. I don't know what one does. Obviously, I didn't feel bad enough to go look him up . . . I suppose I expected him to die. I think a lot of people did. I think probably he did too. So it was just waiting, I suppose. It sounds gruesome but after a while it just got to be no big deal. There was another Steve Earle incident in the paper and the next one you expected to read was, they've found him somewhere.'

This macabre waiting game was played out over and over

again by his family. Having grown up in AA listening to the tragic tales of people hitting rock bottom, Barbara was frantic with worry that that was where her son would end. She called Stacey from Houston nearly every day to ask if she'd seen Steve. 'If she hadn't, we'd send her out to look for him. And she'd go and find him, fetch him to her house, feed him.'

In April, Stacey was at work when she received a frantic call from Mark's sister who worked at *The Tennessean*. According to preliminary wire reports, Steve had been involved in a multi-vehicle pile-up on I-40 near Kingston Springs and they were life-lining him to Vanderbilt. Steve had been on his way to a court date when a gas truck veered across the median and hit an oncoming car head-on, killing the driver instantly. Emergency crews were diverting traffic around the wreck when Steve ploughed into the back of a pickup truck, which in turn smashed into another car. At the moment of impact, the Forerunner Steve was driving flipped over several times and the sunroof sliced into his forehead.

Stacey and Mark raced down to Vanderbilt. Steve was in the emergency room, soaked in blood. He was in terrible pain. The doctors had refused to give him anything to relieve it because he was an IV drug user. After what seemed to Stacey an unnecessary delay, they cut off his suit, put a paper robe on him and stitched up his forehead. Stacey thought he looked like Frankenstein's monster.

'Get him out of here,' they told her unsympathetically.

Downstairs, Mark and Stacey loaded Steve carefully into the front of the car. Lou, who was waiting in the back seat, immediately launched into a tirade of abuse. When she paused for breath, Stacey said to Steve: 'We're going to take you home and you're going to get in bed. You could have concussion or anything.' She still couldn't believe the doctors had released him.

'Well, I can't deal with this pain, so first you've got to take me down to buy rock,' Steve said flatly.

Stacey didn't know whether to scream at him or cry. 'Steve,

this almost killed you today,' she protested. 'Where does this stop?'

But Steve was determined to get his hands on a painkiller, even if it was an illegal one. Stacey was even more determined not to be party to any more insanity. She insisted that Mark drop her off at Mrs Winner's Chicken Restaurant on West End while he took Steve and Lou down to the ghetto. Shortly thereafter Steve could be observed standing on a street corner in South Nashville in a blood-splattered paper robe, his head a grisly mess of seeping stitches, holding out a $10 bill to buy rock.

On and on it went, an insane roller coaster of death-defying stunts. Once, a drug mule almost died in Steve and Stacey's house when he had trouble passing a balloon of heroin with which he had flown up from LA. Stacey had to feed him Dr Pepper and other home remedies before it burst. There was a stage when Stacey joined a support group for families of addicts because she found herself questioning her own sanity.

Mark kept her sane. Stacey called him her blessing. He had been born and raised in Nashville in a secure, happy family and had never smoked a cigarette, drunk a beer or done any form of drug in his life. 'Mark was like the thing that came out of thin air at the best of times. Mark came into the picture at the peak of Steve's drug addiction. I was alone at that point, trying to take it on, and Mark came along and was all of our strengths in a way.' Still, the strain on Mark and Staccy was terrific. According to Stacey, Mark cared for Steve so much that he would drive him in and out of the ghetto, 'let him purchase, then drive him back, because he wanted him to come back alive. Mark would hold Steve's drugs in his pockets and distribute them at certain hours because there was only so much money that we could scrape together to keep him maintained.'

It should be pointed out that Steve and Stacey's stories diverge sharply at this point. Stacey says that she and Mark tried whenever they could to buy back Steve's possessions from the pawn shop owners. After a few years, they were so 'tapped-out money-wise, Mark and I were actually at a point where we were selling our things. I sold a good car to try to get money to maintain [Steve's habit].'

Steve admits that he did borrow money from them but paid most of it back. 'A couple of times I ran it up to a point where I shouldn't have. I mean, they couldn't really afford it.'

Another contentious issue was Steve's beloved '67 Chevelle, which he gave Mark as a gift and Mark sold (Stacey strongly disputes this). 'I pawned a rack of gear to Mark for cash, paid him back for it but didn't pick the equipment up and Stacey took it and sold it. There's a lot of shit that went on then. It was pretty desperate times for her and for me. But I'd bet money on my memory of how it came down.'

There followed a spate of arrests, most of which were dismissed or retired with the help of what one Nashville criminal court clerk called 'high dollar attorneys'. Along with a charge of driving with a suspended licence in January, Steve escaped a criminal charge for the same thing in March and a criminal forfeiture charge in May. Along the way, he had most of his teeth pulled out and implants put in. The sugar content in the drugs he took had literally rotted them to the roots.

'I reached a point where I thought I was going to die, I thought I was supposed to die and I just couldn't figure out what was taking so long.'

Steve was becoming less and less capable of working all the time, but the odd job did still come in. One of them was MCA's Lynyrd Skynyrd tribute album, *Skynyrd Frynds*, which Steve did 'just to get that money'. A week or so before the session, Dotson had contacted Tony and asked him if he could give Steve half of the $7,500 advance at the session. On the day of the recording, Tony gave Steve the money and when their work was done he offered him a ride. They drove into the poorest part of South Nashville, a sinister neighbourhood full of disused buildings and graffiti-covered store fronts. Tony had never seen anything like it. Steve directed him to an abandoned strip mall.

'Let me out here,' he said to Tony. 'They're working on my car.'

Tony was astounded. He twisted around to see if he'd inadvertently missed a cheery new gas station. 'Where at?'

Steve was vague. 'It's round the back.'

'Well, let me drive around the back,' Tony pressed him. 'It's kinda dangerous around here.'

But Steve was insistent. He climbed out of the car and hurried away down the road, a thin manic figure.

A day or two later, on 25 July, Steve was on his way back from pleading guilty to the heroin charge in Lou's rental car when he decided to get some crack and a couple of dilaudids. He was still enrolled on the methadone programme in Chattanooga but he hadn't got it together to go there for a couple of days. After buying crack, he ran into the cocaine dealer he names Harold Mills in the *Doghouse Roses* story, 'A Eulogy of Sorts'. They drove across town to the East Nashville housing project to find their dilaudid connection. Waiting in the parking lot, they were pounced on by cops in an unmarked car. Forty-five minutes after leaving the court, Steve was being charged with trespassing and driving with a suspended licence, as well as drug possession and possession of paraphernalia, including three rocks, a crack pipe and ten syringes.

Watching a television report of the arrest, a vision of the awful street on which he had dropped Steve swam into Tony's mind. 'Oh, my God,' he thought to himself. 'I contributed to that.'

Rick Steinberg, who'd loaned Steve $100 just a few days earlier, thought much the same thing.

Somewhere through the haze, Steve recognized that this latest charge could have serious implications if he appeared in court as scheduled at the end of August. In the weeks that followed he crossed the state line and checked into a motel in Rossville, Georgia, close enough to Chattanooga that he could make regular trips to the methadone clinic. When he couldn't go another day without crack, he would go back to Nashville for a few days, once picking up another charge for driving on a suspended licence. He was in a desperate state. So thin that he wept at the sight of himself, he veered blearily between Fairview, Stacey's house and the street. There were nights when his breathing was so shallow that Stacey held a mirror over his face so that it might mist over and tell her he was still alive. Lou would call the house at three in the morning and ask Mark to go looking for him or tell them she and Steve needed money. And Stacey, who made $80 a night waiting tables, claims that she would give them $40 and keep $40 for herself and Mark. Financially and emotionally, they were bled dry.

It was in this frame of mind that Stacey came to the worst night of her life. It was a mirror night. Earlier, Steve had come stumbling through the front door looking greyer and more fragile than she had ever seen him and, after a series of agonizing convulsions, had passed out on the bed. Since then, Stacey had been in and out of the room with the mirror, praying for the faintest trace of breath. Too exhausted to rest, she finally just sat on the edge of the mattress in the half light, watching Steve jerk in his sleep. 'I really felt that night he wasn't going to wake up. I wished for him to go ahead and sleep for ever. Just so the pain would stop for him. And I said to Mark, "Maybe we should let him go and that way it won't hurt any more and he won't need it any more." I wasn't thinking at all about not wanting to go through it myself. But he had been throwing up all night, everything. It had been a bad night. He'd stand up and convulse and then he'd fall back down again. And really, I prayed for him to die. 'Course it didn't happen and to this day I've had to carry that guilt with me all the time. But I really prayed that it would happen that night . . . I thought about putting a pillow on his face. I wanted for him to stop hurting.'

More than six years on, Stacey still cries uncontrollably at the memory of these desperate thoughts – thoughts she had never confided to a living soul apart from Mark. 'I just wanted for him to stop hurting. I just wanted it all to stop. But it was truly a love wish. It wasn't out of hate.'

14

Outlaw Blues

'To live outside the law you must be honest.'
Bob Dylan, 'Absolutely Sweet Marie'

On a fine September morning in 1994, Steve Earle emerged
blinking from his room at the King's Inn in Chattanooga,
Tennessee, fumbled for a newspaper in the box that housed
the *Chattanooga Times Free Press*, propped himself up and
read it with the aid of a coffee or a Dr Pepper. In a while, he
planned to go over to the methadone clinic for his daily dose
of destiny. Glancing through the newspaper, his eye was caught
by an item bearing his name. He read it quickly, then slowly,
then disbelievingly. A Nashville Criminal Court had sentenced
him, *in absentia*, to an eleven-month, twenty-nine-day jail term
and fined him $2,500 for failing to appear at a 2 September
sentencing hearing on the heroin charge. Judge Tom Shriver
had imposed the maximum penalty.

In that instant, a thousand wild thoughts ran through Steve's
head. Never, as long as there was breath in his body, would
they throw a net over him. He would go to ground and live
a fugitive's life. He would go and live in Ireland, where there
was no extradition treaty. But underneath the addict's bravado
and far, far below the Hell's Angel exterior was a kernel of
Steve that still reasoned and loved. That part of him was weary
to the bone. Tired of being broke, tired of living the dissolute
life he was living, tired of inflicting hurt on his family. It was

that part that finally found the nerve to call his lawyer, Lionel Barrett.

Barrett was full of comforting professionalism. If Steve would only turn himself in, he'd be out the same day, Barrett would make sure of it. Steve thought it over for another week, then, on 11 September, he rode with Barrett to the Criminal Justice Centre in downtown Nashville, just a few blocks from the Ryman.

'This is Steve Earle, turning himself in,' Barrett said as they walked in.

Steve was still sizing up the claustrophobic office, still taking in the smell of stale air and body odour, when the lawyer slipped out the door. Steve turned to follow him. It was only then that he realized that it had been a ploy. The door was locked. 'He just left me! And then I spent two and a half, three hours sitting in the fuckin' processing area in the basement. You don't have *anything*. You're just in a big bullpen and you spend the night there with whoever else is in jail that day and you stay there till they assign you a cell.'

It would be another day and a half before Steve was classified and processed and moved to the fourth floor. Accustomed to the perceived freedom of the streets, where the prison of addiction is invisible, he was almost overwhelmed by helpless desperation. At first he fought the feeling, because acknowledging it would have meant that the system had the upper hand; but it was soon replaced by a much more serious desperation. Cocaine withdrawal was blasting through his brain. Steve had lived through opiate withdrawal a hundred times before, but that, at least, had a physical component to it. Cocaine was another beast altogether. Without crack, Steve was stricken by an unimaginably intense craving and mounting paranoia. Miserable and extremely agitated, he imagined he was also withdrawing from methadone. As it turned out, the methadone detox had hardly begun.

Three days later, Steve was transferred to SJ2, known to inmates as the Blackwood Jail. Situated close to the main jail and next door to the fire department, the Blackwood Jail comprised of four fifty-man cells in an old grocery warehouse. The Tennessee River slid invitingly past. Steve looked and felt close to death. In place of methadone he'd been given the blood pressure medicine Clonadine to which, it transpired, he was hypersensitive. His blood pressure bottomed out dangerously. The Sheriff's department became alarmed. Earlier in the year a high-profile inmate had died of a drug overdose and they didn't want another famous corpse on their hands. They begged the judge to let them transfer him to treatment. He agreed on condition that Steve came up with the $1,100 fee.

Eight days after arriving at the Criminal Justice Centre, Steve was taken to a hospital in Fayetteville, Tennessee, for clinical detoxing. The average heroin detox takes three days, but methadone has a much more savage grip. It was another week before Steve, weak and nauseous, was able to go to a treatment centre. During that time he was kept going by three thoughts: one, there was a bottle of methadone in his fridge at home – as soon as he got a chance he would call Lou and have her smuggle it to him; two, if he didn't like the treatment centre, he could just walk out the front door and go to Ireland if it pleased him (he wasn't aware then that the police force in Hohenwald exists almost solely for the purpose of picking up Buffalo Valley escapees); three, the junkie's eternal quest for a high to match the very first one. 'The junkie in me thought, if I can do this, these nice people are going to help me get high again.'

And underneath he knew that he was only deceiving himself.

The website for Buffalo Valley could as easily be advertising a vacation spot or a spiritual retreat as a recovery centre for addicts. Illustrated by a picture of a single-storey brick building and another of a lake, the accompanying blurb tells interested parties: 'The serenity and spirituality of the recovery programme is enhanced by the abundance of nature and the beauty of the area. Nearby you will find the scenic Buffalo

River, the Tennessee River and the historic Natchez Trace National Parkway . . .'

Steve entered Buffalo Valley with no interest in the scenery and even less interest in getting clean. Coincidentally, Townes would shortly be admitted to a Nashville hospital in a similar frame of mind with regard to alcohol. But Townes lacked Steve's lightness, his hopeful loving soul. Or his will to survive. While Townes, vomiting blood, continued to pursue music's most extreme fringes with the vigour of a Hemingway or a Jimi Hendrix, Steve knew instinctively that poetry stopped at the grave. In his last lonely months at Fairview, he had once or twice contemplated suicide, staring up at the beams and picturing the final exit. But something had always stopped him. Viewed at close quarters, death lost its appeal.

That as much as anything helped Steve to hear the lessons being offered at Buffalo Valley. Initially it was simply a case of thinking that if he behaved himself the judge might free him from jail sooner rather than later. But after ten days his parents and Kelly came to visit him. He hadn't seen them since the Hollywood car wreck nightmare and the hope on their faces stayed with him when they left. Kelly too was touched by the change in him. They sat under a beautiful tree and felt close to him for the first time in years. Then Lou appeared and it was as if a storm had obliterated a sunny day.

After nearly twenty-five years of using drugs, it took time for the Twelve Step message integral to the treatment of addiction to sink in. The Twelve Steps are based on the recovery programme of Alcoholics Anonymous and include: admitting one has a problem, asking for help, self-appraisal, confidential disclosure of one's personal testimony, making amends where hurt or harm has been caused and working with other recovering addicts. These practical principles aim to help addicts take the first steps towards freeing themselves from what the programme refers to as their 'disease'.

For Steve, there was no lights-on revelation. He did have a 'moment of clarity' as the literature put it, but it happened in 'little bitty teeny tiny increments', many of which took place long after he left Buffalo Valley. It would be another six months, for instance, before he realized that an incident he was convinced had taken place, where a SWAT team raided the house he shared with Teresa in LA (a scenario he would later use in *Doghouse Roses*), was a figment of his imagination. The combination of crack cocaine and massive sleep deprivation had created a fair amount of psychosis in the last days of Steve's addiction and the line between fantasy and reality was still very blurred. 'The programme's definition of insanity is doing the same things over and over again and expecting different results . . . and addicts do that. But in my particular case insanity is also hallucinating a SWAT team in your driveway and people in the palm trees. And it doesn't matter whether you induce that psychosis with a chemical or not, it's still psychosis. And if you do it long enough it becomes part of your reality.'

For his parents, who had spent so long staring into the abyss with Steve, it was difficult to comprehend the changes they were witnessing. Prior to going to Buffalo Valley, he had said with brutal honesty: 'I'm going there to get out of jail, I'm not going there for rehab.' Ten days on, it was clear he was thinking differently. Perhaps the most extraordinary change of all was his embracing of the spiritual side of the recovery programme. For years one of his lines had been that he believed in God, he just didn't believe in a God that helped junkies. Now Jack was amazed at what he saw. 'He had always claimed to me that he was agnostic and all of a sudden he was talking pretty seriously about Twelve Steps and acknowledging a higher power, and we just couldn't believe it. And he came out living it.'

Barbara wrote him a letter. 'Steve,' she said, 'I think you know what you have to do.'

There was a guitar at Buffalo Valley to help addicts with the healing process, but because of the associations between music and his habit Steve wasn't allowed to use it. When he started to make progress, his counsellor relented and Lou brought out a cheap Yamaha Steve had purchased shortly before going into jail. With that, he sat down to write for the first time in four and a half years. The result was 'Hard-Core Troubadour' and 'Goodbye', two very different songs. 'Troubadour' was Steve Earle circa 1989, spirited country-rock in which Steve – unrepentantly, one feels – voiced the question he suspected Lou or any other woman caught up in the spin cycle of his life might like to put to him: 'Wherefore art thou Romeo you son of a bitch?'

There was nothing tongue-in-cheek about 'Goodbye'. Completed in forty-five minutes, it was, arguably, the most perfect song Steve had ever written, an achingly sad admission of love lost for all the wrong reasons. 'Was I lost somewhere or just too high/I can't remember if we said goodbye.' He knew even as he wrote it that Teresa was gone for ever.

'"Goodbye" was me at least starting to come to terms with the whole Teresa thing. It really, really upset Lou. She hates that song, *really, really* hates it.'

Steve spent twenty-eight days at Buffalo Valley and then an extra four as staff tried to petition to have him stay longer. Prison is the worst environment possible for a sensitive recovering addict. But the judge was adamant that Steve spend sixty days in orange before he'd even consider reviewing his sentence. He was also insistent that the thirty-three days Steve had spent in treatment not be counted towards his jail-time. Soon the guitar was gone and so were the smiling Buffalo Valley faces and Steve was back behind bars, well enough this time to take in the cold inhumanity of the prison surrounds.

Life quickly took on a hideous routine. In Steve's fifty-man cell, breakfast was at four-thirty a.m., lunch was at ten a.m. and dinner was at 4.30 in the afternoon. Inmates had fifteen minutes to eat. On one memorable day the morning meal consisted of frozen blueberries. They hit Steve's plate like buckshot. 'You couldn't eat 'em. They were harder than a brick bat. So that backfired on 'em. Because what are a bunch of locked up, mostly dopefiend motherfuckers going to do if you give them something on a tray that they can't eat? There were blueberries fuckin' everywhere. It was like blueberry Armageddon . . .'

At midnight, if Steve wasn't locked down, he would go to commissary with his cellmates and buy chips and Cokes and sit there and eat them. 'You weren't supposed to take them back to the cell but we did.' There was a lot of bullying. One inmate had his arm broken over a pair of nail-clippers as Steve looked on. He kept himself to himself, hanging out with two black guys he knew from the street who, for reasons that transcended their drug-forged friendship, watched his back. In between, he threw himself into the Twelve Step programme. Lou came to visit him and supportive letters poured in from Johnny Cash, Waylon Jennings, Hugh Moffat, Emmylou Harris and Richard Dobson, but it was hard not to get depressed. Constitutionally incapable of spending more than thirty days in the same municipality, jail grew increasingly claustrophobic.

'I wasn't doing well in jail. I could go with it for a while and then it would build up and I would be volatile and you can get hurt being volatile.'

When his radio was stolen while he slept, he exploded. In a well-documented exchange, his friend Paul Carver prevented him going on a recovery mission that might have ended in the hospital or the morgue, telling him: 'You're gonna sit your little white ass down and do your little time and then you're gonna get out of here and make me a nice record.'

What Carver may not have known is that a chain of rather bizarre events meant that Steve actually had the opportunity to do just that. Before and during the time he was a fugitive in Chattanooga, he had been visited several times by his old friend Bill Alsobrook with an unlikely business proposition. In the early seventies Alsobrook had been a sound engineer at Nashville's Exit/Inn. His former employer, Owsley Manier, was

298

now co-owner of a little independent label called Winter Harvest Entertainment. His partner was a record executive named Steve Roberts. In the summer of 1994, when Steve Earle was a total pariah on Music Row, they approached Alsobrook about producing an album with him, assuming Steve was still alive or could even make music. According to Manier, Alsobrook was one of the few people to stay in contact with Steve during the dark years – perhaps because he himself had only been clean for two of them.

'Steve was literally on the run and at one point we thought maybe we can record it on the road somewhere, wherever he's hiding out.' Sometimes Bill would drive to Chattanooga and hang around the methadone clinic parking lot until Steve appeared. 'It was crazy but it was fun. We used to meet every night at my house at around midnight and go over how we were going to pull this off . . .'

Perversely, Steve's arrest only encouraged them further. Now at least they knew where to find him. Steve had not given any serious thought to his career in four years, but the new songs, 'Goodbye' and 'Troubadour', had rekindled something in him. Listening to Alsobrook, he felt excited. What if he made an acoustic record? What if he took the songs he had written before 1986 and performed in his solo shows but never recorded, and applied the stripped-down purity of Emmylou Harris's 1980 bluegrass classic, *Roses in the Snow* to them? What if they hired some of the most gifted musicians in Nashville – people like Sam Bush, who had played mandolin on *Copperhead*, or Alsobrook's long-time friends, legendary flat-picking guitarist Norman Blake and Emmy's acoustic bassist, Roy Huskey Jr, who'd quit the Nash Ramblers?

Gradually, the album became more than just a dream. The agreement was actually reached on 23 September, when Steve was still in recovery, and the contract signed on 11 November. He was in jail when he decided that 'Ben McCullough' and 'Tom Ames' Prayer', both written in '75, 'Hometown Blues', written in '77 and 'Nothin' but You' and 'Sometimes She

Forgets', written in the late seventies, should be included. So should 'Goodbye'. He would hold his remaining unrecorded songs, 'CCKMP', 'Hurtin' You, Hurtin' Me' and 'The Unrepentant', back for another album.

From Owsley Manier's point of view, the project was a leap of faith, but it was a leap worth taking – at least financially. He and Roberts knew that *The Hard Way*, *Shut Up and Die Like an Aviator* and *The Essential Steve Earle* had sold in the region of 80,000 units each. If their own record (only the second they'd put on the label) sold half of that, they'd be laughing. The only risk was, if they handed Steve a cheque, would he actually show up?

Any satisfaction Steve gained from these events was diminished by the knowledge that he would be in jail for another six or seven months and life was getting worse by the day. When a police sting brought hundreds of temporary inmates flooding into the jail, Steve and his fifty cellmates were moved into the guard's gym for five days. There was one telephone and the tension was palpable. Hygiene deteriorated, bullying soared. Next Steve was transferred back to the Criminal Justice Centre. To keep from going crazy, he wrote 'Poor Boy', jotting down the lyrics and saving the melody in his head.

And then, as suddenly as it had started, it was over. So many people had written to the judge on Steve's behalf that overnight he relented. Steve was freed without warning at around midnight on 16 November. Emerging unprepared into the neon darkness, he came face to face with the temptation. One way led to the ghetto and the sweet release that lay beyond it. The other led to real life, with all the pain and uncertainty that that implied. Steve held his breath and took the hard road.

When Justin awoke the next morning, Steve was asleep on the couch at Fairview, his skin a ghostly white. He had piled on weight. It had been four months since Justin had last seen him and he felt a rush of emotions, none of which he could probably have put a name to. It had been a strange, cruel few years. Ever since that Christmas Day in 1991, when Steve had come weaving up the drive in a Malcolm X Santa Claus hat and it had hit Justin that something terrible was happening to his father, life had been much tougher. It was no longer easy to be a child.

About the time that *Copperhead Road* was released, Justin first realized that Steve was using drugs. Up until then Steve had always just been an elusive, hero figure in his life. He was absent a lot but when he was home Justin was in heaven. Steve would pick him up and take him to Target and buy him the latest Nintendo game. He made it a point to be around on Justin's birthday. Often he'd hire out Chucky Cheese's, a birthday place for kids, and Justin would invite all his friends and Steve would give them $50 each in coins and they'd play video games to their hearts' content. One afternoon, Steve took him instead to a Nashville club. Justin sat watching a hip hop metal group, while Steve disappeared backstage. After a while, Justin went looking for him. Stumbling around in the dimly lit passages, he heard his father's voice and the words 'eight ball', a measure of cocaine.

That night Justin had gone home and asked Carol what 'eight ball' meant. The only drug he'd really heard about was pot. He had always associated Steve's behaviour and the way in which he kept himself and his various residences with alcohol. Until that day. But even then he never let it bother him 'because it finally came down to: What the fuck am I going to do about it? So I just kinda sat back and watched it happen and disassociated myself with my family name as much as I could for a long time.'

By the time the *Hard Way* came along Steve was home less and less and when he did take Justin out it was usually to the house of one of his friends and he would abandon Justin to the friend's boring kids while he rode away into South Nashville. Each time he reappeared, he seemed a little bit skinnier, a little bit worse. There were days when he literally dozed off on his feet. When Steve moved back to Nashville in 1992,

Justin hoped he might see a bit more of him. In fact he saw less. 'I knew my dad was somewhere in Nashville but he was either in the Shelby bottoms or the Lewis Street bottoms, which are places that, if you're white, you just don't go unless you're copping dope . . . I figured that the only way it was gonna stop was when he dropped dead.'

In his early teens, Justin himself started to court trouble. A lanky mirror-image of his father at the same age, he loathed the music business because he saw the way it destroyed lives. He told himself he was going to be a professional soccer player. At school, he gravitated towards the kids from low-income families because he knew that the 'last thing they gave a fuck about was what was going on on Music Row'. He was forever getting into fights. Many of the kids at school had parents connected to the music business and they'd torture Justin with stories distorted over the dinner table. 'It was hard, especially in Nashville, because it's such a gossip town. Every day there was a fuckin' newspaper brought to me at school by some little mean-hearted kid.' As the list of Steve's misdeeds grew ever longer, Justin began to think about changing his name. Carol was dating a man called T.J. Blackman for a while and if they married, Justin Townes Earle planned to become Justin T. Blackman by deed poll.

With Carol at work all day, Justin had between two in the afternoon and eight or nine at night to run wild through the streets of Nashville. He went crazy with his friends, 'stealing bicycles and shit like that'. Towards the end of 1993, Justin began to be convinced that Steve wasn't going to live much longer. He called his father and asked him if he could move back to Fairview and live with him, Amy and Lou, whom Justin had always adored. The next day Steve picked him up from soccer practice.

One bitter year on, thirteen-year-old Justin stood staring at his father's crumpled form. Then he went quietly out the door and caught the bus to school.

* * *

Steve was released from jail on a year's probation, with urine samples required from him on a weekly basis. Legally, he should have been paroled for a maximum of seven months with urine samples required only once a month, but there was no arguing with the judge. And as loath as Steve was to admit it, he knew that Judge Tom Shriver's decision to jail him had saved his life. He believed wholeheartedly that prison was the furthest thing possible from a solution to drug addiction. His own case was something of miracle. Physically, though, he still didn't feel good and wouldn't for at least six months. Jimbeau Hinson, who saw him shortly after his release, thought he looked 'like Elvis in the last years'. Home in time for Thanksgiving, Steve concentrated only on getting through it.

One of his first actions had been to buy himself a good guitar and start writing, but there were no quick fixes when it came to resuming family life. The sheer weight of psychological trauma that Lou and his children had suffered during his 'vacation in the ghetto' made it impossible for them to continue as if nothing had happened. Lou had still been scarred by her first marriage to Steve when she embarked on a second. 'One thing he told the kids after he got sober and came home, he said, "Look, you guys, all that stuff I did back then, that happened and that was the past and this is the future and we don't need to discuss that again." And, I mean, everybody was in therapy at that point. *Everybody.* Except Ian . . . There was such fallout from all of this. Justin was having problems, Amy was in for depression, *I* went in for depression. Everybody was in rehab for something.'

Steve himself had done a lot of thinking. After years of using drugs to mask every hurt, recovery had taught him that it was not only inevitable but actually healthy to feel pain. 'You're not supposed to hold on to it and you're not supposed to let it get toxic but pain is the way you learn not to do things.' In the past, his conviction that his pain was greater than other people's was at least one of the reasons for his addiction, but he refused to accept Stacey's notion that self-destructiveness was another. He knew that heroin had never enhanced his creativity but at one stage he'd been convinced that artistic inspiration was 'a perk I was owed because of the damage I incurred looking inward at my own pain'. Now he knew that all that it had done was cost him 'four and a half years of creativity in my prime'. For the first time in his life he had regrets – not seeing his boys walk for the first time and destroying his fifth marriage. 'At forty, it becomes clear – especially if you get to be forty the way I did, defying gravity, that what's important is your life and your wife and your kids . . .' he told *Billboard* in March. 'There is an edge in things that you do when you're younger, and you think it's life or death, but if you survive long enough . . . it suddenly dawns on you one day that you didn't have to go through maybe all the shit that you went through, but there ain't nobody in the world that could have told you that when it was goin' on.'

December was spent attending daily Twelve Step meetings and planning the new album, which was to be called *Train A Comin'*. If John Dotson had any doubts about Steve after the experiences of the past few years, they were banished when he heard his new songs. Steve wasn't as different clean as Dotson had envisioned he would be, but he was less hyperactive. He was also less sure of himself, confessing to Dotson that he was worried he had done lasting damage to his voice. The purpose of doing *Train A Comin'* was to ease Steve back into music by doing a low-pressure record.

Partly through adrenalin and enthusiasm, partly to avoid confronting the intricacies of his personal life, Steve filled his days with projects. He renewed his friendship with former manager of Jason and the Scorchers, Jack Emerson, whom he knew from his rockabilly days. Emerson had recently resigned as chief of indie label Praxis and had formed a new partnership with businessman Dub Cornett. Their offices were just along the corridor from Room and Board, the studio where

Steve was set to record *Train A Comin'* and Steve played his new songs for them. He was writing compulsively and looking ahead. One defiantly autobiographical song, 'I Feel Alright', had already given both title and shape to the next record. 'Be careful what you wish for friend/I've been to hell and now I'm back again,' snarled Steve as he sang. After all he had been through the song took a certain panache, but panache was something Steve had always had in spades. Even in his present, weakened state, he could still muster the arrogance and the humour to show two fingers to the establishment on Music Row.

They started *Train A Comin'* on 4 January 1995 and finished it in five days. Sam Bush had broken his arm while out running with his dog, so Steve had called in his long-time friend Peter Rowan, who had toured with Townes and was a veteran member of Bill Monroe's Bluegrass Boys. Rowan was best known for his guitar work but it was his mandolin and tenor vocals that Steve loved. Norman Blake, acoustic bassist Roy Huskey Jr and Steve on guitar and harmonica made up the rest of the new Dukes.

The electricity in the studio on that first morning was as palpable as it had been during the *Guitar Town* sessions. At the very moment that Steve might have been expected to hide behind technology, he chose to do without it. Instead he went for the most organic sound possible – somewhere between the high lonesome music of the Louvin Brothers and the intimacy and immediacy of the old Opry, with the players huddled close around the microphone. It was musicianship stripped to its bare bones, full of raw emotion and intensity. Far from imitating the then vogue for MTV unplugged-type albums, it anticipated by half a decade the back-to-basics roots revival that made the soundtrack of the Coen Brothers movie, *O Brother Where art Thou?* a multi-platinum-selling success story.

Owsley Manier watched Steve work with awe. 'I'll never forget, Steve was in the vocal booth and he had his guitar in there and he was singing, and the players were gathered round on the main floor of the studio, and they just started going. Steve said: "We're going to do this and I'm not looking back." I don't think he overdubbed anything. It was essentially a live performance.'

The night before the third session, Steve wrote 'Mystery Train II', incorporating a mandolin line he'd had lying around for years. Asking Emmy to sing on 'I'm Nothin' without You' and the Melodians' 'Rivers of Babylon' was almost as spontaneous. She and renowned Dylan producer Daniel Lanois were in Nashville doing pre-production on *Wrecking Ball* when Steve sent over the roughs for *Train A Comin'*. It had been years since Emmy had had any kind of conversation with Steve, but when she heard 'Goodbye' she was moved to tears by its mournful beauty. It was 'the saddest song in the world'. That afternoon she and Lanois rang Steve and asked permission to put the song on *Wrecking Ball*. Emmy felt that if they used it, Steve should play on it. 'I just felt like what he was playing was so connected to the feeling in the song.'

On the last day of the *Train A' Comin'* sessions, an ice storm ripped through the streets of Nashville. All they had left to record were the covers – 'The Rivers of Babylon', Townes's 'Tecumseh Valley' and the Beatles tune, 'I'm Looking Through You' – and they were hurrying so that Blake, who had to drive over Mont Eagle Mountain on his way to Georgia, could get home before nightfall. When they wrapped, Steve was exhilarated but still riddled with doubts. He worried that there weren't enough new songs on the album, he worried about how it would be received. He had done what he set out to do – make one of the most spare, personal and under-produced albums to come out of Nashville in years. The die was cast. With the drugs and the technology gone, his artistry was fully exposed.

Steve spent his fortieth birthday in the studio with Emmy and Daniel Lanois. 'If I'd known I would live this long I would have taken better care of myself,' he quipped. Four months on from crack addiction, destitution and the criminal courts, he had finished one album, made a start on another, and was playing his own song on an Emmylou Harris album that would, ultimately, be hailed as a masterpiece.

In the studio, they gathered together in a little folk circle to record, with Lanois on mandolin, Malcolm Burn on an old funky upright piano, Tony Hall on bass, Larry Mullen Jr on hand drums, Steve playing acoustic guitar and Emmy on vocals. When they went back into the control room and listened to it, it was as if something magic had happened. At the core of it, Emmy thought, was Steve's playing, 'that beautiful style of picking that he does'. Steve had only come for the day but he ended up staying all week, playing on the Lucinda Williams song 'Sweet Old World' and the Dylan songs, 'Every Grain of Sand' and 'Deeper Well'. 'Deeper Well' was later re-recorded in a different key.

Guitar Town maestro Richard Bennett came in to play a guitar part on *Wrecking Ball*. The last time he had seen Steve was in 1992 when he had run into him at Harlan Howard's Birthday Bash and invited him over for a coffee. Richard had been sitting at the kitchen table with a newspaper and a cup of coffee when a big black muscle car roared up the driveway and screeched to a halt. It was Steve. The calm quiet with which Richard liked to surround himself was shattered. Steve came striding up the drive in full conversational flow – with himself. As he approached the door, Richard could hear the talking getting louder. '"How ya doing, Steve?" "Great." In he comes. And I think that's all I said, hello and goodbye. For about an hour we sat there drinking coffee. He talked and got up and left and continued talking as he went down the driveway. I went, "Well, see you. Goodbye." That was probably the last time I saw him before he went into the dark.'

Three years on, Steve telephoned Richard from the *Train A Comin'* sessions. Even as he was making one record, he was preparing to make the next. Richard had arrived home one day to be told by his wife, 'You'll never guess who called . . .' Richard was not at all sure that he cared to ring Steve back, but his wife had talked him round. Steve had sounded great on the phone. When Richard heard the animation in Steve's voice as his old employer implored him to come and listen to the *Train A' Comin'* mixes, he felt transported back to *Guitar Town*, as if the intervening years had never happened. But he was cool on the telephone, reluctant to jump back in with Steve. A week later he walked into the *Wrecking Ball* sessions with no idea that Steve would be there, or that his weight had ballooned in prison, or that detoxing meant that his hair and skin were damp with the accumulated poisons of decades of heroin abuse. 'Out of the corner of my eye, I saw this mountain of a redneck in these overalls and his teeth were fucked up and his hair was real lank and I thought, "Who the fuck is this in here with Emmy?" And he came up and said, "Richard, it's Steve," and I felt so bad. Of course, once I got a good look at him, *of course* it was Steve.

In spite of that, Richard was so reassured by this encounter that he agreed to join Ray Kennedy and Richard Dodd as co-producer on *I Feel Alright*, and together they laid down two tracks for the new album before *Train A' Comin'* was even released. Steve had no intention of giving *I Feel Alright* to Winter Harvest, predicting, correctly, that the label would go bust within a few years. There had been approaches by major labels, but he wasn't sure he wanted to go down that route either. Before he could make up his mind, Emerson and Cornett came to him with a plan to launch a label in which all the artists were equal partners. Steve knew it wouldn't work. He was a disciple of *Das Kapital* but he was also a pragmatist and well aware that if one artist consistently made more money than everyone else, resentments would surface. In the end, he and Emerson decided to start a record label of their own. They would call it E-Squared. *I Feel Alright* would be their first project and Emerson's credit cards would provide the start-up capital.

Winter Harvest rushed *Train A Comin'* out in the third week of March. Roberts brought Pam Lewis in to do the publicity on the album. Despite the weight gain and the penchant for blue overalls, to her he was basically the same old Steve. 'I loved the *Train A Comin'* album because it was vintage Steve Earle. It was the closest thing he'd done to *Guitar Town*.'

Professionally, however, she found life difficult. Steve was not easy. 'He can be really rude and he can be really disrespectful and he can be really contrary.' Lewis, who was still trying to deal with the legal fallout that had followed Garth Brooks's decision to go elsewhere for management, found it frustrating, but she would still have taken Steve over Garth any day. '[Steve] doesn't really have a mean bone in his body that I've seen. You know, he can be testy, he can be difficult, but it's almost like this kid that's acting out. There's something underneath that's really very sweet. It's almost like, "I'm a bad boy to get attention." In other words, he doesn't care how he gets the attention as long as he gets it.'

When the album was pressed, Alsobrook drove out to Fairview with a copy, looking, Steve remembers, 'kind of sheepish'. The record had been resequenced without Steve's permission. Steve had wanted 'Mystery Train II' to be the first song on the album, but Manier was concerned that it opened with a fade-up. He was convinced that radio wouldn't play it. At one point he had suggested to Steve that 'Mystery Train' be moved to the back of the album. 'Absolutely not,' snapped Steve. 'The order's the order.' As Manier recalls, 'He was totally intractable on that. He felt very, very strongly about that. And contractually we had the right to put it in any order that we wanted to. So we did.'

When Steve saw the record, he went ballistic. Not even Jimmy Bowen had attempted to tell him how to sequence a record. He was so enraged that he shot up his copy of *Train*

A' Comin' with a .50 calibre muzzle load. 'I called Steve Roberts on the phone and I said, "What the fuck are you doing?" I was screaming and hollering. He said, "Why don't you just call me back after you've calmed down." I said, "Dude, if I were you I'd keep me on the telephone, then you know I'm not coming to your house."'

He told *USA Today* that if he'd had a driver's licence at the time, 'I'd be in jail for assault right now. I probably would have gone off and gone in and hurt somebody.'

With the benefit of hindsight, Manier regrets the bad blood caused, 'but the bottom line was, this album got a Grammy nomination'.

While Dotson assessed the legal options available to them, only to discover that the contract was watertight and they had none, *Train A' Comin'* hit the stores to widespread critical acclaim. 'Superb,' said *Musician*. 'Astonishing,' said *The Tennessean*. 'An awesome re-entry to the recording scene,' gushed the *Chicago Tribune*, describing 'Goodbye', 'Mystery Train II', 'Hometown Blues' and 'Mercenary Song' as gems. *Newsweek* profiled Steve, documenting an amusing encounter with him at the Country Music Hall of Fame. Journalist Karen Schoemer had been walking with Steve among the artefacts – Patsy Cline's cigarette lighter and Elvis's twenty-four-carat gold grand piano – when Steve had panicked, convinced the museum had removed the acoustic guitar and dress suit he had donated to commemorate the release of *Guitar Town*. When they were located, he was relieved.

'Leave it up to Earle, though, to find a glitch. Nothing in his world has ever been perfect. He reads the caption next to the guitar, and a little while later, he wanders back and reads it again. His mood goes from upbeat to agitated. "They've got some s— wrong here," he gripes. "I wonder who wrote this crap. 'Scaled-down model of the Gibson Everly Brothers' Model.' It's a *lot* bigger than an Everly Brothers' model."'

Every interviewer wanted to talk about the drugs. Apart from telling *Billboard* in March that his recent past was 'shit that I don't want to talk about because it isn't anybody's business', Steve was frank about his history, admitting for the first time that he'd been a heroin addict when he made *Guitar Town*. He had been thrilled to find that his voice, far from being ruined by his adventures in the ghetto, was better than ever. 'One thing about it,' he told the *Chicago Tribune*, 'when you're sitting around sticking needles in your arm and smoking crack, then your voice gets some rest, and it just inadvertently did . . . So some good comes out of everything.'

As his confidence increased, so did the outrageous sound-bites. 'Hank Williams couldn't get on country radio nowadays'; Shania Twain was 'the highest-paid lap dancer in Nashville'; there was a picture of Reba McEntire taped to the toilet seat in his office. But his quips didn't disguise his relief and pride at the credibility the record had found. In spite of the sequencing débâcle, *Train* was his most successful album since *Copperhead*, seven years before. Manier was delighted by the praise the album received for its pure sound. 'To this day, a lot of the audiophile magazines use it as a benchmark of an acoustic record in terms of the quality of the sound.'

The challenges of assimilating into family life after decades of addiction went largely unreported. Music was not always the balm it had been in the past. Steve wrote the exquisite, heartfelt 'Valentine's Day' for Lou sitting in the kitchen at eleven p.m. on 13 February. Ostensibly, it was because he didn't have a licence and wasn't able to go out for so much as a doghouse rose, but really the song was about guilt. 'I was trying really desperately at the time that I wrote that to make that marriage work. But it was pretty hopeless. She had a drug thing of her own going on that I didn't know about.'

Slowly but surely he was beginning to see that the main reason he had remarried Lou-Anne was that she was his most efficient co-dependent. 'She loved me *because* I was a junkie. Teresa could live with that . . . but it was really hard on her and really bad for her and after a while she had enough of it and she left. And I completely and totally did that to myself. And it's not like I didn't love everybody else I was with but I loved Teresa more . . .'

Whether or not he made that known to Lou, she sensed it. Steve went with her to a family counsellor and in the middle of the session she doubled up her fist and hit him in the leg so hard that the counsellor's eyes almost bulged from his head. Justin, too, felt a lot of anger towards Steve. To him, the Twelve Step programme was only marginally less evil than the drugs. He found the compulsive necessity of it, the life and death importance of it, reminiscent of the vicious cycle that was going on before. And at the back of his mind was one central question: 'Well, he's clean now, where the fuck is he?'

For all that, Justin was proud that his dad hadn't destroyed himself and any hope of a career like so many other musicians before him. *Train A' Comin'* was by far his favourite album, although he had his own theory on the meaning behind 'Goodbye'. 'There's probably women all over the world that think "Goodbye" was written for them, but I guarantee you "Goodbye" was written for junk . . . He says it's about Teresa but I don't believe it, I really don't.'

Steve launched the first of a series of mini acoustic tours with the *Train A' Comin'* musicians at The Vic in Chicago on 23 August. He had never forgotten the emotional night at Park West during the *Guitar Town* tour when he realized that his dreams had come true, and it felt good to be back in that place. The people and radio stations in Chicago had supported his career longer than any in the USA and he was hopeful that they would continue to do so now. They did. The *Chicago Tribune* named Steve's concert at The Vic No. 1 on their list of the year's best local shows and waxed lyrical about the electricity that passed from Steve to the audience and back again. 'Sometimes that spark becomes as tangible as the tears Steve Earle had to fight back on this night . . . Earle turned his back to the audience during a particularly tumultuous ovation as if to gather himself. He joked, "I'm not that well yet," but the music argued otherwise, as Earle brusquely strummed and sang his mythic tales of Southern sinners, loners and losers through a latticework of virtuoso string accompaniment.'

There was sentimental value in several of the other venues, too, a laying of ghosts and reprising of old glories. He played the Bottom Line in New York, scene of his triumphant *Guitar Town* debut in Manhattan, and the Birchmere in Alexandria, Virginia, which brought mixed emotions. It was after his 1987 solo show there that a local reviewer had described him as 'the best distinctly American songwriter to emerge from any genre in the last couple of years'. But it was at the Birchmere, too, that he had suffered from a crippling panic attack in 1993.

Steve was in Pittsburgh in late August when Dotson telephoned to ask him if he knew who Tim Robbins was.

'Sure,' said Steve, who was a big fan of *Bob Roberts* and *The Shawshank Redemption.*

'Well, he wants to talk to you.'

'Give him my number and have him call me.'

He had read Sister Helen Prejean's eye witness account of the execution of her long-time pen pal, Patrick Sonnier, a convicted killer, in Louisiana's Angola State Prison electric chair. Robbins told him a little more about the film project, which featured Sean Penn and Susan Sarandon, and Steve agreed to consider contributing to the soundtrack. The following day a rough cut of the film arrived at the Philadelphia Folk Festival. When Steve came off stage, he and the band sat down to watch it on the bus. Nobody stirred when they arrived back at the hotel. The power of the story held them spellbound.

Steve wrote 'Ellis Unit One' within the week, as soon as he got home. A chilling tale of man's inhumanity to man told from a guard's perspective, it was by far the most powerful song on an impressive soundtrack. *Q-Magazine* called it a 'career-capping contribution'.

On 13 September, Steve took his place in Nashville history beside his mentors, Townes and Guy, at the Bluebird Café. It was an evening rich with symbolism. For a start, it was Steve's 'clean date'. For one imperfect year he had been free from the addiction that had pursued him since he was a boy. His companions had wrestled with demons of their own in recent years and Townes, his dark hair streaked with iron, his fifty-one-year-old frame frail for his age, sat in a wooden chair between Steve and Guy. His flannel shirt hung loosely on his shoulders. Steve and Guy wore black shirts and blue jeans. Their weathered faces, physicality and mops of unruly hair made them look, for all the world, like outlaws. The club was packed. The proceeds of the evening were going to charity, but most people had come to see three of the finest songwriters ever to come out of Texas. Tickets had sold out in a day.

Over the next four hours, the trio regaled the crowd with blackly comic stories and songs from their most recent albums – Guy's *Dublin Blues*, Townes's *No Deeper Blue* and Steve's *Train A' Comin'*. The bond between all three went to the bone. They were, as Susanna Clark later described them, three 'gentle, crazy and generous souls', linked by pain as well as by the magnificence of their writing. The setlist showed how much Steve had gleaned from each of his mentors – the poetry he had taken from Townes, the storytelling from Guy. Among others, Townes offered 'Katie Belle', 'Tecumseh Valley' and 'Pancho and Lefty', Guy sang 'Baby Took a Limo to Memphis', 'The Cape', 'Randall Knife' and 'Immigrant Eyes' and Steve lent his soul and gravel voice to 'Valentine's Day', 'My Old Friend the Blues', 'I Ain't Never Satisfied' and 'Copperhead Road'. Emmylou Harris joined him for a stunning version of 'Goodbye'. Towards the end of the night, Steve played 'Ellis Unit One'. It was the first time he had performed the song in public and he stumbled a little over the intro. Guy, who had heard it only once, reminded him of the chords. It was a moving gesture that showed that the love and respect between the two men was still strong more than twenty years after they met. At one point, Guy leaned forward and kissed Steve's guitar. 'I love Steve Earle,' he said.

If the lyrics revealed their ragged biographies, the music showed how far they had all come and how true they had stayed to their visions. As Guy said, 'If you wan' good pearls, they're gonna cost ya.'

The return of notoriety and respect brought all the old complications. 'It's good to see you,' Neil Young told Steve in October when he played Farm Aid VIII in Louisville, Kentucky.

'It's good to be seen,' was Steve's droll response.

Soon afterwards the crowds parted and out bounded a small, voluble redhead with a beaming smile. She was an A&R executive at MCA and a huge fan of Steve's. Dub Cornett introduced them. 'Hi,' she greeted him, 'I'm Kelley Walker.'

In the car on the way home, Dotson was surprised to hear Steve talking about MCA, his nemesis, in somewhat positive terms. 'You would make a record for MCA?' Dotson asked in disbelief. 'Nah,' intoned Steve, 'but I'd make a record for Kelley Walker.' And Dotson had the first inkling that Steve had found a new muse.

The past, meanwhile, was catching up with Steve with a vengeance. Teresa Baker popped up at a show in Asheville, North Carolina with a photo of seven-year-old Jessica. She didn't ask for, or expect anything from Steve, she just wanted to show him his daughter. After she'd gone, Steve 'destroyed the picture – left it on the bus – because I didn't want to go home and explain it'. The whole saga had been a hard lesson, well learned. As Steve observed wryly: 'The moral of the story is, don't have sex of any sort anywhere near Johnson City, Tennessee. It's probably not a good idea on any level.'

On 8 November, Steve pleaded guilty to the July 1994 crack cocaine charge. He told a Nashville Criminal Court that staying off drugs was a matter of survival for him. 'It's a day by day thing but I've been clean for about fourteen months and five days now.' Judge Seth Norman was more enlightened on the subject of drugs than many of his counterparts might have been and he sentenced Steve to a year's probation rather than a jail term. He also ordered him to do a show at a local prison, a benefit performance for a drugs-related charity and to stay active in Narcotics Anonymous. He told Steve that he couldn't name one of his songs if he was paid a million dollars to do so, but the important thing was rehabilitation 'and I'm impressed with what you're telling me about yours'.

Steve had taken to rehab with the same fervour he'd once applied to drug taking. With each passing day the possibility of derailment or discouragement was minimized by the rock-solid support system of his Twelve Step programme. He had regular phone conversations with his sponsor and went to Twelve Step meetings on the road, and was pleasantly surprised to find it all worked. For his parents and siblings, there was a lot of enjoyment to be had from getting to know him again. In Houston, Patrick had held his first conversation with Steve in almost five years. 'Just all of a sudden he was aware and was sensitive, and conversations went back and forth and it really hadn't been like that for a long, long time.'

Steve went home to Jacksonville for the first time in years for his grandmother's ninetieth birthday. He wasn't sure he was ready to go to the family farm, with all the old memories, but he dutifully loaded up the kids in the Cadillac and drove north to Texas. The extended family flew in from all over America and they held a double celebration – for Jewel Earle's long life and her grandson's second chance. Steve had always been grandmama's unashamed favourite. She had kept scrapbooks documenting every twist and turn of his career right up until the last days of his addiction when the *National Enquirer* weighed in. Now there was no one happier for him. Surrounded by people who loved him, Steve began to feel much happier himself. The farm, with its peaches and Christmas trees, was the backdrop of his childhood. At nights, Uncle Arlon played the piano and everyone sang or tossed sausage links on the barbecue. They stood around under the hot summer sky until the mosquitoes drove them in.

Days later, the whole family took off to Concan, a vacation favourite in their youth. There was nothing fancy about it but, for Steve's sister Kelly and the other siblings, it was rustic and homely. 'In the daytime we swam, we sunned, we rode horses. At night, there was no TV. We sat around the campfire and listened to Justin play guitar and he played terrible back then. Pretty darned bad. And everyone sang and talked. And then we'd go inside and play poker all night.'

Without the filter of drugs, Dotson also felt that he got to know Steve for the first time, finding him 'the most innately intelligent human being I have ever met, the most determined, insightful and the most sensitive. There are times that paper cuts require stitches. He'll hold up like a rock under things that would crush you and me and melt under a blow dryer. There isn't any in between with that either. He does get hurt. You don't know it sometimes for two or three days. You don't even know what it'll be. It's just that three days after the injuring event he's screaming at you for something. You go, "What is this about?" But it sort of takes a while to wind back to where he was injured. He could overhear something in a restaurant, he could misinterpret something, and it would hammer him into the ground.'

To Dotson, Steve had a habit – particularly in the early days of his recovery – of always looking at the worst case scenario in any situation. Flying to England and Ireland to promote *Train A' Comin'* on 25 November, he was a bundle of nerves. Walking through Logan Airport, he was, Dotson says, 'having serious anxiety about going through customs. He knew he was going to be pulled aside or questioned or he'd be strip-searched. I mean, just the most dire projections about what this trip through customs was going to be. I said, "No, it won't be that bad." He said, "You don't know, you don't know."'

They made two stops before they reached the customs hall so that Steve could compose himself and blot away the perspiration.

'You're going to make them think you're holding,' Dotson chastised him. 'Would you stop already.'

At immigration, they swept through with no questions asked. '*See*,' Dotson said pointedly.

'Oh, they'll get me on the way back,' Steve retorted.

Steve's fragility only underlined the monumental feat that was his recovery. In the year since his release from jail, he had earned a Nashville Music Award nomination for Best Folk Album, performed, appropriately, 'In the Jailhouse Now' on Bob Dylan's tribute album to Jimmie Rodgers, and had at least seventeen cuts by other artists, including Travis Tritt's chart-topping 'Sometimes She Forgets', Confederate Railroad's 'Good Ol' Boy (Gettin' Tough)', Doug Supernaw's 'What'll You Do About Me' and Emmy's 'Goodbye'. Robert Earl Keen, Brother Phelps, the Morales Sisters and Stacey Dean Campbell also recorded his songs. Steve had an office, a desk and a pager. He was in the midst of making *I Feel Alright* and producing hot young Americana band The V-Roys for his own label.

'I'm real, real active and that is how I stay clean,' Steve told music columnist Robert Oermann. 'It's a matter of survival for me.'

On 1 December, he played a comeback concert at the Tennessee Performing Arts Center. It was another evening heavy with symbolism. After years of deriding him for pushing country's boundaries or dismissing him as a rebel without a cause, Music Row's most esteemed citizens had come in all their finery to pay their respects. Under the lights, Steve was still pale and bloated, but his beautiful spirit was intact. The pure, unadulterated passion of his convictions flowed through the music like a prayer. The dark years melted away. It was *Guitar Town* revisited, but without the unconscious anger.

In the middle of a song, the audience erupted. Steve turned around to see a sprightly silver-haired figure wandering out of the wings. Even before he reached centre stage, there was no mistaking the piercing hooded eyes and dignified bearing of the unannounced visitor, and cheers and whistles accompanied his slow progress. It was bluegrass legend Bill Monroe. He had come to welcome Steve home.

For Steve and for the audience, it was a moment of immense poignancy. For more than half a century, Monroe had been the acknowledged patriarch of bluegrass music, an introverted farm boy who had almost single-handedly pioneered a genre. His improvisational mandolin style, 'high lonesome' vocals and proud dedication to excellence made him one of the most influential men in music history. Off stage, Monroe had always had a reputation as a man of few words, so when he walked on to the stage at TPAC, Steve was flattered by the spontaneous show of solidarity. Monroe took the microphone and Steve, like everyone else, was charmed. Five songs later, his mood had moved from excited to frustrated to resigned. He'd lost control of the show. Eventually, Monroe was led from the stage and Steve said sardonically into the mike: 'When the captain's on the bridge, the captain's *on* the bridge.'

It wasn't until Monroe died nine months later, aged eighty-four, that Steve gained any insight into his appearance that night. At Monroe's funeral, a friend told Steve about an incident that occurred years before when Hank Williams, fired from the Grand Ole Opry in August 1952 (four months before his death) because of chronic alcoholism and instability, turned up at the stage door drunk. Monroe was the only performer to go down and shake his hand. Watching the chequered progress of Steve Earle, Monroe was perhaps one of the few to recognize that, far from being the antithesis of Hank Williams and all that he stood for, Steve more purely embodied what Williams considered the most precious ingredient in country music – sincerity – than any starched and pressed Wrangler-wearing Urban Cowboy.

'When a hillbilly sings a crazy song, he feels crazy,' Williams said. 'When he sings, "I Laid My Mother Away", he sees her a-laying right there in the coffin. He sings more sincere than most entertainers because the hillbilly was raised rougher than most entertainers. You got to know a lot about hard work. You got to have smelt a lot of mule manure before you can sing like a hillbilly. The people who has been raised something like the way the hillbilly has knows what he is singing about and appreciates it.'

15

Jailhouse Rock

Steve Earle was afraid. Much more afraid than he had ever been when flick-knife-toting drug dealers tried to get the better of him, or in the seventies when the jealous Mexican shot him in the ribs at the Triple AAA Icehouse in San Antonio, or when police trained their guns on his front door in Nashville, or when he was being airlifted to Vanderbilt after his worst car crash, and more afraid than he'd been when he followed Popeye into the ghostly catacomb on Avenue B in New York. Ahead of him loomed the grim outline of Cold Creek Correctional Facility. In the planning stages, going back to prison had seemed like a novel idea. Steve had to fulfil Judge Seth Norman's stipulation that he perform a show behind bars and Warner Brothers had come up with a proposal to do a live satellite broadcast from Alcatraz. That had blossomed into an MTV special, which they tried to get permission to shoot at Brushy Mountain, a maximum-security prison between Nashville and Knoxville. Taking eighty people and three truck-loads of gear there was, unfortunately, out of the question, so they settled on Cold Creek. It had recently been used for the filming of *The People Vs Larry Flint* with Courtney Love.

It was to Cold Creek that Steve and John Dotson were headed in June 1996. On the way Dotson, as well-turned-out as ever, dark hair groomed, aftershave applied, tried his best to calm Steve down. Steve stayed tense. Dotson gave up trying to distract him when the distant silhouette of the guardhouse loomed into sight. 'When we got off the freeway and got minute by minute closer to the prison, it really rattled him. He was coming to confront the most horrific experience of his life.'

In the first year of his recovery, Steve's achievements had beggared belief. In the history of incarceration, few men can have returned to the outside world with such an overwhelming determination to embrace redemption, or with quite so much to offer the world, both personally and artistically. Far from bemoaning the hand fate had dealt him, Steve was practically bursting with hopeful vitality. The following year, 1996, was no different. A 4 January appearance on the *Today Show* was followed by the third section of the *Train A' Comin'* tour. North West music magazine, *The Rocket*, described the final, sold-out show at the Backstage in Seattle on 19 January as 'phenomenal'. On stage, its reviewer said, Steve was 'everything he was not in the eighties: animated, friendly, talkative, self-depreciating, focused, and compelling from start to finish'. While few people would concur that Steve had been lost for words in the eighties or any other decade, it was obvious that the qualities he possessed in his early twenties – softness, generosity and warmth – were back again, only this time the scattered energy was harnessed. The nearness of death had lent an edge to his playing and given him a new appreciation of the career he had almost thrown away. When Peter Rowan and Norman Blake took centre stage in Seattle, Steve stepped out of the spotlight and, rather than returning to his dressing room, stood in the darkened wings with an expression of bliss on his face, just soaking in the rapture of the crowd.

There was more to come. Ten years after he first attempted to gain entry, Steve made his debut at the Grand Ole Opry, the historic heart of country music. After leaving the Ryman, the Opry had moved out to Opryland, a vast, glittering complex that included a hotel, theme park and conference rooms. Against all expectations, the Opry itself had retained some of its original old-worldy feel. It had its critics but its symbolism as the standard bearer of purism in country music had never lost its value. A cynic might say that it was ironic that, while the relatively clean-cut *Guitar Town* Steve didn't pass muster, the Steve whose life had taken on the tragic proportions of a country song was acceptable. In his current guise, Steve was a living example of the old adage that if you play a country song backwards, you get your house back, your wife back and your dog back. But of course, Steve's welcome at the Opry was predominantly about music. *Guitar Town* had flirted a little too hard with rock and rebellion. *Train A' Comin'* harked back to the roots of hillbilly music. It was traditional music reinvented for a new age.

At the show itself, Emmy sat in on 'Goodbye' and afterwards they went backstage with Tony Brown and talked like old times. The dressing rooms of the Opry were big roomy affairs, with theatrical mirrors and comfortable benches and chairs, and few artists seemed to bother closing their doors. On any given night, Charlie Pride could be seen holding court in one dressing room, Martina McBride or Clay Walker in another and Porter Wagoner would be gliding by like some strange exotic bird. But that particular night belonged to Steve. It marked his acceptance by one of the few authorities he respected.

Much of Steve's newfound confidence and contentment came from the knowledge that in November 1995 he had completed *I Feel Alright*, the first album he'd ever had absolute and total control over from start to finish. It was also his first analog album since the unreleased tracks he'd cut for Epic. Like *The Hard Way*, it was rock as catharsis. Unlike *The Hard Way*, there was plenty of light relief. The pounding guitar rock of 'Feel Alright' and 'The Unrepentant' was interspersed with the jangly Beatles riffs of 'More Than I Can Do' and lonely twelve-bar blues of 'South Nashville Blues'. The Fairfield Four provided gospel backing on 'Valentine's Day' and Lucinda Williams duetted with Steve on 'You're Still Standing There'. Steve did a lot of soul-searching before he added 'CCKMP' and 'The Unrepentant', written before he got clean. When he did add 'CCKMP', he wanted to re-create the eerie echo that had resounded through the house in Larchmont Village the day he wrote it in 1991.

In the early hours of one morning he hurtled into the studio across the hall and asked country band Diamond Rio if they had a tyre iron. 'They said, "Y'all have a flat?"' Steve told *Rolling Stone*. 'And I said, "No, we want to throw it down the stairwell and record it."'

Tyre iron in hand, Steve and Ray Kennedy, who was co-producing, ran a quarter of mile of cables out to a six-storey stairwell. 'I started whacking the shit out of this metal banister with the tyre iron but I couldn't get the low-end sound I wanted. This buddy of mind named Dub was there, and he's so big he could just take the palm of his hand and whomp on the banister, so it went *whoomp-fwoom-fwoom-fwoom*, oscillating up the stairwell. That's the ambient noise on "Cocaine Cannot Kill My Pain".'

Many of the old crew were back on board. Kelley Looney played some of the bass parts and Roy Huskey Jr, Ric Kipp and Springsteen's bass player Garry Tallent played the rest. Richard Bennett lent his production and guitar playing skills to the album, Ken Moore was on organ and Dan Gillis, who had run into Steve at Nashville's Tin Pan Jam in '95, was his tour manager once again.

Richard found everything to be exactly where it was when he left in 1988, 'only healthier'. Steve's songs stripped life down to its marrow. Richard had always considered that a defining point for an artist was how a song would sound if it was played with nothing grander than an acoustic guitar. 'Will it still hold up as a song, or do you need the window dressing around to bolster it up. And his stuff certainly is great with just him and a guitar.'

Steve himself was still coming to terms with the casual cruelty of life without drugs. Richard found that whenever Steve was challenged or forced into a stressful situation in the studio, he used the opt-out clause: 'I'm not that well yet'. Emotionally and physically, he was still very shaky. Aerosmith's Stephen Tyler once said that heroin offers the possibility of 'life without anxiety', but that option was no longer available to Steve. When his father had open-heart surgery for the second time right in the middle of recording, worry and self-reproach consumed him. For all of those reasons, *I Feel Alright* was the most personal album Steve had ever written – his road to recovery laid bare. On the Cold Creek documentary, *To Hell and Back*, he confessed there'd never be another record like it 'because the year in which it was made I changed more than I ever have in my life and probably ever will'.

The release of *I Feel Alright* brought acceptance on a scale Steve could never have dreamed of when he was fighting tooth and nail for the tiniest rock concession on *Exit o*. During the late eighties and early nineties, Nashville had cashed in on the boom precipitated by 'New Country' artists like Steve, Dwight Yoakam, Randy Travis, kd lang, Lyle Lovett and Nanci Griffith and launched, in rapid succession, the next wave of Clint Black, Wynonna Judd, Mary Chapin Carpenter and, of course, Garth Brooks. No one could have predicted then the stratospheric success of Garth, nor that he would enter the mid-nineties as the biggest-selling male artist of all time. By then the line between rock or pop and country had become so blurred as to be almost invisible. The pyrotechnics of Garth's stadium shows were no different from those of Bon Jovi. Often the instrument that once seemed integral to country music, the pedal steel guitar, was missing from the band altogether.

Steve had his own opinion about Garth Brooks: 'Well he really can't sing. He really can't carry a tune in a bucket. His records need a lot of work. He really is tone deaf. He's one of the worst singers I've ever heard in my life. I think Garth Brooks is kind of evil just because he sucks so much energy and money out of the business. But you know, that's country music and I don't have anything to do with what they call country music. I haven't since my second record.'

The cycles that influence music's destiny are as inevitable as the seasons, yet most labels concerned themselves only with churning out Garth Brooks clones. By the time *I Feel Alright* was released, country music was in a markedly different place than it was at the start of Steve's lost years. The polished country-pop of Garth and Clint had been watered down to the point where super-safe, super-clean artists like Clay Walker held sway. The women were more diverse but Country Music Television still played host to an alarming number of blonde Mindy McCready lookalikes. On the positive side, the insipidness of the music and the dominance of country radio had inspired a return to roots and the rapid rise – through indie labels, Triple AAA radio and magazines like *No Depression* – of 'Americana' or 'No Depression' country. After a decade as a musical outlaw, Steve suddenly found that he, Guy and Townes were poster-boys of the Americana movement, along with Emmylou Harris, Buddy and Julie Miller, Gillian Welch and David Rawlings and Lucinda Williams. *Train A' Comin'* reached No. 1 on Gavin's Americana chart. Young bands like Son Volt, the Blood Oranges and Whiskeytown were as likely to be influenced by Townes and Steve as they were by Gram Parsons or the Beatles. Unlike Steve, who'd had to struggle mightily just to get the mixes made harder on *Exit 0*, these bands trampled joyously across musical borders, incorporating a string section on one track and Nirvana on the next.

Having inadvertently precipitated all of this, Steve was at last in a position to capitalize on it. He no longer had to justify his love affair with rock. Now he just told people he made Steve Earle music and that was the end of it. *CD Review* gave *I Feel Alright* a 9 for performance and a 9 for sound quality and *Entertainment Weekly* gave it an A. *Spin* described the album as a 'heaven-sent demo sampler' since 'More Than I Can Do' sounded like an outtake from a Dylan/Beatles session, 'Valentine's Day' had George Jones written all over it, Bruce Springsteen could have recorded 'Now She's Gone' and 'The Unrepentant' was right down Axl Rose's 'self-mythologizing alley . . .'

The drugs still occupied as large a part of every article as the music. Steve remarked to *Q Magazine* that it was a 'real incentive not to fuck up again. Because if I had the blind luck to survive again, I'd have to do all those stupid fucking interviews again and I'm not going to do that.' In April, he was talking to a reporter from the *New York Times* when he came upon his band watching a video of *Pulp Fiction*. The Uma Thurman character had just overdosed on heroin and was about to be administered a life-saving shot of adrenalin. 'None of the junkies I knew were so well-equipped,' Steve told the reporter. 'When they overdosed, they'd usually just die.'

Behind the scenes, Steve, Emerson and Dotson had spent months negotiating a five-album deal with Warner Brothers to distribute Steve's E-Squared records, including *I Feel Alright* and *Train A Comin'*, which they'd bought from Winter Harvest in February. Steve was afraid that it would go out of print. That agreement precipitated a September 1998 lawsuit from Bill Alsobrook, which was still ongoing when he collapsed and died a year later. Legally, Alsobrook was a 'third-party beneficiary' to the transfer. When he did not receive what he felt to be his share, he sued Steve and E-Squared for $120,000.

Owsley Manier still likes and admires Steve, but he feels aggrieved on the late Alsobrook's behalf. 'We rescued [Steve], there's no doubt about it. And not only that, Steve can say what he wants to about it, that's fine, but Bill did come up with those players and Steve had never been in a direction like that before. And the songs were perfect for it. And that was after a lot of contemplation and thinking about a direction to go in to re-emerge. So it was unfortunate.'

Dotson had his own problems with Steve during the thirty-day, twenty-two-city promotional tour they'd done prior to the release of the new album. Triple AAA radio, the Americana format that had come into being and gained power during Steve's long absence from music, liked artists to come to their stations and perform live. Mick Jagger, Elvis Costello, Bruce Springsteen and Lou Reed had all done the radio station circuit. Steve refused. 'I did that early in my career,' he told Dotson, 'I don't do that any more.'

The head of promotion at Triple AAA refused to take no for an answer. She begged and wheedled and Dotson did the same with Steve. Steve would not be moved. There would be no advance press. Journalists could come and review his shows and he would talk on stage but that was it. Few people knew that the main reason he was reluctant to do interviews was that, with very little recovery time under his belt, it was taking all the emotional strength he could rally to deal with the ongoing traumas in his personal life. Physically and psychologically, Lou was still very damaged and with just weeks to go before *I Feel Alright* was released, Steve was by her side at a treatment facility.

At Warner Brothers, meanwhile, relations started to sour. The label heads were already frustrated by Steve's unwillingness to do press and when they found out that Steve and Ray Kennedy were planning to produce the album that Lucinda Williams had been working on with Rick Rubin, himself a source of huge displeasure at Warner, they were furious. According to Dotson, Steve's attitude was: 'Fuck them . . . Tell them whatever you want to tell them.'

Dotson flew to LA to reason with Warner. 'Let's focus on what's right,' he said. 'When he leaves the cities, we're getting tremendous press . . . At some point he's got to stop answering questions like, "Where have you been and how long did you do heroin?" and let the music speak for itself.'

It was an impassioned speech and at the end of it he felt that Warner was back onside. But the label would not let up on the live radio performance. Dotson told Steve, 'If you don't want to do it, you don't want to do it and I'll tell them you don't want to do it but the doors will shut, the lights will go off with the first single on the album. Is that really what you want?' Pushed into a corner, Steve had little choice but to agree to appear on a Los Angeles radio station. Not even Dotson seemed capable of understanding that touring without the safe haven of drugs was still very new to him. Many of Steve's reservations about Triple AAA radio had to do with not wanting to add the pressure of live broadcasts to an already daunting schedule. 'It may have been foolish on my part but I just couldn't physically do it.'

On Easter Sunday, Kelley Walker moved to Nashville to work for E-Squared and, in lieu of a larger salary, took up residence in an apartment Steve had rented near Music Row. In the months since their meeting they'd begun a flirtation over the phone ('I flirted with her but then I flirted with everybody') and Steve had run up a $2,000 bill. But talking was all they did. That changed fairly quickly after Walker started doing A&R for his label. On stage he would joke, 'Lou-Anne and I decided to get married again because our divorce didn't work out,' but he was deeply unhappy at home.

He was in Amsterdam in May when his stepdaughter Amy rang him in tears to tell him that her sister had been killed in a car wreck by a drunk driver.

'Please come home, Daddy, I need you,' Lou says Amy pleaded.

But Steve, who was on the last night of an acclaimed European tour that had taken in Norway, Scotland and York, Cambridge and the Shepherd's Bush Empire in London, was so worried about cancelling the few dates he had in the USA before he went home that not even the appeal of his stepdaughter could bring him home. 'If I do, people will think I'm using again,' he told Amy. It was a legitimate concern. Added to which, Steve would have been liable for thousands of dollars' worth of cancellation charges. Lou suspected that there was another reason Steve stayed away. She did some investigating and confirmed what she'd already guessed: Steve was having an affair. 'Of course, Steve denied it. He said, "No, that's not true." The next thing I knew, a reporter was calling the house, "How do you feel about Steve filing for divorce?" Well, I didn't know he'd filed for divorce. He just beat me to the lawyers is all I can say.'

With that, the longest, most tempestuous relationship of Steve's life came finally to an end. He and Lou had, as Lou put it, 'lived out a novel together', but it had become toxic. Walker was not the cause of their divorce, she was merely the latest factor in it. It had become too easy for Steve and Lou to hurt each other. After her first divorce from Steve, Lou had made several tearful phone calls to his sister Kelly to tell her about Steve's cheating ways with Teresa. Kelly had felt somewhat bemused to be the recipient of these calls. 'These women, they steal him from another woman . . . It's like, get with the programme. If it's happened once or twice or three or four times, it's going to happen again.'

Whether or not this was a life lesson Lou should have absorbed, she was deeply wounded when Steve left her for another woman a second time. 'All I ever did was love Steve and try to support him and give up part of myself, which I will never do again.'

'Don't hit her. Don't do anything stupid,' Dotson told Steve when he received the call about the second divorce, knowing that his client could be volatile and his erstwhile sister-in-law dangerously unpredictable. 'If you need a place to go, I live in a security building.'

Days later, Steve walked into his office with his bags packed. 'Need your place starting tonight, hoss,' he announced. Dotson had always considered Steve to be the incarnation of Charles Schultz's cartoon character Pigpen, so he moved out and went to stay with his girlfriend. He knew that there would be tears if he tried to cohabit with Steve. 'I had to get a professional cleaning service to come in and put it back in shape after he left. And pay a $300 phone bill.'

Lou, Amy, Ian and Justin moved back to downtown Nashville and made an appointment with a family therapist. Over the years, Lou had grown to hate Fairview. It was too far from Nashville and too full of memories, wonderful and horrific. 'I had not realized how detrimental it was to all of us. It was like living in hell. I can't describe it any other way.'

It was to hell Steve went on 26 June – or his definition of it, at any rate. 'This ain't going to be no beach party,' he drawled to the MTV cameraman after crossing the razor-wire perimeter of Cold Creek Correctional Facility in West Tennessee. Black t-shirt stretched over his 265 pound bulk, hair hanging lankly beside muttonchop sideburns, he strode towards the stony white walls and crashing steel gates of the prison looking as though he belonged there.

Perhaps there never will be another performance like the one Steve gave at Cold Creek. Outwardly, he looked as intimidating as he'd been at the most insane heights of his post-*Hard Way* success, dark glasses concealing his eyes, meaty hands gripping the skull and crossbones on the fretboard of his guitar. But under the white sheen of sweat, his faith and humanity and urgent need to reach out and touch people and change their lives came through on every note. When he played 'Guitar Town', the prisoners were dancing in the aisles. They punched the air with Custer's drumbeats on 'The Unrepentant'. But when Steve introduced 'Ellis Unit One' by saying that he'd felt less proud to be Texan after learning that twenty-three of the fifty-six people who were executed in the USA in 1995 met their end on Ellis Unit One in Huntsville, Texas, you could have cut the silence with a knife.

In the documentary, the songs were interspersed with the cautionary tales of a group of inmates, their young, almost clean-cut faces stricken with the awfulness of their plight. Twenty-one-year-old Robert was a lifer, convicted of first-degree murder. His voice cracked as he described prison life as 'as type of hell – you've gotta stay, you can't leave'. Joseph, twenty-two, serving twenty years for second-degree murder, told the camera: 'You're lonely, you don't trust nobody. Because if you trust people, you can get killed.' He had a gentle face and a wife and kids back home. He was paying the ultimate price for a marijuana scam that went wrong when a friend pulled a gun. Most haunting of all was the desperation of Mario, a handsome twenty-two-year-old black man serving fifteen years 'confined in a cage' like an animal. 'I've been here for four years. I think it's time to go. I'm ready to go *now*.'

Mario was one of the seventy or so per cent of Cold Creek's five hundred inmates who had come to prison by way of drugs. Later, Steve stood in the shadow of the guard tower and the razor-wire and asked, 'If anybody out there thinks they can handle a drug problem, can you handle living in here? This is the good thing that can happen. The other alternatives are mental institutions where you stay for the rest of your life – and the cemetery.'

Back in Nashville, Dotson redoubled his efforts to finalize the Canadian section of the *I Feel Alright* tour, which was scheduled for August. Under Canadian immigration laws, the entire tour had to be booked and all contracts signed before the necessary entry permits could be considered. Since Steve had been convicted of drug offences, an FBI report was also required. All went smoothly until Immigration received the FBI report detailing his 1988 trial for assaulting a police officer and 1987 charge for carrying a concealed weapon at Norfolk International Airport. At that point, they stalled.

With days to go before the first show in Vancouver, Dotson managed to persuade them that, since the Dallas case had been adjudicated, it was a non-issue. They refused to budge on the Virginia Beach charge. Dotson enlisted the aid of a local attorney and was shocked to find that although Steve had pleaded not guilty, he had failed to make an October 1988 court appearance in Virginia Beach. An arrest warrant had been issued and had been active for eight years. In Dotson's fevered imagination, 'if Steve had driven through Virginia with a tail-light out and gotten pulled over, he would have gone straight to State Pen. But what hacked off the Canadian Government is that he had gone in and out of Canada [several] times since both of these convictions and did not bother to tell them. And they were really angry.'

Steve was angry with Dotson. 'You didn't need to tell them,' he insisted.

'Yes, we did,' Dotson said stubbornly. 'These are legal obligations.'

With $200,000 in possible concert cancellation charges hanging over his head, Dotson sent the Virginia Beach attorney back to the courthouse. It turned out that the case had never been adjudicated. The attorney argued that Steve had been denied due process and had the charges against him dismissed. Twenty-four hours before the Vancouver show, the Canadian permits were issued.

Dotson telephoned Steve in Vancouver. 'I don't ever do this but I'm going to tell you, I just saved your ass,' he said.

'If you're going to invent a crisis so that you can ride in on your white horse and save my ass, fuck you,' Steve shouted. Fifteen minutes later, he called Dotson back 'to tell me how much angrier he was at me and that I could either wait till he got home to kick my ass or I could come out on the road and face the music in person. I got on an aeroplane and went to Canada to meet him. *What?* What did he have to say to me? "*&!!#**^@ . . ." When we got home, he fired me.'

But Steve maintains that he would never have fired Dotson over such a trivial incident, particularly since the Canadian tour went ahead and nothing was lost. Nor did he hold a grudge against Dotson for apparently using Steve's recovery as an excuse for his reluctance to do live radio broadcasts when talking to Warner (something Dotson denies). The real reason he fired Dotson was, he says, because he believed his manager was alienating people at Warner Brothers. *I Feel Alright* was on its way to selling 100,000 copies and Steve wanted the label behind him. He felt that certain people cringed when Dotson walked through the door. 'That had become evident to me. It was a decision I was very slow to make after the complaints started coming in and they started immediately.'

Years later, when Dotson ran into Teresa in Austin, he observed ruefully to her that he should have set some boundaries in his relationship with Steve. Teresa, he says, responded that Steve didn't recognize boundaries. 'Boundaries are a target for him.' It was an uncanny echo of Lou's comment that Steve 'does not respect boundaries. If you say, "Steve, this is a line in the sand that I'm going to draw for my personal protection because I don't want to go there with you," he will, when you least expect it, cross it.'

Dotson remains resentful about his sacking, not least because he feels he 'waded in' when no one else wanted Steve and ended up with less than $80,000 for three and a half years of service. Many of the choices he made were in the hope of some long-term benefit to his niece Amy, but the acrimony surrounding Lou and Steve's divorce tainted Lou's relationship with Dotson and to this day they don't speak. In a letter outlining his position, Dotson wrote:

I wish Steve nothing but success because, as I told you, the world would be poorer for the lack of his voice and unique, wonderful work . . . I am only one of the many people who have given their attention, effort, total energy, heart and uncompromising belief to open and reopen and reopen and reopen doors for him over the years. Maybe it is too much to hope that he could appreciate how much has been given by so many people in keeping his voice alive and a place at the table. The distinguished alumni association of which I am part can continue to hope, even in the absence of expectation.

Regards,
John Dotson

Steve returned to Fairview to find a fresh family crisis brewing. His revolver was missing. What made him particularly upset was that there was little doubt who had taken it. Ever since his break-up with Lou, Justin, wired with teenage fury, had gone rapidly off the rails. He wasn't speaking to Steve. His appearances at school were infrequent and he was showing an unhealthy inclination towards arson and illicit substances. As Stacey says, Steve was 'staring himself in the mirror for a while'.

Confronted about the gun, Justin adopted a stance of insolent innocence. Steve knew he was lying. He ransacked the house in a bid to find it. When repeated searches of the house turned up nothing, he made the decision to dispatch Justin to Three Springs, the 'wilderness camp' where he had sent Nick's son Cole. In Cole's case, he'd had no option. In 1990, when Cole was living at Fairview, he stole Teresa's rental car and Grace's credit card in a bid to escape to Texas. As his legal guardian, the judge had given Steve two choices: pay for a private teenage boot camp or Cole would be sent to a correctional facility for juvenile delinquents. Steve paid for Three Springs: 'It was expensive, it was a fortune – I could have sent him to college.' In all, Cole spent nearly eighteen months there. After his release, he did well until he finished high school, at which time he moved out of Fairview and burgled some thirty-two houses, including Steve's. He has been in jail on and off ever since.

Despite this appalling outcome, Steve sent Justin, to Three Springs in September. 'I said, "I can't get you to tell me the truth but I can get you to [do this]." And I still have problems with the fact that I did that. Because I mean, the place is a pretty horrible place.'

At Three Springs, Justin had to wear an orange jumpsuit,

just as his father had in jail. He called Steve as soon as he arrived and told him where he had hidden the gun but Steve refused to let him come home. Justin was forced to accept that he'd be in a work camp for the next four months, a terrifying prospect made bearable only by the fact that six other kids from his neighbourhood had also been condemned to Three Springs. 'We were all chained together so we could work on the roads. It was kinda scary being chained to a criminal who's behind you with a pickaxe in his hand. I was fourteen years old when I went in. Basically, the place is put there to shock kids into "This is what you're heading for if you don't straighten your act out." It didn't work. It didn't work for anyone I knew.'

At Fairview, Steve took a cutting torch to the only two guns he still owned. Once he'd been vehemently opposed to the anti-handgun lobby. He had even bought the party line of the ultra-right-wing National Rifle Association, albeit with his own left-wing ideology thrown in. 'I interpreted the right to bear arms as something that was put in to facilitate a revolution if the government got oppressive.' Even after he came out of jail, he carried a pistol every time he drove into town. Gradually, though, he came to see that guns were not synonymous with liberty. There was a moral issue on the line. 'In other words, if somebody's going to kill me, am I prepared to take someone's life because mine is at stake? Well, at one time I was. I was totally capable of it. And I'm really lucky I didn't kill someone when I was out running around carrying guns all the time and out of my mind on dope.'

At times, though, it seemed as if the past would never stop biting at his heels, reminding him, in the most excruciating way possible, how much havoc his addiction had caused. Apart from the obvious conclusions to be drawn from the behaviour of Justin, trying to out-rebel his father, Steve had to attend a June trial for driving on a revoked licence in April 1994 when he had crashed on I-40. Then there were the scavengers who tried to sell the guitars and motorbikes he had hocked in his worst days back to him at ten times the price. It made Patrick mad, the number of people willing to trade on the guilt Steve so clearly laboured under to take advantage of him. Worst of all, in his opinion, were a couple of the ex-wives. 'It's pretty amazing the people that will openly come and tell him to his face: "You *owe* me this."'

But even Pat, who had spent most of his adult years protecting Steve just as Steve protected him, had to accept that confronting the demons his brother had always fled from was something Steve would have to do alone.

On New Year's Day, 1997, Townes Van Zandt slipped from consciousness. His youngest son Will came upon his motionless form and ran, white-faced, to call his mother, Jeanene, who at the very moment was on the phone to Susanna Clark. 'Mom, you better look at Dad, he looks dead!' he cried. Jeanene still had the receiver in her hand when she rushed into the room, but as she later recalled on the internet site, *Around-Townes*, 'as soon as I passed through the doorway I knew his spirit was no longer in the room . . .'

Death had hovered about Townes for days. On Christmas Eve, he had suffered a violent fall, injuring his hip, but had refused to visit a doctor. It was New Year's Eve before Jeanene, to whom he was no longer married, coaxed him into seeking medical attention. By then Townes could barely walk. His hip had become a black and blue circle of pain. At the hospital, doctors diagnosed a broken hip. They admitted him there and then and he was wheeled into surgery at one-thirty a.m. When Jeanene came to collect him later that day, she took him a flask of alcohol to quell the shakes that were wracking his wasted body. Back home, Townes had been quiet but he seemed more peaceful. Jeanene brought him a plate of cheese and crackers and his daughter Katie Belle sat by his side. Will wandered in and out of the room. At ten p.m., as Jeanene was on the phone to Susanna Clark, updating her on Townes's condition, Townes had suffered a massive heart attack. Jeanene dialled 911 and attempted to resuscitate him, and emergency crews took over fifteen minutes later. They detected a faint heartbeat on the way to the hospital, but it faded away. Townes never regained consciousness.

It was New Year's Day – the forty-fifth anniversary of the death of Hank Williams, Townes's hero.

Steve called as soon as he heard the news. Susanna Clark answered the phone. She and Guy had driven over to comfort Jeanene. 'Steve, you don't need to come out here,' Susanna said to him. 'We're handling it.'

'I *need* to be there,' Steve said.

He had a strong feeling of déjà-vu as he drove out to the house on Old Hickory Lake. It was the Clarks' seventies songwriter haven, which they had later sold to Townes. For the rest of the day, he took turns with Susanna at fielding the phones as friends, fans and journalists called from across the globe. Susanna was thankful for Steve's support. 'He was nice. He's a good guy. He'll let you cry when you need to cry.' Privately, Steve was more worried about the tall, hunched figure of Guy. Guy had a tendency to internalize things anyway and now, with the shock of his best friend's death, he seemed more shut down than ever.

The house was thick with memories. This was the place where Steve had honed his craft, where he'd sat at the feet of his mentors with a cheap guitar and more hunger to learn and sheer willpower than any of them had ever witnessed. It was the scene of all of those intense, Malt Duck-fuelled nights – when the artistic energy in the house was, as Susanna had often said, 'like Paris in the twenties'. It was the house where Townes and Guy had taught him to be a songwriter. Awkwardly at first and then with deep affection, Steve, Guy and Susanna reminisced about the magic and the craziness that was Townes. It had frightened Guy sometimes, the weird characters that latched on to Townes – 'serious bad guys'. He had often wondered if it was some sort of 'noblesse oblige' thing on Townes's part. Once, when Guy was visiting Townes at a farm he owned, Townes's 'schizoid' Eskimo neighbour, now long since dead, had taken it into his head that Townes's guitar player was being offensive towards him. He stormed into his house and emerged with a rifle. The guitarist, he screamed, was going to die.

Guy, Townes and the guitarist watched impassively from the window. 'I'm gonna go talk to him,' Townes announced suddenly. 'You wait here with the shotgun. If he shoots me, kill him.'

'Okay, man,' drawled Guy. He had become accustomed to such scenes. Townes always seemed to attract, and be attracted to, the deranged, the unhinged, the downright psychotic.

Songwriter Mickey Newbury called Steve in distress on the day Townes died. He was convinced that he had contributed to the wounding of Townes's psyche by selling his publishing contract to Kevin Eggars early in his career. 'I think he'd still be alive if I hadn't done that,' he said. Steve understood that the subtext of Newbury's distress was simply that he had recognized that, beneath the mad bravado, Townes was a vulnerable as a fawn, and Newbury was blaming himself for not doing more to protect him. Steve, too, felt a great tide of rage rushing through him at the managers and record companies who had taken advantage of his friend's lack of business savvy.

'There are reasons why nobody knew who Townes was until relatively late in his life and after he was dead. He was incredibly mismanaged. It was just amazing how incompetent and how criminal it was.'

Guy believed that in art, as in life, Townes had been far more aware of what he was doing than his choices might have led some people to believe. 'Townes's work was always inspiring for me and always will be. Sure, some of his songs should have done better, but the reality is, even though they're masterpiece songs, they're not what gets played on the radio. And even [the commercial success of] 'Pancho and Lefty' was a fluke. It's got to be. But still, what a wonderful thing to have happened and I wish it had happened more.'

Two weeks later, Steve flew to Glasgow for the start of a two-month-long solo tour. Justin went with him. He had emerged unrepentant from Three Springs shortly before his birthday on 4 January. The last thing he and his friends talked about before leaving was getting the money together to get some dope to sell for profit. Lou found she could no longer handle him and he was soon back with Steve. 'In town, he started getting into so much trouble that she handed him off to his mother and Carol handed him off to me. She called. So I'd had a year and a half clean, Lou and I had split up and all of that had gone on, and [six] months after that I had an out-of-control four-teen-year-old boy on my hands, and it was a pain in the ass to take a fourteen-year-old to Europe. He went all over Europe, hated every second of it. 'Course now when he's talking to girls he tells them all about Europe.'

In Slovenia, Steve gave Justin his own room and Justin repaid him by raiding his mini bar and refilling all the bottles with water. Looking back, Justin concedes that he was a 'horrible little shit' at that age. 'I did everything that I possibly could to get into trouble . . . Then when people tried to explain to me that it was wrong, I could not find any reason why it was wrong. I was just awful.'

From Scotland, Steve flew to Denmark, Sweden and Norway, accompanied by JT, Dan Gillis and alt-country band, the Delevantes. Dan had become his manager when Dotson vacated the position. 'It's your turn,' Steve had told him. 'Do you want to do it or not?' Dan did.

On the road, Steve threw himself into work and activism like he once had into heroin, finding he had an abundance of time, money and energy now that he didn't have to forage for drugs. The first V-Roys album was out and Steve had signed or was in the process of signing 6-String Drag, Cheri Knight and Ross Rice. He and Jack Emerson had renegotiated the

Warner deal so that E-Squared existed as a free-standing label, distributed by independent Warner subsidiary ADA.

In Nashville and outside of it, he found himself thinking more and more about the death penalty. Writing 'Ellis Unit One' for *Dead Man Walking* had, as one might have expected, drawn him back into the campaign to abolish capital punishment. Up until 1993, his main involvement with the death penalty had simply been his correspondence with Jonathan Wayne Nobles and a handful of other inmates on Death Row. That had come to an abrupt end when he received a phone call from an organization which worked to convince death penalty volunteers to change their minds on the grounds that it made it easier for the state to kill people. The charity wanted Steve to contact a volunteer in Alabama and try to talk him round. Steve, however, was at the worst stage of his addiction and it was some days before he summoned the wherewithal to return the call. When he did, the volunteer was dead. Stricken with guilt, Steve stopped writing to Nobles and the other inmates and stopped thinking about the death penalty altogether. It was only in 1996, when he attended the *Dead Man Walking* concert in LA, a benefit for Murder Victims Families' for Reconciliation (MVFR), that he became convinced that he could make a positive contribution to the abolition movement. He met the inspirational members of another organization, Journey of Hope: From Violence to Healing, all of whom were relatives of Death Row inmates or Death Row inmates who had been found to be innocent. Their commitment to healing rather than revenge made him feel that the very least he could do was dedicate himself to their cause. In his music, Steve had always championed the dispossessed, but he himself had never felt that way. 'A champion is someone who actually does something about it and I've only lately become an activist,' he said.

Throughout the European tour of 1997, Steve spoke about the death penalty whenever he performed, never preaching to the crowd, but simply pointing out, with clear-eyed eloquence, the fundamental unfairness of a justice system that targeted ethnic minorities and the poorest of the poor. And because it came from Steve, people listened. What it all boiled down to, Steve told his audiences, is that he didn't want the United States goverment killing people in his name. 'Nobody fuckin' asked me.'

Kelley Walker flew over and met Steve in Dublin and stayed until the tour ended in March. It was with some relief that Steve put her and Justin on the plane. Author Joanna Serraris relays his monologue on the subject of children at a Nighttown show in Rotterdam in her book, *Steve Earle in Quotes*.

'Kids – when they're little, they're cute. And the reason they're so cute is so you won't kill them. And then the hope is that you become attached to them, so that when they stop being cute, you won't kill them either. So far it's working.'

With his family gone, Steve went on a pilgrimage to the Irish town of Galway, a bohemian gathering place for artists and musicians, where Townes had played his last show. He rented a cottage in Bardow, on the Connemara Road, and fell in love with the place. It was, Steve said, his 'kind of town. I walked into a coffee bar there and they had books from floor to ceiling, they had good espresso and they had beautiful women and I would've married any of them!' Perhaps fortunately, he resisted. Alone but for the sea winds, he began to write. Townes's presence was everywhere. In the last months of his life, Townes had touched down in many of the places Steve played on his own tour and the memory of his hero's dark poetry still lingered in them. After shows, people pressed photographs of Townes into Steve's hand. Already Townes was more famous in death than he had been in life. What really counted was his musical legacy. The indelible imprint of his commitment to songwriting as literature was on a whole generation of artists. And on his protégé. Even Steve's guitar playing was a combination of Townes's flat picking style and Townes's and John Prine's finger picking style. Steve used those lessons again in Galway to write a tribute worthy of his mentor, 'Fort Worth Blues'. In graceful lines, he summed up Townes's life-long dilemma.

> *You used to say the highway was your home*
> *But we both know that ain't true*
> *It's just the only place a man can go*
> *When he don't know where he's travelling to*

Steve stayed in Galway until mid-May and wrote two-thirds of his seventh album there. On all of his records Steve had what he referred to as a 'state of me' song. On *El Corazon*, it was 'Christmas Time in Washington', the profound life lessons of a forty-two-year-old man who had been to hell and realized that there had to be a better option. Written on the night of the US elections, it was a moving expression of Steve's disillusionment with American politics and of his continuing inability to understand why anyone needed to go hungry in the richest country in the world. He called on the heroes of America's past – Martin Luther King, feminist Emma Golden, Malcolm X and Woody Guthrie – to 'come back to us now'. Months later, when *El Corazon* was released, Steve was asked by a reporter if he considered himself to be, like Guthrie, a link in what Dylan called the chain between American song-writing and the tradition of storytelling. Steve immediately responded that the difference between himself and Guthrie was that Guthrie was working class. 'Me, I can more easily identify with Bob Dylan – to be middle class but feel guilty about it, and be a radical only for that reason.'

Jimbeau Hinson once said that Steve's great gift was his ability to reflect life back to the listener, and when Steve returned to the States he did that again, only this time the life was that of Townes. He performed 'Fort Worth Blues' at the Austin City Limits memorial to Townes Van Zandt. So powerful was his performance that tears started pouring down the face of Nanci Griffith, who was sitting beside him on the stage. 'I thought, I'm not going to wipe my face, I'm not going to distract this. This is Steve's deal. But it was overwhelming. And no matter how many times I hear him play it, I feel that way. It's the same with "Christmas Time in Washington". He's just a brilliant writer.'

Steve had always said that Townes had been a good teacher and a bad role model and he'd reaped the whirlwind of both. He thanked God and the programme for saving him, but he knew he still shared his mentor's self-destructive streak. At Emmylou Harris's house, he confided to Susanna Clark that, when it came to drugs and alcohol, there was never enough for him of anything, so he dare not do anything. Susanna knew that it was probably true. 'I always trusted that Steve would get his wheels hanging right over the edge of the precipice just before he said, "Whoops. Time to take care of myself." And he came through it, and beautifully, I might add. A fine human being. Very mature human being. Still talks a lot.'

16

Execution Song

In November 1997, a month after its release, *El Corazon* went to No. 1 on *No Depression*'s top forty chart, one place ahead of Bob Dylan's *Time Out of Mind*. Around the same time, it went to No. 1 on Gavin's Americana chart and entered the top five on the Triple AAA chart. Over in Europe, the single 'Telephone Road', released in December, went straight to the top of the Country Music Radio charts. The boost it gave Steve was enormous. He still believed that Townes Van Zandt was the world's greatest songwriter, but he no longer under-valued himself. 'I used to see Dylan as doing something that was way out of my reach and now I see him as just a very, very good songwriter. Which doesn't mean that I think less of him, it just means I think more of myself. That sounds arro-gant but it's not really meant to be. Being arrogant will kill you, but not knowing your own worth is just as, and maybe more toxic sometimes.'

With *El Corazon*, Steve had pushed the boundaries of what was musically acceptable in Nashville further than he had on any previous album. Rock, grunge, old-time country and blue-grass melded into a glorious whole that seemed steeped in the revolutionary spirit of the sixties, coffeehouse activism brought to life. When he sang 'the unions have been busted but they cannot break our will', or conjured up the rage and optimism that fuelled the Civil Rights movement with the words, 'marching into Selma as the bells of freedom ring' it was a virtual incitement to disenchanted Americans to light a fire under Congress. The reviewers thrilled to its genre-bending energy. 'An American songwriter treasure,' raved *Guitar World Acoustic.* Listening to Steve's back catalogue on stage, Kelley Looney was struck by the 'inescapable trap for detail' in Steve's mind. 'The everyday things that are the essence of someone, he gets that in his songs.' Country star Wade Hayes described Steve's songs as 'almost evil. I love that, though. His lyrics are so real. He paints a picture like I've never heard anyone else paint a picture.'

The making of *El Corazon* was as cathartic a process as *I Feel Alright* had been for Steve. The songs themselves were therapeutic. 'NYC' was hitchhiking for grownups, written with the realization that Steve would never be far enough from the temptations of addiction to be able to live in the city he'd always dreamed of moving to. 'Taneytown' started life as a song about a slow-witted black youth who is taunted by white racists until, in panic and confusion, he kills a man; and went on to become a moving short story. The bluegrass song, 'I Still Carry You Around', hinted at Teresa, whom he still ached for after all these years. They had not spoken since 1992, but Steve had continued to care for her long past that date. 'You don't fall completely out of love with anybody. If you do, you didn't do it right.'

But Steve had too many things demanding immediate attention for the past to occupy his time for long. Justin, for example. The reason his fifteen-year-old son came to play guitar on the rock track, 'Here I Am', was purely accidental. Justin had owned a guitar since he was seven but it had only recently come out of the closet. In Europe, he had grown a little closer to his father and, while Steve was recording *El Corazon*, Justin took to hanging around the studio with his friends and working out Mance Lipscomb licks on guitar. It turned out he was a natural. Where Steve had taken fifteen years to learn every lick of 'So Different Blues', Justin learned it overnight. One afternoon Steve suggested that Justin pick up Ray Kennedy's guitar and try his hand at 'Here I Am'. They recorded it in two takes.

While all of this was going on, Steve and Ray Kennedy were gaining considerable renown as producers. Operating under the label 'the twangtrust', they used the Beatles as their guiding influences and their Room and Board studio was cluttered with Fab Four memorabilia. To Steve's mind, 'They were very, very, very good and they came along at a time when the state of the art in recording had been achieved. Nothing's been done anywhere to make records sound better, in my opinion, since 1962 or '3.' The twangtrust's organic approach to production would see them named Producer of the Year at the 1999 Nashville Music Awards for Lucinda Williams's slice of deep Southern soul, *Car Wheels on a Gravel Road*. Williams would go on to win a Grammy for it. Recording the album, however, had been one of the least happy studio experiences of Steve's life. While Lucinda found Steve sexist and overbearing, Steve found that Lucinda's angst and neuroses in the studio dramatically impaired his quest to make the recording process one of ease and fun. But the tears had all been worth it.

Accepting their producer award, Kennedy turned to Steve, bearded and attired in a champagne-hued designer suit, and joked: 'Remember when we started and we said we wanted to break all the rules and piss everybody off? It didn't work.'

In fact, Steve was about to confound his critics once again by doing the very last thing they expected: embracing traditionalism. Since leaving jail he had become obsessed with bluegrass music and had spent much of the past year getting to know to Delano Floyd 'Del' McCoury and his son Ronnie, whose Del McCoury Band were the very best in bluegrass. He'd written 'I Still Carry You Around' specifically so that he could call in the McCourys to play on it. Now he had something bigger in mind. 'I said to Del, "If I wrote a blue-grass record and recorded it, would you tour with me to support it?" And Del said, "Yeah." I guess he thought it would be six years, but six months later I had the songs.'

The band that accompanied Steve on the *El Corazon* tour was one of the best line-ups of his career. Looney was back on bass and Steve had borrowed New Orleans jazz drummer Brady Blade and guitarist Buddy Miller from Emmy's band, Spyboy. It was an inspired decision. Smooth-talking, hyperactive Brady Blade was Aaron Neville's nephew and one of the most prodigiously gifted drummers in America, and Miller's guitar style bordered on artistry. He and wife Julie Miller, who opened for Steve on the tour, had recorded several celebrated albums of their own in a home studio overrun with cats. Steve adored the Millers. He thought they were 'like Desi and Lucy on acid. It's cool. I envy that.'

The Millers' unique, almost telepathic musicianship was made all the more extraordinary because Julie suffered from the crippling nerve disease, fibromyalgia. The pain was so excruciating that she spent whole days in bed and there came a night in New Jersey when she overslept. Steve has never forgotten the vision that flew out from the wings while he was on stage, her electro-magnetic back support stuffed under her clothes. She'd forgotten to take it off. 'She comes out, her hair's all messed up and the wire's hanging out of the bottom of her dress and I went, "Oh, the electric girl!"'

It was in Seabright, New Jersey that Steve finally shared a stage with Bruce Springsteen. On 6 February 1998, as gales battered the shoreline, the Boss made a surprise appearance at the venue were Steve was performing. 'They'll let anyone in here,' joked Steve as Springsteen took the stage, his cropped hair and tanned and buffed working man's physique contrasting starkly with Steve's heavy-set frame and overlong hair. Yet it was Steve who seemed the more authentic working man – the kind of working man never likely to have the luxury of going to the gym. Springsteen was the perfect musician – the clean-living rock star, the consummate chronicler of welfare line blues, but Steve had lived the life.

Those, though, were the superficial things. Their grit-laden voices, Springsteen's wrenched from the bottom of his soul and Steve's from the depths of his rabble-rousing past, lent electrifying life to Carl Perkins's 'Everybody's Trying to be My Baby', the Rolling Stones' 'Sweet Virginia', 'Guitar Town', 'I ain't Ever Satisfied', 'Dead Flowers' and 'Johnny Come Lately'. When the whoops and whistles died down, Steve introduced his band, including the grinning Springsteen among the Dukes. Springsteen's support was as meaningful and historic in its way as Bill Monroe's visit to the stage in Nashville or Steve's debut at the Grand Ole Opry. He had been a continuous thread in Steve's life, both as an influence and a motivating force. *Guitar Town* had been written after a Springsteen concert, and Steve had never forgotten Springsteen's endorsement of his performance of 'State Trooper' at the Palace in 1989. In the media, comparisons of the two artists had never ended. As recently as September, a British reviewer had observed that *El Corazon* 'marked Steve out as the finest chronicler of blue-collar rock since Bruce Springsteen'. But Steve had never achieved the mainstream success of Springsteen.

Bill Bennett, formerly head of promotion at UNI, had worked with Springsteen for a couple of years and found that, on and off the stage, he had the heart of a poet. 'Steve, on the other hand, is definitely a poet but he's got the heart and soul of a bandit or an outlaw. He's not endearing. Bruce Springsteen is endearing. But, you know, drug addiction is a part of Steve that could be very unattractive to be around. And Bruce was always, even at the height of his popularity, self-effacing. Kind of the blue-collar man and proud to be that. Steve was kinda more pissed off about everything.'

To Tony Brown, the hypothetical argument of whether or not Steve could have been as big as Springsteen if he hadn't been his own worst enemy was redundant for one simple reason: 'He was his own worst enemy.' None of it mattered except the body of work Steve had created, the music he had honoured and the integrity he had clung to in his blackest hour. He would be remembered, Tony thought, as one of the greatest songwriters America had ever seen and as an artist who had made a difference. 'Like Jimmie Rodgers. Nobody plays Jimmie Rodgers records like they play Louis Armstrong or Patsy Cline or Ella Fitzgerald or Sara Vaughan but they remember him as an artist who made a difference.'

Sara Sharpe had never heard of Steve Earle and only barely knew about Springsteen when she joined the movement to abolish the death penalty in the mid-nineties. For ten isolating years, she had lived with her husband Curtis in South Pittsburgh, Tennessee and watched no television, heard little music and had scant contact with the outside world. Once Sara had had ambitions of becoming an actress. The daughter of a professor of philosophy and religion and an artistic mother, she had moved to Tennessee from Wisconsin when she was two and was still a child when she knew she wanted to act. As a young adult, she bore more than a passing resemblance to Sissy Spacek, with vivid blue eyes and a warm, calm manner. She went to university to study theatre but life took an unexpected turn. She and Curtis found themselves being drawn into a cult, which seemed, for a time, like the answer.

Sara emerged six years later as if from a time warp. Slowly she began to rebuild her life, having two children, Trenna and Jacob, and auditioning for commercials and bit parts. She and Curtis separated. A passionate opponent of capital punishment, she became a volunteer for the Tennessee Coalition Against State Killing (TCASK) and it was there that she first heard Steve Earle's name. Her ambition was to bring the Journey of Hope, an annual two-week abolition campaign, to Tennessee and it occurred to her that it would be even more effective if Steve Earle was on board. For several months her efforts to contact him were thwarted, but then she heard that he was travelling on the Texas Journey in June 1998.

The day that Sara flew to Texas to join the journey her flights were repeatedly delayed, and it was two in the morning when she finally walked into the arrivals hall. 'The airport was absolutely deserted. And then I see this guy walking towards me. And as he got closer I could see the Journey of Hope emblem on his shirt. And he finally just marches right up to me, sticks out his hand and says, "I'm Steve Earle." I said, "No you're not!" And he said, "Yes, I am!" And later he told me, "I was so tired at that point, Sara, I wasn't even sure myself." And we've laughed about it ever since.'

Steve knew immediately that his heart was in trouble again. Driving back to the base, he played her the Iris DeMent duet he had recorded for *The Mountain* over and over again. He was absolutely carried away with it. Sara smiled to herself in the darkness. She thought it was cute.

The Journey of Hope brought together an extraordinary group of people, made unique by their commitment to ending violence through healing and reconciliation when their own experiences should have left them hellbent on revenge. Sonia 'Sunny' Jacobs had spent seventeen years on Death Row in Florida – five of them in solitary confinement – for murders she did not commit. Her partner, Jesse, was executed by the chair they call 'Old Sparky' in a now notorious incident where the chair malfunctioned three times and his head caught fire before he died. Sunny's story was tragic but it was only one of many. Bill Pelke had spent years fighting to overturn the death sentence of one of the girls who stabbed his grandmother thirty-three times for $10. George White had been sentenced to life imprisonment in 1985 for the murder of his wife, despite the fact that he himself had been shot three times and left for dead in the same attack. It was seven years before his conviction was quashed by an appeal court, at which the original trial was described as 'a mockery and a sham'.

'You couldn't shoot yourself once, never mind three times,' Steve said about White's case. 'Pulling the trigger that second time, I don't think anyone could physically do it. I don't think there's anyone that badass on the whole planet. And I don't wanna meet 'em if there is.'

For Steve and Sara, it was a life-changing week and they bonded very quickly. Quite apart from the daily mindspin of the Journey, Sara was riveted by Steve himself. 'I was utterly charmed. He is so endlessly charming. But I also just thought, OH MY GOD! We were in San Antonio and Steve took the whole crew down to the Riverwalk. There was this huge parade of abolitionists marching down the Riverwalk and Steve was going back and forth, from the front of the line to the back of the line. It was just really this manic energy. But he just didn't want to miss anything. He wanted to be at the back *and* the front of the line at the same time. I've never seen anything like it.'

The emotions Steve felt that week were encapsulated in his June 11 e-mail to his website.

I've got a minute to write so here goes – we are in Austin. San Antonio was great. Sister Helen is with us now, and the crowds are good. My home town came through! Tonight the state of Texas is preparing to kill Clifford Boggus. The guards are filling the syringes and checking the straps on the gurney. By now they have rehearsed this murder until they could destroy Cliff Boggus in their sleep. We on the Journey are preparing, as well there are boxes of t-shirts and books to load, as well as boxes of candles. Some of us are on their way to Huntsville to hold a vigil outside the walls. The rest of us will gather at the capital here in Austin. I'll sing 'Ellis Unit One'. This is as close as I've ever been to a state-sanctioned homicide – the most aware I've ever been – the most plugged in – God help us.

He left the next day to rejoin the Dukes in Memphis on the last leg of the *El Corazon* tour, knowing that life would never quite be the same. Sara's lovely face and soothing voice were imprinted on his memory. Sara had guessed that Steve had a crush on her, but knew he was living with Kelley Walker and doubted anything would come of it. 'He had said really wonderful things about the woman he was dating and he did nothing that I would call flirtatious that week at all. *Nothing.* He went to bed early.' Later she realized that Steve had done little things to be close to her that week. For instance, when the activists went out each morning to speak at churches and schools, he made sure that he and Sara travelled in the same van together. 'He was orchestrating things.'

Unbeknownst to Sara and perhaps even to himself, Steve was falling in love again.

Steve spent most of August and September in the studio recording *The Mountain*. He had fallen out with Warner Bros over the album. The $450,000 advance that was scheduled in his contract was withdrawn with almost no notice and Steve found himself scrambling to find the money to pay for the record himself. *El Corazon* had not sold any more units than *I Feel Alright* – around 100,000 – and there was talk of dropping him. Steve managed to negotiate himself out of his deal with Warner Bros, emerging relatively unscathed from the whole experience. But his interactions with the label had confirmed several of his long-held opinions about Music Row. 'Basically it got down to Warner telling me I couldn't make a bluegrass record,' Steve told *No Depression*. 'My attitude was, what part of fuck you do you not understand? *Fuck*, or *you?*' Opening the South by Southwest Music and Media Conference in a red I'm from *@#&* Outer Space t-shirt some months later, he proffered free advice on the music industry. 'I like all my snakes in one basket,' he said of the corporate mergers gobbling up smaller labels across America. As for the major labels, why, musicians had no more in common with them than 'Michelangelo had with the Vatican'.

Back in Nashville, Steve and Jack Emerson decided that,

rather than embark on another failed dance with Music Row, they would approach former Mercury chief Danny Goldberg with a deal that would allow E-Squared to operate as an independent label with major label resources. E-Squared now had five bands on its roster. Under the terms of the agreement, Goldberg's record company, Artemis, would absorb the $100,000 debt Steve was to incur making *The Mountain*.

None of the ennui of corporate deal-making casts a shadow over *The Mountain*. The opening song, 'Texas Eagle', simply bursts out of the box in a hail of joyous fiddle-playing and lightning guitar work. 'A masterpiece', Emmylou Harris called it. '*The Mountain* rocks!' said *No Depression*. With Steve keeping up with the virtuoso musicianship of the Del McCoury Band, his voice reaching effortlessly for the higher range occupied by bluegrass singers, 'Carrie Brown' and 'The Mountain' already sounded like standards. So evocative was the combination of the old-timey Appalachian music and Steve's lyrics that it was if 'The Texas Eagle' was pulling out of the studio. The destruction of 'the mountain' in the title track was like the loss of a family friend.

In between takes, Steve and Sara talked on the phone and she was there for him the day that he received the letter that some part of him had always known was inevitable. Jonathan Wayne Nobles, now a friend after a decade's worth of correspondence, wanted him to witness his execution.

In 1989, when Steve first started writing to Death Row inmates, Jon had already been on Ellis Unit One for four years. He had been sentenced to die for the vicious murders of two girls he had gone to a college with the intention of raping. One girl's boyfriend lost an eye in the attack. A methamphetamine addict, Jon was nicknamed 'The Animal' when he first arrived at Ellis. He was violent and hateful, with a penchant for destroying property and cutting himself with razor blades just so he could lure guards into his cell to do the same to them. Over the years, he changed profoundly, thanks in part to a religious conversion. An interest in Catholicism led to him becoming a lay member of the Dominican Order of Preachers and he began ministering to other inmates.

During the time of their correspondence, Steve saw clear evidence of Jon's transformation in his letters and Jon, doubtless, was encouraged by Steve's support. But it went both ways. For Steve, Jon was both a cautionary tale, a continual reminder of where Steve himself could so nearly have headed, and one of the few people in Steve's post-junkie world who had been to the most hideous corners of drugs and life and survived to tell the tale. Now Steve had to watch him die.

In September 1998, Steve visited Jon for ten consecutive days, speaking to him through the inch-thick, wire-reinforced glass of his visiting area cage. On the day of his execution, Jon was wheeled into the death chamber on a gurney, leather straps restraining his chest and limbs. He twisted his head towards the witnesses' gallery until he saw his friend. The sight of Steve seemed to give him strength. 'Steve, I can't believe I had to go through all of this just to see you in a suit coat,' he said wryly. He read a verse from Corinthians and then, with a nod to the executioner, he began to sing 'Silent Night'. Steve forced himself to watch, his stomach clenched in horror. When Jon reached the line 'mother and child', Steve saw all the air burst from his lungs. 'He gave a shout: "Huh!" It looked like an invisible cinder block had been dropped on his chest. His head hit his chest so violently that his glasses, a pair of heavy, plastic prison-issue glasses, flew off.' Six minutes later, the doctor consulted his watch. Jon was dead.

The prison service dispatched Jonathan Wayne Nobles's ashes to Steve in an urn. Under the words 'cause of death' on the certificate the coroner had written: 'Homicide.'

Two days after leaving Huntsville, Steve played the first Campaign for a Landmine Free World show in Washington

DC. Part furious, part heartbroken, Steve played as loud as he could. 'The set didn't have anything to it except aggression. Just the loudest things I could think of to play. And then I threw my guitar into the drum kit at the end of it.'

On 10 November, he flew to Galway for two months to be alone with his thoughts and to work on his book of short stories, *Doghouse Roses*. For more than a decade Steve had yearned to publish prose, and references to a short story about a man who takes ten years to hitchhike to California crop up in his interviews from 1987 onwards. The luxury of having 3,000 words to tell a story rather than the thirty or so required for a song appealed to him. When he was first released from jail, he had painstakingly re-created 'Wheeler County', the hitchhiker's story, which had been lost for ever when he pawned a computer to buy drugs. 'The Internationale' and 'Taneytown' followed. Not surprisingly, 'The Witness', a searing account of an execution, was one of the first stories he wrote when he got to Galway Bay.

The death of Jon amid the clinical inhumanity of Death Row had left Steve in strange frame of mind. His emotions were very close to the surface. He longed for Sara too, not knowing if his feelings would ever be returned. She had been reunited with her husband Curtis. Without knowing what else to do, he took long walks in the rough sea wind and in between wrote more intensely than he ever had before – working on both *Doghouse Roses* and a new album, *Transcendental Blues*. Steve had always been more of a narrative songwriter. He found poetry more elusive. 'Tom Ames' Prayer' and 'Ben McCulloch' came easier to him than 'My Old Friend the Blues' or 'Valentine's Day'. With short fiction, the discipline was very different. His short story, 'The Red Suitcase', was written in two or three days after an encounter with a homeless man in Fargo, North Dakota. But for the most part short fiction was unpredictable and required hours and hours in the seat. By comparison, songs were easy. They could be written in an afternoon.

Unless he was writing for a specific project, Steve had a tendency to write songs when he came across a guitar he hadn't played in a while and found that there was a song 'hiding in there'. This superstition of Steve's regarding the ghosts of songs hiding in guitars had been observed by John Dotson when he was managing Steve. 'We would go shopping and he would buy guitars based on the fact that there was a song in the guitar. At first, I thought it was kind of a ruse because he used to go to McCabe's [Guitar Shop] every time we went to Santa Monica and every time he'd play seven or eight guitars. Sometimes he wouldn't buy one and sometimes he would play four and buy two. Initially, it seemed very random to me, but as I observed it over a period of time I realized it wasn't random at all. He would go back to the hotel room and emerge a few hours later with a song.'

By the time Steve left Galway, he had the backbone of *Doghouse Roses* written and the makings of a *Transcendental Blues*. He felt driven. 'I'm really really aware of my mortality at this point in my life. And not in any negative way. It's just, I lost four and a half years and I can't get 'em back and I just don't see any reason not to write. I've got a gift and I'm supposed to use it.'

When Steve returned to Nashville shortly before Christmas, his parents and Kelley Walker were at Fairview. Walker and Steve were no longer getting along. 'Kelley wanted to get married and have kids and I just didn't see myself doing that with Kelley. Living with her was great.'

Steve's parents had moved into Fairview when Barbara broke her ankle and the owners of the Franklin, Tennessee, apartment complex she had been managing used it as an excuse to get rid of her. Steve was more than happy to have his parents living at Fairview, where they could take care of the house while he was on the road and keep an eye on Justin, who seemed determined to follow in Steve's worst footsteps. Walker had no influence over Steve's sons at all.

But even as Barbara and Jack suffered palpitations at the prospect of Justin going down the same drug-strewn path as his father, Justin was fretting about Ian. His half-brother was barely thirteen and already simmering with the same fury Justin had felt towards Steve at the same age. Justin felt very protective towards Ian and his stepsister Amy. 'I'm grown and I've made it through the whole adolescent pissed-off thing but Steve's still got Ian sitting at home who's pissed off and needs him around. Because Ian's big enough that if he gets pissed off and becomes a criminal, like I did in the early stages, he . . . could kill somebody.' Justin had always felt that, as a child, Ian had coped best with Steve's addiction because he was too young to understand what was going on. But now that he was older, Ian needed his father and Justin knew without being told that his brother couldn't understand why Steve was still not there for him.

'Ian's got a long road ahead of him as far as this shit goes and Steve's got to realize that. He hasn't yet. Everybody has but him.'

Ian and Justin were not the only ones trying to get to know Steve in the aftermath of addiction, although for most of the family there was much more pleasure than pain in the acquaintance. The Earle siblings were in very different places from the ones where they had been when *Guitar Town* was released. Mark was now director of Lubbock Airport, Texas, with an annual operating budget of $10 million, a capital budget of $30 million and 3,000 acres to oversee. He was also on the board of the Vietnam archives at Texas Tech. Kelly, the liveliest, sunniest and in many ways most innately artistic Earle, was living in Cape Cod and sewing theatrical costumes, just as her grandmother had before her. She was also researching Jewel Earle's memoirs and venturing into alternative healing. Patrick was Steve's production manager and worked three times as hard as anyone else lest anyone think he'd got the job through nepotism.

Of all his siblings, it was Steve's relationship with Stacey that was the most complex, largely because they had never resolved their vastly differing perceptions of what went on when Steve was on the street. Even as Stacey started to achieve recognition as a songwriter in her own right with the release of her albums *Simple Gearle* and *Dance with the One that Brung You*, there was no narrowing of the distance between them. Stacey was still traumatized by some of the things that had gone on, and hurt that Steve seemed to blame her for perpetuating his addiction. Steve, meanwhile, was under the impression that in public, Stacey claimed some credit for his recovery. It irritated him because he felt that she really hadn't been there for him. 'She wasn't around.'

Even with music, there was little common ground. Stacey believed that she and Steve communicated through songs. Steve, on the other hand, felt that the songs that Stacey had written about his addiction were based on her perception of events, 'which I don't think is real. Believe me, that's a hard thing for me, but I still, to this day, don't buy into her version of what happened.' He had written 'When I Fall', the duet he performs with Stacey on *Transcendental Blues*, after seeing a parallel between his relationship with Stacey and the relationship of the brother and sister in the movie *You Can Count on Me*. 'The song's about me and Stacey and there are two viewpoints in the song. The verse she sings is geared towards her viewpoint, which I don't even think is completely accurate and don't totally agree with.'

Their mother was of the opinion that the root of the problem was that Steve and Stacey were too alike. They let pride get in the way. 'Stacey doesn't want anybody to say that Steve helped her do what she does, but she shoots herself in the foot sometimes because there's things he could help her with, but she's afraid of what he'll say . . . She worries more about what he says than anybody else and yet she won't let him do a thing. He thinks she doesn't care about anything he says.'

The truth was, they both cared a great deal. Steve had an

immense regard for the progress Stacey had made a songwriter; Stacey clung on to his small kindnesses. 'Even through all his addictions, when all that mess was going on, he was always very giving. Usually, you have one focus: get up in the morning and get high. You don't care about anybody around you. He had those moments. They were there. But somehow he . . . never lost his heart.'

Steve's huge heart and his infinite generosity were, his family agreed, his best attributes, but it concerned them that it extended so excessively to his ex-lovers. As far as his family could see, he never divorced his wives. Carol-Ann had received alimony from him for a decade longer than the court had ordered him to pay her because he was worried that she wouldn't manage without the money, and even Lou acknowledged that if there was a hint that his children needed something, Steve was on the doorstep with his chequebook. Stacey believed that Steve needed to 'look again through the divorce papers and draw the line . . . You've got to lay the guilt down and move on and start living again.'

Since her divorce from Steve, Lou had enrolled on a degree course in psychology and would later change to law. She and Steve observed a guarded friendship, each nervous that the other might inflict further hurt. There was a part of Lou that still viewed Steve as the beautiful man he had seemed the night she met him, but she still wrestled with the bitterness that she had come to feel. 'I've always seen something in Steve that's greater than what he sees in himself. To this day, I don't think Steve sees it. He covers it up with bullshit. If he ever got serious about becoming the person he wanted to be, it would be really unbelievable but Steve's a very, very scared person in some ways. He can only get so far in discovering who he is and then he stops.'

The Mountain was released on 23 February 1999, prompting a feud with *Billboard*. The industry bible had failed to include the record on its Country Album chart despite the fact that it had sold enough units in its first week to be at No. 13. Since E-Squared was not planning to release a single to country radio, the album was not considered country. 'To say Steve Earle on this record isn't country is like saying Robert Johnson isn't the blues,' said Brad Hunt, retail consultant for E-Squared. The problem was fixed the following week.

On a brighter note, *El Corazon* had been nominated for a Grammy. On 1 March, Steve embarked on *The Mountain* tour with five nights at Nashville's famous Station Inn, a low-ceilinged bluegrass haunt soaked in the music of bluegrass artists from Bill Monroe to Gillian Welch. After that came a blur of dates which covered Virginia, Kentucky, North Carolina, New York, Texas, Canada and Kansas. It was at Merle Fest, the North Carolina traditional music festival, that the first major fissures appeared in Steve's relationship with Del McCoury. For reasons of irrefutable commercial logic, the organizers of the festival had seen fit to put the Del McCoury Band on the main stage when they were performing with Steve and on a smaller stage when they were performing without him. As the reigning king of bluegrass, Del McCoury had taken it as a personal affront – something he would later deny in interviews. Instead he maintained in the media that the reason he pulled out of the *Mountain* tour in May 1999 just days before Steve and the McCourys were due to appear on *Letterman* and leave for Europe was because he objected to Steve's bad language on stage.

Steve, who was convinced that the real reason for McCoury's fit of pique was his lesser billing at Merle Fest, suddenly found himself being held to ransom. 'I was sitting there with all these contracts . . . When you cancel shows you have to reimburse the promoters for any out of pocket expenses and the adver-tising's one of them. It would have been a fortune. It would have ruined me.' He had no option but to renegotiate the McCoury Band's contract and give in to Del's principal demand, that he had more time in the European shows. To Steve, it was a 'disaster. I mean, when we came over to start playing, it was the one criticism consistently of the show. It was just too long.'

The antipathy between the two men was so deep that Steve would finish the US tour with a new band of Bluegrass Dukes. McCoury's quoted opinions on the vulgarity his erstwhile collaborator had brought into bluegrass so infuriated Steve that he inserted a sly reference to them into *Transcendental Blues*: 'There's no room in vulgarity for bluegrass.' He still had a lot of respect for Del McCoury's musicianship but suggested that McCoury 'should have more respect for me'. Del and Ronnie McCoury now refuse do interviews on the subject of either Steve Earle or *The Mountain*.

Rather than taking a much-needed vacation, Steve devoted a full two weeks of April 1999 to the Journey of Hope in Tennessee, beginning with a benefit concert at the Ryman. Jackson Browne, the Indigo Girls and Emmylou Harris were also on the bill. There, Steve played 'Over Yonder (Jonathan's Song)', an achingly sad memoir of his friend Jon Noble's life, told in the voice of Jon himself.

Steve left Nashville the next morning for Memphis, the first stop on the Tennessee Journey of Hope. Over the next two weeks, he would sleep uncomplainingly on floors, couches and rusting asylum-type cots in disused school gymnasia, drive vans and convert streetlights into instant power sources for unplanned rallies. He would find comfort in the shared experiences of Death Row survivors and other Journey members' friends and in telling Jonathan's story to anyone who would listen in churches and schools from Memphis to Knoxville. He would rise at six in the morning and walk through the halls where the Journey members still slept, picking out the songs that spilled like poetry from his guitar – 'Halo Round the Moon', 'Lonelier than This' and 'Another Town'. And he would fall utterly and hopelessly in love. This time, though, the love was unconditional. If the Del McCoury episode had showed that in many ways Steve's life since September 1995 was subject to the same patterns of behaviour that had defined it before that date – only this time without the drugs, his feelings for Sara showed that on a deeper level he had fundamentally changed. He loved Sara so much that he knew that even if they could never be together, loving her would be enough.

17

Fearless Heart

'If ever there was a person who came to live out
loud, it's Steve. He came to live out loud, that's
the only way I know to put it.'
Sara Sharpe, Nashville, March 2002

The road from Jacksonville, Texas, to Earle's Chapel is little changed from the days of Steve's youth. It is a little wider, its surface a little shinier, but it is still untroubled by traffic and flanked by peach trees and dark-hued vegetation which, in the summer, fills the air with the sweet smell of humidity and verdant, irrepressible life. An interested traveller would find that even this short stretch of highway wends its way through a host of Earle family memories, over the hill where Steve used to race his bike, past the roadside store where Booster Earle sold his produce, and alongside the fields where Steve ran bare-foot and shirtless in the summer, mimicking Tarzan, his cultural icon before the Beatles.

It was along this road that Steve was headed in July 2000. He had driven from the airport in a luxury hire car – its grandeur somewhat diminished by an ever-increasing collection of What-A-Burger wrappers and Dr Pepper bottles, their meaty crumbs and pink droplets sneaking on to the carpet – with Sara at his side and Justin in the back seat. Steve himself was freshly showered and dressed in a Gap t-shirt and baggy shorts. His hair was neatly combed and he was smoking a pipe, the smouldering contents of which were floating down to join the debris on the floor. Apart from his Fear No Evil tattoo and the skull ring on his callused hands, he gave every impression of being the most respectable citizen in Jacksonville – which, at that particular moment, he might well have been. He was on his way to the farm for a double celebration – his grandmother's ninety-fifth birthday and the Earle family Homecoming, for which his relations had flown in from across America. Steve Earle was going back to his roots.

The previous night, Steve, Stacey and Justin, ably assisted by Mark Earle, had played an informal show in the intimate confines of Roland's Next Door, a quaint venue housed in the old Palace Theatre in downtown Jacksonville. As a boy, the Palace had been the only place where Steve ever saw a movie indoors. Jack and Barbara mostly took their five children to the drive-in because it was cheaper.

'I saw *Woodstock: The Movie* when it came out, and a little older than that I started going out and taking acid and watching *2001*,' Steve reminisced as he drove.

'*2001* on acid!' said Justin. 'God, I couldn't handle that.'

'It was a thing,' Steve agreed.

'I'm just a little more mentally stable than that,' continued Justin with a degree of self-righteousness to which he was not exactly entitled, being sleepy-eyed and hungover after a four a.m. poker session.

'That was the thing to do,' Steve explained. 'And the weird thing about it was, there's absolutely no need to do that with that movie. That's one of the most psychedelic movies ever made.'

He pulled off the tarmac and bumped over the track that leads to the family farm. Under the trees, thirty or so of the Earle clan were gathered, some tending to the smoking barbecue or drinking iced drinks in deck chairs, others playing pitch 'n' washers in the shade. Only Uncle Arlon, who had died recently and was much mourned, was missing. On the hot porch of the rustic A-frame house where Jack's sister Bettye had spent most of her life, Kelly and the aunts were making flower arrangements for the Homecoming church service. Inside, Barbara and Bettye were preparing lunch. There were thick slices of East Texas tomatoes, mixed bean salads, burgers, steaks and sausages. From the yard came the sound of laughter and the voluble – at times ear-splitting – chatter of multiple Earles, all of whom had something to say. There was an overwhelming sense of family and community. It was that, more than anything, which provided the clue to Steve's against-the-odds recovery. Throughout his ordeal, he had had an addict's most valuable survival tools: spiritual faith and a loving family to come back to.

Although it went unspoken, the Earles were also in Jacksonville for the weekend to give thanks for Steve's recovery. Jewel Earle, particularly, was thrilled to see him. He was the golden grandchild. Kelly had often marvelled at the pleasure it had given Jewel whenever Steve returned from Nashville. 'If any of us came to visit, Grandmama would be leaning out the door and we all got our own special bear hug. It was love, it was just liquid love. You knew that if no other place in the world, this person was just so happy to see you alive. But when Steve came, how could this be any more concentrated? But it was.'

On Sunday morning, the whole family went over to Earle's Chapel for the Homecoming Memorial Service. A little white programme welcomed them as the 'fifth and sixth generation descendants of Elijah and Mary Elizabeth Earle', here to pay 'tribute to their pioneer heritage'. Sun streamed through the pine-framed windows of the chapel as the family knelt in prayer. After the reading, the 'Earle Family Singers', with Mark Stuart at the piano and Steve – a warm healthy figure in the midst of them all, bearded and in a cobalt-blue shirt – sang 'Church in the Wildwood', 'Blest be the Tie' and 'Amazing Grace' – their rich voices ringing out across the pretty cemetery where Elijah Earle lay buried: 'Grace hath bro't me safe thus far, And grace will lead me home . . .'

*   *   *

It had been a long time coming, but Steve Earle finally felt at peace. The first, gentle tendrils of it had stolen over him a year and a half earlier – 10 May 1999, to be precise – in a moment of typical drama. Steve had been buckled into his seat, on a plane bound for Sweden, when his cellphone rang. He had forgotten to turn it off. Steve, who had been sitting there fuming about how Del McCoury had virtually gone on 'strike' until his demands were met for the forthcoming European tour, snatched up the phone as the plane prepared to pull out of the gate. It was Sara announcing her separation from Curtis. She had no idea where she was going to go or what she was going to do.

Instantly, Steve's emotions were thrown into confusion. It was the phone call he'd scarcely dared hope he would ever receive, but the timing couldn't have been more difficult. Even as he spoke, the plane was lumbering towards the runway and Steve was committed to a month-long tour of Europe. The only thing he could do was offer to support Sara and be a friend to her in any way that he could, and he started by lending her the money to rent a house in Sewanee, Tennessee. Over the next four weeks, they spoke for hundreds of hours on the phone and Steve flew back to Nashville via Troy, New York, where Sara was at a conference teaching acting skills to courtroom attorneys. This time it was Sara whose emotions were hit for six. She felt very strongly that before she could embark on any sort of relationship with Steve, she had to be sure that she was genuinely in love with him and not just drawn in by his magnetic personality. 'At one point I asked him to go away for a while and he did so very, very lovingly, and it meant so much to me because he's not a terribly patient man and I think when Steve decides he wants something, he really fuckin' wants it. He really goes for it. And I think that applies to people too sometimes. So the fact that he just sort of let me go so easily and so lovingly and it was very hard for him, I know – was a really amazing gift.'

Sara and her children, Trenna and Jacob, moved into a log

cabin deep in the woods of Sewanee, on the top of Mont Eagle mountain midway between Nashville and Chattanooga, and Steve stayed with a friend nearby and visited Sara as often as she'd let him. 'She was pretty much keeping me at arm's length and I was really dangerous because I didn't have a girlfriend!' As the months went on, Steve progressed to a blow-up mattress in Sara's living room, a situation that continued for quite some time without Steve, former scourge of unattached women across the globe, ever complaining, until, half a year on, their relationship could safely be called official. To celebrate, Steve took Sara to the Balsam Mountain Inn in North Carolina, one of the most breathtakingly lovely places in America, for what Sara recalls as 'an amazingly romantic weekend . . .'

In Sewanee, Steve Earle lived the kind of life he hadn't experienced since early childhood. For the best part of a year, he and Sara had stayed tucked away in the cabin in Sewanee, never watching TV and rarely listening to music. Sara had the distinct impression that, as someone who had required incessant stimulation all his life, Steve was interested in exploring that side of himself. During the recording of *Transcendental Blues*, he commuted back and forth to Nashville, but whenever he was at home on Mont Eagle mountain he simply fished, wrote poetry and 'watched dogs chase cars'. The relationship that he and Sara managed to build in this tranquil, homely environment – where there were always children playing and pots of vegetable soup bubbling away on the stove – was very different from the explosive couplings of Steve's past, born amid the chaos of his career and addiction. It was not without its mercurial moments, but at its heart was a solid core of love and respect. But with seven broken marriages between them, Steve and Sara had made the decision to go to a therapist in Sewanee for couples counselling before any problems started. As Steve observed to one journalist, 'When you've been married six times, as I have, you figure out that it's at least partly your fault.' It was only later that Sara realized that their time in Sewanee had been a turning point in Steve's life. 'I think it probably did change him. If he is better able to relax now, that's probably why.' Before they left, Steve wrote a haiku that Sara loved so much she had it framed for him.

> *Atop this mountain it's easy to be small*
> *Down below it's tougher.*

Transcendental Blues was released on 6 June 2000, a month before the Earle family Homecoming, and went straight to No. 1 on the Americana charts. To Barbara Earle, all her son's albums had a woman behind them and this one was no different. 'Steve tells me, "Well, some of them are just songs," and I say, "No, they're not!" I know what caused every one of them to happen. You can tell if you listen to the songs exactly what he was thinking, and this album is Sara's album.'

Transcendental Blues owed its psychedelic opening to Steve's love affair with *Sgt Pepper* and the Beatles in general. A copy of *Revolver* had lain on the console throughout recording, inspiring the bass parts, drums and mix, although musically the album acknowledged no boundaries whatsoever. It roared freely between rock, bluegrass, folk, country and the Celtic roots of renowned Irish accordionist Sharon Shannon and her band the Woodchoppers. When it came time to tour the album, however, it was rock music that dominated Steve's live shows. Watching Steve and the *Transcendental* Dukes (Kelley Looney on bass, Will Rigby on drums and former Blackheart and Del Lord Eric 'Roscoe' Amble on guitar) at London's Shepherd's Bush Empire on 19 September 2000, *Times* critic David Sinclair drew a comparison with Neil Young and Crazy Horse and said that they could 'fairly claim to be the most righteous defenders of the rock 'n' roll faith currently at large on the live circuit'.

After the formality and traditionalism of bluegrass, Steve revelled in indulging that part of himself that longed to 'go out on stage and grab my amplifier stack and perform an unnatural act with my guitar . . . My deal with all that is, I started playing electric guitar relatively late in life, my late twenties, and I like noise music. I always have. The raw power intrigues me . . . And that part of it is about rock 'n' roll and about sex . . . it's not about anything else. It's about picking up girls. It's very overt, there's nothing subtle about it. It is sexual and it's extremely primal. It's a release. You feel better immediately. It's one of those things. And I have a hard time doing without that sometimes.'

Off stage, Steve made a huge effort to improve his relationship with Justin. For a long time he'd imagined he was doing the best he could to get through to his eldest son, who was becoming more and more rebellious all the time. It was only when Sara pulled him up at a Fourth of July party that he realized that he needed to work harder at it. 'She said, "You need to do something before he's gone, because he's about to be gone and you're going to spend years reeling him back in. Not to mention that he may react and get himself hurt out there." Because he was doing some dumb shit.'

It was Sara's idea that Steve enrol Justin in the famous Old Town School of Folk Music in Chicago and exchange his experience and reputation as an artist for Justin's tuition. It was, Steve later admitted, the best thing he ever did. In Chicago, he roomed with Justin and presided over a course entitled: 'The Relationship Between Traditional Material and Contemporary Songs; Or the Cool Shit to Steal, Tracing the Roots of American Music'. Justin enrolled in a selection of courses. Over the months, the change in him was striking. Ultimately, he would drop out of the Old Town School in less than a year, but the time that he spent there went a long way towards soothing the lingering resentment he felt towards his father and gave him the confidence to pursue a career as a singer-songwriter in his own right. To Justin, every day spent there was worth it just for the memory of performing three songs with Steve on stage at the Old Town School. 'And that show did something. Since that show, everything I've done musically stage presence-wise and guitar playing-wise has just shot to another level. I think what it was was the competition of being on stage with Dad, trying to upstage him. But it worked.'

Perhaps because his new life with Sara was a constant reminder of the fragility and importance of family bonds, and perhaps because guilt still gnawed at him more than it ought to have, Justin wasn't the only family member to whom Steve made an effort to reach out. Whether or not it was conscious, there was a sense that he was pulling his family back to him, re-creating the loving support network that had sustained him before fame and addiction got in the way. Early in 2001, he took steps to heal the divide with Stacey by inviting her to open for him at a host of US dates. It meant more to her than he could have possibly imagined. 'It has made me so content. It was the last little thing I needed other than maybe finding this child [the one she gave up for adoption] to say I've had a complete life . . . I went and played a song for him two weeks ago in his hotel room and he looked at me and said, "It's a great song." He's never said that before.'

His recovery continued to amaze her as much as his artistry. 'For him to take that on and clean up, there's no way for you and I to understand how big that is. I smoke cigarettes and drink coffee and just the thought of letting go of this coffee cup and these cigarettes just really sends me out of my mind. So imagine giving up cigarettes, coffee and drugs. Especially crack. So I put all of that stuff together and I have to say, he is my hero. There's no room for complaining for anybody if you have that to compare to. Our family probably feels more blessed than anybody, not only because he's clean and he's well; we also endured it and got through it. Dad and I were sitting around one night talking about it and then we both just got quiet and sat there and grinned at each other. It's amazing.'

Somewhere in the labyrinth that is London's Barbican Centre, a line of at least a hundred people waited for Steve to sign their copies of *Doghouse Roses*, his long-awaited book of short stories. It had been published in the spring and fall of 2001 by two respected literary houses, Houghton & Mifflin in the States and Secker & Warburg in Britain, and had already received a fair selection of favourable reviews. 'Could be I'm just some Big City sucker for a hard-rocking, Nietzsche-reading, Che Guevara-quoting redneck country singer,' Mark Jacobson wrote in *Men's Journal*, 'but . . . if Steve Earle isn't a Great American, he'll have to do until the real thing comes along.' Other writers who were Earle fans included horror maestro Stephen King, Nick Hornby who had profiled him in the *New Yorker*, and Michael Ondaatje whose novel, *Anil's Ghost*, refers to 'Fearless Heart'.

Beside the stack of books was a stand bearing the fruits of Steve's life. The top shelf featured more copies of *Doghouse Roses* and the second *Together at the Bluebird*, a live recording of Steve's 1995 Bluebird Café performance with Townes and Guy. *Transcendental Blues* was on the third shelf, with *The Devil's Right Hand: An Introduction to Steve Earle* (MCA) and Tony Brown's compilation – *The Essential Steve Earle* – occupied the next one down. The fifth shelf was taken up by *El Corazon*, *The Mountain* and *Shut Up and Die Like an Aviator*, the sixth by *Guitar Town* and *Copperhead Road*. Last but not least was *Beyond Nashville*, a compilation album of Americana artists with Gram Parsons, Steve Earle and Emmylou Harris's names prominently displayed.

Steve was appearing at the Barbican in November 2001 as part of its *Beyond Nashville* season, and was to do one show with Justin and Stacey as part of a mini 'Earle Family Values' tour, and a solo performance on the second night following a Blind Boys of Alabama concert. For Justin, it was another quantum leap towards becoming an artist in his own right. At nineteen, he already had a sizeable share of his father's potent alchemy of charm and charisma and was six foot four inches of lean muscle, untamed hair and blues musician style. He'd written at least half the songs necessary for a planned first album and had mastered enough of Mance Lipscomb's guitar licks to be preternaturally confident about his own abilities. 'It's when I started getting into fingerstyle that I lost Steve. He couldn't show me anything now. I've gotten to the point where I'm secure enough in what I play to where I can be a little arrogant and say, "Fuck you. You don't know anything I don't." And so I run from his help. Everything he tells me to do, especially on guitar, I do the exact opposite to see if it works out. Usually it does!'

Justin was living out the same rock 'n' roll dream as his father at the same age – with one essential difference. He had vowed to himself that if he ever 'screwed up' and made a girl pregnant, he'd give up music. 'Because there's no fuckin' way in hell that any kid of mine's gonna grow up like I did. Father out on the road and a mother scrounging to keep the household in order. I won't let it happen is all.'

For all his youthful conceit, Justin couldn't have helped but feel proud of his father – six years clean and producing some of the best work of his life. Apart from *Doghouse Roses*, Steve had, in the past six years, written some eighty-five songs. That in itself required a superhuman work ethic, but he'd also completed 365 haikus, several draft chapters of a novel about Hank Williams's doctor, co-produced with Ray Kennedy dozens of records at E-Squared, completed at least half of a play about Karla Faye Tucker, the first woman to be executed in Texas since 1863, and stood vigil outside the Nashville prison where Tennessee had once again resumed executions. He had also volunteered his time for the January 2002 Campaign for a Landmine Free World tour with Emmy, Nanci Griffith and John Prine. Griffith was astounded by his accomplishments. 'Whatever it is Steve Earle is doing, he is obsessed with it. The work he is doing with the abolitionist movement is extraordinary work and just a totally admirable thing.'

Because *Transcendental Blues* had been a resounding commercial success, it would have been logical to assume that Steve was growing wealthier by the day, particularly since the publishing royalties from his prolific songwriting output were now going directly to him since he had left Warner Chappell. What is more, after years of making very little money touring, he'd reached the point where he consistently made $10,000 or $15,000 per show. He'd spent a lot of it because he travelled with a large crew and two buses but even so, since leaving jail, he'd never made less than $500,000 annually even in the light years and in 2000 he'd grossed $1.5 million and paid $190,000 to the taxman.

There were several reasons why Steve was not in fact as rich as some of his ex-wives might have suspected. For one thing, Steve had never recouped a dime from MCA Records and doubted he ever would. But the principal reason was his overheads, many of them avoidable. Stacey had a theory that needing to be needed was just another of Steve's addictions. 'He seems to support anybody who stands in his path. If anybody needs something badly – I'm talking about a single mom or something – he will clothe her entire family.' Steve admits that there's a degree of truth in this statement. 'I support my parents, Justin, Ian, and Lou and Amy because I basically pay the rent on that household plus $1,800 a month – $4,500 a month goes into that house. I still make Kelley Walker's truck payment. I pay for my dad's car, Sara's car, Sara's kids are in private schools. I've got an illegitimate child [Jessica Montana Baker] that I pay for in East Tennessee; that's $1,500 a month. My expenses are about $35,000 a month. I've got to make $35,000 before I see the first dime.'

In his time as manager, John Dotson had found that, alimony aside, Steve could spend money faster than anyone he'd ever seen in his life. 'He can spend $200 in an airport gift shop and buy nothing, $5,000 on guitars.' Dan Gillis had noticed the same thing. At tour stops, for instance, Steve did his personal laundry at the Gap and Urban Outfitters. 'He always was a good shopper . . . I asked him about it once, about two years after he got out of jail, and he said, "You know, I should be dead. What the hell have I got to lose? I'm going to spend it like I've got it and not worry about it."'

Recently though, Steve had begun to rethink his approach to spending and worry a little about his complete lack of provision for the future. He was very aware that he couldn't make records for ever and was giving some thought to slowing down and cutting at least some things from his life – E-Squared, for example. 'I have less interest in the record label than I probably do in anything in my life right now.' He found it comforting when money came from other outlets – journalism, for one. 'I'm locked into a situation now where I have to work and there really isn't any money saved. There's my guitar collection and that's it. And so I'm going to have to start doing some sort of planning on my pension or something that'll at least give me the option to walk away. Because I'm getting uncomfortable with not having the option to say, "All you guys are going to have to go and find something else to do for a living." You know, because I could make a lot more money if I took care of fewer people than I do. For right now, I'm okay with it. But I've got to start thinking about it.'

It was Tony Brown who came up with the idea of holding a *Guitar Town* reunion concert. More than a decade and a half after it was first released, *Guitar Town* had gone Gold and MCA were planning to reissue the album as an analog remaster. Steve was writing new liner notes for it. A recent *Billboard* review had observed that, 'As one of the most groundbreaking country records ever made, *Guitar Town* is in some way a promise of both Earle's boundless potential and Nashville's possibilities as the Guitar Town. While Earle has more than kept his promise, Nashville, unfortunately, has not.' Tony planned to rectify the situation by holding a reunion concert at the Ryman on 6 February 2002 with as many of the original Dukes as would agree to play. Apart from recognizing the album as a classic that had helped to change the course of country music, it would raise money for two charities.

On 5 February the day before the reunion show, Steve

arrived in Nashville from Ireland. He rushed home to spend a few precious hours with Sara, his bonsai trees and his beloved Blue Heeler puppy, Beau, before rushing out again for rehearsals. Home was Fairview, a house that over the years had provided shelter for so many hopeful, dysfunctional or downright dangerous characters, and was so immersed in Earle family history – some sordid, some tragic, some enchanting – that it had taken on the metaphorical significance of Wuthering Heights or Manderley. Sara had never imagined that she could live at Fairview, the backdrop of three broken marriages. But when Steve's parents moved into Nashville to be close to Jack's doctors and Steve and Sara grew tired of looking for their dream house, they moved into Fairview as a temporary measure. Now Sara was glad that they did. 'It's a great house and I think we've done a lot with the house and for the house and I think he feels really good about it again.'

The fact that more than two years on the house radiated homeliness, with light pouring through every window, bookcases creaking under the weight of Steve's plethora of interests and dogs and cats rushing manically through the comfy living room, had a lot to do with Sara. When Steve raced in off the road, she would follow protectively in his wake, like a breeze sifting through the rubble in the aftermath a tornado. On the morning of the reunion concert rehearsals, she had been shuttling children to school, catching up with Steve and trying to find accommodation for an unexpected guest, but she was doing everything possible to keep things calm and simple. 'I don't know if there's ever been a coming together of two more extremely opposite people. If Steve is at this end of the spectrum, I'm way the hell down there. I have spent a lifetime trying, in some way, *not* to ruffle feathers, *not* to upset people. I'm the quintessential people pleaser. And people pleasing is really – in some very important ways, I think – very foreign to Steve. Not in all ways. But he's not afraid to say what he thinks and, in fact, I think it's impossible for him *not* to say what he thinks . . . I used to think he was so rash that there was no way he was getting it right. Because he'd meet a person, size 'em up and make a definitive comment and I'd think, that's impossible and unfair to boot. But history has proven that he's generally pretty close to target.'

Much of Sara's time since the move had been devoted to the creation of the not-for-profit theatre project, Broadaxe Theatre, that she and Steve had first envisioned up on Balsam Mountain in North Carolina. Their first production had been Cuban-American playwright Maria Irene Fornes's drama *Mud*, which opened at Nashville's Bongo After Hours Theatre on 14 September 2001. Behind the scenes, the production of both *Mud* and Broadaxe's second project, *The Vampire Monologues*, had been a test of Steve and Sara's relationship, partly because of all the usual complications associated with artists attempting to become administrators, partly because of the differences in their personalities. Justin describes his father as 'very loving, very frantic . . . very, very knowledgeable but still extremely capable of talking out of his ass. It's definitely an Earle thing . . . to, if you don't know exactly what's going on, just come up with a wild idea of what it is.'

It was that trait of Steve's with which Sara had the most difficulty. 'I find it really frustrating sometimes because he speaks in the definitive, whether or not he knows what he's talking about. Generally, he does. I mean, he knows so much. He's got this amazing steel trap mind and once information goes in, it doesn't come out. But obviously there are some things he doesn't know . . . And sometimes I just have to say, "STOP! You might want to preface that statement with, 'What I believe is . . .' or, 'Here's how I see it.'" But that's not the way Steve operates. It's just full steam ahead in every way.'

The most contentious issue in their relationship was television. Steve loved it, Sara couldn't stand it. Steve had a habit of taking over dinner party conversations, Sara liked to hear other people talk. In the time that she had been with Steve she had come across many of the habits and emotional cycles that had derailed his other relationships – business and personal. Some of them were more troubling than others. It was less worrying that he was still capable of the stream of chatter that had amazed Susanna Clark back in the 1975, than it was that he still had a penchant for taking things to the wall in the way that had always terrified Lou. But Steve was also endlessly kind, endlessly generous, romantic and very, very funny. The side of him capable of writing songs like 'Fort Worth Blues' was the side that could spend dozens of patient hours tending to his bonsai trees, taking care of babies or playing with his puppy. It was that side of him with which Sara was quite hopelessly in love. The difference between Sara and most of the other women who had chequered Steve's life was that she, like Teresa, was not dependent on Steve for an identity. She had a life of her own, a career of her own and an unshakeable faith in who she was and what she stood for that allowed her to balance the positive side of Steve with the negative without ever having to compromise herself. 'I think that he has one of the biggest hearts in the world – an amazing heart. I think that he can speak in a way that is borderline verbally abusive and I think that's one of the things that he most needs to work on. It's never malicious or horrible, but he opens his mouth and whatever threatens to come out does, in fact, come out. Inevitably. There are very few filters. Sometimes that's a good thing and sometimes it's pretty difficult. It's put him in some sticky situations . . .

'Living with him is the most exhilarating thing I've ever done. It's also absolutely the hardest. It's a huge challenge. It's very worth it. There have been times when I've said, "I can't do it. I can't hang." But I never think that for very long because, *God* . . . he tries *so* hard, and not only does he try, he makes progress. And I know beyond a shadow of a doubt, if I go to Steve as my partner and say, "You know what, this is not working for me. This that you do really hurts me and we need to take a serious look at it," he takes a *very* serious look at it. And that's quite something. From a man I would not consistently describe as a good listener, I do feel heard. Sometimes

I really have to shake him and say, "STOP! You have to listen to me." And he will. If he didn't, I think I would just run screaming off into the woods.'

After decades of stormy relationships, Sara's gentle insistence that they treat each other with dignity and kindness had brought a measure of stability and happiness to Steve's life that would have been unimaginable even two years before. Steve believed that he'd lived with only 'two truly challenging women in my life – Teresa and Sara. Two people that actually made me do things that I wasn't capable of before I met them.' Sara had worked so hard to improve Steve's relationship with his children – he had taken Ian on the road with him during the *Transcendental Blues* tour and he now employed Justin as a guitar tech – that she had even won the approval of the ex-wives, 'Salt of the earth', Carol called her. Even Lou-Anne, who was constantly at loggerheads with Steve over Ian's upbringing, had to admit that Sara had done wonders for Steve and the children, although she remained somewhat cynical about Steve himself. 'He's always played with fire and will continue to do so.' Whether or not that was true, Steve was still dealing with the after-shocks of the days when he did start blazes on a regular basis. Apart from the custody battle looming with Lou and the inevitable health problems associated with a quarter of a century of drug addiction, he had made up his mind that he would finally have to meet his fourteen-year-old daughter, Jessica Montana Baker, because her mother had told her that Steve Earle was her father. To the casual observer, Steve's life was as complicated as it ever was in the bad old days, only now there were no drugs or jail sentences involved. But as he told Sara, '*comparatively*, this is fuckin' Club Med'.

For all of that, Sara felt more loved than she ever had in her life. She doubted she would marry Steve, purely because she'd lost faith in marriage as an institution, but she knew that he had picked her up when she was at her most vulnerable and given her the strength to follow her dreams. 'I really credit him, ultimately, with reminding me, first of all that I am an artist and, more importantly, that there are two ways to approach one's art and that is fearlessly and uncompromisingly. How do you repay somebody for something like that? I have no idea. I really don't. It's amazing to be loved like that. I feel incredibly fortunate and incredibly blessed and I hope that in some way I've given him something too.'

At the far end of the corridor at Soundcheck, the main door flew open and in came a noisy blur of black and red and grey speckles. Richard Bennett and Tony Brown watched the vision approach with the same incredulous smiles they would almost certainly have been wearing when they met Steve Earle more than fifteen years previously. Steve, wearing his Gap laundry – a grey duffle coat over a red sweatshirt – was being dragged down the passage by his dog Beau, talking as he came about airline delays, weather nightmares and Galway. 'It's my favourite place in the world,' he told Richard Bennett by way of a greeting. 'It sort of took the place of San Miguel de Allende for me. Every dog has a bandana round its neck and a frisby in its mouth. And there is the right proportion of espresso machines to population density!'

He swept past them and into the warehouse-sized rehearsal hall, where Harry Stinson and keyboard player John Jarvis were setting up. Not all of the *Guitar Town* Dukes had been available for the reunion show. Ken Moore had recently married and taken a teaching position in LA, Emory Gordy Jr had hedged his bets for months before sending Tony a refusal, and Paul Franklin, who'd played many of the steel parts on the original album, was in bed with flu. Bucky Baxter was on the road with Ryan Adams and, perhaps fortunately, booked up for the evening. He and Steve had had a major fall out over the producer credits for the Jimmie Rodgers tribute album. But, Mike McAdam was on rhythm guitar and Gary Morse was standing in for Paul and Bucky Baxter. Glen Worf was on bass guitar.

Steve moved around the rehearsal studio with the same nervous energy he'd had the day he walked into Bishops' Pub in November 1974 and introduced himself to Guy Clark. Between checking amplifiers, he fussed over Beau – 'the love of his life', Sara called the dog – whom he had already trained to do several jaw-dropping tricks. The most startling of them was one where Steve pretended to whip a gun out of holster and shoot him: 'Bang!' At that point Beau, who had his owner's flair for melodrama, would give an eerily convincing death jolt, roll on to his back and close his eyes. It was a benign echo of the days when real-life gun tricks were the stock in trade of Steve's outlaw existence and it showed that while he had retained the handsome writerly demeanour he had taken on during *The Mountain* tour, the rebel in him still lurked beneath the surface. 'Steve likes putting himself through the fire,' Jimbeau Hinson had observed. 'It's part of his rebel image. He's living out his legend in his lifetime.'

Steve called over Tony, Richard and Harry Stinson and they gathered around Steve in a close circle. He wanted to play them his latest song, the subject of which was John Walker Lindh, the American member of the Taliban. 'They can't get Bin Laden so they're going to get him,' Steve told them. He picked up his guitar and perched on the edge of the riser. Musically, the song was as affecting as 'Christmas Time in Washington', lyrically, it was explosive, not least because it was written from the standpoint of an Islamic martyr. Even more controversially, Steve had written part of the chorus in Arabic. It made for uncomfortable listening and at the end of it nobody commented. Steve, who clearly relished the idea that 'this will be the song that gets me kicked out of the country', told the gathered musicians that 'John Walker' was one of five tracks he had already laid down for his next album, *Jerusalem*, to be released close to the first anniversary of the September 11 attacks on New York. 'Amerika Version 6.0.' was another. 'There's times to write songs about girls and there's times when there's just too much going on,' Steve said firmly, 'and this is going to be one of those too much going on records.'

Chuckling to himself, Tony Brown found a seat so he could watch the rehearsal. A small, perfectly formed man in a brown cashmere sweater and soft suede jacket, it amused him that Steve still found so much pleasure in controversy. He watched Steve stride around the stage reminiscing about the summer of 1986 when he was riding the Oaks' bus back and forth to California. Despite this grandstanding, there was, at forty-seven, something unmistakably intellectual about Steve. 'Steve Earle turned out exactly the way I thought he would,' Brown said. 'He looks like a college professor.'

The musicians settled down to rehearse and the timeless sound of *Guitar Town* flowed into the room. Over the next few hours, the rehearsal room took on the temperature of the snowstorm lashing Nashville outside, but the musicians played on, filling the space with a furious rush of notes and bringing the album to vivid life. Afterwards the band were uplifted. For Stinson, Jarvis and Bennett in particular, there was a sense that they were part of musical history. From Richard's standpoint, Steve was 'a mild genius. He's brilliant. So if you combine all of that with having something good to say and knowing how to craft it in a way that gets it across, you've got somebody who can really write some good songs. To me, he's a folk troubadour first. There's other styles that he absorbs and spits back out, bluegrass or his rock 'n' roll thing or country, but I think he's a troubadour first. He's a folk singer. Every single one of those songs you can take back down to him and his guitar or a little mandolin. They're folk songs.'

The reunion concert programme called *Guitar Town* 'the album that changed country music forever' and the crowd at the Ryman on 6 February provided vocal testimony to that truth. When the first swaggering bass notes of 'Guitar Town' rolled from Richard Bennett's guitar, they went into a delirium of nostalgia. Country singer Terri Clark all but leapt from her seat. 'I've been listening to these songs for fifteen years,' she gushed to her companions as Steve, dark hair swept back, a black velvet shirt pulled tight across his shoulders, prepared to enjoy the reception he had more than earned.

Susanna Clark wasn't the only one going into raptures. Half of Music Row had turned out for the show. Lucinda Williams sat beside Tony Brown, and long-term fans like Noel Fox and Steve's opening act, flame-haired Patty Griffin, were in the audience. Steve's parents, Sara and her children and Ian and Justin sat close to the stage as Steve and the Dukes brought 'Someday', 'Good Ol' Boy', 'Hillbilly Highway', 'Down the Road' and 'Little Rock 'n' Roller' to vivid life. Fifteen years after *Guitar Town* was released, the songs were still as fresh as the day they were written, alternately arrogant, poignant and wickedly humorous, thumbing their nose at state troopers, bankers and anyone else who threatened to deny a man the right to put his back to the riser and make his stand. Each new song was laden with memories – for Steve and for the audience – their lyrics so familiar that it was hard that believe that there was a time when you might not have known them. From 'Hey, pretty baby, are you ready for me' to 'Nothin' ever happens around my home town', they were masterly précis of the flawed intensity of young love and the meaning inherent in the smallest of lives.

'Mr Earle, we surely do appreciate you,' shouted a fan.

'And my ex-wives appreciate you!' retorted Steve.

In between songs, he recalled those tumultuous years in the seventies when the support of Townes and Guy had contrasted starkly with the hostile reception he had from Music Row. 'One of the problems I always ran into when I got to Nashville was that everybody was telling me, "Bring me songs that are up tempo and positive." And the problem with that is life ain't always up tempo and positive.'

With that, Steve slid into the first tender notes of 'My Old Friend the Blues'. Every soulful twist and lyric confirmed how engrained Steve's music had become in the language of country and how profoundly it had influenced alternative country's course until, in 2002, a whole new movement had sprung up from it and Ryan Adams, a scruffy, soul-bearing, hard-living incarnation of Steve at the same age, was on the world stage capitalizing on it the way Steve never had a chance to do.

Ultimately what mattered was Steve's clear-eyed humanity and commitment to making a difference. Guy Clark held the view that songwriting was not a competitive sport, and that Steve could not be compared to anyone else but simply followed in the tradition of great American songwriters like Guthrie, Dylan and Springsteen in lending a voice to the powerless and the disenfranchised and finding poetry in their nightmares as well as in their dreams. If Steve had, along the way, the appetite for life of Charlie Parker, Janis Joplin or the Beats, his courage to halt at the graveside with his great integrity still intact had taught a generation of outsiders that revolution for the sake of it is always better than rebelling without a cause, and a generation of addicts that it is not only possible to survive but to go on and create something beautiful.

For his encore, Steve did solo performances of 'Now She's Gone', 'Valentine's Day', 'Billy Austin' and Townes Van Zandt's 'Mr Mudd and Mr Gold', the song he had sung in defiance the day that his would-be mentor first saw him play in Houston more than twenty years before. And just to show that, even though Nashville had belatedly decided to honour his contribution to country music the rocker in him was still intact, Steve called in the Dukes and they launched into a rocking version of The Stones' 'Dead Flowers'. Steve sang 'I'll be down in my basement room with my needle and spoon' with almost as much glee as he had in the bad old days. The difference was in the spirit. Shot through with humour and Richard Bennett's guitar playing, it was no longer a tale of decadence and drugs but a rousing, foot-stomping honky-tonk song. By the end of it, the audience were dancing in the aisles of the Ryman.

'I'm so proud,' Jack Earle said with feeling, 'so proud.'

Afterwards, Steve sank into the squashy cushions of the

dressing room sofa while stars, friends and Music Row power players came in to congratulate him. His hair was damp with sweat and his black t-shirt rode up over his tattooed biceps. On the table beside him was a bouquet of pink and yellow roses sent by Stacey, the card inscribed 'To Steve Earle (Bubba)'. Everyone wanted to see him or be close to him, but Steve did not, as one might have expected, hold court. He hugged people, thanked them sincerely and then was quiet. Given a choice, he would have preferred to be alone with his thoughts, to take in all that had happened since that long-ago night in Chicago when he first knew that his dreams had come true. Everything had come full circle.

Gradually, though, the beautiful hordes thinned and only Steve's immediate family and a few industry hangers-on remained. Suddenly starving, Steve and Sara, Jack and Barbara and all the children decided that they'd like nothing more than to go to the Waffle House for a simple, down-home Southern dinner of scrambled eggs, black coffee, raison toast and waffles. But there were commitments. Tony Brown had booked a table at Music Row's favourite restaurant, the Sunset Grill, and the Earles were expected there. Somewhat reluctantly, Steve let go of the Waffle House idea. Tomorrow was another day and there were songs and plays and novels to write and love, in all its shades, to go back to.

Fittingly, Sara had the last word. 'There just is no one else on the planet like Steve Earle. He's a force of nature. He is the stuff that legends are made of, I really believe that. And that's a helluva journey for anyone.'

Acknowledgements

I first raised the idea of a biography with Steve Earle in May 1999. We had just spent a week together in the intense environment of the Journey of Hope, a state-wide tour by Death Row survivors and relatives of Death Row inmates to campaign against capital punishment. Steve had been there to talk about the shattering experience of witnessing the execution of a long-time friend; I had been there to research *Walking After Midnight*, a book documenting the lifelong quest of artists like Steve and Emmylou Harris to make music that challenged and uplifted the human spirit. The Journey itself had been a life-changing experience for me, partly because it is a life-changing experience for anyone involved with it, partly because the abolitionists were some of the most amazing people I'd ever met and partly because any concentrated period of time spent with Steve Earle is unforgettable. Over the ensuing months, it became apparent to me not only that Steve's life had been far more incredible than even the most in-depth interviews with him suggested, but also that he had a unique ability to confront himself and his past with absolute candour, huge intelligence and a lot of humour. It took another year for me to persuade him that consenting to a biography when you've been married six times and had a drug habit lasting nearly a quarter of a century was a good idea. During that time it became more and more obvious that, for any biographer to attempt to tell the whole truth about Steve Earle, two things needed to happen. Firstly, the book had to be unauthorized. Without the freedom to approach the people whose lives Steve had touched with such dramatic, beautiful or even horrific consequences, it would not be honest. On the other hand, a biography which did not have complete access to Steve and his family would not be honest either.

It is a measure of Steve's courage and the unswerving frankness with which he approaches everything, that he agreed to both. And it is a measure of his big heart that he not only agreed but spent hundreds of patient hours talking to me on tour buses, late at night after gigs when he was absolutely exhausted, over breakfasts, London lunches and American dinners. He opened his home and his life to me and encouraged his family to do the same, and it was an unforgettable experience. For all of those reasons and more, thanks seems a very inadequate word but I mean it with all of my heart.

Steve aside, there are three people without whom this book would not have been possible. Everyone at Fourth Estate has put an enormous amount of effort into producing this book but I am forever indebted to Clive Priddle, the most amazing, most diligent editor on the planet. If I promise not to write any more golf books, can I stay at Fourth Estate forever? Thanks also to my agent, Sara Menguc, for always believing in me. Lastly and most importantly, thanks to Kellie Santin. You're the best. The absolute best.

Because of the nature of some of the events in Steve's life, many of the interviews in this book have required a degree of candour and personal courage that has often been extremely difficult for the people concerned. For that reason, I am particularly grateful to Kelly (you're an inspiration), Stacey, Justin, Jack, Barbara, Patrick and Mark Earle, to the wonderful Sara Sharpe and to two of Steve's ex-wives, Lou-Anne and Carol-Ann. Thanks also to Tony Brown, Richard Bennett, Guy and

Susanna Clark, Harry Stinson, Mike McAdam, David Simone, Bill Bennett, John Lomax, John Dotson, Teresa Ensenat, Mark Stuart, Noel Fox, Rick Steinberg, Charlie Mullins, Elisa Sanders, Dan Gillis and Pam Lewis. Thanks to Mitzi Angel and Kate Balmforth for the editorial support and to Julian Humphries for the fantastic cover. Finally, thanks to my mom, dad and sister Lisa for always being there for me. I couldn't have done it without you.

Index

Huskey Jr, Roy 299, 305, 324

In Cold Blood (Capote) 27–9, 228, 255

Jacobs, Sonia 'Sunny' 351
Jarvis, John 128, 190, 380, 382
Jason and the Scorchers 97, 304
Jennings, Waylon 63, 115, 147, 160, 170, 298
Jetton, Robert 138
Johnson, Robert 62
Jones, George 59, 100, 135–6, 141
Joplin, Janis 36, 44, 46
Journey of Hope: From Violence to Healing 341, 350–1, 352, 362
Juanita 13
Judd, Wynonna 325
Junky (Burroughs) 53, 18, 224, 246

Keen, Robert Earl 318
Kelly, Jimmy 166
Kelly's Pub 43
Kennedy, Bobby 34
Kennedy, John F. 16, 19, 22
Kennedy, Ray 308, 324, 328, 347, 373
Kerouac, Jack 104, 131
Kerrville Folk Festival 57
Kilzer, John 193
King, Doug 39
Kling, Reno 98, 143, 161, 179
Knopfler, Mark 102
Korean War 8
Kreck, Dr 43

lang, kd 136, 197, 325
Lanois, Daniel 299, 306
Late, Great Townes Van Zandt, The (Van Zandt) 48
Leadon, Bernie 175
Lee, Albert 128
Lee, Johnny 93
Lennon, John 20, 31
Lewis, Pam 81, 83, 121, 130, 131, 132, 144, 178, 258, 309
Lindh, John Walker 381
Lipscomb, Mance 346–7, 373
Live at the Old Quarter (Van Zandt) 81, 100–1
Lohmann, Macayla 110–13, 118, 137
Lomax III, John 60–1, 65, 99, 101, 104, 118, 119, 121, 125–6, 177, 178, 202
Londin, Larrie 102, 123
Looney, Kelley 233, 244, 324, 346, 348, 369
Lorimar Publishing Inc 170
Louvin Brothers 111, 305
Lovett, Lyle 49, 109–10, 134, 135, 136, 197, 325
Lowe, Mick 235
LSI 93, 100
Lust for Life (Gogh) 83
Lynn, Loretta 58, 59, 116–17, 131

MacColl, Neil 191, 192, 193, 196
MacGowan, Shane 196
Maddox, David 177
Mandrell, Barbara 59, 62